VOLUME FIFTY TWO

Advances in Experimental
SOCIAL PSYCHOLOGY

SERIES EDITORS

JAMES M. OLSON

MARK P. ZANNA

Advances in Experimental
SOCIAL PSYCHOLOGY

Edited by

JAMES M. OLSON

Department of Psychology
University of Western Ontario
London, Ontario, Canada

MARK P. ZANNA

Department of Psychology
University of Waterloo
Waterloo, Ontario, Canada

AMSTERDAM • BOSTON • HEIDELBERG • LONDON
NEW YORK • OXFORD • PARIS • SAN DIEGO
SAN FRANCISCO • SINGAPORE • SYDNEY • TOKYO
Academic Press is an imprint of Elsevier

Academic Press is an imprint of Elsevier
225 Wyman Street, Waltham, MA 02451, USA
525 B Street, Suite 1800, San Diego, CA 92101-4495, USA
125 London Wall, London, EC2Y 5AS, UK
The Boulevard, Langford Lane, Kidlington, Oxford OX5 1GB, UK

First edition 2015

ISBN: 978-0-12-802247-4
ISSN: 0065-2601

For information on all Academic Press publications
visit our website at store.elsevier.com

Working together
to grow libraries in
developing countries

www.elsevier.com • www.bookaid.org

CONTENTS

CONTRIBUTORS

Manuela Barreto
Department of Psychology, University of Exeter, Exeter, United Kingdom, and Lisbon University Institute (CIS-ISCTE/IUL), Lisbon, Portugal

Naomi Ellemers
Institute of Psychology, Leiden University, Leiden, The Netherlands

Jeff Greenberg
Department of Psychology, University of Arizona, Tucson, Arizona, USA

Ying-yi Hong
Nanyang Technological University, Nanyang Business School, Singapore, Singapore

Shinobu Kitayama
University of Michigan, Ann Arbor, Michigan, USA

Malgorzata Kossowska
Jagiellonian University, Department of Psychology, Kraków, Poland

Arie W. Kruglanski
University of Maryland, Department of Psychology, College Park, Maryland, USA

Hannah U. Nohlen
Faculty of Social and Behavioral Sciences, Social Psychology Program, University of Amsterdam, Amsterdam, The Netherlands

Antonio Pierro
University of Rome "La Sapienza", Department of Social and Developmental Psychology, Rome, Italy

Tom Pyszczynski
Department of Psychology, University of Colorado Colorado Springs, Colorado Springs, Colorado, USA

Arne Roets
Ghent University, Department of Developmental, Personality, and Social Psychology, Ghent, Belgium

Iris K. Schneider
Department of Psychology, University of Southern California, Los Angeles, California, USA, and Department of Psychology, VU University Amsterdam, Amsterdam, The Netherlands

Sheldon Solomon
Department of Psychology, Skidmore College, Saratoga Springs, New York, USA

Steven Tompson
University of Michigan, Ann Arbor, Michigan, USA

Frenk van Harreveld
Faculty of Social and Behavioral Sciences, Social Psychology Program, University of Amsterdam, Amsterdam, The Netherlands

CHAPTER ONE

Thirty Years of Terror Management Theory: From Genesis to Revelation

Tom Pyszczynski*,1, Sheldon Solomon†, Jeff Greenberg‡
*Department of Psychology, University of Colorado Colorado Springs, Colorado, USA
†Department of Psychology, Skidmore College, Saratoga Springs, New York, USA
‡Department of Psychology, University of Arizona, Tucson, Arizona, USA
1Corresponding author: e-mail address: tpyszczy@uccs.edu

Contents

Advances in Experimental Social Psychology, Volume 52
ISSN 0065-2601
http://dx.doi.org/10.1016/bs.aesp.2015.03.001

Abstract

Terror management theory posits that human awareness of the inevitability of death exerts a profound influence on diverse aspects of human thought, emotion, motivation, and behavior. People manage the potential for anxiety that results from this awareness by maintaining: (1) faith in the absolute validity of their cultural worldviews and (2) self-esteem by living up to the standards of value that are part of their worldviews. In this chapter, we take stock of the past 30 years of research and conceptual development inspired by this theory. After a brief review of evidence supporting the theory's fundamental propositions, we discuss extensions of the theory to shed light on: (1) the psychological mechanisms through which thoughts of death affect subsequent thought and behavior; (2) how the anxiety-buffering systems develop over childhood and beyond; (3) how awareness of death influenced the evolution of mind, culture, morality, and religion; (4) how death concerns lead people to distance from their physical bodies and seek solace in concepts of mind and spirit; and (5) the role of death concerns in maladaptive and pathological behavior. We also consider various criticisms of the theory and alternative conceptualizations that have been proposed. We conclude with a discussion of what we view as the most pressing issues for further research and theory development that have been inspired by the theory's first 30 years.

And the Lord God commanded the man, saying, . . . of the tree of the knowledge . . . thou shalt not eat of it: for in the day that thou eatest thereof thou shalt surely die. . . And when the woman saw that the tree was . . . to be desired to make one wise, she took of the fruit thereof, and did eat, and gave also unto her husband with her; and he did eat. And the eyes of them both were opened, and they knew that they were naked . . . And unto Adam he said, Because thou hast . . . eaten of the tree . . . cursed is the ground for thy sake; In the sweat of thy face shalt thou eat bread, till thou return unto the ground; for out of it wast thou taken: for dust thou art, and unto dust shalt thou return.

Genesis Chapters 2 and 3, King James Version

And I saw the dead, small and great, stand before God; and . . . the dead were judged . . . according to their works . . . And God shall wipe away all tears from their eyes; and there shall be no more death. . .

Revelation 20 and 21, King James Version

1. INTRODUCTION: PURPOSE AND GOALS OF THE THEORY

Terror Management Theory (TMT; Greenberg, Pyszczynski, & Solomon, 1986; Solomon, Greenberg, & Pyszczynski, 1991, 2015) was originally developed 30 years ago to address three broad questions about the roots of human motivation and behavior: (1) Why do people need self-esteem? (2) Why do people need to believe that out of all the possible ways of understanding the world, theirs is the one that happens to be correct? (3) Why do people who are different from each other have such a hard time peacefully coexisting? Back then, the three of us had recently finished our graduate studies in experimental social psychology and were beginning to settle into academic positions. Social cognition was flourishing, as many psychologists attempted to explain virtually all human behavior in terms of the workings (and sometimes mis-workings) of an information processing system; computers as a metaphor for the functioning of the human mind dominated the field. Emotions and motives, when they were discussed, were viewed as particular types of information deployed by cognitive systems to guide behavior. Indeed, it was not unusual to engage in discussions with respected proponents of this approach who, while acknowledging that cognitive analyses had not yet reached the point where they could provide comprehensive explanations for *all* behavior, argued that eventually such information processing perspectives would eliminate the need for motivational and emotional constructs in psychological theorizing.

While intrigued by many of the new ideas and methods that came out of the purely cognitive approach, we also felt that some important things were missing from the social psychological discourse in the early 1980s.[1] For starters, the field consisted almost exclusively of a plethora of mini-theories focused on explicating the concrete details of psychological processes rather than tackling broad questions about *why people behave the way they do*. It seemed to us that social psychologists were more devoted to explaining the findings of laboratory experiments than elucidating the real world phenomena that these experiments were purportedly designed to help us understand (Greenberg, Solomon, Pyszczynski, & Steinberg, 1988). Indeed, students in our classes bemoaned the lack of central organizing principles for grasping the long lists of fascinating findings about human behavior that were cataloged by the textbooks of the day. In addition, social psychology seemed intellectually isolated, both from other related academic disciplines and from previous developments in the field of psychology itself. In particular, psychological science had all but outlawed consideration of

---

[1] Whether our criticisms of the state of social psychology in the early 1980s were reasonable and justified is a question that is open to debate and obviously a matter of personal and professional opinion. We discuss these impressions here because they were important to *us* at the time and played an important role in what we hoped to accomplish with TMT. Whether these concerns continue to apply to the field today is another open question that we think worthy of discussion and debate.

psychoanalytic and existential ideas in theory construction and empirical research. Yet when we first encountered and seriously entertained such ideas *after* completing our graduate education, we were stunned by their relevance to the questions that social psychologists pondered and to the panoply of pressing problems that plagued people in their daily lives.

TMT was our attempt to redress some of what we thought was missing from the field of social psychology at that time. We aimed at producing a theory focused on basic "why" questions regarding the roots of social motivation and behavior. We sought to bring together ideas, old and new, to illustrate important insights that could be gleaned from various sources rarely given much credence within academic psychology. We also hoped to show that applying state of the art experimental methods to test such ideas would infuse them with new life by establishing their empirical credibility. We wanted to develop a theory that was integrative and synthetic; a theory that would shed light on diverse and superficially disparate human phenomena that would itself be refined due to engagement with these phenomena and the conceptual and empirical traditions that surrounded them. Although we didn't realize it at the time, TMT was part of an emerging wave of broader and more integrative theories within social psychology, including self-determination theory (Deci & Ryan, 1980) and evolutionary psychology (e.g., Buss, 1989). In the Enlightenment tradition, we wanted the theory to provide insights about the human condition that could be useful for fostering personal growth and social progress; accordingly, we concluded our first presentation of the theory in *Advances in Experimental Social Psychology* (Solomon et al., 1991, p. 146) with a section entitled, "Toward an Applied Experimental Social Psychology."

We also wanted to draw attention to the problem of death and the possibility that the uniquely human awareness of this existential certainty might play an important role in life. We had never encountered even passing reference to existential concerns in the psychological literature of the day. But given how hard humans (and indeed, all forms of life) usually strive to stay alive, it seemed extremely unlikely to us that knowledge of the inevitability of death would *not* have vital cognitive, emotional, and behavioral consequences. TMT posits that the fear of death lies at the root of some very important psychological motives. To clarify a common misconception, though, our view has never been that the fear of death is the *only* motivational force that drives human behavior; e.g., in our first TMT chapter in *Advances*, we noted that "...it is important to acknowledge that this theory focuses on one particular motive... many other factors, both historical and psychological, need to be considered to fully understand the determinants of any particular human behavior" (Solomon et al., 1991, p. 149). Rather, we argue that attempts to explain human behavior that ignore this fear neglect an extremely important aspect of the human condition and are thus fundamentally incomplete. In a related vein, we never claimed that TMT explains *everything* that needs to be known about *anything*; rather, we argue that TMT sheds important new light on crucial aspects of most of what people think, feel, and do. For this reason, we designed TMT with an eye toward interfacing with other social psychological theory and research.

We begin this chapter marking the 30th anniversary of the initial publication of TMT (Greenberg et al., 1986) with this brief overview of the concerns and goals that fueled the development of the theory as a prelude to an assessment of the current state of the theory, which is our primary aim here. How well has the theoretical and empirical work derived from TMT over the past three decades addressed these concerns and met the goals we set for it? More importantly, how well does the theory do what theories are supposed to do? Does TMT provide a useful way of integrating findings across diverse literatures in social psychology? Does it shed new light on these issues and direct us to new phenomena not apparent from the perspective of other theories? Does it serve a generative function and suggest novel directions for both empirical research and conceptual refinement? Does it suggest potentially useful ways of addressing important individual and societal problems?

Toward these ends, we start with an overview of the theory and a very brief review of the empirical evidence for its fundamental propositions. We then consider a series of distinct conceptual extensions that have emerged from the theory's core propositions to interface with other theory and research to explain: (1) the cognitive and motivational mechanisms through which awareness of death affects human thought and action; (2) the development of terror management processes and the anxiety-buffering system over the course of childhood and individual life spans; (3) the evolution of human mind and culture; (4) how these processes affect the way human beings relate to their bodies and the rest of the natural world; and (5) the role that mismanagement of existential terror plays in psychological dysfunction. We then consider the most important and influential critiques of TMT and alternative explanations for our research findings. Finally, we close with a consideration of some of the most important questions that have emerged from the first 30 years of TMT research that we think are especially important for furthering our understanding of these issues.

2. THE INTELLECTUAL ROOTS OF TERROR MANAGEMENT THEORY

TMT was initially inspired by Becker (1973), a cultural anthropologist whose life work centered on integrating and synthesizing what he believed were the most important ideas and insights afforded by diverse scholarly traditions focused on understanding human nature. He drew heavily from psychology, psychoanalysis, existential philosophy, sociology, anthropology, and the humanities to propose what he hoped would become a "general science of man." Becker was especially influenced by the work of Otto Rank, Sigmund Freud, Gregory Zilborg, Norman Brown, William James, Erich Fromm, George Herbert Mead, Robert Jay Lifton, Erving Goffman, Søren Kierkegaard, and Friedrich Nietzsche, all thinkers whose ideas have made essential contributions to understanding human nature, but were generally viewed as difficult to test empirically and therefore given little attention within scientific psychology. We were struck, however, by the relevance of their thinking to the issues that we and other social psychologists were focused on and to the many social problems that people have faced throughout history that continued to be pressing issues for contemporary society. Consequently, we thought it would be worthwhile to try to incorporate these ideas within contemporary social psychological discourse.

This led to our initial presentation of TMT in a chapter reviewing the empirical literature on the need for self-esteem and its influence on diverse aspects of human behavior (Greenberg et al., 1986). In addition to providing a simple explanation of what self-esteem is, Becker's work addressed the previously unasked question of *why* people need self-esteem. Following Becker, TMT defined self-esteem as the individual's assessment of the extent to which he or she was living up to the standards of value associated with the cultural worldview to which he or she subscribed, and posited that self-esteem functions to buffer the anxiety that results from awareness of the inevitability of death.

Our initial goals for this paper were to: (1) argue that addressing the question of why people need self-esteem is imperative for understanding an undeniably important aspect of human nature; (2) propose a plausible and provocative answer to this question; and (3) assert that awareness of the inevitability of death has a profound influence on many aspects of life. We also hoped to remind fellow social psychologists that there was a long history of scholarly work in psychology and other disciplines that offered valuable insights that ought not be ignored if our discipline is to be a truly cumulative and progressive enterprise. Moreover, we realized that recent methodological developments within experimental psychology could be deployed to test hypotheses derived from TMT and other ideas that previous generations of psychologists had deemed untestable. We also realized that recent developments within the field of social psychology fit well with these ideas and could shed new light on them that would facilitate their further refinement and specification. This instigated a program of research and theory development that has kept us and many others busy over the past 30 years.

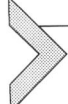

3. FUNDAMENTAL PROPOSITIONS OF TERROR MANAGEMENT THEORY

Although most psychological perspectives emphasize either the similarities (e.g., evolutionary and behavioral theories) or differences (e.g., cognitive and humanistic theories) between human beings and other animals, TMT focuses on the interplay between these similarities and differences. Although humankind shares many evolutionary adaptations with other species, including diverse bodily and motivational systems that ultimately function to keep us alive, our capacity for symbolic and abstract thought make us different from all other living entities. Such sophisticated intelligence is adaptive because it increases behavioral flexibility and helps us solve diverse challenges; however, it also inevitably makes human beings realize that they will someday die, and that death can come at any time for any number of unpredictable and uncontrollable reasons. TMT posits that awareness of death in an animal designed by natural selection to avoid premature termination creates the potential for intense primal fear, which we refer to as *terror* to underscore its potency and connection to death. This potential for terror in response to awareness of a basic fact of life would seriously impede successful goal-directed behavior and perhaps survival itself unless effectively managed. Although fear in response to proximal threats to survival has obvious adaptive value in facilitating behavior that averts death, terror in response to awareness of the long-term inevitability of an inescapable fate is another matter—and the focal problem addressed by TMT.

People use the same intellectual abilities that give rise to their awareness of the inevitability of death to manage their potential for terror with ideas, beliefs, values, and concepts. Specifically, they invent, absorb, and cling to *cultural worldviews*, which are sets of ideas that provide: (1) a theory of reality that gives life meaning, purpose, and significance; (2) standards by which human behavior can be assessed and have value; and (3) the hope of literal or symbolic immortality to those who believe in and live up to the standards of their cultural worldview. *Literal immortality* entails believing that one will continue to exist after death, usually in a form that transcends the limitations of the physical bodies we inhabit. It typically reflects the religious aspects of cultural worldviews, which promise heaven, reincarnation, or the myriad other types of afterlives that people have aspired to since the earliest days of our species. *Symbolic immortality* entails being part of something greater than oneself that continues to exist after one's own death and on into eternity. People acquire symbolic immortality by being valued contributors to the worlds in which they live and leaving reminders that they were here, such as families, fortunes, monuments, or anything else that persists after they are gone, whether tangible (e.g., books, pictures, music) or intangible (e.g., memories, histories, ideas).

Qualifying for either literal or symbolic immortality requires that people maintain faith in their cultural worldviews and live up to the standards of value that are part of them. Doing so provides the sense that one is a valuable participant in a meaningful universe, which is the essence of self-esteem. Uncertainty regarding the validity of one's worldview or one's value within the context of the standards it provides undermines the efficacy of these psychological structures as a shield against existential terror. And because there are many possible ways of understanding reality and there are rarely objective metrics of how well one is meeting cultural standards, people require consensual validation of their worldviews and self-esteem from others to effectively buffer anxiety. Others who share one's worldview or evaluate one positively increase this certainty, but others with different worldviews or who evaluate one negatively decrease this certainty. Consequently, people are motivated to seek consensual validation of their worldviews from others and avoid or dismiss any disconfirmation of these structures that may come their way. The power of consensual validation depends on the value of the others whose worldview and evaluations impinge on us. Accordingly, people exaggerate the value of those who share their worldview or who provide positive evaluations and denigrate the value of those with diverging worldviews or who provide negative evaluations.

Although there are other elements of the theory that address how this dual component (i.e., cultural worldview and self-esteem) anxiety-buffering system develops and functions, these are its core propositions. Over the years, a variety of theoretical modules regarding specific aspects of these processes have emerged that we believe elucidate the evolution, development, and functioning of the anxiety-buffering system. We discuss these developments in a later section of this paper in which we promote the utility of conceptual interconnectedness across theories. But first we present empirical evidence for the theory's fundamental propositions. This research provided initial support for the viability of the theory and posed questions that led to theoretical refinements and the emergence of some of the theoretical modules to be discussed later.

4. RESEARCH ON THE FUNDAMENTAL PROPOSITIONS OF TERROR MANAGEMENT THEORY

Our research strategy for assessing the empirical validity of TMT follows the time-honored tradition of logically deducing hypotheses from the theory and subjecting them to experimental tests. As with most theories, no single hypothesis captures the entirety of the phenomena that TMT seeks to explain or the processes it posits. Therefore, we rely on a set of distinct logical deductions from the theory that yield hypotheses that converge on the core ideas to evaluate the theory's fit with empirical reality. These "building block" hypotheses have been combined with each other to yield more complex predictions that further enhance the convergence across distinct deductions from the theory. Although the fundamental propositions of TMT are relatively simple, they entail claims that involve processes that are involved in many diverse forms of behavior. Thus, our strategy was to test the hypotheses derived from the theory by applying them to a correspondingly diverse range of behavioral domains. Support for these hypotheses has been highly consistent across these domains.

4.1 Anxiety-Buffer Hypothesis

One of the most straightforward implications of TMT is that if a psychological structure serves an anxiety-buffering function, then increasing the strength of that entity should reduce anxiety in threatening situations. When we embarked on this research, studies had already shown that self-esteem was negatively correlated with anxiety (for a review, see Greenberg et al., 1986), threats to self-esteem increase anxiety and negative affect (e.g., Burish & Houston, 1979), and defending self-esteem reduces anxiety produced by self-esteem threats (McFarland & Ross, 1982). But TMT posits that self-esteem is a general anxiety buffer, so the effects of enhancing it should extend to threats in other domains unrelated to the one in which self-esteem is damaged. In particular, elevated self-esteem should reduce anxiety related to thoughts of death.

In the initial test of the anxiety-buffer hypothesis, Greenberg, Simon, Pyszczynski, Solomon, and Chatel (1992) randomly assigned participants to receive positive or neutral feedback on a personality inventory to increase their self-esteem or leave it unaltered, respectively; manipulation checks confirmed that it did. They then viewed a video clip of graphic depictions of death or a neutral film. Whereas neutral self-esteem participants showed a significant increase in self-reported anxiety in response to the death–related video, those who received a self-esteem boost did not. A follow-up study with different manipulations of self-esteem (high scores on a supposed IQ test) and threat (anticipating painful electric shocks) showed the same effect on galvanic skin response, a physiological measure of autonomic arousal associated with anxiety.[2] Subsequent studies demonstrated that both manipulated and chronically high levels of self-esteem mitigated defensive reactions to reminders of death (e.g., Greenberg et al., 1993). Taken together, these studies confirm that self-esteem does indeed buffer anxiety and that this effect extends beyond self-esteem-related threats.

4.2 Mortality Salience Hypothesis

Far and away the most oft-tested implication of TMT is that reminders of death (mortality salience, MS) should increase one's need for the protection provided by one's worldview, self-esteem, and close attachments and therefore increase one's commitment to or striving for them. Consequently, MS is predicted to lead to more positive responses to anyone or anything that bolsters them and more negative responses to anyone or anything that threatens them. Support for this hypothesis comes from studies showing that MS increases motivation to enhance and defend diverse aspects of these components of the cultural anxiety buffer. A now 5-year-old meta-analytic review of 277 studies concluded that this is a moderate to strong effect ($r^2 = 0.35$) that is among the top 20% of the strongest effects in the field of social psychology (Burke, Martens, & Faucher, 2010). This burgeoning

---

[2] We used threat of electric shock because of its independence from threat to self-esteem and its compatibility with a procedure that allowed us to measure a physiological indicator of anxiety. But we should note that although the threat of being shocked may indeed conjure the threat of possible death, it may also raise a fear of pain. Because our developmental analysis posits self-esteem as a general source of protection, we consider it an open question whether it is a general anxiety-buffer that extends beyond direct threats of death and to terror management resources.

literature is so large that we can provide only a few illustrative examples here. MS increases: worldview defense in the form of harsher punishment for moral transgressors (e.g., Rosenblatt, Greenberg, Solomon, Pyszczynski, & Lyon, 1989); more positive evaluations of those who praise one's culture and more negative evaluations of those who criticize it (e.g., Greenberg et al., 1990); greater in-group bias (e.g., Castano, Yzerbyt, Paladino, & Sacchi, 2002); less aggression toward those who share one's worldview and more aggression toward those with worldviews different from one's own (e.g., McGregor et al., 1998); greater support for violent solutions to ethnic, religious, and international conflicts (e.g., Hirschberger & Ein-Dor, 2006; Pyszczynski, Abdollahi, Solomon, Greenberg, & Weise, 2006); increased anxiety when handling cultural icons in a disrespectful way (e.g., Greenberg, Simon, Porteus, Pyszczynski, & Solomon, 1995); more positive evaluations of essays that argue that humans are different from other animals and more negative evaluations of essays that argue that humans are similar to other animals (e.g., Goldenberg et al., 2001); and increased preference for well-structured information and greater dislike for poorly structured information (e.g., Landau, Greenberg, & Solomon, 2004). MS also increases self-esteem striving in the form of increased self-serving attributional biases (e.g., Mikulincer & Florian, 2002); effort and risk taking on activities that are central to one's self-esteem (e.g., Taubman-Ben-Ari, Florian, & Mikulincer, 1999; Peters, Greenberg, Williams, & Schneider, 2005); desire for fame (e.g., Greenberg, Kosloff, Solomon, Cohen, & Landau, 2010); preferences for self-esteem enhancing romantic partners (e.g., Kosloff, Greenberg, Sullivan, & Weise, 2010); and behavior in line with both chronic and situationally primed standards (e.g., Rothschild, Abdollahi, & Pyszczynski, 2009). MS increases attachment motivation, as indicated by: greater attraction to romantic partners (e.g., Mikulincer, Florian, & Hirschberger, 2003); greater willingness to instigate social interactions (e.g., Taubman-Ben-Ari, Findler, & Mikulincer, 2002); increased desire for intimacy in romantic relationships (e.g., Mikulincer & Florian, 2000); more positive associations with one's parents (e.g., Cox et al., 2008, Studies 4 and 5); greater desire for children (e.g., Wisman & Goldenberg, 2005); and larger allocation of resources to maintain contact with attachment figures (e.g., Cox et al., 2008, Study 6).

4.3 Death Thought Accessibility Hypothesis I

It also follows from the theory that threats to any component of a person's anxiety buffer should increase the accessibility of death-related thoughts.

Threats to worldviews, self-esteem, and close attachments increase the number of incomplete word stems completed in death-related ways and reduce latencies for recognizing death-related words but not other negative or neutral words on a linguistic decision task (e.g., Hayes, Schimel, Faucher, & Williams, 2008). Moreover, the same conditions that increase death thought accessibility (DTA) also increase defense of one's worldview and striving for self-esteem and close attachments (e.g., Greenberg, Pyszczynski, Solomon, Simon, & Breus, 1994). Defending one's worldview, bolstering one's self-esteem, or thinking about attachment figures decreases DTA (Harmon-Jones et al., 1997). The DTA literature is also quite substantial and had reached over 80 studies back in 2010 (see Hayes, Schimel, Arndt, & Faucher, 2010).

4.4 Combining the Hypotheses

Various combinations of these three core hypotheses have also been tested. For example, affirming one's self-esteem, worldview, or attachments eliminates the increase in DTA and defense of other anxiety-buffer components that MS produces in the absence of such affirmation (e.g., Arndt, Greenberg, Pyszczynski, & Solomon, 1997; Arndt, Greenberg, Solomon, Pyszczynski, & Simon, 1997; Harmon-Jones et al., 1997). Giving participants supposed evidence supporting the existence of an afterlife eliminates the effect of MS on both worldview defense and self-esteem striving (Dechesne et al., 2003), and affirming one's religious faith has similar effects among those with an intrinsic religious orientation (Jonas & Fischer, 2006). This body of research documents the dynamic relation between DTA and the various components of the anxiety buffer posited by TMT.

5. TERROR MANAGEMENT THEORY AND CONCEPTUAL INTERCONNECTIONS

As empirical support for the theory's fundamental propositions grew and we examined an expanding array of phenomena from a TMT perspective, important questions arose that took us considerably beyond the core ideas. What are the finer grained processes through which death-related thoughts lead people to think, feel, and behave as they do? Considering that young children are clearly not capable of conceptualizing death, how does the anxiety-buffering system develop in early childhood and across the life span? How do death-related anxiety and the mechanisms that manage it interact with motive systems that produce growth, development, and self-expansion? How did awareness of death, which TMT posits as a central turning point in the evolution of our species, affect the evolution of mind and culture? How do cultural concepts of mind and soul relate to physical bodies? What produces variability in the content and effectiveness of the worldviews and standards of value that people use to manage their anxiety? What happens when the anxiety-buffering system breaks down? The fact that the theory led to these and many other questions, along with plausible and testable potential answers to them, is testament to its generative power.

These questions led to theoretical refinements, which led to conceptual interfaces with other theories and research, both within social psychology and beyond. Although these conceptual refinements were developed with an eye toward compatibility with both the core propositions of the theory and knowledge from other domains of psychology and related disciplines, they each dealt with unique processes and, to some extent, are independent of each other. We believe that conceptual interconnectedness across theoretical constructions is a useful way of promoting integration across research domains toward a more complete understanding of human behavior. Conceptual interconnectivity is also likely to increase the generative power of a theory, in that advances in understanding often come from focusing on the intersection of differing ideas and phenomena. The ultimate explanatory power of a theory can be best appreciated by considering the entire explanatory network with which it interfaces.

Because TMT was initially developed as an attempt to understand the roots of many of the motives that other theories use as a point of departure (e.g., self-esteem, meaning, belonging), it was important that it could effectively interface with other theories that addressed these and related phenomena. Over the years, research has been conducted that used TMT to build on ideas from many other theories, including social identity theory (e.g., Castano et al., 2002), cognitive dissonance theory (e.g., Jonas, Greenberg, & Frey, 2003), optimal distinctiveness theory (e.g., Simon et al., 1997), objective self-awareness theory (e.g., Arndt, Greenberg, Simon, Pyszczynski, & Solomon, 1998), just world theory (e.g., Hirschberger, 2006), objectification theory (Goldenberg, McCoy, Pyszczynski, Greenberg, & Solomon, 2000), self-determination theory (e.g., Vail, Arndt, Motyl, & Pyszczynski, 2012; Vail, Juhl, et al., 2012), ironic process theory (e.g., Arndt, Greenberg, Solomon, et al., 1997), reactance theory (e.g., Solomon, Pyszczynski, & Greenberg, 2004), attribution theory (e.g., Mikulincer & Florian, 2002), balance theory (e.g., Landau et al., 2004), ego depletion theory (e.g., Gailliot, Schmeichel, & Baumeister, 2006), and lay epistemology theory (e.g., Dechesne & Kruglanski, 2004). Indeed, even the staunchest critics of TMT seem to have constructed their alternative accounts using essential elements of TMT, including the concept of worldview defense and importance of time passing between threat induction and defense assessment (e.g., McGregor, Zanna, Holmes, & Spencer, 2001; van den Bos & Miedema, 2000).

We now turn to a discussion of what we view as the most central conceptual interfaces that have emerged regarding TMT-related issues.

5.1 Psychological Mechanisms Through Which Thoughts of Death Affect Behavior

Initial tests of terror management hypotheses produced consistently supportive results, showing that boosting self-esteem reduced anxiety and anxiety-related behavior (Greenberg et al., 1992, 1993) and that reminders of mortality led to harsher evaluation of moral transgressors (Rosenblatt et al., 1989), greater in-group bias (Greenberg et al., 1990), and more negative evaluations of those who criticized one's culture and more positive evaluations of those who praised it (Greenberg et al., 1990). But soon after our initial findings were published, German psychologist Randolph Ochsmann contacted us to report that he was unable to replicate the MS effect. After consulting about the details of the procedures he was using, it became apparent that his MS induction was much more intensive than ours. When he tried the study again with the simpler MS induction we had been using, he replicated the effects of MS on evaluations of moral transgressors and found that they generalized to other types of transgressions beyond the effects of evaluations of a prostitute that we had reported (Ochsmann & Mathy, 1994).

These observations led us to suspect that, contrary to the usual dose–response relationship, milder MS inductions might produce stronger effects than more intensive ones. This was confirmed in a study that directly compared the two open-ended questions about death we had been using with a more intensive induction in which, after answering our two questions about death, participants were asked to vividly imagine they were on their deathbed, with only a few days remaining to live (Greenberg et al., 1994). Whereas the milder MS induction produced the usual effect on worldview defense, the more intensive one did not.

Though initially puzzling, this pattern of results shed a glimmer of light on some troublesome inconsistencies in results from our own research: whereas studies conducted by one of us yielded very consistent MS effects, those conducted by another did not. Looking more carefully at the details of these studies, we realized that all of the successful MS effects came from studies in which substantial intervening tasks (filler or affect measures and experimental instructions) were placed between the MS manipulation and the dependent variable; but when the dependent variable was assessed immediately after the MS manipulation, significant effects were not found. This raised the possibility that when people are actively contemplating the problem of death, they do not cling to their worldviews—and made us wonder what else they might be doing to cope with death under such conditions. This led to studies comparing the immediate and delayed effects of MS, which showed that worldview defense occurred only when a delay and distraction separated the MS manipulation and assessment of defensive responses (Greenberg et al., 1994, Studies 2 and 3). But why would a delay between MS induction and worldview defense assessment be needed for these effects to emerge—and what were people doing immediately after being reminded of their mortality?

These questions led to the development of the dual defense model that posits distinct defensive tactics for coping with thoughts of death when they are in current focal attention and when they are on the fringes of consciousness—highly accessible but not in current focal attention (Pyszczynski, Greenberg, & Solomon, 1999). We reasoned that when thoughts of death are in focal attention, people might cope with them in a seemingly rational manner that "makes sense" and directly addresses the problem. For example, when consciously thinking about death, people deny their vulnerability, exaggerate their health and hardiness, or simply suppress such thoughts. This enables them to convince themselves that death is a problem for the distant future and of little relevance to them now. We refer to these as *proximal defenses* because their content is logically related to the problem of death and addresses this threat directly.

Proximal defenses remove death thoughts from focal attention but do nothing to negate the fact that death is our inevitable fate. The fact that we will someday die is a bit of declarative knowledge, similar to our address or phone number—something that rarely occupies conscious attention but can easily and quickly be brought to mind. Such thoughts linger on the fringes of consciousness, in a state of high accessibility, always ready to enter consciousness (Wegner, 1994). People push these implicit thoughts further away from consciousness with *distal defenses* that entail viewing themselves as valuable contributors to a meaningful world; these distal defenses are the core components of the anxiety-buffering system specified by TMT. They prevent death-related thoughts from entering conscious attention by reducing their accessibility before they can reach consciousness.

The idea that worldview defense and self-esteem striving occur when thoughts of death are outside of conscious attention explains why people have little or no awareness of these processes and why many people are able to honestly say that they rarely think about death. When thoughts of mortality enter consciousness, people push the problem into the distant future by convincing themselves of their health and hardiness or simply suppressing such thoughts by seeking distractions (Wegner, 1994). Once these thoughts are banished from consciousness and people are no longer aware of them, the suppression is relaxed, which makes it possible for these thoughts to become more accessible. But they then activate distal defenses to reduce the accessibility of these thoughts and further reduce the likelihood that they will enter consciousness. The greater the accessibility of death-related thoughts outside of conscious awareness, the more vigorous the distal defenses. Thus, proximal and distal defenses work together to keep death thoughts out of consciousness and keep people unaware of the influence that they exert from the fringes of consciousness. This, in turn, enables them to maintain an illusion of objectivity and rationality about their thoughts and feelings (Pyszczynski & Greenberg, 1987) and be unaware of the role these defensive processes play in protecting them from the problem of death.

A large and growing body of evidence supports the dual defense model. Whereas the distal defenses of clinging to one's worldview and self-esteem striving emerge only when there is a delay and distraction separating the death reminder and assessment of defensive responses, the proximal defenses of denying one's vulnerability and suppressing death-related thoughts emerge immediately after death reminders (e.g., Arndt, Greenberg, Pyszczynski, et al., 1997; Arndt, Greenberg, Solomon, et al., 1997; Greenberg, Arndt, Simon, Pyszczynski, & Solomon, 2000). The two exceptions are that distal defenses occur immediately after *subliminal* death reminders or if cognitive load is high during the MS induction (Arndt, Greenberg, Pyszczynski, et al., 1997; Arndt, Greenberg, Solomon, et al., 1997); this provides further evidence that these defenses emerge when thoughts of death are accessible but not in conscious attention. Research also shows that threats to one's worldview, self-esteem, and attachments increase DTA (for a review, see Hayes et al., 2010). Importantly, stimuli that increase death thought accessibility increase commitment to one's worldview and self-esteem striving, which in turn reduces death thought accessibility to baseline levels (e.g., Arndt, Greenberg, Pyszczynski, et al., 1997;

Harmon-Jones et al., 1997). Although we generally avoid assessing both death thought accessibility and worldview defense in the same study because of the possibility that the DTA assessment would prime thoughts of death and thus contaminate control participants, several recent studies have done this and shown that DTA mediates the relation between MS and worldview defense (e.g., Das, Bushman, Bezemer, Kerkhof, & Cermeulen, 2009). MS also increases the accessibility of concepts that are central to one's worldview and thus especially useful for defusing the threat of death (Arndt, Greenberg, & Cook, 2002).

Support for the dual defense model has been obtained across a diverse range of applications of TMT, particularly in research inspired by the Terror Management Theory Health Model (TMTHM; Goldenberg & Arndt, 2008), which posits that people generally respond in health-promoting ways via proximal defenses immediately after death reminders but in self-esteem enhancing and cultural worldview bolstering ways via distal defenses after being distracted from thoughts of death. For example, in one study, participants chose a more protective sunscreen than controls immediately after a death reminder (presumably to protect themselves from skin cancer), but if there was a delay after the reminder, people who value a tan as a basis of self-worth chose a less protective one. For a more comprehensive review of the literatures on the dual defense model and TMTHM, see Goldenberg and Arndt (2008).

Recent studies suggest that there may be other ways people cope with their fear of death in addition to the particular proximal and distal defenses specified by TMT and the dual process model. DeWall and Baumeister (2007) showed that reminders of death increase attention to positive affect, presumably to counteract the anxiety that could otherwise arise; specifically, MS increased completions of word stems with positively valenced affective words and marginally decreased completions with negatively valenced affective words. In a related vein, MacDonald and Lipp (2008) found that MS produced a significant reduction in the attentional bias for fear-relevant stimuli that was obtained in the absence of MS. Research also suggests that alcohol and other drugs may sometimes serve a terror management function. Ein-Dor et al. (2014) showed that a death reminder increased the likelihood of participants consuming an alcoholic beverage shortly thereafter, and Chatard and Selimbegović (2011) and Nagar and Rabinovitz (in press) showed that MS increased cannabis users' desire to get high and that cannabis use reduced the accessibility of death-related thoughts. These responses all seem to fit within the category of proximal defenses that likely divert attention from these troubling thoughts. However, they could also be distal defenses because alcohol and drug consumption can serve as sources of self-worth for some people in certain social contexts. Clearly, these and other possible ways of coping with thoughts of death merit further exploration.

Somewhat surprisingly, the MS inductions used in TMT research do not typically produce measureable signs of anxiety, distress, or negative affect. When we designed the first MS study, we gave little thought to whether healthy young adults writing about death in the safety of our labs would consciously experience fear. On the one hand, fear of death is the central motivating force in the theory. On the other hand, Becker posited that this fear is largely unconscious, and people have presumably spent their lives investing in cultural worldviews and striving for self-esteem to minimize their experience of that fear. Our first six MS studies showed no hint of either elevated self-reports of fear or anxiety and no increase in autonomic or cardiovascular indicators of arousal. Hundreds of studies have subsequently similarly failed to find an impact of MS on self-reported affect relative to various control conditions; one study (Arndt, Allen, & Greenberg, 2001) found a small increase in corrugator activity during subliminal presentation of death primes, but it didn't persist beyond the primes, and this activation did not mediate the increased worldview defense the death primes produced.

Of course, encounters with death often do produce strong emotional reactions. Threat of immanent death from disease, violence, or airplane turbulence can quickly generate feelings of terror and palpable signs of physiological arousal. Even healthy people sometimes awaken in the safety of their bedrooms terrified by dreams or ruminations about their inevitable fate. The consistent finding that our MS induction did not produce negative affect but did increase worldview defense and self-esteem striving led us to posit that these and other relatively subtle death reminders produce a *potential* for anxiety or negative affect that is quickly averted by the activation of terror management defenses. This lack of consciously experienced affect in the many studies demonstrating that MS increased worldview defense was one of the findings that led us to infer that responses to MS were not simply the result of negative affect or anxiety that any unpleasant event could produce. Indeed, in the first of many studies directly comparing the effect of MS with reminders of other aversive events, we found that whereas thoughts of taking an important exam or worries about life after college produced significant increases in negative affect but no increase in worldview defense, thoughts of death did not increase negative affect but did increase worldview defense;

this research also found that negative affect in response to MS was associated with lower rather than higher levels of worldview defense (-0.50; Greenberg et al., 1995).

Greenberg et al. (2003) provided more direct evidence for the proposition that it is the potential for anxiety rather than consciously experienced anxiety that drives MS effects by showing that giving participants a placebo believed to block the experience of anxiety for an hour eliminated the MS effect (measured within the hour) obtained in the absence of this placebo. In other words, if participants didn't believe they could get anxious, they had no need to bolster faith in their worldview in response to MS. If actual arousal or anxiety was driving the increased worldview defense that MS produced, the misattribution of arousal literature (e.g., Storms & Nisbett, 1970) suggests that these instructions might have led to *increased* defensiveness, similar to what has been found in many previous studies in which participants who are experiencing arousal were told that a placebo pill would make them feel relaxed, which increased their subjective experience of emotion (e.g., Zanna & Cooper, 1974). These ideas fit the general view that many behaviors, including psychological defenses, are motivated not by the direct experience of affect, but rather the anticipation of that affect (e.g., Baumeister, Vohs, DeWall, & Zhang, 2007; Erdelyi & Goldberg, 1979).

Lambert et al. (2014) recently reported four studies that did detect increased affect in response to an MS induction using a more refined measure of fear rather than general negative affect, consisting of a subset of items from the PANAS (fearful, afraid, scared, frightened). They also showed that this increased fear mediated a *decrease* in self-esteem in response to MS. It is not clear what to make of these findings in light of the hundreds of studies that did not find a difference in reported general negative affect between MS and control conditions[3] and the fact that *decreased* self-esteem in response to MS runs counter to what would be predicted from TMT and has not been

---

[3] Lambert et al. (2014) argue that previous research has not provided a fair test of the possibility that the MS manipulation used in TMT research produces increases in subjectively experienced affect. In addition to arguing that the mostly widely used affect measure in these studies, the PANAS-X, is not specific enough to pick up the subjective fear that they view as the most likely response to thoughts of death, they argue that the large majority of MS studies entail comparison with other aversive events rather than a true neutral control condition. Although this is true of the majority of studies (to respond to reviewer and critic concerns about alternative explanations), over 20 studies have compared MS to neutral controls such as watching television or eating food. In addition, the majority of studies using aversive controls found no differences on affect but differences on the primary dependent variables, which suggests that the differential effects of MS were not the results of differential affective reactions.

found in previous research; TMT predicts that, if anything, MS should *increase* self-esteem striving, which makes this decrease in reported self-esteem difficult to interpret from the perspective of the theory. Their study did show that, as in many previous studies, MS increased worldview defense along with self-reported fear; but, importantly, this increased fear did not mediate worldview defense, much as the small increase in corrugator activity in response to subliminal death primes did not mediate worldview defense in Arndt et al. (2001). It is unclear what if anything these findings imply regarding the processes through which MS increases defensiveness.

Other recent research has shown that MS leads to activation of brain regions associated with affect, such as the right amygdala, anterior cingulate cortex, and right caudate nucleus (Quirin et al., 2012). Tritt, Inzlicht, and Harmon-Jones (2012) argue that this evidence challenges our conclusion that MS does not produce affect and that affect does not mediate defensive responses to it. But activation of brain regions associated with affect is not the same as the subjective experience of affect. Perhaps MS produces some form of implicit affect, or unconscious signal of impending affect, but that's essentially what we mean by the concept of potential affect. Regardless of what one calls it, though, it makes perfect sense that some sort of neural activation would be involved in signaling the potential for affect. But there is still no evidence that subjectively experienced emotion mediates MS effects. Nonetheless, these recent findings indicate that further research on the role of affect and arousal in MS effects is surely warranted.

It is important to realize, though, that TMT is not a theory of MS effects *per se*; rather, the MS research is one line of evidence regarding TMT's claims about the role of awareness of death in life. Indeed, the theory is mute as to whether particular reminders of death will or will not arouse measureable subjective affect; presumably this depends on how threatening and intense the death reminders is. Consequently, although it would certainly change our understanding of the mechanisms through which MS effects are produced, the basic theory would not be fundamentally altered or called into question if MS effects were found to be mediated by affect and/or arousal (as some researchers who equate the theory with the MS evidence have implicitly implied or explicitly claimed).

5.2 Development of the Anxiety-Buffering System

The fact that children are clearly not aware of death in their earliest years of life, nor are they aware of themselves or capable of the conceptualizing even the most rudimentary elements of cultural worldviews, raises the question of how awareness of death and the anxiety-buffering capacities of worldviews and self-esteem develop. Our analysis of how children develop the capacity to use beliefs, values, and self-esteem to manage anxiety builds on the work of Otto Rank, Karen Horney, Harry Stack Sullivan, Jean Piaget, Ernest Becker, John Bowlby, and other developmental theorists. The core idea is that these more sophisticated anxiety-buffering capacities develop out of the attachment system that evolved to insure the survival of offspring too immature to survive on their own.

Human infants are born helpless, unable to meet their own needs, and prone to experience and express distress when those needs are unmet. From the beginning, the child innately fears what could harm and ultimately kill it. These innate fears protect the child from premature death. Parents and caregivers respond to children's distress signals by holding, rocking, and comforting them, while doing what must be done to meet their needs. These interactions produce strong affectional bonds that provide comfort to parent and child alike. As the child's cognitive abilities develop, internal representations of the parent are formed which serve as an additional source of security. Then as the child's behavioral capacities increase, the parents' displays of affection gradually become more contingent on the child's behavior. Whereas in the early months of life, children receive affection from the parents for simply existing, as they become increasingly capable, the parents reserve their more enthusiastic displays of affection for increasingly sophisticated behavior—crawling, walking, simple verbalizations, then phrases, sentences, and behavior that later must comport with the parents' beliefs and values. Through this process, children learn that meeting their parents' versions of their culture's values brings love and protection, whereas falling short of their standards can bring rebukes and apparent withdrawal of affection. In this way, children learn that they are safe when they live up to the parents' standards and are in jeopardy when they fall short of them. Because the parents' values reflect those of the culture at large, the child's emotional well-being soon becomes dependent on living up to the values of the cultural worldview.

Children subsequently develop awareness of themselves as unique beings with minds and experiences that are distinct from anyone else. They also come to realize that there are limits to their parents' power and ability to protect them, and that their parents, like everyone else, themselves included, are mortal. These unwelcome realizations create a need for a basis of security broader than what the parents can provide by themselves. To help them cope with their increasing fears, children are taught about deities that make it possible for them and those they love to move on to a better mode of existence when they die. They also learn about secular institutions, their ethnic and religious heritage, their nation, and various other cultural institutions that give life meaning and permanence that they can be part of if they stay in the good graces of others. Through these interactions with their parents, family, clergy, teachers, and peers, they gradually become indoctrinated into the cultural worldview that relieves anxiety by giving meaning to life and value to themselves. Although this security is initially based on the parents' love, it is gradually transferred to the culture at large, and in most cases, the protective providence of the deity and spirit world that is part of the cultural worldview. Thus, what starts as an innate threat management system that protects preverbal children form things that could kill them adds explicit death-denying components as children become more and more aware of death.

In the one direct empirical evaluation of this developmental account of which we are aware, Florian and Mikulincer (1998a) assessed the effect of responding to a series of questions about death on 7- and 11-year-old Israeli children's attitudes toward other children who were either Israeli or recent immigrants from Russia. The death reminders affected both groups' attitudes toward the other children, but in different ways. Whereas the youngest children's evaluations of both groups became more negative in response to the death reminders, the older children exhibited the typical pattern of worldview defense found among adults: they became more positive in their evaluation of the fellow Israeli children but more negative in their evaluation of the recent immigrants. These findings suggest that the use of in-group favoritism to manage death concerns probably emerges between the ages of 7 and 11.

Research has also shown that attachment relationships continue to be important sources of existential security long after people have begun using their worldviews and self-esteem for this protection. A large body of evidence documents the use of romantic relationships to manage death fears (for a review, see Mikulincer, Florian, & Hirschberger, 2004). MS increases interest in romantic relationships, willingness to compromise to have them, and expressions of love for one's partner. Thoughts of separation from romantic partners increase DTA, and thoughts of intimacy with one's partner decrease DTA and the worldview defense that thoughts of death otherwise produce. Other research shows that adults continue to use their parents as terror management resources and that parents get protection from death concerns from their children through the sense of self-worth and symbolic immortality afforded by offspring who continue into future generations (e.g., Cox et al., 2008; Wisman & Goldenberg, 2005).

But as is clear from the attachment literature, children vary in how securely they bond with their parents and, therefore, in the extent to which they associate security with pleasing their parents and, later, living up to their internalized versions of the cultural worldview. Insecure attachments likely force alternative ways of managing anxiety, which can interfere with their relationships with others, ability to buy into important aspects of the cultural worldview, and obtain security by maintaining a positive self-image. Although most people learn to manage anxiety by maintaining a positive self-image, those with less fortunate childhood experiences may be less able to do so and, therefore, turn to other less adaptive ways of finding security. In some cases, people seem to seek security in a negative self-image. Indeed, there are relatively rare instances where people appear to hope to be remembered for things that they themselves realize are moral atrocities, as documented in the writings of the Columbine High School and Virginia Tech mass murderers, who seemed to want their horrific actions to achieve an ignorable sort of immortality. This suggests that those who feel rejected by others and unable to garner attention for their positive qualities may attempt to leave their mark on perpetuity by dramatically violating cultural values. Perhaps difficulties in the initial development of the capacity to be comforted by close relationships, self-esteem, and culturally shared meanings increase the likelihood of such deviant behavior in later life.

It also seems clear that many people show developmental changes in the way they cope with death in their later years. We propose that this transition is instigated by the increased proximity to death that is inherent in old age, coupled with the reduced ability to meet the standards through which people maintained self-esteem in their younger years, the changes in dominant worldview promoted by the now dominant younger generation, and the loss of the close relationships (due to death and illness) that were previous bases of security. Older adults are less prone than young persons to respond to MS with harsher judgments of moral transgressors and those who criticize their worldviews (e.g., Maxfield et al., 2007). Instead, older adults are more likely to respond to MS by increasing their prosocial generative concern for future generations (Maxfield et al., 2014). These developmental shifts are most apparent among older adults with high levels of executive functioning (Maxfield, Pyszczynski, Greenberg, Pepin, & Davis, 2011); the finding that older adults with low levels of executive functioning continue to respond to death reminders the same way younger adults do suggests that intact executive functioning may be necessary to facilitate such changes in how one relates to and copes with the increased proximity to death associated with aging.

5.3 The Body, Nature, and Physicality

TMT posits that people cope with knowledge of the inevitability of death by living their lives in a symbolic world of meaning in which they are enduringly significant beings rather than mere animals fated only to obliteration when they die. A major component of most culture's solution to this problem is to imbue life with mind and spirit, an essence that transcends the body and is not dependent on it. This makes it possible to construe ourselves as continuing to exist after our bodies have perished. Because bodies are the clear culprits in death, people identify their selves more with their minds and spirits than with their bodies, which are often viewed as mere containers for the more essential immaterial self.

Because our physical bodies are a continual reminder of our vulnerability and mortality, we distance ourselves from our animal nature as best we can. An important line of research spearheaded by Jamie Goldenberg (for a review, see Goldenberg, 2012) has demonstrated the many ways people engage in this process. MS increases denial of similarities between humans and other animals, disgust in response to bodily products, distancing from animals and animalistic activities, and even avoidance of physical sensations. MS also increases dislike of nonhuman animals (Beatson & Halloran, 2007) and support for killing them (Lifshin, Greenberg, & Sullivan, 2014), as a way of feeling superior to them. Additionally, DTA is increased when people are reminded of bodily products, disgusting things, and the physical (but not romantic) aspects of sex. These propensities are particularly strong for people high in neuroticism or who have recently been reminded of their similarity to other animals. Recent evidence that MS increases belief in an afterlife primarily among people who are high in mind–body dualism or when dualistic thinking has been experimentally enhanced (Heflick, Goldenberg, Hart, & Kamp, 2015) supports the idea that separating the mind or soul from the body facilitates belief in literal immortality. These diverse lines of research provide converging evidence for the proposition that people distance from their bodies and invest their selves in abstract concepts of mind and spirit because of the undeniable fact that bodies die.

This tendency to distance from our animal nature helps explain the ambivalence that people feel about sex despite the great potential for pleasure that it entails. Cultures vary widely in both the content and restrictiveness of their rules regarding sexual conduct. Some restrict sex as something that should occur only between married men and women, in private and in the dark, sometimes through a hole in a sheet, done only for the purpose of procreation. Other cultures encourage sharing sex partners, expressing one's carnal desires whenever and wherever one likes, in whatever way strikes one's fancy, either alone or with others present. However, even the most sexually permissive cultures attach important cultural meaning to sex, making it an expression of transcendent love, a means of spiritual fulfillment, one's duty to replenish the group, or an athletic contest of some sort. Most other theories that address these issues (e.g., Buss, 1984) view sexual ambivalence as the result of innate intuitions and cultural restrictions that evolved to facilitate group harmony and prevent disputes over mates. While not disputing this function, TMT views the universal existence of these cultural norms as attempts to distance ourselves from our animal nature, of which sex is a rather striking reminder.

This analysis also provides an explanation for the near universal tendency to place greater emphasis on beauty and purity in women than men. This may be due to the more obvious role that women's bodies play in the creaturely activity of reproduction—menstruation, pregnancy, giving birth, and lactation are all creaturely activities that make many people squeamish. Or it could result from the power men have over women in most cultures. Support for these ideas is provided by studies showing that reminders of death or one's creaturely nature increase distancing from and derogation of pregnant, menstruating, breast-feeding, or sexually provocative women (for a review, see Goldenberg, 2012). Other studies have shown that witnessing a woman accidentally drop a tampon from her purse leads both men and women to derogate her and distance from her, while also increasing the importance that they place on the value of physical beauty for women in general (Roberts, Goldenberg, Manly, & Pyzsczynski, 2002). Cultures reduce the threatening nature of reproductive processes by putting women on pedestals, treating them as objects of beauty to be admired, and placing greater value on virginity and purity for women than men. Thus, MS leads to devaluing of women who are overtly sexual but not women who are modestly clothed and wholesomely attractive. For example, in a recent study (Morris & Goldenberg, 2015), MS led men to report lower liking for photos depicting sexually provocative women posed next to physical objects, compared to a non-MS control condition. Interestingly, if these provocative women were objectified (quite literally) by fusing them with the objects,

MS actually led men to report more liking for the photos, compared to a non-MS control condition. Presumably, the objectification reduced the threat of the provocative women, which increased liking under conditions of MS.

5.4 The Evolution of Mind and Culture

Although the primary goal of TMT is to explain contemporary psychological functioning, from its earliest incarnations, the theory also provided an analysis of how the awareness of death affected the emergence and content of culture (Solomon et al., 1991, Solomon, Greenberg, Schimel, Arndt, & Pyszczynski, 2004). Thus, like most religions and contemporary evolutionary psychology, TMT provides an "origin story" for humankind—something that the theory posits is appealing because it provides meaning for human existence. The TMT analysis builds on evolutionary theory and is consistent with most variations of this approach, although it adds additional forces that are given little attention by most evolutionary psychologists. Perhaps the biggest point of departure from most, but not all (e.g., Deacon, 1997; Langer, 1967), evolutionary analyses is that TMT draws attention to the importance of the *internal environment of the human mind* as exerting adaptive pressures that affected human nature and culture (Pyszczynski, Sullivan, & Greenberg, 2014). TMT also places greater emphasis on the role of human ingenuity in solving both internal and external adaptive challenges and the impact that these human inventions played in the development of mind and culture.

Consistent with all evolutionary accounts of the origins of our species, TMT posits that the sophisticated cognitive abilities unique to our species were selected for because they facilitated our ability to survive, reproduce, and care for our young, which ultimately led to the propagation of the genes responsible for these successes into future generations. In particular, these cognitive capabilities increased the flexibility of our ancestors' capacity to respond to the diverse and rapidly changing environments that they inhabited. This culminated in a new form of behavior regulation, in which linguistic concepts of current self and standards of personal value served as monitors that signaled the need to adjust behavior to keep it on track in the pursuit of important goals (Becker, 1971; Carver & Scheier, 1981a, 1981b; Pyszczynski, Greenberg, Solomon, & Hamilton, 1990). Although generally highly adaptive, these sophisticated intellectual capacities made our ancestors aware that death was inevitable, for themselves and for all other humans, and that death could come at any time for any number of reasons. The juxtaposition of this awareness with the strong desire for life that came with the diverse adaptations that facilitated surviving long enough to reproduce and care for offspring created the potential for terror. Such terror would have seriously impeded effective goal-directed behavior, and eventually reproduction and gene perpetuation, unless effectively managed. Whereas fear in response to clear and present danger is adaptive because it motivates behavior to avert such threats, terror in response to awareness of the long-term inevitability of death has little direct utility because there is nothing that can be done to avoid this fate.

5.4.1 Gods, Morality, and Death

TMT posits that our ancestors used the same sophisticated cognitive abilities that gave rise to the problem of terror to create a partial solution to it—they invented ideas that enabled them to live with relative equanimity in spite of their awareness of the inevitability of death. This awareness emerged around the same time our ancestors were using their newfound intelligence to answer questions about how the world works and how to survive and prosper in it with other members of their groups. Beliefs and values that helped minimize their fears were especially appealing and likely to be communicated and spread to others and eventually became institutionalized as cultural knowledge. As cognitive capacities continued to evolve and people became more adept at using them, human life became increasingly dependent on the cultural world of symbols, ideas, and values; this likely influenced the further evolution of the human brain, in that those who were best able to adapt to and prosper in the cultural environments of ideas, values, rules, and deities were more likely to have their genes be propagated into future generations (Baumeister, 2005). Our species was gradually transformed from groups of conspecifics who responded to the challenges of the external environment, to *social animals* that worked together to prosper in the external environment and therefore were forced to adapt to the challenges of living in groups, to *cultural animals* that lived in a world of symbols, words, ideas, and values, populated by spirits and deities, that they themselves invented to ward off their fears.

Early presentations of TMT did not address the question of where these cultural beliefs and values came from, other than to say they were invented to help manage terror. More recently (e.g., Greenberg et al., 2014; Pyszczynski & Kesebir, 2012), we built on theorists who emphasize the dialectic interplay between natural selection and cultural innovation (e.g., Deacon, 1997; Haidt & Joseph, 2004; Shweder & Haidt, 1993) to further explicate the content of the beliefs and values that our ancestors invented to assuage their fears. For example, Boyer (2001), Atran (2002), and others have argued that the concept of spirits and deities emerged as a nonadaptive side effect of the evolved human tendency to perceive mental states and agency in other humans. Application of these mind-concepts to other natural phenomena is claimed to be responsible for the emergence of concepts of gods and religions, which themselves are claimed to serve no adaptive function. Others argue that religion emerged to facilitate social cooperation within groups by creating a sense of fictive kinship (e.g., Bering, 2006). Although these views are sometimes presented as alternatives to the view that religion functions to manage death-related fear (e.g., Kirkpatrick & Navarrete, 2006), we view them as complementary to the TMT analysis. Concepts of spirits and deities may have indeed initially emerged as our ancestors applied cognitive tools that had evolved to facilitate social interaction to help them understand the workings of what we now view as the nonpersonal forces of nature. As awareness of death emerged, these primitive intuitions and concepts were then used as the building blocks for the more complex death-denying beliefs about deities and spirits that became central to culture. Because spiritual entities could not be directly observed, people relied on the shared beliefs of others within their group to validate their belief in them. This shared need for validation of their belief in invisible entities that protected people from existential fears encouraged people to congregate in groups, engage in shared rituals, and build tangible monuments to the gods that they created. Consistent with these ideas, research has shown that reminders of death increase belief in deities, spirits, and an afterlife (for a review, see Vail et al., 2010), as well as estimates of social consensus for one's attitudes (Pyszczynski et al., 1996).

Experiential knowledge that resulted from parent–child and other person-to-person interactions was another likely source of inspiration for the content of religious beliefs. As discussed in Section 5.2, children's initial protection from distress and fear comes from meeting the wishes of their seemingly omnipotent parents. Experiences such as these may have inspired initial conceptualizations of even more powerful deities and how to procure and maintain their protection. The idea that God is an attachment figure that substitutes for our parents has been suggested by scholars of varying theoretical orientations over the years (e.g., Freud, 1930; Kirkpatrick, 2005). Viewing socialization experiences with parents who guarded our well-being in our early years as providing intuitive inspiration for the cultural innovation of omnipotent gods who control access to the afterlife helps explain the specific characteristics of the deities that cultures created. Perhaps some of the variability of conceptions of gods across cultures and historical epochs reflects differences in parenting practices—and this variability in concepts of gods likely influenced later cultural values regarding optimal parenting.

Another likely source of inspiration for the images of deities that our ancestors created may have been other powerful figures with whom they interacted, such as chiefs, shamans, and kings, who likely enjoyed the fawning fealty that many religions assume their deities similarly require from their followers. This helps explain the despotic, egotistical, and occasionally benevolent character attributed to the various gods that have populated human cultural history. As Wright (2009) suggested, religious conceptions often reflect social and political realities that people were facing at the time, with vengeful gods emerging during times of conflict and more benevolent ones flourishing during times of peace, when cooperation and commerce between different tribes were needed. As Feurbach (1841/1989) put it, "Man created God in his own image."

The central point of the TMT analysis of the evolution of mind and culture is that the emergence of awareness of the inevitability of death was the cataclysmic problem that brought the experiential world of our prehuman ancestors into play as grist for the solutions to existential problems developed by the inquisitive minds of our newly emerging species. From this point on, explanations for how the world works that helped assuage death-related fears had a distinct advantage and became increasingly popular. The fear of death and corresponding hope for immortality had a powerful influence on the sorts of beliefs and values that people sought. Before this point, explanations for how the world works that were effective in meeting people's tangible needs for food, water, warmth, and safety from predators and rival bands of humans were most desirable and adaptive. Moral and social structures functioned primarily to preserve peace within the group and facilitate dominance over other groups; this is the essence of the explanations for the ongoing function of morality and religion proffered by most contemporary theories (e.g., Bering, 2006; Graham et al., 2013; Norenzayan et al., in press). While not disputing these accounts of the earlier precursors to contemporary morality and religion, TMT adds that emerging awareness of death altered the psychological landscape such that beliefs and values that were effective in managing existential terror gained a distinct advantage. Morality, which initially functioned to keep one in the good graces of others, now became the primary basis for admission to the afterlife.

Consistent with this view, MS increases behavior and attitudes in line with all five of the moral intuitions posited by Moral Foundations Theory (Haidt & Joseph, 2004): fairness, harm, loyalty, authority, and sanctity (for a review, see Pyszczynski & Kesebir, 2012). Other research (Bassett, Van Tongeren, Green, Sonntag, & Kilpatrick, 2014) has shown that MS polarizes moral judgments, exaggerating the differences typically found between conservatives and liberals (e.g., Graham, Haidt, & Nosek, 2009). Additionally, priming the concept of god, which TMT posits is the prepotent line of existential defense for many people, increases charitable giving and benevolent judgments of others and decreases cheating (for a review, see Norenzayan et al., in press). From the perspective of TMT, thoughts of one's deity increase morality by activating efforts to defeat death by qualifying for the literal immortality that is believed to depend on staying in the deity's good graces by behaving in a moral manner.

Continuing cognitive evolution probably accelerated the pace at which cultural knowledge was created and codified, which in turn likely created further adaptive advantage for brain structures that promoted sophisticated intellectual abilities. With increasing civilization, scholarly, scientific, and religious traditions (which for most of human history were the same thing) expanded in varying directions. As these intellectual traditions increased in influence, the ideas, beliefs, narratives, and values that constituted cultural worldviews came under increasing scrutiny, and pressures to make the many pieces of the puzzle fit together increased. Thus, elaborate cosmologies emerged that tried to explain everything—usually by invoking an all-knowing all-powerful deity who created the universe and whose desires and dictates became the ultimate answer to all questions. Why are we here? Because the gods wanted us and therefore created us! What should we do? Whatever the gods want us to do! Why? In order to attain everlasting life and avoid eternal damnation. Thus, the cultural revolution of 40,000 years ago likely involved a gradual shift in the motives that drove human behavior, especially those involving morality, from staying in the good graces of other humans to transcending death.

The idea that experiential knowledge gleaned from socialization and interactions with others inspired the kinds of gods that cultures created may help explain the parallels between the literal and symbolic modes of immortality that we have often noticed over the years but not explicitly discussed in previous presentations of TMT. The two modes of immortality may have built on and influenced each other over thousands of years of cultural evolution, such that qualifying for either requires the same things: faith in the cultural worldview and heroically exemplifying its standards. Just as most religions teach that literal immortality in the form of a blissful afterlife is granted to those who believe in their teachings and live up to their value, the hope of symbolic immortality typically depends on leaving a lasting positive contribution to one's culture that will be remembered long after one dies.

5.5 Terror Management and Psychological Disorder

TMT posits that psychological equanimity requires a well-functioning anxiety buffer that entails faith in one's worldview, self-esteem, and close interpersonal attachments. Threats to any of these anxiety-buffer components signal a potential for anxiety that typically engenders defensive efforts to restore the integrity of the system and thus ward off this anxiety. From this perspective, many of the vicissitudes of thought, emotion, and behavior in daily life reflect attempts to respond to fluctuations in the functioning of this system. But the effectiveness of this anxiety-buffering system varies across persons and situations, leaving some people secure and confident and others riddled with anxiety. TMT follows many previous theories in suggesting that many forms of psychological dysfunction and disorder result from, or are exacerbated by, ineffective control of anxiety and reflect maladaptive attempts to cope with such malfunctions.

Consistent with the idea that many psychological disorders result from an inability to effectively manage anxiety, high levels of anxiety are central components of many DSM-V diagnoses, including not only the many problems that fall under the blanket category of anxiety disorders but also others where anxiety itself is not the defining feature, such as depression, posttraumatic stress disorder (PTSD), obsessive–compulsive disorder, substance abuse, sexual difficulties, and schizophrenia. Anxiety is widely recognized as a common comorbid problem associated with many psychological disorders. And high levels of anxiety or neuroticism have been found to be associated with a wide range of other undesirable psychological states and traits, such as guilt, shame, uncertainty, shyness, procrastination, academic difficulties, and interpersonal problems. Although most of this research is correlational, difficulties controlling anxiety seem likely to play at least some role in the etiology of diverse psychological problems.

Research has shown that reminders of death increase the severity of psychological symptoms of some disorders. For example, Strachan et al. (2007) found that MS led diagnosed spider phobics to judge spiders depicted in photos as more dangerous and to spend less time looking at them, people high in obsessive–compulsive tendencies to spend more time and use more soap and water when washing their hands, and people high in social anxiety to become more avoidant of social interactions. Following Yalom (1980), Strachan et al. (2007) interpreted their findings as reflecting participants' tendency to focalize their fear of death onto smaller objects that are easier to control. Although there is nothing, one can do to avoid death, spiders, germs, and embarrassing interactions with others can be avoided if one is sufficiently vigilant.

Additional research found that concerns about death underlie psychological dissociation in response to trauma, and that individuals who experience intense fear of death during a traumatic event are especially likely to dissociate and subsequently develop PTSD (Gershuny, Cloitre, & Otto, 2003). Moreover, in 2005, New Yorkers reminded of their mortality and then asked to recall how they felt during the 9/11 terrorist attacks, or when they watched video footage of the attacks, reported greater dissociative reactions, such as feeling like they were outside of their own body, compared to a control group of students who thought about being in pain or an upcoming exam (Kosloff et al., 2006). These dissociative reactions in turn led to more anxieties about the future.

Another study (Abdollahi, Pyszczynski, Maxfield, & Luszczynska, 2011a, 2011b) tracked people who had survived a traumatic earthquake in Zarand, Iran, in 2005, in which over 1500 people perished and almost 7000 had to evacuate their homes. When reminded of their own death or the earthquake a month later, survivors who did not dissociate in the aftermath of the earthquake responded without anxiety. They instead responded to MS by expressing negativity toward foreigners, a typical defensive maneuver to manage terror. However, survivors who did dissociate during the earthquake, when reminded of their mortality or the quake a month later, reported a great deal of anxiety and did not express antipathy toward foreigners. The usual means of terror management, bolstering one's own group at the expense of others, was apparently unavailable to the survivors who had dissociated. And 2 years later, these high dissociators were far more likely to have developed PTSD than those who had not dissociated and continued to show atypical responses to MS. This absence of defensive response to MS mediated the relation between dissociation at the time of the quake and PTSD 2 years later, suggesting that this disruption of normal terror management defenses plays an important role in the emergence of this disorder. Similar results have been found for Polish victims of domestic violence

(Kesebir et al., 2011) and survivors of a civil war in the Ivory Coast (Chatard et al., 2012).

6. SUMMARY OF TERROR MANAGEMENT THEORY AND RESEARCH

According to TMT, the uniquely human awareness of death gives rise to potentially paralyzing terror that is assuaged by embracing cultural worldviews and meeting or exceeding the standards of value associated with them (i.e., self-esteem) in pursuit of literal and/or symbolic immortality. Convergent empirical support for TMT was originally obtained by studies demonstrating that: momentarily elevated or dispositionally high self-esteem reduces anxiety, autonomic arousal, and defensive cognitive distortions produced by psychological and physical threats; making MS increases defense of the cultural worldview and self-esteem striving; and threats to cherished cultural beliefs or self-esteem increase the accessibility of implicit death thoughts (DTA).

Subsequent theoretical and empirical inquiry has led to: an elucidation of the psychological mechanisms underlying MS effects, culminating in the development of a dual-process model of proximal and distal defenses that are instigated in response to conscious and unconscious death thoughts, respectively; a developmental account of how the anxiety-buffering system emerges over time as an elaboration of infant attachment to primary caretakers; a research program devoted to explaining how existential concerns foster discomfort with physical bodies and bodily processes, particularly sex; important additions to contemporary understanding of how mind, culture, morality, religion, and other aspects of culture evolved in the early days of our species and continue to change to this day; and a model of psychopathology as terror mismanagement.

7. CRITICISMS OF AND ALTERNATIVES TO TERROR MANAGEMENT THEORY

Despite the large body of research inspired by TMT, the theory also has attracted its share of criticism. This has sometimes been a little disturbing to us—because condemnation of the theory threatens our cherished beliefs and self-esteem, leaving us flooded with highly accessible death-related ideation, which is compounded by the constant reminders of death that litter our papers. But critical skepticism is essential for scientific progress. We're convinced that constructive critiques of TMT and associated research have played an invaluable role in promoting the theory's development and refinement. In the following section, we discuss what we believe are the most important and influential criticisms of the theory and alternative explanations for the associated research. We organize our discussion around Martin and van den Bos's (2014) recent overview of criticisms of TMT, because both of these authors have been long time critics of the theory and are, as Stephen Colbert would put it, particularly persistent "worthy adversaries."

7.1 Falsifiability and Insularity

One criticism Martin and van den Bos (2014) lodge against TMT is that the theory is not falsifiable because "conflicting results are not integrated into the theory," "alternative explanations have been ignored," and it is problematic that "mortality salience can heighten self-interest … as well as prosocial interest … can make people more lenient … as well as more punitive … it can increase tolerance … or it can increase aggression … [and] lead to health-promoting or health-endangering behavior" (pp. 52–53). However, Martin and van den Bos neglected to mention that TMT hypotheses have to our knowledge always been derived from the core propositions of TMT. The theory emphasizes the role of the cultural worldview and bases of self-worth in determining how people will manage the potential terror of death. Thus, the effects of MS are never really main effects. Indeed, we began examining the moderating role of individual differences in worldview defense in response to MS in our second MS study (Rosenblatt et al., 1989, Study 2) and have continued ever since. When surprising results have occurred, as those reported to us by Ochsmann, we have then sought to understand those anomalies by exploring relevant process in a more refined way. This is, according to Thomas Kuhn in *The Structure of Scientific Revolutions* (1962), how "normal science" proceeds; i.e., anomalous findings draw attention to areas of inquiry that foster either theoretical refinement if the anomaly can be explained by the addition of internally consistent assumptions that are then verified empirically, or abandonment of the theory entirely if the anomalous findings are ultimately inexplicable without additional assumptions at odds with the theory.

To give another example, Greenberg et al. (1990) found that low authoritarians did not derogate an attitudinally different other in response to MS. This led us to hypothesize that because political liberals value tolerance as part of their worldview, they will not derogate a different other after MS; moreover, MS might lead them to increase their tolerance of a different other. We then found support for these hypotheses in two studies (Greenberg et al., 1992). In the first, MS led conservatives to be more harsh toward a liberal, but tended to lead liberals to become less harsh toward a conservative. We then considered an alternative explanation that MS led all these participants to be supportive of conservative views. So in a second study, we tested the valuing tolerance hypothesis by priming the value of tolerance, a value to which virtually all Americans pay at least lip service. We predicted and found that this prime led MS participants to become less harsh toward an anti-American essay writer (Greenberg et al., 1992, Study 2).

We agree with Martin and van den Bos that it is often difficult to predict exactly how people will respond to reminders of death (or any other threat for that matter). People are complex animals who differ in biological temperament, in the content of their cultural worldviews, and in the particular aspects of the worldview that they internalize as their own. And situations vary in terms of which beliefs and values are most salient. People are thus likely to have multiple and sometimes conflicting elements of their worldviews to rely on for terror management purposes, making it difficult to make *a priori* predictions of which one they will gravitate toward.

Accordingly, we have devoted considerable attention to specifying individual differences, such as self-esteem (e.g., Harmon-Jones et al., 1997), attachment style (e.g., Mikulincer & Florian, 2000), personal need for structure (e.g., Dechesne, Janssen, & van Knippenberg, 2000), and right wing authoritarianism (e.g., Greenberg et al., 1990), that determine which of the many possible sources of security different people gravitate toward when faced with existential threat. Other research has documented the important role that momentary accessibility of beliefs and values plays in this process, and has shown, for example, that MS can lead to diametrically opposed responses, such as increased support for either war or peace, and greed or prosocial behavior, depending on which values have recently been primed (for reviews, see Anson, Pyszczynski, Solomon, & Greenberg, 2009; Rothschild et al., 2009). Although TMT doesn't stipulate which of the many possible sources of security particular people will gravitate toward in specific situations, research is making progress toward providing such specification. It now seems reasonably clear that people cope with death by clinging to values in which they are highly invested and that are high in momentary accessibility. Still, we agree that even more precise elucidation of which anxiety-buffer elements will be used in any given instance is needed. Ironically, the theories that have been proposed as alternatives to TMT provide even less basis for predicting the specific nature of responses to threats, and most invoke concepts so undifferentiated (e.g., meaning, approach motivation, certainty) that there is no conceptual basis at all for making specific predictions. This is an issue for all complex multidimensional theories that entail dynamic interactions among their components (e.g., predicting when cognitive dissonance will produce changes in attitudes, behavior, or adopting additional cognitions). Like all theories, TMT is a tool for expanding our understanding of nature, which requires refinement in response to empirical findings, rather than provides an immutable oracle that requires no additional input to generate accurate predictions.

Martin and van den Bos's next claim, that we "ignore alternative interpretations," is simply untrue. A substantial portion of the empirical research that we and others have conducted over the years was undertaken with the explicit goal of answering questions raised by reviewers and critics, involving issues such as the role of affect in the MS effect (e.g., Greenberg et al., 2003, 1995), the cognitive processes through which thoughts of death affect behavior (e.g., Arndt, Greenberg, Pyszczynski, et al., 1997; Arndt, Greenberg, Solomon, et al., 1997), whether the increase in DTA produced by worldview and self-esteem threats is specific to death or simply reflects general negativity (e.g., Schimel, Hayes, Williams, & Jahrig, 2007), various alternative explanations for MS effects (e.g., Greenberg et al., 1995), and the interface of defensive and growth-oriented motives (e.g., Vail, Juhl, et al., 2012). We've devoted entire papers to responding to critical assessments of TMT (e.g., Landau, Solomon, Pyszczynski, & Greenberg, 2007; Pyszczynski, Abdollahi, et al., 2006; Pyszczynski, Greenberg, Solomon, & Maxfield, 2006; Solomon, Greenberg, & Pyszczynski, 1997), including an extensive response to an issue of *Psychological Inquiry* devoted entirely to critiques of TMT. Although we find some critiques of TMT misguided, we have done our best to respond to them and explain why we find them unconvincing, to examine them empirically (e.g., we have used uncertainty salience as a comparison condition in over 20 studies), and incorporated some of the issues they raise into our conceptual analysis.

7.2 Consistency with Evolutionary and Biological Perspectives

Another common claim is that TMT is not consistent with modern evolutionary theory. Some have taken us to task for the statement that awareness of the inevitability of death is terrifying for "an animal instinctively driven toward self-preservation and continued experience" (Solomon et al., 1991, p. 95), arguing that evolution produces specific solutions to specific environmental challenges rather than general all-purpose adaptations or "instincts." Our use of the term "self-preservation instinct" was intended to give credit to the psychoanalytic roots of TMT's fear of death construct in Zilborg's (1943) analysis of the fear of death. We included the self-preservation construct in the theory to provide a simple explanation of why knowledge of death would inevitably create fear; ironically, we assumed this would be the *least* controversial aspect of the theory, because it seems obvious that people want to stay alive. However, some evolutionary psychologists (e.g., Buss, 1997; Fessler & Navarrete, 2005) pointed out that a unified motive oriented to stay alive is unlikely if one takes a modular approach to thinking about evolution. Because the specifics of how the motivation to stay alive emerged is not particularly germane to the main points of the theory, we changed our verbiage to refer to a "general inclination to stay alive" rather than an instinct, noting that the vast majority of bodily systems ultimately function to keep organisms alive long enough to reproduce and care for their offspring. We suspect that in humans and other cognitively complex species, a general motive to stay alive arises as an emergent property of specific life-supporting adaptations in specific organ systems, especially the brain; see Deacon (1997) and Langer (1967) for similar arguments. But whether one conceptualizes this inclination to stay alive as a series of inter-related adaptations that serve the same function (survival so that genes can be passed on) or a single emergent motive that results from these specific adaptations is largely irrelevant to the rest of the theory and the major points it makes.

Others have argued that fear is a useful adaptation and that evolution would never produce adaptations (i.e., cultural worldviews and self-esteem as anxiety buffers) that undermine something as functional as fear (Fessler & Navarrete, 2005; Kirkpatrick & Navarrete, 2006; Leary, 2004). Although we of course agree that fear is an adaptive emotion that evolved because it stimulates adaptive life-preserving behavior, it is clear that people do a lot of things to minimize their fears, some of which are adaptive (e.g., taking deep breaths; seeking help from others) and some of which are not (e.g., consuming large amounts of alcohol; exaggerating one's abilities). It is also clear that many antagonistic systems exist throughout the body to put the brakes on adaptive responses to prevent too much of an otherwise good thing. But this criticism misses the point: TMT views cultural worldviews and self-esteem as means to manage the fear produced by the ever-present knowledge of the inevitability of death rather than immediate threats to continued existence. Although fear in response to imminent threats is usually adaptive, fear in response to awareness of an inevitable unavoidable future event is generally not. This is why we argue that our ancestors invented ways of managing their fear of death.

More recently, Tritt et al. (2012) have taken the opposite tack, arguing that it is unlikely a system designed specifically to deal with the problem of death could be a product of evolution given that more primitive and domain general systems exist to respond to simpler challenges that require less cognitive complexity than what is needed to cognize death. We agree to a certain extent. Specifically, while death awareness (and the potential for terror engendered by this awareness) is a uniquely human problem, different from all other fears, the terror management system developed by building on more primitive systems that evolved to respond to simpler problems. Although our initial discussions of how the anxiety-buffering system emerged in early humans did not go very far into the details of this process beyond positing that it emerged in response to awareness of the inevitability of death, we certainly never disputed the idea that both biological and cultural evolution build on earlier adaptations to previous adaptive challenges.

But this does not imply that understanding the primitive building blocks of the human adaptation to awareness of the inevitability of death explains the system that ultimately emerged to deal with it. It is widely agreed, for example, that humankind's complex visual apparatus evolved out of very primitive light sensitive cells in far simpler species, but no one would suggest that this provides a comprehensive explanation for the workings of the eye and visual cortex. We argue that although interesting and useful in its own right, identifying the primitive aspects or biological underpinnings that served as the foundation of the system that our ancestors constructed to deal with their burgeoning awareness of death is insufficient to provide a useful understanding of that system.

Frankly, we're puzzled by the general lack of attention given to the problem of death by most evolutionary psychologists. We question evolutionary psychologists' near exclusive emphasis on adaptation to features in the external physical and social environment, because there is nothing in Darwin's or any other evolutionary theory that limits evolution to adaptation to external features. Indeed, it is clear that internal adaptive challenges are also subject to natural selection, as when physical features of organs change over time in response to mutations that make them more compatible with other organs or their products or processes. What is somewhat unique is that TMT focuses on the impact of an idea (i.e., the inevitability of death), a product of the human mind, as an important influence on other ideas generated by people that are spread within and across groups, which then may make particular biological features of the brain more adaptive, which therefore themselves change over time in response to this idea (see Varki & Brower, 2013, for a similar evolutionary account of the central role of death denial in human mentation).

7.3 Cultural Differences

Hypotheses derived from TMT have been tested and supported in experiments conducted in over 25 countries the world over. Although most of these studies were conducted with participants from Western cultures, others were conducted in the Middle East and North Africa (e.g., Israel, Palestine, Iran, Ivory Coast, Turkey), Asia (e.g., Japan, Korea, China, India, Hong Kong, Tibet), Latin America (Mexico, Costa Rica), and at least one was conducted with bicultural Aboriginal Australians. Nevertheless, Martin and van den Bos (2014) argue that TMT trivializes culture and glosses over cultural differences. We find this claim a little strange because we have—long before it became fashionable to do so in social psychology—always emphasized the importance of culture and cultural differences in bases of self-esteem. They argue that MS effects are less consistent and of smaller magnitude on the average in non-Western cultures and that several studies in non-Western cultures have failed to find any MS effects at all (Yen & Cheng, 2010).

Although we agree that much more research is needed in non-Western cultures and there is much to be learned about cultural variations in dealing with death, theory-predicted effects have been found in studies conducted in *all* of the Asian countries in which TMT research has been conducted. Research conducted in East Asian cultures has shown that MS increases nationalism, negative evaluations of those who criticize one's culture, support for military action to defend one's country, in-group bias in job allocations, and the appeal of material goods (for a review, see Park & Pyszczynski, in press), much like what has been found in research conducted in Western cultures. TMT posits that people from different cultures deal with the awareness of death in different ways, depending on the nature of their cultural worldviews. Thus, findings that people from individualistic cultures respond to reminders of death by striving to maximize their individual value while people from collectivist cultures respond by striving to maximize their collective value (e.g., Kashima, Halloran, Yuki, & Kashima, 2004) are *exactly* what is predicted by the theory. In related vein, Wakimoto (2006) found that MS led Japanese students who were strongly enculturated to the Japanese interdependent worldview to respond to success in a self-effacing manner but reduced self-effacement among those less enculturated to the Japanese worldview. Similarly, a study of multicultural Aboriginal Australians found that MS increased collectivist responses when their aboriginal identity was primed and individualistic responses when their Australian identity was primed (Halloran & Kashima, 2004).

Although TMT posits that the fear of death and cultural meaning systems that mange this fear are universal, the content of these meaning systems are viewed as culture specific, thus leading to cultural variations in how they are manifested. Given that East Asian cultures value collective over individual identity and view modesty and humility as virtues, what would appear to reflect a lack of self-esteem striving within a Western context may actually reflect attempts to demonstrate one's value by behaving in a modest nonself-aggrandizing way in a more collectivist cultural context. This issue is not unique to TMT and has been debated extensively in the literature on cultural differences in the self. Whereas some have argued that the self-esteem motive is a uniquely Western phenomenon that is largely absent in East Asian cultures (e.g., Heine, Lehman, Markus, & Kitayama, 1999), others have argued that apparent cultural differences in self-esteem striving reflect differences in what cultures value as prototypic of a good person (Sedikedes, Gaertner, & Vevea, 2005). Clearly, TMT falls in the latter camp. Ever-increasing trends toward globalization and infiltration of values from other cultures complicate matters further, making it even more difficult to specify exactly which values people from different cultures in specific situations will be oriented toward when motivated to demonstrate their value.

It is also possible that some cultures are more accepting of death than others. For example, Yen and Cheng (2010) assert that many Asians view death as a natural and even desirable part of life. Viewing life and death as part of the same process is a central tenet of many forms of Buddhism and other Eastern religions. However, many Americans also claim not to fear death. We have found that what people consciously report about death bears no clear relation to how they respond to reminders of mortality. And we are skeptical that it's biologically possible not to fear death. Of course, strong terror management resources can help people endure reminders of mortality without need for additional defense. For example, recent studies suggest that Buddhism, meditative states, and mindfulness may have such protective value. We found that although MS increases derogation of a person who criticizes Korea among Korean non-Buddhists, this effect does not occur among Korean Buddhists (Park & Pyszczynski, in press). Interestingly, the effect of MS on derogation of a person who criticized Korea was eliminated among another sample of Korean non-Buddhists after a 45-min Zen meditation training exercise (Park & Pyszczynski, in press). Similarly, Niemec et al. (2010) found MS effects among persons low but not high in dispositional mindfulness, a state that is a central goal of most meditation practices. These findings may help explain some of the differences in responses to MS between people from Eastern and Western cultures that research has sometimes (though not always) found.

7.4 What's so Special About Death?

In the early days of the theory, many psychologists told us that, because they themselves are not afraid of death, it is unlikely that the fear of death could play a significant role in much of what people do. As data came in, documenting the wide-ranging effects that reminders of death have on people, the focus of criticisms shifted to the implausibility of a system which functions to manage this one specific fear. Indeed, TMT's focus on the fear of death runs counter to a long history of domain general theorizing in psychology that emphasizes very broad motives and processes that cut across the specific content of people thoughts and fears.

Far and away the most common critique of TMT consists of attempts to reduce the problem of death to a specific instance of some other more general threat. Rather than arguing that death is not threatening, more recent critics argue that death is a specific case of a more general threat, which is the "real reason" thoughts of death produce the effects they do. The most popular and influential of these alternatives argue that death is threatening because of the uncertainty it entails (e.g., Hohman & Hogg, 2011; McGregor et al., 2001; van den Bos & Miedema, 2000); because it undermines meaning (Heine, Proulx, & Vohs, 2006); because it is largely uncontrollable (Fritsche, Jonas, & Fankhanel, 2008); or because it threatens social relationships and belonging (e.g., Leary, 2004; Navarrete & Fessler, 2005).

People fear death for many reasons, including those proposed as alternatives TMT (Florian & Mikulincer, 1998b). But the problem of death cannot be reduced to any one of these specific features. It encompasses *all* these concerns and many others: the absence of experience, the cessation of bodily functions, bodily decay, burial or cremation, not being involved in future events, and the possibility of continuation of consciousness after during burial or during cremation. From the perspective of TMT, though, the most basic problem with death is that it entails *not living*, which is the prerequisite for all other human needs, motives, and desires. As we stated in the initial presentations of the theory, from the perspective of TMT, it is the *terror of absolute annihilation*, the fear of not being, that is most disturbing about death (e.g., Solomon et al., 1991, p. 96).

Nonetheless, we agree that certainty, meaning, control, and interpersonal relationships are important motives in their own right. However, positing that these motives also play important roles in managing the terror of death is quite different than claiming that they are the "real reason" people fear death. Cultural worldviews buffer anxiety by imbuing existence with *meaning*, the possibility of attaining personal value (self-esteem), and the hope of transcending death. To effectively *control* death anxiety, people require faith (i.e., *certainty*) in the validity of their worldviews and self-concepts. Because the most important aspects of worldviews cannot be directly observed and some violate direct sensory experience, people require *consensual validation* of their worldviews and self-concepts from others to maintain the *certainty* that enables these structures to manage their fears; thus, acceptance from *other people* is essential for effective terror management.

This in no way implies, though, that effective anxiety-buffer functioning is the *only* reason people need meaning, certainty, control, or other people. Effective goal-directed behavior clearly requires these psychosocial resources; these constructs play central roles in most contemporary theories of self-regulation (e.g., Bandura, 1986; Carver & Scheier, 1981a, 1981b). The central claim of TMT is that in addition to the pragmatic functions they serve, these psychological entities are part of the system through which people control existential fear. As discussed above, the terror management system builds on more primitive systems that initially evolved to serve more concrete pragmatic functions. TMT posits that awareness of death changes the way the motives for meaning, certainty, control, and interpersonal connections operate. These needs extend beyond their pragmatic function to that of maintaining a conception of reality and one's contributions to it that detoxify death.

Purely pragmatic motives that serve to facilitate effective action would orient people toward the most accurate meanings possible and toward connections with people who are most useful for meeting their pragmatic needs.

Although people *sometimes* seek accurate meanings that fit well with observable reality, they also sometimes go to great lengths to believe things that conflict with the information provided by their senses and to connect with those who help them to maintain these counter-experiential beliefs. Death-denying motives help explain such departures from practical utility.

7.5 Do Other Threats Produce Effects Similar to Mortality Salience?

Soon after our initial MS studies (Greenberg et al., 1990; Rosenblatt et al., 1989) were published, critics asked whether these effects were driven by thoughts of death, *per se*, or whether any aversive event or negative affective state yields the same effects. This led us to begin contrasting MS with control conditions in which participants were given parallel inductions regarding other unpleasant and threatening events, such as failure, uncertainty, worries about the future, general anxieties, meaninglessness, giving a speech in front of a large audience, social exclusion, paralysis, and physical pain; our strategy was to make the MS and control inductions parallel to each other but vary the specific aversive event about which participants were asked. The first of these studies showed that thoughts of worries about life after college did increase negative affect but did not increase worldview defense; thoughts of death, on the other hand, did not produce negative affect but did increase worldview defense (Greenberg et al., 1995). Well over 100 other studies have shown that MS produces effects different from thoughts of these other threats. These studies make it clear that not just any aversive event or threat leads to the effects that MS produces.

However, more recent studies have shown that other types of threats, such as personal dilemmas (e.g., McGregor et al., 2001), thoughts of being uncertain (van den Bos & Miedema, 2000), or not having control (Fritsche et al., 2008), disconfirmation of expectations (Proulx & Heine, 2008), and even abstract art and absurdist literature (e.g., Proulx & Heine, 2009), sometimes produce effects parallel to those of MS. Critics of TMT view these studies as evidence that the problem of death is a specific instance of these other threats. These are interesting findings, but there are important issues to consider regarding their implications for TMT.

Prior to the development of TMT, there were already substantial literatures showing that people respond defensively to threats to their self-esteem and meaning systems: e.g., self-serving biases, cognitive dissonance, just world beliefs, and other motivated cognitive distortions. Thus, it is not surprising that research continues to show that threats to these psychological entities produce defensive reactions. TMT was developed, in part, to explain *why* people need self-esteem and certainty regarding their meaning systems. We developed the MS hypothesis as *one of several converging approaches* to assessing the proposition that self-esteem and cultural worldviews provide protection from death-related anxiety. The purpose of the MS hypothesis is to serve as a tool for assessing the validity of TMT, rather than the purpose of TMT being to provide an explanation for the MS effect. A compelling alternative to TMT needs to go beyond providing an alternative explanation for one line of evidence regarding the theory and address the literature in its entirety.

But because the MS research is central to the TMT literature, it is clearly important to understand the nature of the effects demonstrated there. What should be made of this mixed evidence? Looking only at the pattern of empirical results and ignoring conceptual arguments, one could summarize the existing literature by saying it shows that in the vast majority studies, MS produces different effects from many aversive control conditions, but that some studies have found other threats producing effects paralleling a subset of the effects of MS. Among that majority of studies, MS has been found to produce different effects than making salient threats of uncertainty, pain, loss of control, failure, meaninglessness, and attachment disruptions. If 100 studies found aspirin to have different effects than acetaminophen, and 40 studies found similar effects, it would not make sense to conclude that aspirin is just one version of acetaminophen and the same processes are triggered by both. Pertinent to this point, Martens, Burke, Schimel, and Faucher (2011) found in a meta-analysis that whereas MS effects get stronger with longer delays, effects of threats to meaning and certainty get weaker, suggesting that different processes are often if not always involved.

In addition, given the impossibility of accepting the null hypothesis, it cannot be concluded that MS produces the *same* effect as these other threats. Given that all of the threats of interest here are abstract psychological states, it is always possible that studies that find no difference between MS and other threats have used ineffective manipulations of one or the other threat or insensitive dependent measures, lack of statistical power, or have other problems that prevent them from finding real effects. But this is not a very satisfying answer to the question of whether MS is the same or different from other threats.

This begs the question of whether the processes that produce defensive responses to other threats are at least sometimes the same as those involved in MS effects. From the perspective of TMT, similar processes might be involved if other threats increase the accessibility of death-related thoughts. Because a large body of literature has shown that threats to worldviews, self-esteem, and attachments increase the accessibility of death related but not other aversive thoughts (for a review, see Hayes et al., 2010), it is possible that at least some of the defensive responses are caused by threats to the anxiety buffer, which increase DTA and produce defensive responses for this reason.

Some researchers, for example, McGregor et al. (2001), van den Bos and Miedema (2000), and Proulx and Heine (2009), report that the other threats they have investigated increase worldview defense but do not increase DTA. However, some of these studies used procedures that varied from ours in small but theoretically significant ways. For example, McGregor et al. (2001, Studies 3 and 4) found that a temporal discontinuity manipulation (specifically, asking university student participants how they might think about a childhood memory 35 years in the future) produced increased cultural worldview defense comparable to an MS induction, but did not increase DTA. It seemed to us that asking people to think about themselves in the distant future could plausibly conjure up intimations of mortality; and when we examined the materials from this study, we noticed that the supposedly neutral passage between the temporal discontinuity manipulation and the assessment of cultural worldview defense made explicit reference to death, which could keep death thoughts in focal attention and suppress DTA accordingly. Chaudry, Tison, and Solomon (2002) consequently replicated the McGregor et al. study with the neutral passage from our experiments and found that the temporal discontinuity manipulation produced the same increase in DTA as a traditional MS induction. McGregor and colleagues then replicated the finding that temporal discontinuity increases DTA in their lab (Ian McGregor, personal communication to Sheldon Solomon, October 16, 2001).

Other studies used DTA measures different from those used in most TMT research that appear to be considerably less sensitive. Whereas the word stems used in our measure are designed so that there are generally just two possible words to complete each critical item which can be completed by filling in two additional letters, the measures used in many of the studies conducted by others had multiple possible completions, were more open-ended, and had more open letters. Weber, Zhang, Schimel, and Blatter (2015) found that some of the manipulations of meaning threat used by Proulx and colleagues (Proulx & Heine, 2009; Randles, Heine, & Santos, 2013) yielded increased DTA when our usual more sensitive measure was used. Thus, the possibility that these other threats produce effects parallel to MS because they produce a subtle increase in DTA remains.

Besides the possibility that other psychological threats produce effects similar to MS because they increase DTA (in which case such findings would follow directly from TMT), it is also not clear how these alternative explanations for MS effects would account for the dramatic and reliable difference in the nature of proximal defenses that emerge immediately after MS and distal defenses that emerge when thoughts of death are accessible but not in focal attention. Why would threats to certainty, meaning, control, or belonging lead to behavior aimed at increasing one's health and longevity immediately after they are perceived but to behavior aimed at shoring up one's worldview, self-esteem, or attachments after a delay or distraction? And, why would this difference evaporate and worldview defense emerge immediately after these threats when they are presented subliminally (see Arndt, Cook, & Routledge, 2004, for a review of this literature)? Indeed, although researchers testing alternatives to TMT include a delay and distraction after their threat inductions, it is not at all clear why this would be needed from their perspectives; rather than providing a theoretical rationale for their use of a delay, these researchers simply cite our studies showing that MS effects on worldview defense require a delay or distraction between the threat induction and measurement of defense. Their explanations of why uncertainty and meaning threats produce defensive responses make a little more sense when people are consciously contemplating these threats, yet that is precisely when symbolic terror management defenses do *not* occur.

Tests of other TMT hypotheses also undermine these alternative views. Many studies have shown that threats to self-esteem, worldviews, and close relationships increase DTA, and that boosts to each of these anxiety-buffer components reduce both DTA- and MS-induced defense. Anxiety-buffer threats increase DTA while not increasing the accessibility of other negative thoughts (Hayes et al., 2010), and evidence for an afterlife reduces worldview defense in response to MS (e.g., Dechesne et al., 2003). The fact that threats to these anxiety-buffer components activate and respond to content specifically focused on death, and that bolstering these components reduces DTA, shows that death is central to these processes. Studies have also shown that DTA mediates the relation between MS and worldview defense (e.g., Cohen, Sullivan, Solomon, Greenberg, & Ogilvie, 2011; Das, Bushman, Bezemer, Kerkhof, & Vermeulen, 2009; Vail, Arndt, et al., 2012). It is not at all clear how any of the alternatives to TMT would explain these findings. Although critics usually restrict their focus to the MS effect itself, a viable alternative to TMT needs to account for all of the TMT literature.

7.6 Conceptual Problems with Alternatives to TMT

Because we have provided extensive critiques of most alternatives to TMT elsewhere (e.g., Landau, Solomon, Pyszczynski, & Greenberg, 2007; Pyszczynski, Abdollahi, et al., 2006; Pyszczynski, Greenberg, et al., 2006; Solomon et al., 1997), here we discuss only the most serious issues that render them conceptually implausible. Because we've yet to see responses to our critiques of these alternative perspectives, we again invite the proponents of these alternatives to address the issues we raise so that we can better understand their reasoning.

7.6.1 Uncertainty

Some theorists argue that uncertainty about either when and how death will occur or what happens afterward (e.g., Hohman & Hogg, 2011) or general personal uncertainty activated by reminders of death (e.g., McGregor, 2006; van den Bos & Miedema, 2000) underlies the MS effects that have been documented in the literature. However, death is one of the few truly certain things in life. Although uncertainty surrounding death is *one* of the many things that are troubling about it, there are certainly many other terrifying aspects of death. Besides, people don't always prefer certainty over uncertainty. Research has shown that people actively avoid certainty in many situations, usually when they fear unpleasant truths. Avoiding diagnostic medical tests, self-handicapping, and gambling are all examples of active avoidance of certainty. Unrealistic optimism in many domains of life, including those related to one's health and longevity, is well documented (e.g., Weinstein & Klein, 1996). And although some people might believe they would like to know with certainty what happens after death, we suspect their enthusiasm for such knowledge would wane if the answers were not to their liking. As we've asked uncertainty theorists before (Pyszczynski et al., 2010, p. 7550): "Would people rather believe there certainly is not an afterlife or that there *might* be one? Would they rather believe they will certainly be forgotten a few years after they die, or that their memory *might* live on indefinitely? Would it be comforting for people to know that they were absolutely certain to die a painful death a year from today, or would they prefer the possibility that they will live a happy and productive life into their 90s and then die painlessly in their sleep?" Do uncertainty theorists really believe that people would prefer to know with certainty they will never find a loving partner or succeed in their career, as opposed to holding out hope that they might? Would people rather be certain they are stupid, unattractive, and untalented or remain hopeful about these domains? Our point here is that the motive to avoid undesirable information is often more powerful than the motive for certain knowledge, and this seems especially true with matters of life and death. Uncertainty theories leave us uncertain as to when uncertainty will be avoided and when it will be sought.

7.6.2 Meaning Threat

It has also been argued that thoughts of death are threatening because they undermine meaning. In their Meaning Maintenance Model (MMM), Heine et al. (2006, p. 90) define meaning as "what connects things to other things in expected ways – anything and any way that things can be connected." Because human beings are meaning-making animals, threats to meaning lead to attempts to restore meaning, which sometimes extend to domains unrelated to the original disruption. They argue that thoughts of death produce the effects they do because they undermine meaning frameworks and, importantly, are not different in any significant way (except perhaps extremity) from any other expectancy disconfirmation or perceptual anomaly.

But is it plausible that the major reason death is threatening is that it undermines meaning? We simply don't understand how thoughts of death, regardless of their content, are a threat to "any way that things can be connected" (Heine et al., 2006, p. 90). The inevitability of death is a fact of life, part of the meaning system of all but the youngest children, and surely part of the meaning systems of all who have ever participated in MS experiments. Another meaning that can be affixed to death that fits the MMM definition of meaning quite well is that all consciousness ends at the moment of death, never to be regained, and that in a short time all remnants of our existence will be lost. Although unpleasant, this meaning fits better with observable reality than what most people believe. Yet people avoid meanings such as this and exert considerable energy to preserve more pleasing, but less likely, meanings. A fatal flaw of the MMM is that it has no conceptual basis for predicting a preference between these two or any other alternative meanings.[4]

Although people sometimes say death robs life of meaning, it is not the MMM's very general "relationships among things" sort of meaning to which

---

[4] Although the vast majority of people hold comforting beliefs entailing some form of life after death, some people do accept the less comforting idea that consciousness ends at death. It's important to be clear that although TMT posits a motive to believe comforting things about death, this does not mean that this motive will outweigh all other forces and sources of information. The biological worldview espoused by most of today's scientists is compelling to many people for reasons that may outweigh the desire to believe in an afterlife. TMT suggests that accepting worldviews that do not include literal immortality requires greater commitment to symbolic immortality or other ways of coping with the problem of death.

they are alluding. Rather, this usually refers to the sort of cosmic significance that TMT posits people use to shield themselves from the terror of nonexistence. From our perspective, the MMM has the problem backward: people do not fear death because it undermines meaning, but rather, need life to be meaningful to protect themselves from the fear of death. Both ontologically and phylogenetically, it seems highly unlikely that the capacity to view life as cosmically significant precedes the capacity to be frightened by the prospect of death, which would be necessary if the fear of death was a response to threats to cosmic meaning.

Importantly, not just any meaning will do when it comes to dealing with death—or most other problems for that matter. People work hard to preserve the culturally transmitted meanings our ancestors invented to enable them to cope with knowledge that death is an inevitable fact of life. Research shows that MS (and other threats when they have such effects) increases belief in an afterlife, deities, supernatural powers, nationalism, and the value of one's attachment figures. The MMM provides no specification of which meanings people seek and which they avoid and no basis for predicting the direction of people's responses to threats. Recent refinement of the model (Proulx & Inzlicht, 2012) that posits an initial preference for restoring meaning on the threatened dimension, which generalizes to other domains only if the specific threat is not resolved, is a step in the right direction, but further specification of what determines the preferred content of meaning-making efforts and further consideration of the functions of different levels and types of meaning are still needed.

7.6.3 Explaining MMM Effects

We suspect that the types of expectancy disconfirmations and perceptual discrepancies studied in MMM research do not motivate people toward any specific types of meaning because they involve processes different from those activated by MS. One sensible way to understand expectancy disconfirmations and perceptual discrepancies is that they arouse dissonance. And dissonance motivates efforts to defend beliefs and affirm values. Indeed, evidence shows that arousal mediates the effects in these studies. In contrast, evidence suggests that MS does not produce physiological arousal and that arousal does not mediate its effects.

Another way to understand these effects builds on research showing that disconfirmed expectancies instigate inferential processes aimed at resolving the disrupted meaning that such disconfirmations produce. For example, Pyszczynski and Greenberg (1981) found that unexpected behavior from an attractive female confederate prompted questions to her that were relevant to the unexpected behavior over the more interesting things that college men were likely to ask in the absence of the unexpected behavior. Wong and Weiner (1981) found that unexpected behavior increased interest in "why" questions. This research raises the possibility that the effects produced by the expectancy violations and perceptual anomalies in MMM research (e.g., Randles et al., 2013) are due to a general increase in epistemic motivation and inferential processing. This of course is quite different from the directional effects posited by TMT. Consistent with this general increased epistemic activity explanation, recent studies have found that perceptual anomalies used in MMM studies improve artificial grammar learning (Proulx & Heine, 2009), which is one sign of greater processing capacity being devoted to incoming information. On the other hand, Trémolière, De Neys, and Bonnefon (2014) have shown that MS improves performance on logical syllogisms when conclusions support one's worldview but inhibits performance when conclusions violate one's worldview. Future research should compare the effects of MS with those of expectancy disconfirmation and perceptual anomalies on these measures of general epistemic activity and the more specific worldview confirming attitudes that are predicted by TMT as one strategy for determining whether the same or different processes are involved in these effects—and how they might be related.

7.6.4 Death Is Not Living

We agree that uncertainty about death, lack of clear understanding of what it means, the loss of control that it entails, and the severing of social bonds are among the many reasons that people fear death. Indeed, research suggests that people vary in which aspects of death they report to be most troubling (e.g., Florian & Mikulincer, 1998b). Death is a complex, multifaceted, and very troubling aspect of human existence. TMT maintains that the most basic reason death is upsetting and motivating is because it undermines the most basic motive of all, which is a prerequisite for all other need satisfaction—staying alive. More specifically, death is a unique motivator because: (a) most biological systems function to keep the organism alive, thus averting death; (b) death must be avoided to enhance opportunities for reproduction and care of offspring, both essential for gene perpetuation; (c) death is the only absolutely inevitable future event; and (d) death threatens to undermine all human desires, whether for pleasure, belonging, certainty, meaning, control, competence, self-actualization, or growth. Human beings are the only species sufficiently cognitively complex to be aware of the inevitability of their own demise and the only species with the cognitive wherewithal to invent conceptions of reality that deny the finality of this fate.

7.7 Threat-General and Threat-Specific Theories

The most recent trend in alternatives to the TMT analysis of the role of death in life are models positing very general biological mechanisms through which *all* threats produce their effects (e.g., Jonas et al., 2014; McGregor, 2006; Tritt et al., 2012). These models view all threats as functionally equivalent and posit mechanisms that reduce anxiety produced by perceived discrepancies to explain the effects of all threats and discrepancies. McGregor's (2006) Reactive Approach Motivation (RAM) model was the first of these and seems to be the prototype upon which other models have built. From this perspective, threats of all kinds are reduced to conflicts or discrepancies between actual and expected or desired states, which activate the Behavioral Inhibitory System (BIS; Gray & McNaughton, 2000) and produce a subjective state of anxious uncertainty. The BIS produces an orienting response that disrupts ongoing behavior and motivates efforts to resolve the discrepancy in question. If a resolution of the focal discrepancy is not forthcoming, the RAM model posits a rapid switch to the approach-oriented Behavioral Activation System (BAS) that refocuses the organism toward approaching other goals. This switch to approach motivation is claimed to relieve the distress activated by the original disruption, and thus either resolve the problem or provide a palliative to the distress produced. From the RAM perspective, activation of approach motivation is the central mechanism that resolves the distress produced by all threats, including thoughts of death. Jonas et al. (2014) posit a somewhat different view, with threats activating the BIS so as to facilitate a more rapid return to the BAS and the goal-oriented behavior.

It seems unlikely to us, though, that there are no meaningful differences in the processes involved in terror management, cognitive dissonance, perceptual discrepancies, and the many other effects that Tritt et al., Jonas et al., and McGregor argue are produced by the same underlying process. There are large and complex literatures surrounding all of these effects that cannot be comprehensively explained by simple alternation between approach and avoidance motivation. For example, there are no theoretical mechanisms in any of these models to explain why choice and foreseeable aversive consequences play a role in dissonance processes or the interplay between worldviews, self-esteem, and attachments in terror management processes. The different moderating and mediating variables for these effects also suggest that single process models are unlikely to provide adequate explanations. The contents of cognition play important roles that cannot be ignored if one hopes to explain the literature surrounding any of these processes.

Although proponents of these models offer some evidence of similarity in the neurological correlates of some aspects of some of these effects, the evidence that the processes are the same is far from compelling. For example, Tritt et al. cite evidence suggesting that activation of the right amygdala anterior cingulate gyrus is the common shared neural pathway through which threats produce their effects. But there is also evidence of activation of distinct neural structures in response to MS that does not appear to occur in response to other threats (e.g., Agroskin, Klackl, & Jonas, 2014; Quirin et al., 2012). The literature on neurological underpinnings of these processes is far too tentative to make sweeping generalizations such as these. Even if many of the neurological structures involved in responses to these different types of threats did turn out to share common pathways, it is virtually certain that there are also unique aspects of each, at neural, and all other levels of analysis. Minimally, there must be neurological underpinnings of the contents of consciousness that differentiate the diverse array of events that these models attempt to encompass.

Turning to the more specific claims of these models, it is implausible that all of the findings from TMT research result from activation of approach motivation. The large literature documenting the tendency of people to move away from reminders of their animal nature when mortality is salient is especially difficult to construe as approach focused: finding the physical aspects of sex less appealing, *withdrawing* from both pleasant and unpleasant physical sensations, *distancing* from a breast-feeding mother, and *avoiding* breast self-examinations (for a review, see Goldenberg, 2012) provide just a few examples. Indeed, many responses to MS involve negative evaluations, derogation, or distancing from a person who is different from oneself or who violates cultural values (e.g., Greenberg et al., 1990). Although threat-general theorists argue that aggression is an approach-oriented behavior, citing Harmon-Jones and Peterson (2008), and this might help account for findings in which MS increases actual aggression (McGregor et al., 1998), it is a major stretch to construe all negative evaluations as approach oriented. MS has also been shown to increase distress when handling a flag or crucifix disrespectfully (Greenberg et al., 1995), distancing from one's own ethnic group (Arndt et al., 2002), disdain for abstract art (Landau et al., 2006), opposition to immigration (Weise, Arciszewski, Verlhiac, Pyszczynski, &

Greenberg, 2012), derogation of a sexually provocative woman (Landau et al., 2006), and giving harsher punishment to a moral transgressor (Florian & Mikulincer, 1997), none of which can easily be construed as approach-motivated behavior.

Taken literally, the RAM model predicts the opposite of what was found in all these studies. Perhaps proponents would argue that these cases of overt avoidance involve upholding values or standards of some sort, and that the apparent avoidant nature of these attitudes and actions is ultimately serving approach motives. But this sort of argument would obscure any meaning or utility of the distinction between approach and avoidance, and illustrates the looseness and inability to generate *a priori* predictions from this perspective. It's hard to imagine how a theory that views activation of approach motivation as the proximal source of relief from threat could generate any of the predictions made by TMT, or any *a priori* predictions regarding specific responses to particular threats (cf. Shepherd, Kay, Landau, & Keefer, 2011).

It is also important to recognize that most, if not all, behavior involves simultaneous activation of both approach and avoidance systems. For example, theory and research (Wegner, 1994) suggest that suppressing unpleasant thoughts (avoidance motivation) entails the generation of distractions (approach). And pursuing most goals requires simultaneous avoidance of appealing impediments to approaching the goal (Kuhl & Beckman, 1985)—as when avoiding extreme statements in order to craft a convincing argument. Similarly, the proximal and distal defenses documented in the TMT literature seem to involve coordinated activation of both approach and avoidance motivation, as in the case of the proximal defense of intending to go to the gym to exercise and the distal defense of supporting war to eliminate an enemy. Although one can assess the relative activation of brain regions more associated with approach or avoidance, it is important to realize that most if not all behavior involves a blend of both approach and avoidance, and presumably activation of brain centers involved with both.

Tritt et al. (2012) argue that it is likely that the systems for responding to complex abstract threats evolved in a way that built on earlier more primitive systems for coping with more concrete threats. This is a good point with which we concur. Although our original conceptualization of TMT didn't address the precursors upon which the terror management system was built, we never claimed that it emerged out of nowhere; we provided a more thorough discussion of possible scenarios through which these processes might have emerged among our ancestors in Pyszczynski and Kesebir (2012), Pyszczynski et al. (2014), and Section 5.4.

Our perspective differs from that of Tritt et al. in placing much greater emphasis on human innovation, cultural evolution, and the specific contents of conscious and nonconscious ideation. Modern humans' approach to dealing with death builds on the approach our ancestors invented that has been passed down and modified over the millennia by further human innovations that became institutionalized in our cultures. These cultural innovations changed the environment to which human brains must adapt and thus likely affected biological evolution as well. Importantly, though, being built upon more primitive adaptations in no way implies that the terror management system is the same as the various other systems that also built on these earlier adaptations.

These general threat-compensation models are conceptualized at a different, more concrete, level of abstraction than TMT, focusing on neurological underpinnings and biological processes. For example, Tritt et al. (2012, p. 716) describe their model as a "biologically informed, mechanistic elucidation of threat-compensation processes" that provides an improvement over the "meta-physical explanations" (p. 727) provided by TMT. Beyond the apparent misunderstanding of the term "meta-physics," these authors conflate reductionism with science. As many others have pointed out before us, psychological processes cannot be reduced to or explained by their neurological substrates (see, e.g., Jaynes, 1976). And although progressing at an impressive pace, current understanding of how neurological locations and events relate to psychological processes involving meanings and behavior is still in its infancy and far from able to produce confident conclusions regarding subtle distinctions in meaning, beliefs, or values.

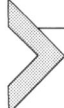

8. ISSUES FOR FUTURE RESEARCH AND THEORY DEVELOPMENT

Although there are many issues for which further research and theoretical specification are needed, here we briefly discuss what we see as some of the most pressing ones.

8.1 The Relation Between Thoughts of Death and Other Threats

The biggest point of contention between proponents and critics of TMT is how the problem of death relates to other threats. We presented our analysis of this relation and discussed the major problems with alternative accounts in previous sections. But there is still much to be learned about this relation.

Perhaps the most pressing question is whether the mechanism through which MS produces its effects is the same as those invoked by other threats. Although the evidence is mixed as to whether other threats produce the same or different effects as MS, and there is compelling evidence that MS effects are at least partially mediated by DTA, the mechanisms through which other threats produce their effects is less clear. What role, if any, does DTA play in these other effects? If DTA does not mediate them, does increased accessibility of thoughts about these other threats play a role? If so, do defensive responses reduce the accessibility of those thoughts, as they do for death-related thoughts? Or are responses to other types of threats the result of a general increase in epistemic activity that spills over to the domain in which effects are assessed?

A related question is whether the time course for responses to other types of threats is the same or different from that typically found for MS—and, if not, what that tells us about the process. Because some level of delay and distraction has been included in most studies of the effects of other threats, it is unclear whether similar or different effects emerge immediately after exposure to them. Recent research also shows that threats to meaning increase DTA and worldview defense only when they produce increases in self-reported negative affect (Weber, Zhang, Schimel, & Blatter, 2015). Studies directly comparing the immediate and delayed effects of MS and various other threats on DTA, the accessibility of other relevant cognitions, affect, and defensive responses would be especially useful for addressing this question.

A related question concerns the growing body of research documenting effects of thoughts of threatening events that are directly associated with death but also involve other threatening content, often of a political or ideological nature. For example, it has been shown that reminders of terrorist attacks (e.g., Landau et al., 2004), bombed out buildings (Vail, Arndt, et al., 2012; Vail, Juhl, et al., 2012), nuclear accidents (Selimbegović, Chatard, Er-Rafiy, & Pyszczynski, 2014), natural disasters (Kesebir & Pyszczynski, 2014), and the Holocaust in Nazi Germany and Japanese occupation of Korea (e.g., Hirschberger, Lifshin, Seeman, Ein-Dor, & Pyszczynski, 2014) produce increases in various forms of worldview defense similar to that produced by MS. Some of these studies show that thoughts of these events also increase DTA (e.g., Landau et al., 2004); one showed that defense was mediated by DTA, but another did not find such mediation (Selimbegović et al., 2014). Although we suspect that death-related ideation is part of what drives these effects, these other threats are likely to also activate thoughts and emotions regarding the specific type of event in question. As Arndt et al. (2002) have shown, other thoughts activated along with those directly related to death appear to influence the specific domains from which security is sought. Specification of the dynamics of these processes is an important issue for further theory development and research.

8.2 Variations in How Death Is Construed

Because TMT emphasizes the role of unconscious death-related ideation, we've tended to assume that it is simply the idea of death or nonexistence from which people must defend themselves. The fact that in our first few studies, we attempted but did not find relations between the content of participants' responses to the open-ended MS manipulation and the level of worldview defense they exhibited supported this assumption; so we soon stopped looking for such relations. But failing to find effects does not mean they do not exist. More recent findings of cultural differences in some aspects of responses to death-related thoughts have led to us to think about the possibility that different ways of construing death have different consequences. Indeed, Eastern religions often view life and death as part of the same process and advocate accepting one's mortality as a major spiritual task. In a related vein, many (but certainly not all) patients with terminal diseases report having made peace with their mortality, and research has shown that older adults generally report less fear of death than middle-aged persons (Fortner & Niemeyer, 1999) and that older adults with high levels of executive functioning do not show the harsher responses to moral transgressors and worldview criticizers that younger persons do, though they are still affected by them (e.g., Maxfield et al., 2007). This suggests that investigating the consequences of different ways of construing death may be a fruitful avenue for future research.

Recent studies conducted in the Netherlands (Doojse, Rutjens, & Pyszczynski, 2015) show that a substantial minority of participants report feelings of acceptance or curiosity when reminded of death and that these responses are associated with lower levels of worldview defense. Follow-up experiments showed that MS inductions that encourage participants to think about death with acceptance or curiosity eliminate the effects found with the more typical open-ended MS induction, and also increase organ donation willingness. This line of research raises the question of whether such inductions actually eliminate death-related fear, albeit temporarily, or if these ways of thinking about death are a particularly effective way of defending against it. Interestingly, Abdollahi (2006) began his exploration of terror management processes when he noted that many of the Muslim students in his classes responded to his presentation of TMT by insisting that they actually look forward to death because of the paradise that they were certain would follow; similar responses are sometimes found in American students' responses to MS in our own studies. Despite this, Abdollahi (2006) replicated five different types of defensive responses to MS among Iranian students and community dwellers. This suggests that the relation between conscious construal of death and how it affect one's behavior is likely a complex one—and certainly worthy of additional investigation.

8.3 Where Will People Turn for Protection?

TMT posits that people protect themselves from death-related anxiety by maintaining faith in and living up to the standards of their cultural worldviews. But cultural worldviews are complex, multifaceted constructions that each person abstracts from the diverse range of information to which they are exposed and experiences they have over the course of their lives. What determines which of these diverse worldview elements a person will turn to for protection in any given situation? This question is at the root of the discussion over whether MS produces a shift toward conservative and dogmatic attitudes, which tend to provide high levels of structure and certainty, or toward one's preexisting worldview, which presumably was adopted because of the security it provides (e.g., Anson et al., 2009; Jost, Fitzsimons, & Kay, 2004).

It has already been well established that individual differences in worldview and sources of self-esteem, along with recent priming of specific worldview elements, are important predictors of these responses. We have also assumed that the relative importance of particular beliefs and values to one's worldview is a major determinant. But a more precise conceptual answer to this question would be that people gravitate toward whatever worldview elements are most associated with safety and security. This probably depends on features inherent in the worldview element as well as one's socialization history with respect to the diverse teachings of one's culture. For example, research shows that behaviors related to morality are especially important determinants of how people evaluate both self and others (e.g., Skitka et al., 2005). We suspect this is because most cultures teach that one's moral actions are the most important, if not the only, factor that determines one's eligibility for literal immortality. It is also likely that one's parents, significant others, and the culture at large place different emphasis on particular beliefs and values, which influences the extent to which one relies on them for security. A reliable way of measuring or manipulating the security value of particular worldview elements would be an important step toward making more precise predictions about where people will turn for protection when existential threat is heightened.

8.4 Alternate Ways to Feel Protected from Death

Related to the issue of how a given individual will respond to the threat of mortality is the nature of the interplay between different forms of immortality striving. The first elaborate written story, *The Epic of Gilgamesh*, concerned Gilgamesh's search for immortality through an afterlife, through an elixir that eliminates death, and through accomplishments that yielded lasting fame. And humans have been seeking literal immortality, eternal life without death, and symbolic immortality ever since.

TMT and research have focused primarily on striving for literal and symbolic immortality, and found plenty of evidence for both. In addition, Dechesne et al. (2003) demonstrated that increased confidence in literal immortality reduces self-esteem striving in response to reminders of death. Furthermore, recent studies (Lifshin, Weise, Soenke, & Greenberg, 2015) have shown that literal immortality via an immortal soul reduces defensive reactions to the prospect of humanity becoming extinct. These findings suggest that these two forms of immortality belief can substitute for each other.

Recently, we have started to examine Gilgamesh's third plan for immortality, finding a way not to die. Indeed, recent advances in understanding the biological processes through which death occurs have made it now possible to resuscitate people up to 4 h after clinical death (Parnia, 2013). Biologists have been making strides toward the possibility of indefinite life extension (ILE) by increasing our understanding and hopefully eventually controlling the biological processes that produce aging (De Grey & Rae, 2008). While debates rage about the feasibility and desirability of ILE, we have begun to study the psychological impact of considering this as a plausible possibility. Preliminary findings suggest that: as investment in literal immortality beliefs increases, support for ILE decreases; American males are generally more on board the ILE train, whereas women are more supportive of literal immortality; if ILE is presented as plausible, people tend to become less invested in literal immortality beliefs; MS increases people's ambivalence about life-extending technologies, making them both view them as more plausible and have more doubts about the objectivity of the scientists exploring these ideas. These studies just scratch the surface of the ways in which hopes of ILE, literal, and symbolic immortality may interact. As we approach this brave new world, we believe it is important to continue assessing the relations among these approaches to quelling the terror of death.

8.5 Variation in Anxiety-Buffer Functioning and Psychological Disorder

The TMT analysis of psychological dysfunction posits that ineffective anxiety-buffer functioning is responsible for many psychological disorders, and research has shown that PTSD and depression are associated with the absence of normal defenses to MS (Pyszczynski & Kesebir, 2011; Simon, Arndt, Greenberg, Pyszczynski, & Solomon, 1998). But it has yet to be determined whether these atypical responses are directly related to an overabundance of anxiety or the specific psychological symptoms that we claim are driven by this lack of protection. There is some evidence that people with phobias and obsessive–compulsive tendencies exhibit these symptoms to a greater extent after being reminded of their mortality. But these studies reflect only a few disorders directly related to anxiety—are other dysfunctional behaviors the result of ineffective terror management? And many questions remain about the antecedents and consequences of such dysfunctional responses to threat. It also seems likely that people without symptoms of significant psychological disorders vary in the effectiveness of their anxiety-buffering system. New strategies for assessing and manipulating anxiety-buffer effectiveness are needed to further research on these issues.

8.6 Better Modes of Dealing with Death?

From the perspective of TMT, the fear of death is a universal aspect of human experience, as is the system of managing it through worldviews, self-esteem, and close interpersonal attachments. But as documented in diverse lines of research, there is considerable variability in how individuals within and across cultures approach this problem. Although we claim that some version of a system for managing the fear of death is present in all cultures and passed on to children through the socialization process, we suspect that some people transcend the anxiety-buffering systems of their cultures and find new, perhaps better, ways of dealing with the problem of death. Finding better ways to live life without fear or its troublesome consequences has been the explicit goal of all religions and many philosophies probably since the earliest days of our species. This elusive goal continues to be pursued today, in the form of psychotherapies, programs for psychological harmony, spiritual growth, and self-actualization. Perhaps the ultimate question for future exploration regarding the existential quagmire of mortality is whether any of these practices actually help, and, if so, how they do so.

9. CONCLUSION

TMT has come a long way over the past 30 years. Both terror management research and the number of researchers contributing to it have been increasing exponentially in the last decade (see tmt.missouri.edu). In fact, when we entered "terror management" in a Psych Info search, we were startled to find, from January 2014 to January 2015 alone, 53 publications (excluding dissertations). Although a handful of these were not empirical papers, these publications reported a total of 83 supportive studies! Clearly, to paraphrase a popular paraphrase of Mark Twain, "rumors of TMT's death are greatly exaggerated." The theory and associated research programs continue to engage the interest of scholars in myriad academic disciplines; generate testable hypotheses that produce empirical findings in accord with theory; widen the scope of conceptual domains to which TMT is now applied (e.g., law, consumer behavior, political preferences, robotics); and advance the ongoing refinement of the theory in light of novel empirical findings. Like all theories, there will come a time when TMT will be supplanted by a more potent theoretical perspective, but in the meantime, the theory is continuing to contribute to progress in understanding important aspects of human behavior.

REFERENCES

Abdollahi, A. (2006). Terror management in Iran. In *Presented at meeting of the International Society for Political Psychology, Barcelona, Spain, July.*

Abdollahi, A., Pyszczynski, T., Maxfield, M., & Lusyszczynska, A. (2011). Posttraumatic stress reactions as a disruption in anxiety-buffer functioning: Dissociation and responses to mortality salience as predictors of severity of post-traumatic symptoms. *Psychological Trauma: Theory, Research, Practice, and Policy, 3,* 329–341.

Abdollahi, A., Pyszczynski, T., Maxfield, M., & Luszczynska, A. (2011). Anxiety buffer disruption theory: The relationship between dissociation, anxiety-buffer functioning and severity of posttraumatic symptoms. *Psychological Trauma: Theory, Research, Practice, and Policy, 3,* 329–341.

Agroskin, D., Klackl, J., & Jonas, E. (2014). *Avoiding death by avoiding cultural otherness: Neural evidence for a mediational role of avoidance motivation in mortality effects on cultural closed mindedness.* Unpublished manuscript, Salzburg, Austria: University of Salzburg.

Anson, J., Pyszczynski, T., Solomon, S., & Greenberg, J. (2009). Political ideology in the 21st century: A terror management perspective on maintenance and change of the status quo.

In J. T. Jost, A. C. Kay, & H. Thoristottir (Eds.), *Social and psychological bases of ideology and system justification*. New York: Oxford University Press.

Arndt, J., Allen, J. J. B., & Greenberg, J. (2001). Traces of terror: Subliminal death primes and facial electromyographic indices of affect. *Motivation and Emotion, 25*, 253–277.

Arndt, J., Cook, A., & Routledge, C. (2004). The blueprint of terror management: Understanding the cognitive architecture of psychological defense against the awareness of death. In J. Greenberg, S. L. Koole, & T. Pyszczynski (Eds.), *Handbook of experimental existential psychology* (pp. 35–53). New York: Guilford.

Arndt, J., Greenberg, J., & Cook, A. (2002). Mortality salience and the spreading activation of worldview-relevant constructs: Exploring the cognitive architecture of terror management. *Journal of Experimental Psychology: General, 131*, 307–324.

Arndt, J., Greenberg, J., Pyszczynski, T., & Solomon, S. (1997). Subliminal exposure to death-related stimuli increases defense of the cultural worldview. *Psychological Science, 8*, 379–385. http://dx.doi.org/10.1111/j.1467-9280.1997.tb00429.x.

Arndt, J., Greenberg, J., Simon, L., Pyszczynski, T., & Solomon, S. (1998). Terror management and self-awareness: Evidence that mortality salience provokes avoidance of the self-focused state. *Personality and Social Psychological Bulletin, 24*, 1216–1227.

Arndt, J., Greenberg, J., Solomon, S., Pyszczynski, T., & Simon, L. (1997). Suppression, accessibility of death-related thoughts, and cultural worldview defense: Exploring the psychodynamics of terror management. *Journal of Personality and Social Psychology, 73*, 5–18.

Atran, S. (2002). *In gods we trust: The evolutionary landscape of religion*. Oxford, England: Oxford University Press.

Bandura, A. (1986). *Social foundations of thought and action: A social cognitive theory*. Englewood Cliffs, NJ: Prentice Hall, ISBN: 0-13-815614-X.

Bassett, J. F., Van Tongeren, D. R., Green, J. D., Sonntag, M. E., & Kilpatrick, H. (2014). The interactive effects of mortality salience and political orientation on moral judgments. *British Journal of Social Psychology*. http://dx.doi.org/10.1111/bjso.12086.

Baumeister, R. F. (2005). *The cultural animal: Human nature, meaning, and social life*. New York: Oxford University Press.

Baumeister, R. F., Vohs, K. D., DeWall, C. N., & Zhang, L. (2007). How emotion shapes behavior: Feedback, anticipation, and reflection, rather than direct causation. *Personality and Social Psychology Review, 11*(2), 167–203.

Beatson, R. M., & Halloran, M. J. (2007). Humans rule! The effects of creatureliness reminders, mortality salience and self-esteem on attitudes towards animals. *British Journal of Social Psychology, 46*, 619–632.

Becker, E. (1971). *The birth and death of meaning* (2nd ed.). New York: The Free Press.

Becker, E. (1973). *The denial of death*. New York: Simon & Schuster.

Bering, J. M. (2006). The folk psychology of souls. *Behavioral and Brain Sciences, 29*, 453–462.

Boyer, P. (2001). *Religion explained: The evolutionary origins of religious thought*. New York: Basic Books.

Burish, T. G., & Houston, B. K. (1979). Causal projection, similarity projection, and coping with threat to self-esteem. *Journal of Personality, 47*, 57–70.

Burke, B. L., Martens, A., & Faucher, E. H. (2010). Two decades of terror management theory: A meta-analysis of mortality salience research. *Personality and Social Psychology Review, 14*, 155–195. http://dx.doi.org/10.1177/1088868309352321.

Buss, D. M. (1984). Evolutionary biology and personality psychology: Toward a conception of human nature and individual differences. *American Psychologist, 39*, 1135–1147.

Buss, D. M. (1989). Toward an evolutionary psychology of human mating. *Behavioral and Brain Sciences, 12*, 39–49, Author's response to 27 commentators.

Buss, D. M. (1997). Human motivation in evolutionary perspective: Grounding terror management theory. *Psychological Inquiry, 8*(1), 22–26.

Carver, C. S., & Scheier, M. F. (1981a). *Attention and self-regulation: A control theory approach to human behavior.* New York: Springer-Verlag.

Carver, C. S., & Scheier, M. F. (1981b). Self-consciousness and reactance. *Journal of Research in Personality, 15,* 16–29.

Castano, E., Yzerbyt, V., Paladino, M., & Sacchi, S. (2002). I belong, therefore, I exist: Ingroup identification, ingroup entitativity, and ingroup bias. *Personality and Social Psychology Bulletin, 28,* 135–143.

Chatard, A., Pyszczynski, T., Arndt, J., Selimbegović, L., Konan, P., & Van Der Linden, M. (2012). Extent of trauma exposure and PTSD symptom severity as predictors of anxiety-buffer functioning. *Psychological Trauma: Theory, Research, Practice, and Policy, 4,* 47–55.

Chatard, A., & Selimbegović, L. (2011). When self-destructive thoughts flash through the mind: Failure to meet standards affects the accessibility of suicide-related thoughts. *Journal of Personality and Social Psychology, 100,* 587–605.

Chaudry, N., Tison, J., & Solomon, S. (2002). What'd death got to do with it? The role of existential uncertainty in implicit death thoughts. In *Paper presented at the meeting of the American Psychological Society, New Orleans, LA.*

Cohen, F., Sullivan, D., Solomon, S., Greenberg, J., & Ogilvie, D. M. (2011). Finding everland: Flight fantasies and the desire to transcend mortality. *Journal of Experimental Social Psychology, 47,* 88–102.

Cox, C., Arndt, J., Pyszczynski, T., Greenberg, J., Abdollahi, A., & Solomon, S. (2008). Terror management and adults' attachment to their parents: The safe haven remains. *Journal of Personality and Social Psychology, 94,* 696–717.

Das, E., Bushman, B. J., Bezemer, M. D., Kerkhof, P., & Vermeulen, I. E. (2009). How terrorism news reports increase prejudice against outgroups: A terror management account. *Journal of Experimental Social Psychology, 45,* 453–459. http://dx.doi.org/10.1016/j.jesp.2008.12.001.

De Grey, A., & Rae, M. (2008). *Ending aging: The rejuvenation breakthroughs that could reverse human aging in our lifetime.* New York, NY: St. Martins Griffin.

Deacon, T. (1997). *The symbolic species: The co-evolution of language and the human brain.* London: Penguin Books.

Dechesne, M., Janssen, J., & van Knippenberg, A. (2000). Defense and distancing as terror management strategies: The moderating role of need for structure and permeability of group boundaries. *Journal of Personality and Social Psychology, 79,* 923–932.

Dechesne, M., & Kruglanski, A. W. (2004). Terror's epistemic consequences: Existential threats and the quest for certainty and closure. In J. Greenberg, S. L. Koole, & T. Pyszczynski (Eds.), *Handbook of experimental psychology* (pp. 247–262). New York: Guilford.

Dechesne, M., Pyszczynski, T., Arndt, J., Ransom, S., Sheldon, K. M., van Knippenberg, A., et al. (2003). Literal and symbolic immortality: The effect of evidence of literal immortality on self-esteem striving in response to mortality salience. *Journal of Personality and Social Psychology, 84,* 722–737.

Deci, E. L., & Ryan, R. M. (1980). The empirical exploration of intrinsic motivational processes. In L. Berkowitz (Ed.), *Advances in experimental social psychology: Vol. 13* (pp. 39–80). New York: Academic Press.

DeWall, C. N., & Baumeister, R. F. (2007). From terror to joy: Automatic tuning to positive affective information following mortality salience. *Psychological Science, 18,* 984–990.

Doojse, B., Rutjens, B., & Pyszczynski, T. (2015). *Variations in death construal and defensive responses to mortality salience.* Unpublished manuscript, Amsterdam, The Netherlands: University of Amsterdam.

Ein-Dor, T., Hirscheberger, G., Perry, A., Levy, N., Perry, R., Cohen, R., et al. (2014). Implicit death primes increase alcohol consumption. *Health Psychology, 33*(7), 748–751.

Erdelyi, M. H., & Goldberg, B. (1979). Let's not sweep repression under the rug: Toward a cognitive psychology of repression. In J. F. Kihlstrom, & F. J. Evans (Eds.), *Functional disorders of memory.* Hillsdale, NJ: Erlbaum.

Fessler, D. M. T., & Navarrete, C. D. (2005). The effect of age on death disgust: A critique of terror management perspectives. *Evolutionary Psychology*, *3*, 276–297.

Feurbach, L. (1841/1989). *The essence of Christianity*. Amherst, NY: Prometheus.

Florian, V., & Mikulincer, M. (1997). Fear of death and the judgment of social transgressions: A multidimensional test of terror management theory. *Journal of Personality and Social Psychology*, *73*, 369–380. http://dx.doi.org/10.1037/0022-3514.73.2.369.

Florian, V., & Mikulincer, M. (1998a). Terror management in childhood: Does death conceptualization moderate the effects of mortality salience on acceptance of similar and different others. *Personality and Social Psychology Bulletin*, *24*, 1104–1112.

Florian, V., & Mikulincer, M. (1998b). Symbolic immortality and the management of the terror of death. *Journal of Personality and Social Psychology*, *74*, 725–734.

Fortner, B. V., & Neimeyer, R. A. (1999). Death anxiety in older adults: A quantitative review. *Death Studies*, *23*, 387–411.

Freud, S. (1930). *Civilization and its discontents*. London: Penguin.

Fritsche, I., Jonas, E., & Fankhanel, T. (2008). The role of control motivation in mortality salience effects on ingroup support and defense. *Journal of Personality and Social Psychology*, *95*, 524–541. http://dx.doi.org/10.1037/a0012666.

Gailliot, M. T., Schmeichel, B. J., & Baumeister, R. F. (2006). Self-regulatory processes defend against the threat of death: Effects of self-control depletion and trait self-control on thoughts and fears of dying. *Journal of Personality and Social Psychology*, *91*, 49–62.

Gershuny, B. S., Cloitre, M., & Otto, M. W. (2003). Peritraumatic dissociation and PTSD severity: Do event-related fears about death and control mediate their relation? *Behaviour Research and Therapy*, *41*, 157–166.

Goldenberg, J. L. (2012). A body of terror: Denial of death and the creaturely body. In P. R. Shaver, & M. Mikulincer (Eds.), *Meaning, mortality, and choice: The social psychology of existential concerns* (pp. 93–110). Washington, DC: American Psychological Association.

Goldenberg, J. L., & Arndt, J. (2008). The implications of death for health: A terror management health model for behavioral health promotion. *Psychological Review*, *115*, 1032–1053.

Goldenberg, J. L., McCoy, S. K., Pyszczynski, T., Greenberg, J., & Solomon, S. (2000). The body as a source of self-esteem: The effects of mortality salience on identification with one's body, interest in sex, and appearance monitoring. *Journal of Personality and Social Psychology*, *79*, 118–130.

Goldenberg, J. L., Pyszczynski, T., Greenberg, J., Solomon, S., Kluck, B., & Cornwell, R. (2001). I am not an animal: Mortality salience, disgust, and the denial of human creatureliness. *Journal of Experimental Psychology: General*, *130*, 427–435.

Graham, J., Haidt, J., Koleva, S., Motyl, M., Iyer, R., Wojcik, S., et al. (2013). Moral foundations theory: The pragmatic validity of moral pluralism. *Advances in Experimental Social Psychology*, *47*, 55–130. http://dx.doi.org/10.1016/B978-0-12-407236-7.00002-4.

Graham, J., Haidt, J., & Nosek, B. A. (2009). Liberals and conservatives rely on different sets of moral foundations. *Journal of Personality and Social Psychology*, *96*, 1029–1046. http://dx.doi.org/10.1037/a0015141.

Gray, J. A., & McNaughton, N. (2000). *The neuropsychology of anxiety*. Oxford, England: Oxford University Press.

Greenberg, J., Arndt, J., Simon, L., Pyszczynski, T., & Solomon, S. (2000). Proximal and distal defenses in response to reminders of one's mortality: Evidence of a temporal sequence. *Personality and Social Psychology Bulletin*, *26*, 91–99.

Greenberg, J., Kosloff, S., Solomon, S., Cohen, F., & Landau, M. J. (2010). Toward understanding the fame game: The effect of mortality salience on the appeal of fame. *Self and Identity*, *9*, 1–18.

Greenberg, J., Martens, A., Jonas, E., Eisenstadt, D., Pyszczynski, T., & Solomon, S. (2003). Psychological defense in anticipation of anxiety: Eliminating the potential for anxiety eliminates the effect of mortality salience on worldview defense. *Psychological Science*, *14*, 516–519. http://dx.doi.org/10.1111/1467-9280.03454.

Greenberg, J., Pyszczynski, T., & Solomon, S. (1986). The causes and consequences of a need for self-esteem: A terror management theory. In R. F. Baumeister (Ed.), *Public self and private self* (pp. 189–212). New York: Springer.

Greenberg, J., Pyszczynski, T., Solomon, S., Pinel, E., Simon, L., & Jordan, K. (1993). Effects of self-esteem on vulnerability-denying defensive distortions: Further evidence of an anxiety-buffering function of self-esteem. *Journal of Experimental Social Psychology*, *29*, 229–251.

Greenberg, J., Pyszczynski, T., Solomon, S., Simon, L., & Breus, M. (1994). Role of consciousness and the accessibility of death-related thoughts in mortality salience effects. *Journal of Personality and Social Psychology*, *67*, 627–637. http://dx.doi.org/10.1037/0022-3514.67.4.627.

Greenberg, J., Pyszczynski, T., Veeder, M., Kirkland, S., & Solomon, S. (1990). Evidence for terror management theory II: Effects of mortality salience on reactions to those who explicitly and implicitly threaten the cultural worldview. *Journal of Personality and Social Psychology*, *58*, 308–318.

Greenberg, J., Simon, L., Porteus, J., Pyszczynski, T., & Solomon, S. (1995). Evidence of a terror management function of cultural icons: The effects of mortality salience on the inappropriate use of cherished cultural symbols. *Personality and Social Psychology Bulletin*, *21*, 1221–1228.

Greenberg, J., Simon, L., Pyszczynski, T., Solomon, S., & Chatel, D. (1992). Terror management and tolerance: Does mortality salience always intensify negative reactions to others who threaten one's worldview? *Journal of Personality and Social Psychology*, *63*, 212–220.

Greenberg, J., Solomon, S., Pyszczynski, T., & Steinberg, L. (1988). A reply to Greenwald et al.: Under what conditions does research obstruct theory progress? *Psychological Review*, *95*, 566–571.

Greenberg, J., Vail, K., & Pyszczynski, T. (2014). Chapter three-terror management theory and research: How the desire for death transcendence drives our strivings for meaning and significance. *Advances in Motivation Science*, *1*, 85–134. http://dx.doi.org/10.1016/bs.adms.2014.08.003.

Haidt, J., & Joseph, C. (2004). Intuitive ethics: How innately prepared intuitions generate culturally variable virtues. *Daedalus*, *133*(4), 55–66, Special issue on human nature.

Halloran, M. J., & Kashima, E. S. (2004). Social identity and worldview validation: The effects of ingroup identity primes and mortality salience on value endorsement. *Personality and Social Psychology Bulletin*, *30*, 915–925.

Harmon-Jones, E., Simon, L., Greenberg, J., Pyszczynski, T., Solomon, S., & McGregor, H. (1997). Terror management theory and self-esteem: Evidence that increased self-esteem reduces mortality salience effects. *Journal of Personality and Social Psychology*, *72*, 24–36.

Harmon-Jones, E., & Peterson, C. K. (2008). Effect of trait and state approach motivation on aggressive inclinations. *Journal of Research in Personality*, *42*, 1381–1385. http://dx.doi.org/10.1016/j.jrp.2008.05.001.

Hayes, J., Schimel, J., Arndt, J., & Faucher, E. H. (2010). A theoretical and empirical review of the death-thought accessibility concept in terror management research. *Psychological Bulletin*, *136*, 699–739. http://dx.doi.org/10.1037/a0020524.

Hayes, J., Schimel, J., Faucher, E. H., & Williams, T. J. (2008). Evidence for the DTA hypothesis II: Threatening self-esteem increase death-thought accessibility. *Journal of Experimental Social Psychology*, *44*, 600–613. http://dx.doi.org/10.1016/j.jesp.2008.01.004.

Heflick, N. A., Goldenberg, J. L., Hart, J., & Kamp, S. M. (2015). Death awareness and body-self dualism: A why and how of afterlife belief. *European Journal of Social Psychology*, *45*(2), 267–275.

Heine, S. H., Lehman, D. R., Markus, H. R., & Kitayama, S. (1999). Is there a universal need for positive self-regard? *Psychological Review*, *106*, 766–794.

Heine, S., Proulx, T., & Vohs, K. D. (2006). The meaning maintenance model: On the coherence of social motivations. *Personality and Social Psychology Review*, *10*, 88–110.

Hirschberger, G. (2006). Terror management and attributions of blame to innocent victims: reconciling compassionate and defensive responses. *Journal of Personality and Social Psychology*, *91*, 832–844. http://dx.doi.org/10.1037/0022-3514.91.5.832.

Hirschberger, G., & Ein-Dor, T. (2006). Defenders of a lost cause: Terror management and violent resistance to the disengagement plan. *Personality and Social Psychology Bulletin*, *32*, 761–769.

Hirschberger, G., Lifshin, U., Seeman, S., Ein-Dor, T., & Pyszczynski, T. (2014). *Historical trauma and unsupportive allies: An experimental test of siege mentality*. Unpublished manuscript, Herzlya, Israel: Herzlya Interdisciplinary Institute.

Hohman, Z. P., & Hogg, M. A. (2011). Fear and uncertainty in the face of death: The role of life after death in group identification. *European Journal of Social Psychology*, *41*, 751–760.

Jaynes, J. (1976). *The origin of consciousness in the breakdown of the bicameral mind*. New York: Houghton Mifflin.

Jonas, E., & Fischer, P. (2006). Terror management and religion: Evidence through intrinsic religiousness, mitigated worldview defense after mortality salience. *Journal of Personality and Social Psychology*, *91*, 553–567.

Jonas, E., Greenberg, J., & Frey, D. (2003). Connecting terror management and dissonance theories: Evidence that mortality salience increases the preference for supportive information after decisions. *Personality and Social Psychology Bulletin*, *29*, 1181–1189.

Jonas, E., McGregor, I., Klackl, J., Agroskin, D., Fritsche, I., Holbrook, C., et al. (2014). Threat and defense: From anxiety to approach. In J. M. Olson, & M. P. Zanna (Eds.), *Advances in experimental social psychology: Vol. 49* (pp. 219–286). San Diego, CA: Academic Press.

Jost, J. T., Fitzsimons, G., & Kay, A. C. (2004). The ideological animal: A comparison of system justification, terror management, and just world theories. In J. Greenberg, S. L. Koole, & T. Pyszczynski (Eds.), *Handbook of experimental existential psychology* (pp. 263–283). New York: Guilford.

Kashima, E. S., Halloran, M., Yuki, M., & Kashima, Y. (2004). The effects of personal and collective mortality salience on individualism: Comparing Australians and Japanese with higher and lower self-esteem. *Journal of Experimental Social Psychology*, *40*, 384–392.

Kesebir, P., Luszczynska, A., Kesebir, P., Luszczynska, A., Pyszczynski, T., & Benight, C. (2011). Posttraumatic stress disorder involves disrupted anxiety-buffer mechanisms. *Journal of Social and Clinical Psychology*, *30*, 819–841.

Kesebir, P., & Pyszczynski, T. (2014). Meaning as a buffer for existential anxiety. In P. Russo-Netzer, & A. Batthyany (Eds.), *Meaning in existential and positive psychology*. New York: Free Press.

Kirkpatrick, L. A. (2005). Evolutionary psychology: An emerging new foundation for the psychology of religion. In R. F. Paloutzian, & C. L. Park (Eds.), *Handbook of the psychology of religion and spirituality* (pp. 101–119). New York: Guilford.

Kirkpatrick, L. A., & Navarrete, C. D. (2006). Reports of my death anxiety have been greatly exaggerated: A critique of terror management theory from an evolutionary perspective. *Psychological Inquiry*, *17*, 288–298.

Kosloff, S., Greenberg, J., Sullivan, D., & Weise, D. (2010). Of trophies and pillars: Exploring the terror management functions of short-term and long-term relationship partners. *Personality and Social Psychology Bulletin*, *36*, 1037–1051.

Kosloff, S., Solomon, S., Greenberg, J., Cohen, F., Gershuny, B., Routledge, C., et al. (2006). Fatal distraction: The impact of mortality salience on dissociative responses to 9/11 and subsequent anxiety sensitivity. *Basic and Applied Social Psychology, 28,* 349–356.

Kuhl, J., & Beckman, J. (1985). *Action control: From cognition to action.* New York: Springer.

Kuhn, T. S. (1996). *The structure of scientific revolutions* (3rd ed.). Chicago: University of Chicago Press.

Lambert, A. J., Eadeh, F. R., Peak, S. A., Scherer, L. D., Schott, J. P., & Slochower, J. M. (2014). Toward a greater understanding of the emotional dynamics of the mortality salience manipulation: Revisiting the "affect-free": Claim of terror management research. *Journal of Personality and Social Psychology, 106,* 655–678.

Landau, M. J., Greenberg, J., & Solomon, S. (2004). The motivational underpinnings of religion. *Behavioral and Brain Sciences, 27,* 743–744. http://dx.doi.org/10.1017/S0140525X0435017X.

Landau, M., Johns, M., Greenberg, J., Solomon, S., Pyszczynski, T., & Martens, A. (2006). Windows into nothingness: Terror management, meaninglessness, and negative reactions to modern art. *Journal of Personality and Social Psychology, 87*(2), 190–210.

Landau, M. J., Solomon, S., Pyszczynski, T., & Greenberg, J. (2007). On the compatibility of terror management theory and perspectives on human evolution. *Evolutionary Psychology, 5,* 476–519.

Langer, S. K. (1967). *Mind: An essay on human feeling.* Baltimore: Johns Hopkins University Press.

Leary, M. R. (2004). The function of self-esteem in terror management theory and sociometer theory: Comment on Pyszczynski et al. (2004). *Psychological Bulletin, 130,* 478–482.

Lifshin, U., Greenberg, J., & Sullivan, D. (2014). *Killing animals to feel transcendent of death.* Unpublished manuscript, University of Arizona.

Lifshin, U., Weise, D., Soenke, M., & Greenberg, J. (2015). *The effect of literal and symbolic immortality beliefs on perceptions of end-of-the world scenarios.* Unpublished manuscript, University of Arizona.

MacDonald, G., & Lipp, O. V. (2008). Mortality salience eliminates attentional bias for fear-relevant animals. *Motivation and Emotion, 32,* 243–250.

Martens, A., Burke, B. L., Schimel, J., & Faucher, E. H. (2011). Same but different: Meta-analytically examining the uniqueness of mortality salience effects. *European Journal of Social Psychology, 41*(1), 6–10. http://dx.doi.org/10.1002/ejsp.767.

Martin, L., & van den Bos, K. (2014). Beyond terror: Toward a paradigm shift in the study of threat and culture. *European Journal of Social Psychology, 25,* 32–70.

Maxfield, M., Greenberg, J., Pyszczynski, T., Weise, D. R., Kosloff, S., Abeyta, A., et al. (2014). Increases in generative concern among older adults following reminders of mortality. *International Journal of Aging and Human Development, 79,* 1–21.

Maxfield, M., Pyszczynski, T., Cox, C., Kluck, B., Greenberg, J., Solomon, S., et al. (2007). Age related differences in responses to thoughts of one's own death: Mortality salience and judgments of moral transgressions. *Psychology and Aging, 22,* 341–353.

Maxfield, M., Pyszczynski, T., Greenberg, J., Pepin, R., & Davis, H. P. (2011). The moderating role of executive functioning in older adults' responses to a reminder of mortality. *Psychology and Aging, 27,* 256–263.

McFarland, C., & Ross, M. (1982). Impact of causal attributions on affective reactions to success and failure. *Journal of Personality and Social Psychology, 43,* 937–946. http://dx.doi.org/10.1037/0022-3514.43.5.937.

McGregor, I. (2006). Offensive defensiveness: Toward an integrative neuroscience of personal uncertainty, and other poignant self-threats. *Psychological Inquiry, 17,* 299–308.

McGregor, H. A., Lieberman, J. D., Greenberg, J., Solomon, S., Arndt, J., Simon, L., et al. (1998). Terror management and aggression: Evidence that mortality salience motivates aggression against worldview-threatening others. *Journal of Personality and Social Psychology, 74*(3), 590.

McGregor, I., Zanna, M. P., Holmes, J. G., & Spencer, S. J. (2001). Compensatory conviction in the face of personal uncertainty: Going to extremes and being oneself. *Journal of Personality and Social Psychology, 80,* 472–488.

Mikulincer, M., & Florian, V. (2000). Exploring individual differences in reactions to mortality salience: Does attachment style regulate terror management mechanisms? *Journal of Personality and Social Psychology, 79,* 260–273.

Mikulincer, M., & Florian, V. (2002). The effects of mortality salience on self-serving attributions: Evidence for the function of self-esteem as a terror management mechanism. *Basic and Applied Social Psychology, 24,* 261–271.

Mikulincer, M., Florian, V., & Hirschberger, G. (2003). The existential function of close relationships: Introducing death into the science of love. *Personality and Social Psychology Review, 7,* 20–40.

Mikulincer, M., Florian, V., & Hirschberger, G. (2004). The terror of death and the quest for love: An existential perspective on close relationships. In J. Greenberg, S. L. Koole, & T. Pyszczynski (Eds.), *Handbook of experimental existential psychology* (pp. 287–304). New York: Guilford.

Morris, K. L., & Goldenberg, J. L. (2015). Objects become her: The role of mortality salience on men's attraction to literally objectified women. *Journal of Experimental and Social Psychology, 56,* 69–72.

Nagar, M., & Rabinovitz, S. (in press). Smoke your troubles away: Exploring the effects of death cognitions on cannabis craving and consumption. *Journal of Psychoactive Drugs.*

Navarrete, C. D., & Fessler, D. M. T. (2005). Normative bias and adaptive challenges: A relational approach to coalitional psychology and a critique of terror management theory. *Evolutionary Psychology, 3,* 297–325.

Niemiec, R., Kashdan, T. B., Breen, W. E., Brown, K. W., Cozzolino, P. J., Levesque-Bristol, C., et al. (2010). Being present in the face of existential threat: The role of trait mindfulness in reducing defensive responses to mortality salience. *Journal of Personality and Social Psychology, 99,* 344–365.

Norenzayan, A., Shariff, A. F., Gervais, W. M., Willard, A., McNamara, R., Slingerland, E., et al. (in press). The cultural evolution of prosocial religions. *Behavioral and Brain Sciences.*

Ochsmann, R., & Mathy, M. (1994). *Depreciating of and distancing from foreigners: Effects of mortality salience.* Unpublished manuscript, Mainz, Germany: Universitat Mainz.

Park, Y. C., & Pyszczynski, T. (in press). *Meditation, Buddhism, and ortality salience effects.* Unpublished manuscript, New York: Taylor & Francis: University of Colorado Colorado Springs

Park, Y. C., & Pyszczynski, T. (in press). Cultural universals and differences in dealing with death. In L. A. Harvell & G. S. Nisbet (Eds.), *Denying death: An interdisciplinary approach to terror management theory.*

Parnia, S. (2013). *Erasing death: The science that is rewriting boundaries between life and death.* New York, NY: HarperOne.

Peters, H. J., Greenberg, J., Williams, J. M., & Schneider, N. R. (2005). Applying terror management theory to performance: Can reminding individuals of their mortality increase strength output? *Journal of Sport & Exercise Psychology, 27,* 111–116.

Proulx, T., & Heine, S. J. (2008). The case of the transmogrifying experimenter: Affirmation of a moral schema following implicit change detection. *Psychological Science, 19,* 1294–1300.

Proulx, T., & Heine, S. J. (2009). Connections from Kafka: Exposure to meaning threats improves implicit learning of an artificial grammar. *Psychological Science, 20,* 1125–1131. http://dx.doi.org/10.1111/j.1467-9280.2009.02414.x.

Proulx, T., & Inzlicht, M. (2012). Moderated disanxiousuncertlibrium: Specifying the moderating and neuroaffective determinants of violation-compensation effects. *Psychological Inquiry, 23,* 386–396. http://dx.doi.org/10.1080/1047840X.2012.734912.

Pyszczynski, T., Abdollahi, A., Solomon, S., Greenberg, J., Cohen, F., & Weise, D. (2006). Mortality salience, martyrdom, and military might: The great satan versus the axis of evil. *Personality and Social Psychology Bulletin, 32,* 525–537.

Pyszczynski, T. A., & Greenberg, J. (1981). Role of disconfirmed expectancies in the instigation of attributional processing. *Journal of Personality and Social Psychology, 40,* 31–38.

Pyszczynski, T., & Greenberg, J. (1987). Self-regulatory preservation and the depressive self-focusing style: A self-awareness theory of reactive depression. *Psychological Bulletin, 102,* 122–138.

Pyszczynski, T., Greenberg, J., & Solomon, S. (1999). A dual-process model of defense against conscious and unconscious death-related thoughts: An extension of terror management theory. *Psychological Review, 106,* 835–845.

Pyszczynski, T., Greenberg, J., Solomon, S., & Hamilton, J. (1990). A terror management analysis of self-awareness and anxiety: The hierarchy of terror. *Anxiety Research, 2,* 177–195.

Pyszczynski, T., Greenberg, J., Solomon, S., & Maxfield, M. (2006). On the unique psychological import of the human awareness of mortality: Theme and variations. *Psychological Inquiry, 17,* 328–356.

Pyszczynski, T., & Kesebir, P. (2011). Anxiety buffer disruption theory: A terror management theory account of posttraumatic stress disorder. *Anxiety, Stress, and Coping, 24,* 3–26.

Pyszczynski, T., & Kesebir, P. (2012). Culture, ideology, morality, and religion: Death changes everything. In M. Mikulincer & P. Shaver (Eds.), *The social psychology of meaning, mortality, and choice* (pp. 75–91). Washington, DC: American Psychological Association.

Pyszczynski, T., Motyl, M. S., Vail, K. E., Hirschberger, G., Arndt, J., & Kesebir, P. (2010). *A collateral advantage of drawing attention to the problem of global warming: Increased support for peacemaking and decreased support for war.* Unpublished manuscript, University of Colorado at Colorado Springs.

Pyszczynski, T., Sullivan, D., & Greenberg, J. (2014). Experimental existential psychology: Living in the shadow of the facts of life. In E. Borgida, & J. Bargh (Eds.), *American Psychological Association handbook of personality and social psychology.* Washington, DC: American Psychological Association.

Pyszczynski, T., Wicklund, R. A., Floresky, S., Gauch, G., Koch, S., Solomon, S., et al. (1996). Whistling in the dark: Exaggerated estimates of social consensus in response to incidental reminders of mortality. *Psychological Science, 7,* 332–336.

Quirin, M., Loktyushin, A., Arndt, J., Kustermann, E., Lo, Y., Kuhl, J., et al. (2012). Existential neuroscience: A functional magnetic resonance imaging investigation of neural responses to reminders of one's mortality. *Social Cognitive and Affective Neuroscience, 7,* 193–198.

Randles, D., Heine, S. J., & Santos, N. (2013). The common pain of surrealism and death: Acetaminephin reduces compensatory affirmation following meaning threats. *Psychological Science, 24,* 966–973.

Roberts, T.-A., Goldenberg, J. L., Manly, C., & Pyszczynski, T. (2002). "Feminine Protection": The effects of menstruation on attitudes toward women. *Psychology of Women Quarterly, 26,* 131–139.

Rosenblatt, A., Greenberg, J., Solomon, S., Pyszczynski, T., & Lyon, D. (1989). Evidence for terror management theory: I. The effects of mortality salience on reactions to those who violate or uphold cultural values. *Journal of Personality and Social Psychology, 57,* 681–690.

Rothschild, Z., Abdollahi, A., & Pyszczynski, T. (2009). Does peace have a prayer? The effect of mortality salience, compassionate values and religious fundamentalism on hostility toward out-groups. *Journal of Experimental Social Psychology, 45,* 816–827.

Schimel, J., Hayes, J., Williams, T. J., & Jahrig, J. (2007). Is death really the worm at the core? Converging evidence that worldview threat increases death-thought accessibility. *Journal of Personality and Social Psychology, 92*, 789–803.

Sedikedes, C., Gaertner, L., & Vevea, J. L. (2005). Pan-cultural self-enhancement reloaded: A meta-analytic reply to Heine. *Journal of Personality and Social Psychology, 89*, 539–551.

Selimbegović, L., Chatard, A., Er-Rafiy, A., & Pyszczynski, T. (2014). *The paradoxical effect of nuclear accident reminders on support for nuclear power.* Unpublished manuscript, Poitiers, France: University of Poitiers.

Shepherd, S., Kay, A. C., Landau, M. J., & Keefer, L. A. (2011). Evidence for the specificity of control motivations in worldview defense: Distinguishing compensatory control from uncertainty management and terror management processes. *Journal of Experimental Social Psychology, 47*, 949–958.

Shweder, R., & Haidt, J. (1993). The future of moral psychology: Truth, intuition, and the pluralist way. *Psychological Science, 4*, 360–365.

Simon, L., Arndt, J., Greenberg, J., Pyszczynski, T., & Solomon, S. (1998). Terror management and meaning: Evidence that the opportunity to defend the worldview in response to mortality salience increases the meaningfulness of life in the mildly depressed. *Journal of Personality, 66*(3), 359–382. http://dx.doi.org/10.1111/1467-6494.00016.

Simon, L., Greenberg, J., Harmon-Jones, E., Solomon, S., Pyszczynski, T., Arndt, J., et al. (1997). Terror management and cognitive-experiential self-theory: Evidence that terror management occurs in the experiential system. *Journal of Personality and Social Psychology, 72*, 1132–1146.

Skitka, L. J., Bauman, C. W., & Sargis, E. G. (2005). Moral conviction: Another contributor to attitude strength or something more? *Journal of Personality and Social Psychology, 88*, 895–917. http://dx.doi.org/10.1037/0022-3514.88.6.895.

Solomon, S., Greenberg, J., & Pyszczynski, T. (1991). A terror management theory of social behavior: The psychological functions of self-esteem and cultural worldviews. *Advances in Experimental Social Psychology, 24*, 93–159.

Solomon, S., Greenberg, J., & Pyszczynski, T. (2004). The cultural animal: Twenty years of terror management theory and research. In J. Greenberg, S. L. Koole, & T. Pyszczynski (Eds.), *Handbook of experimental existential psychology* (pp. 13–34).

Solomon, S., Greenberg, J., & Pyszczynski, T. (1997). Return of the living dead. *Psychological Inquiry, 8*, 59–71.

Solomon, S., Greenberg, J., & Pyszczynski, T. (2015). *The worm at the core: The role of death in life.* New York: Random House.

Solomon, S., Greenberg, J., Schimel, J., Arndt, J., & Pyszczynski, T. (2004). Human awareness of death and the evolution of culture. In M. Schaller, & C. Crandal (Eds.), *The psychological foundations of culture* (pp. 15–40). Mahwah, NJ: Erlbaum.

Storms, M. D., & Nisbett, R. E. (1970). Insomnia and the attribution process. *Journal of Personality and Social Psychology, 16*, 319–328. http://dx.doi.org/10.1037/h0029835.

Strachan, E., Schimel, J., Arndt, J., Williams, T., Solomon, S., Pyszczynski, T., et al. (2007). Terror mismanagement: Evidence that mortality salience exacerbates phobic and compulsive behaviors. *Personality and Social Psychology Bulletin, 33*, 1137–1151.

Taubman Ben-Ari, O., Florian, V., & Mikulincer, M. (1999). The impact of mortality salience on reckless driving: A test of terror management mechanisms. *Journal of Personality and Social Psychology, 76*, 35–45.

Taubman-Ben-Ari, O., Findler, L., & Mikulincer, M. (2002). The effects of mortality salience on relationship strivings and beliefs: The moderating role of attachment style. *British Journal of Social Psychology, 41*(3), 419–441.

Trémolière, B., De Neys, W. D., & Bonnefon, J. F. (2014). The grim reasoner: Analytical reasoning under mortality salience. *Thinking & Reasoning, 20*, 333–351.

Tritt, S. M., Inzlicht, M., & Harmon-Jones, E. (2012). Toward a biological understanding of mortality salience (and other threat compensation processes). *Social Cognition, 6,* 715–733.

Vail, K. E., Arndt, J., Motyl, M., & Pyszczynski, T. (2012). The aftermath of destruction: Images of destroyed buildings increase support for war, dogmatism, and death thought accessibility. *Journal of Experimental Social Psychology, 48,* 1069–1081.

Vail, K. E., Juhl, J., Arndt, J., Vess, M. K., Routledge, C., & Rutjens, B. T. (2012). When death is good for life: Considering the positive trajectories of terror management. *Personality and Social Psychology Review, 16*(4), 303–329.

Vail, K. E., Rothschild, Z. K., Weise, D., Solomon, S., Pyszczynski, T., & Greenberg, J. (2010). A terror management analysis of the psychological functions of religion. *Personality and Social Psychology Review, 14,* 84–94.

van den Bos, K., & Miedema, J. (2000). Toward understanding why fairness matters: The influence of mortality salience on reactions to procedural fairness. *Journal of Personality and Social Psychology, 79,* 355–366.

Varki, A., & Brower, D. (2013). *Denial: Self deception, false beliefs, and the origins of the human mind.* New York: Twelve.

Wakimoto, R. (2006). Mortality salience effects on modesty and relative self-effacement. *Asian Journal of Social Psychology, 9,* 176–183.

Weber, D., Zhang, R., Schimel, J., & Blatter, J. (2015). *Finding death in meaninglessness: Evidence that death thought accessibility increases in response to meaning threats.* Edmonton, AL, Canada: University of Alberta. Unpublished manuscript.

Wegner, D. M. (1994). Ironic process theory of mental control. *Psychological Review, 101,* 34–52.

Weinstein, N. D., & Klein, W. M. (1996). Unrealistic optimism: Present and future. *Journal of Social and Clinical Psychology, 15*(1), 1–8.

Weise, D. R., Arciszewski, T., Verlhiac, J., Pyszczynski, T., & Greenberg, J. (2012). Terror management and attitudes towards immigrants: Differential effects of mortality salience for low and high right-wing authoritarians. *European Psychologist, 17,* 63–72.

Wisman, A., & Goldenberg, J. L. (2005). From the grave to the cradle: Evidence that mortality salience engenders a desire for offspring. *Journal of Personality and Social Psychology, 89,* 46–61.

Wong, P. T. P., & Weiner, B. (1981). When people ask "why" questions, and the heuristics of attributional search. *Journal of Personality and Social Psychology, 40,* 650–663.

Wright, R. (2009). *The evolution of God.* New York: Little, Brown.

Yalom, I. (1980). *Existential psychotherapy.* New York: Basic Books.

Yen, C. L., & Cheng, C. P. (2010). Terror management among Taiwanese: Worldview defence or resigning to fate? *Asian Journal of Social Psychology, 13,* 185–194.

Zanna, M. P., & Cooper, J. (1974). Dissonance and the pill: An attribution approach to studying the arousal properties of dissonance. *Journal of Personality and Social Psychology, 29,* 703–709. http://dx.doi.org/10.1037/h0036651.

Zilborg, G. (1943). *Mind, medicine, and man.* New York: Harcourt Brace.

CHAPTER TWO

A Biosocial Model of Affective Decision Making: Implications for Dissonance, Motivation, and Culture

Shinobu Kitayama[1], Steven Tompson
University of Michigan, Ann Arbor, Michigan, USA
[1]Corresponding author: e-mail address: kitayama@umich.edu

Contents

Advances in Experimental Social Psychology, Volume 52
ISSN 0065-2601
http://dx.doi.org/10.1016/bs.aesp.2015.04.001

Abstract

Drawing on recent advances in both neuroscience and animal behavior, we propose a biosocial model of affective decision making, which holds that when people face a conflict between two competing behavioral options (e.g., go vs. no-go, approach vs. avoidance), they develop a new affective disposition that resolves the conflict. This newly emerging affect will enable one to select a response while forming the basis for an elaborate cognition that justifies the selected response. The model reconceptualizes cognitive dissonance as fundamentally affective and involving both predecisional and postdecisional components. Furthermore, by postulating both top-down and bottom-up neural pathways to regulate the sensitivity to behavioral conflict, it integrates prior evidence on factors that moderate dissonance, including action orientation, self-affirmation, mortality salience, and culture. It also offers new insights into a disparate set of motivational phenomena including animal behaviors that mimic cognitive dissonance, sunk-cost fallacy, addiction, and ego-depletion. Lastly, the biosocial model has implications for how humans may be affectively and motivationally attached to symbols of culture. Directions for future research are discussed.

1. INTRODUCTION

1.1 Behavioral Conflict, Affect, and Motivation

People are conflicted in many different situations. Conflicts can happen when they face important decisions. Conflicts may also happen when they work on a demanding task such as climbing to reach the summit of a mountain. Similar conflicts will also be evident when one is confronting a loss of money, health, or a loved one through gambling, smoking, or using alcohol or illicit drugs. In all these cases, from decision making to mountain climbing, and from gambling to illicit drug use, a conflict arises because the two behavioral options are equally appealing for different reasons, but one course of action (choosing to work for one company; continuing to work on a demanding task or to gamble) precludes the other (choosing to work for the other company; stopping work on a demanding task or giving up gambling).

More often than not, the climbers continue to climb and the gamblers to gamble. Moreover, they often appear to be even more attracted to the endeavor as a result of their desire to discontinue it. For example, the climbers appear to be more attracted than ever to reaching the summit as a result of experiencing the behavioral conflict. Could the climbers be more committed to climbing because they wanted to quit? More paradoxically, in some cases, people appear to be psychologically depleted (much like the climbers who are physically exhausted) after working on a highly demanding task, as if they have used up limited "muscle power" for self-control. Under such conditions, they find other impulses and temptations irresistible and difficult to control (Baumeister, Vohs, & Tice, 2007). Is this effect (called "ego-depletion") related to the commitment of our climbers? Why are our climbers not "depleted" after having worked so hard to climb?

The thesis advanced in the current article is that the behavioral conflict associated with any demanding task or important decision is highly instrumental in determining subsequent decisions and behaviors, with an assortment of affective and motivational consequences. We propose that humans inherit from nonhuman animals certain brain circuitries that detect behavioral conflict. Once detected, the conflict initiates an active search for incentives associated with one of the response options to select and to pursue. Exactly what incentives are identified depends on what incentives are available and salient. The gamblers may be surrounded by a lot of attractive cues built into any Casino, and, likewise, the climbers may know how breathtaking the view from the summit would be. The gamblers may therefore become addicted to gambling, and the climbers may be more attracted to the endeavor. In contrast, people may be distracted if salient incentives are irrelevant to what they do. In such cases, they may appear being "depleted." Although some of these phenomena, especially those involving post-decisional increases of commitment, have traditionally been studied under the rubric of cognitive dissonance (Aronson & Mills, 1959), we argue that the relevant brain circuitries responsible for these effects are largely subcortical and thus arguably precognitive. They can best be characterized as affective. We share these circuitries with rodents, birds, and nonhuman primates. The resulting affective dynamic is relevant in understanding the observations made above for the gamblers, the climbers, and the person who has been "depleted." Moreover, this analysis will shed new light on the nature of all types of both decision making and decision rationalization.

Our thesis is couched initially in terms of cognitive dissonance theory. We will show that the above affective dynamic offers an important insight into a variety of phenomena covered in the dissonance literature of the last half century. Importantly, our analysis will go beyond the traditional confines of dissonance theory. We will use the same theoretical model to understand several different phenomena, including addiction and self-control or the failure thereof. Importantly, the model is open to sociocultural influences and conditioning. This makes it possible to use the model to illuminate how people may be emotionally attached to symbolic systems of culture.

1.2 Dissonance Revolution

Our discussion starts with cognitive dissonance—one of the most prominent topics in social psychology. The central thesis of cognitive dissonance theory (Festinger, 1957) is that when two beliefs are inconsistent, individuals experience negatively arousing cognitive conflict (called dissonance). Because the dissonance is aversive, the individuals try to reduce it by changing one or the other beliefs. For example, when making a difficult decision, individuals show attitude change that justifies the decision. In this case, individuals who face such a decision are conflicted because not all beliefs are consistent with the decision. For example, they may have beliefs favoring the option that is rejected. The individuals are therefore motivated to reduce the conflict by justifying the decision they have made. The justification is typically achieved by changing their attitudes and beliefs so that the new attitudes and beliefs are consistent with and justify the decision that has been made. Notably, the resulting attitude change can be long lasting (Sharot, Fleming, Yu, Koster, & Dolan, 2012). By nature, then, we may be rationalizing beings, ready to justify what we have done after the fact.

Dissonance theory revolutionized social psychology by emphasizing the role of cognition in social behavior. More importantly, it also provided the first testable framework in which to conceptualize how cognition could be motivated and how the motivated cognition could yield some intriguing forms of social behavior. The theory enabled us, both in and outside of social psychology, to reflect on potentially unflattering aspects of the human mind. Indeed, the influence of dissonance theory went far beyond the field of social psychology. The term dissonance has since become incorporated into the English vernacular.

1.3 Charting the Terrain

As a scientific hypothesis, dissonance theory has been tested with three primary experimental paradigms (Aronson, 1969). First, a *free-choice dissonance paradigm* tests the degree to which choice leads to attitude change that justifies the choice (Brehm, 1956). By definition, difficult choices involve competing choice options that are almost equally attractive and thus difficult to choose between. The more difficult the choice, the greater dissonance would be expected to be. To reduce the resulting dissonance, the chooser will increase her preference for chosen options and decrease her preference for rejected options. Researchers have also used an *effort justification paradigm*. When people invest considerable effort to obtain a positive outcome (e.g., climbing a mountain), they supposedly experience dissonance because knowing that one worked so hard is inconsistent with the possibility that the work (e.g., climbing) is valueless (Aronson & Mills, 1959). The individuals typically justify their effort by increasing their commitment to the task. Third, in an *induced compliance paradigm*, individuals are led to commit an action that contradicts their beliefs or preexisting attitudes. The action therefore produces a conflict with their preexisting attitudes and beliefs. In order to reduce the resulting dissonance, the individuals change their attitudes and beliefs so that they are better aligned with their action (Festinger & Carlsmith, 1959). These three paradigms (free choice, effort justification, and induced compliance) account for the bulk of dissonance research conducted over the last half century.

Researchers have extended Festinger's original formulation by elaborating on different theoretical possibilities (Harmon-Jones & Mills, 1999). This effort was motivated by the need to account for some important boundary conditions and moderating variables that were uncovered through extensive research over the decades. An emerging consensus is that a justification effect is typically magnified when a decision entails aversive consequences for someone else (as when fellow students may suffer from one's decision to endorse a tuition increase) (Cooper & Fazio, 1984), or when action orientation is induced (Harmon-Jones, Amodio, & Harmon-Jones, 2009). Conversely, the justification effect is often mitigated when one's self has been affirmed (Steele, 1988). Moreover, recent cross-cultural research shows that conditions in which a justification effect occurs vary across cultures. Specifically, whereas European Americans show a justification effect when a decision is personal and private, Asians show the effect primarily when the decision is social and public (Kitayama, Snibbe, Markus, & Suzuki, 2004).

One novel development in recent years comes from neuroscience. Several published studies have addressed brain mechanisms involved in dissonance (Harmon-Jones, Harmon-Jones, Fearn, Sigelman, & Johnson, 2008; Jarcho, Berkman, & Lieberman, 2011; Kitayama, Chua, Tompson, & Han, 2013; van Veen, Krug, Schooler, & Carter, 2009). This work has shown that dissonance may be based on a network of various brain functions such as conflict detection, reward processing, self-referential processing, and self-regulation, among others. But implications of this newly emerging evidence have yet to be fully articulated and evaluated. In particular, it is not clear how key social psychological constructs in the dissonance literature such as dissonance, attitude or preference, effort, and justification may be mapped onto, and redefined in terms of, known brain mechanisms. Nor is it clear whether there might emerge any novel insights or testable implications through this effort to reformulate dissonance from the neuroscience perspective.

Also important is an effort to explore dissonance among nonhuman animals. Since pioneering work by Lawrence and Festinger (1962), dissonance effects have been repeatedly demonstrated with nonhuman animals, including rodents (Lydall, Gilmour, & Dwyer, 2010), monkeys (Egan, Bloom, & Santos, 2010), pigeons (Clement, Feltus, Kaiser, & Zentall, 2010), and starlings (Kacelnik & Marsh, 2002). All these nonhuman animals are not capable of using language and, thus, supposedly also deprived of any higher-order beliefs. This animal literature therefore calls into question all theoretical accounts, including the original theory by Festinger (1957) and its reformulation in terms of self-perception processes (Bem, 1967), that posit sophisticated cognitive beliefs as necessary elements of dissonance. It is possible that cognitive beliefs often participate in the process of dissonance arousal and reduction (Stone & Cooper, 2001). However, such beliefs may be neither necessary nor sufficient. The fact that humans with little or no episodic memory capacity show a full-fledged dissonance effect (Lieberman, Ochsner, Gilbert, & Schacter, 2001) also underscores the secondary role of cognition since episodic memory is supposedly required to cognitively process prior experience that feeds into dissonance (e.g., having chosen one option over the other). There may be something else, other than cognitive beliefs, that defines the core of dissonance, but this "something else" has yet to be clearly defined and explicated.

We should bear in mind there is one curious omission from previous theorizing on dissonance. As noted earlier, although dissonance theory has spawned hundreds, if not thousands, of experiments, all this work focuses on how the decision maker might resolve a cognitive conflict posed by the decision she has made. The reason for this may in part be due to an insistence of Festinger (1957) that for dissonance to arise, a decision must be final and irreversible. It is possible that an irreversible decision entails a strong commitment to it and, most likely, an equally strong tendency to act on it (Lewin, 1947); so all information contradicting it could be a cause of a much larger conflict. Thus, it is possible that the finality or reversibility of a decision is an important contributing factor to dissonance (Knox & Inkster, 1968). However, it is debatable whether no behavioral conflict is involved when decisions are not final. In fact, we propose that behavioral conflict can be quite intense and consequential even before any decisions are made.

Because of its emphasis on postdecisional processes, dissonance theory is agnostic about how the decision is made. To fill this important gap, subsequent researchers have proposed cognitively elaborate decision mechanisms that offer insights into dissonance effects (Shultz & Lepper, 1996; Simon, Krawczyk, & Holyoak, 2004). However, these models minimize the significance of affect or motivation. Moreover, they are hard pressed to account for the simple fact that seemingly identical effects are present in nonhuman animals that are cognitively far less equipped than human decision makers. In short, it is unknown whether postdecisional dissonance might be related to preceding decision mechanisms and, if so, how the two mechanisms might be related. In the current paper, we propose that the same conflict resolution mechanisms may be implicated in how decisions are made, as well as how they are justified once they have been made.

Last, but not least, one important strength of dissonance theory is its breadth. Ironically, however, after the theory lost its initial traction in the 1980s and 1990s, much of the literature on motivation has proceeded without considering potential implications of dissonance-related mechanisms. Some of the affective and motivational phenomena that have been investigated without consideration of dissonance processes include behaviors of nonhuman animals that appear to show a type of "work ethic" (Clement et al., 2010), ego-depletion (Baumeister et al., 2007), and addiction (Flagel et al., 2010). It remains to be seen how such diverse phenomena might be integrated within a coherent theoretical framework.

2. THE BIOSOCIAL MODEL
2.1 Key Propositions

To address the gaps in the literature noted earlier, we propose a new model of affective decision making called the biosocial model. As illustrated in Figure 1, the model is composed of four core propositions: negatively arousing behavioral conflict, active search for positive incentives, recursive loop, and top-down/bottom-down regulation.

2.1.1 Negatively Arousing Behavioral Conflict
We assume that difficult decisions and demanding tasks cause a behavioral conflict, which is negatively arousing. This complex of both behavioral

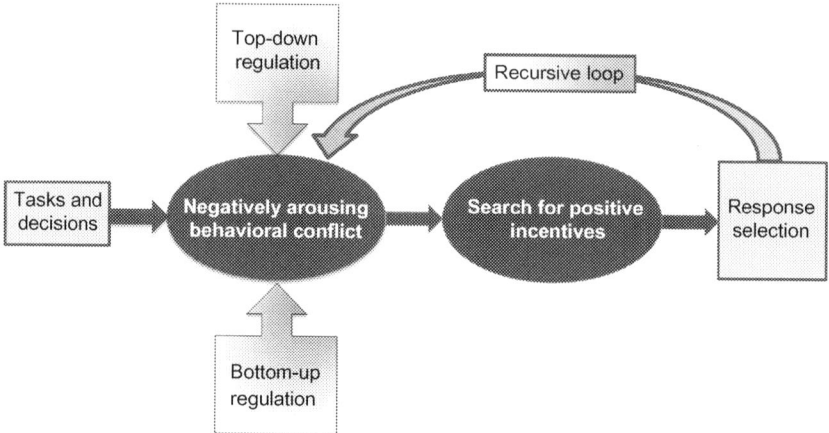

Figure 1 The biosocial model of affective decision making. Demanding tasks and difficult decisions induce behavioral conflict, which is negatively arousing. To reduce the negatively arousing conflict, available behavioral options are parsed for unique positive incentives. Once identified, such incentives resolve the conflict, tame the negative arousal, and enable one to select a response. This decision mechanism may be recursively engaged. The conflict detection system is regulated by both top-down and bottom-up neural pathways. dACC and aINS play significant roles in detecting negatively arousing behavioral conflict. Incentive processing is likely carried out at reward-processing areas including vSTR and om/vmPFC. Top-down regulation of dACC (behavioral conflict detection) is likely subserved by left dlPFC, whereas the amygdala and the midbrain DA system are likely implicated in the bottom-up regulation of dACC.

conflict and negative arousal constitutes the core of dissonance as proposed by Festinger. Whereas the original theory suggested that dissonance by definition was confined to conflict that is generated by a decision and, thus, the dissonance is construed to be postdecisional, the current model emphasizes that dissonance is inherent in the decision itself. As we shall see, the model hypothesizes that the same dissonance mechanism can be recursively engaged. It therefore can be extended to cover postdecisional dissonance phenomena.

A behavioral conflict emerges once a decision is required to select between mutually incompatible responses or when a task is too demanding that there arises a temptation to stop and quit. At the most primitive level, this conflict is apparent when nonhuman animals seek a reward ("go" response) that can be attained only by overcoming certain difficulties ("no-go" response). Of course, in many cases involving human adults, the conflict can be more elaborate and informed by cognitive beliefs. For example, a similar conflict is apparent when one is induced by an experimenter to agree with a counter-attitudinal position or when one is choosing between two equally attractive vacation plans. However, no matter how elaborate the background beliefs might be, the resulting conflict is constituted at the level of behavioral response, whether overt (e.g., approach vs. avoidance) or covert (e.g., approval vs. disapproval). The biosocial model therefore assumes that the core of dissonance lies in this conflict between different behavioral representations (Zajonc & Markus, 1984).

2.1.2 Search for Positive Incentives

Consistent with the original dissonance theory, the biosocial model assumes that behavioral conflict is negatively arousing. As a consequence, the decision maker, both human and nonhuman animals alike, is motivated to reduce it. Unlike the original dissonance theory, the biosocial model holds that resolving behavioral conflict, rather than resolving cognitive inconsistency, is the core of dissonance reduction. It is hypothesized that the negatively arousing behavioral conflict is best reduced by identifying positive, appetitive incentives in one of the response options. By identifying such incentives, the decision maker will be able to reduce the negative arousal while resolving the conflict. Importantly, this affective information produces a potent appetitive response tendency, which would enable the decision maker to either achieve a clear-cut decision if this process is engaged before the decision or reinforce the decision-consistent attitude if it is engaged afterward. It is worth emphasizing that implications of the basic principle proposed here, namely, that of behavioral conflict leading to an active search for positive incentives, goes beyond dissonance itself. As we shall see, it covers various motivational phenomena, including sunk-cost fallacy, addiction, and ego-depletion. It further sheds a new light on how and why humans may become motivationally and affectively attached to religion, tradition, and other forms of cultural symbol.

Much of the process involved in both arousal and reduction of dissonance can be entirely precognitive. That is, positive, appetitive information that is identified during a decision may be no more than a transitory activation of subcortical reward-processing regions of the brain (Berridge & Robinson, 1995; Zajonc, 1980). It should be noted, however, that especially in the case of human adults, the precognitive affective information may be cognitively encoded and elaborated to form the basis of a new full-fledged attitude. The initial affect that is produced to resolve the dissonance promotes a certain behavioral response while at the same time yielding a congruent attitude. Thus, the resulting attitude will inevitably be suitable for justifying the decision or response that is being developed. As implied by the original dissonance theory, the biosocial model predicts that post-decisional justification is likely to be quite common and powerful. However, unlike the original dissonance theory, the biosocial model holds that the "affective seed" for justification is formed during the decision and plays a critical role in informing subsequent cognitive rationalizations.

2.1.3 Recursive Loop

According to the biosocial model, the decision mechanism specified in terms of the first three propositions is sometimes (but not always) recursively engaged to magnify the initial decision-based attitude change. This recursion may account for certain important phenomena that involve post-decisional processes (Cooper & Fazio, 1984). For example, people rationalize their decisions more if they learn that the decisions are irreversible (Knox & Inkster, 1968). The current model suggests that once a decision is made, it by itself can be a source of a new behavioral conflict, which in turn will initiate another round of a search for positive incentives. This conflict may be larger if the initial decision is irreversible, thereby producing a stronger response tendency that may be pitted against any competing response tendencies.

Moreover, through the recursion, both existing conflicts and associated negative emotional arousal are likely to be consciously registered and subjectively experienced. As a consequence, these experiences themselves may become the target of conscious reflection and interpretation. One important consequence of this is that the negative arousal evoked by behavioral conflict may be interpreted in terms of other events in the environment. For example, the negative arousal may be misattributed to external events. When this misattribution happens, the effort to reduce the negative arousal may dissipate (Cooper & Fazio, 1984; Zanna & Cooper, 1974).

2.1.4 Top-Down/Bottom-Up Regulation

The biosocial model holds that the magnitude of behavioral conflict (i.e., dissonance) is modulated by a variety of situational factors. For example, imagine someone who is driving a car on a busy street. In such situations, the person will be more careful than usual. To put it differently, she will recruit self-regulatory regions of her brain to "tighten the belt" of the conflict detection system (which is required to detect an error so as to preempt any serious accidents). She is thus using her higher-order goal of "driving carefully" to regulate her conflict detection system. This pathway may therefore be called top-down. When the conflict detection system is upregulated, behavioral conflicts will be more likely to be taken note of and thus can initiate a more vigorous search for positive incentives. Conversely, if the system is downregulated (as when the driver is relaxed), the conflicts may not be noticed even if they exist, thus entailing no downstream effects including the search for positive incentives.

An analogous regulatory process may happen bottom-up. For example, the same person may be exposed to a cue indicating certain threats impinging on her (e.g., a police car passing her car at high speed). Such a cue will promptly increase the level of alertness and, as a consequence, enhance the sensitivity of the conflict detection system. In this case, it is the immediate emotional reaction of fear that is regulating the conflict detection system. Thus, the mechanism is said to be bottom-up. As we shall see, both top-down and bottom-up regulatory pathways for the sensitivity of the conflict detection system are important in understanding an assortment of variables that have been proposed as moderators of dissonance effects, including action orientation, self-affirmation, mortality salience, and culture.

2.2 Moving Forward

With this overview in mind, we now turn to each key component of the biosocial model in some detail. This review is divided into several major sections. To begin, we will discuss the core proposed mechanism of affective decision making, composed of negatively arousing behavioral conflict followed by a search for positive incentives in terms of key brain substrates that support it (Section 3). We will show that the same mechanism is responsible, not only for phenomena traditionally subsumed under the rubric of cognitive dissonance, but also an assortment of disparate phenomena including animal behavior that mimics cognitive dissonance, addiction, and ego-depletion. Next, we will discuss neural mechanisms involved in both the top-down (Section 4) and the bottom-up regulation of dissonance (Section 5). Finally, we will discuss the nature of a recursive loop involved in affective decision making, which has implications for postdecisional effects such as effects of aversive consequences and misattribution (Section 6). Taken together, we will show that the biosocial model integrates insights from both dissonance theory as originally formulated and all subsequent elaborations. Moreover, the model offers important new insights on apparently unrelated motivational phenomena. One strength of the model is to provide a single framework that is well grounded in current knowledge of how the brain functions. This framework will be applicable to a wide range of affective and motivational effects. In the concluding section, we will explicate additional implications of the model and suggest directions for future research on biosocial processes involved in dissonance in particular and affective decision making in general.

3. NEURAL SUBSTRATES OF AFFECTIVE DECISION MAKING

3.1 Behavioral Conflict and Negative Arousal

Numerous studies in cognitive neuroscience demonstrate the critical role of the dorsal anterior cingulate cortex (dACC; illustrated in Figure 2) in the detection of behavioral conflict in a variety of conflict-inducing paradigms such as Stroop tasks and flanker tasks (Botvinick, Cohen, & Carter, 2004; Bush, Luu, & Posner, 2000; Carter & van Veen, 2007; Shenhav, Straccia, Cohen, & Botvinick, 2014; but also see Izuma & Adolph, 2013). An event-related potential (ERP) component marking the detection of behavioral conflict, called error-related negativity (ERN), is thought to be derived from dACC (Carter & van Veen, 2007), although the issue is far from settled (Agam et al., 2011). It stands to reason that behavioral conflicts associated with demanding tasks or important decisions are also detected by the dACC. Consistent with this analysis, several researchers have proposed that dACC

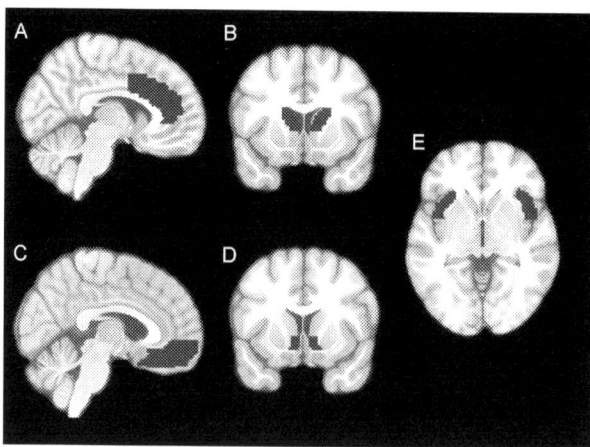

Figure 2 Some key brain regions involved in arousal and reduction of dissonance as specified in the biosocial model. (A) Dorsal anterior cingulate cortex (dACC). (B) Caudate nuclei. (C) Orbital/ventral medial prefrontal cortex (om/vmPFC). (D) Ventral striatum/nucleus accumbens (vSTR/Nacc). (E) Anterior insula (aINS).

constitutes a key neural substrate of dissonance (Harmon-Jones & Harmon-Jones, 2008; Kitayama et al., 2013; van Veen et al., 2009).

dACC is also important in detecting reward prediction errors. When individuals anticipate a certain reward outcome (e.g., earning $5 in a gamble), there arises a negative reward prediction error if they fail to get the outcome. Conversely, if the outcome is better than anticipated, there arises a positive reward prediction error (Walsh & Anderson, 2012).[1] A negative reward prediction error signals the outcome being less than expected. This error signal may interrupt and suspend an approach tendency to achieve the reward and, as such, lends itself to a go versus no-go behavioral conflict. For the purpose of the current discussion, then, we hypothesize that negative reward prediction error can be subsumed under a larger category of behavioral conflict.

Anatomically, dACC is densely connected with the anterior part of the insula cortex (anterior insula or aINS) (see Figure 2). aINS is thought to map visceral bodily sensations (Damasio & Carvalho, 2013; Immordino-Yang, Yang, & Damasio, 2014; Singer, Critchley, & Preuschoff, 2009), which may then be cognitively interpreted to yield subjective feelings (Immordino-Yang et al., 2014; Schachter, 1964). In particular, aINS shows strong activation during the experience of certain negative states or emotions such as pain and disgust (Damasio & Carvalho, 2013). The network including dACC and aINS is activated during the experience of social pain that is caused by social exclusion (Eisenberger & Lieberman, 2004). This network also responds to vicarious pain or empathy for in-group members (Han et al., 2009; Singer, 2004; Xu, Zuo, Wang, & Han, 2009). The network including dACC and aINS is therefore characterized as a "neural alarm system" (Eisenberger & Lieberman, 2004). Further, both dACC and aINS are correlated with autonomic arousal, which is known to occur when dissonance is induced (Croyle & Cooper, 1983; Elkin & Leippe, 1986; Losch & Cacioppo, 1990).

Altogether, we may hypothesize that when trying to make a difficult decision or working on a demanding task, dACC detects behavioral conflict, and this activation quickly spreads to aINS to make the conflict negatively

---

[1] Existing research on animal behavior suggests that ACC also encodes reward values of different actions or incentive cues. Thus, laboratory animals with permanent or transient ACC lesions cannot perform optimally when seeking rewards (Amiez, Joseph, & Procyk, 2006; Hillman & Bilkey, 2012; Kennerley, Walton, Behrens, Buckley, & Rushworth, 2006). The function of ACC to encode reward values makes this region suitable for the detection of reward-related conflicts, such as when one has to engage in a costly action (e.g., effort or investment) to achieve a certain desirable goal.

arousing. This negative arousal shares much in common with experiences of social pain. Moreover, aINS is known to respond to disappointment and regret (Chua, Gonzalez, Taylor, Welsh, & Liberzon, 2009). We may thus suggest that the complex encompassing dACC and aINS constitutes the core of negatively arousing behavioral conflict, or dissonance as formulated by Festinger (1957). All subsequent dissonance researchers have conceptualized dissonance as an aversive state (Cooper & Fazio, 1984; Harmon-Jones et al., 2009; Steele, 1988) that has a negatively arousing motivational potential (Elliot & Devine, 1994). The current model adds to the previous conclusion by proposing that the network of dACC and aINS supports this aversive motivational state.

Evidence for the proposal above comes from a recent neuroimaging study (Kitayama et al., 2013), in which American undergraduates were scanned while making choices between many pairs of popular music CDs.[2] They had been told that one of the chosen CDs would be given to them as a gift at the end of the session. To investigate the effect of choice difficulty on brain activity, half of the CD pairs were composed of two CDs that had been rated by each participant to be nearly equally likable, whereas the remaining half consisted of two CDs that had been rated to be very dissimilar in likability. In support of the hypothesis that dissonance entails strong activation of the network consisting of both ACC and aINS, this

---

[2] Chen and Risen argue that a certain statistical artifact may be involved in a justification effect observed in the free-choice paradigm (Chen & Risen, 2010). Specifically, in this paradigm, individuals are typically asked to rate a limited set of options. They are then given a choice between two options that are similarly rated. The same rating task is administered again after the choice. It is assumed that the prechoice rating is error-free. In reality, however, there may be measurement error such that even though the two options appear very close in liking in the first rating task, their true likability might in fact be further away from one another. In this case, the truly more favored option may be both selected and ranked higher in the subsequent measurement. This stochastic mechanism, if sufficiently powerful, will ensure what appears to be a justification effect. There is a debate regarding how serious this potential artifact might be (Izuma & Murayama, 2013; Kitayama, Tompson, & Chua, 2014). We should bear in mind, however, that especially when measurement error is minimized with careful experimental control, the artifact is likely to be negligible. We pointed out elsewhere that if such an artifact is always involved, there should emerge a sizable effect of apparent justification even when dissonance is predicted to be minimal (Kimel, Lopez-Duran, & Kitayama, 2014). As shown in numerous studies—especially behavioral studies involving only one choice (which are reviewed later Sections 5.3 and 5.4), a justification effect that is observed in one condition of a given study disappears in another condition of the same study, depending on dissonance-increasing or dissonance-depressing experimental manipulations. The absence of any justification effect in at least one condition within a study shows that measurement error is negligible within the study under discussion. Hence, a justification effect observed in all other conditions of the study can hardly be due to any statistical artifact.

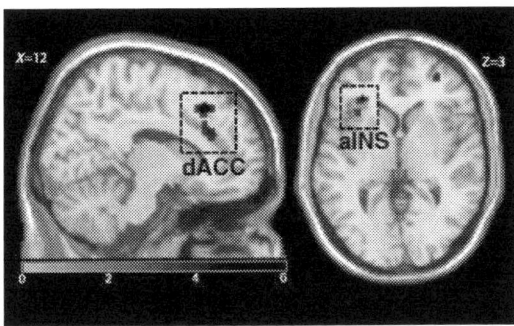

Figure 3 Areas of the brain that are activated by difficult choices, relative to easy choices in a free-choice dissonance study by Kitayama et al. (2013). *Reprinted from Kitayama et al. (2013) with permission from Elsevier.*

study observed strong activations in these two areas (illustrated in Figure 3) during difficult (as compared to easy) choices. Another recent study tested Japanese participants and also found that choice difficulty was positively correlated with dACC activation during choice (Izuma et al., 2013).

In another fMRI study, van Veen and colleagues (2009) adopted an induced compliance paradigm (Cooper & Fazio, 1984). American college undergraduates first worked on an extremely boring task in the unpleasant scanner environment for 40 min. Afterward, they were asked to indicate whether they would endorse a series of sentences by pressing a response key. Some of the sentences focused on the first phase of the study (I feel calm and peaceful in the scanner), whereas the rest were irrelevant to the latter (The weather is very bad today). They were asked to respond as if they enjoyed the first phase of the study. Half of the participants were told that every time they indicated this attitude they would receive one dollar (control condition). The remaining half were told that in the scanner control room a patient scheduled to be scanned after the participants was waiting. The person was so anxious and worried, so the participants were told that the experimenter would like them to respond as if they enjoyed the study. In that way, the patient would feel at ease. They were told that the patient would be watching the participants' responses in the control room (dissonance condition). Because one's own action can have unintended, potentially negative effects on the patient, the decision to act that way should produce conflict between conforming to the request from the experimenter and resisting the pressure so as to avoid negative effects on the patient. As may be expected, van Veen and colleagues observed an increased activation

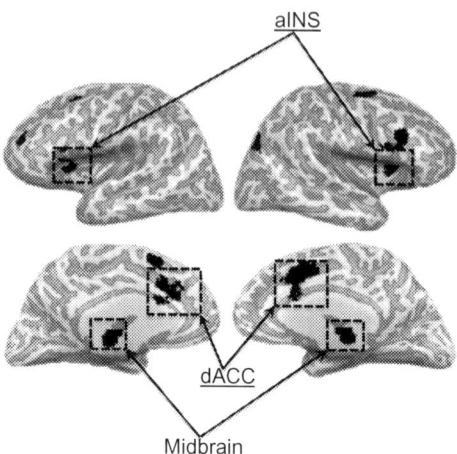

Figure 4 Areas of the brain that are activated by target sentences (vs. control sentences) in the dissonance condition as compared to the control condition in an induced compliance study performed by van Veen et al. (2009). The dorsal anterior cingulate cortex (dACC) and the anterior insula (aINS) in combination constitute the core of dissonance. The activation of the midbrain area may indicate successful effort to find positive features of the preceding, seemingly boring task (see Section 3.3, Page 92). *Reprinted from van Veen et al. (2009) with permission from Macmillan Publishers Ltd., copyright 2009.*

of both dACC and aINS, while the participants were reading the critical sentences relative to reading the control sentences in the dissonance condition. Their primary results are shown in Figure 4.

3.2 Making Decisions: Reward Processing and Response Selection

Once negatively arousing behavioral conflict (i.e., dissonance) is aroused, it will motivate a search for positive incentives that are unique to one of the available response options. For example, when choosing between a rock CD and a modern jazz CD, the decision maker might think of his plan to host a party next week and imagine how much better the rock music would be for the occasion than the jazz music. For another example, think about a climber, who saw a ridge in front of him and anticipated arriving at the summit only to realize that he still had a long way to go. Every time this happens, his goal to reach the summit is interrupted. This interruption, caused by a negative prediction error indicating that the outcome (just another ridge) was worse than expected (summit), results in a conflict between the two behaviors (i.e., continuing to climb vs. quitting), which would prompt him to look for added incentives in the endeavor. Once found and recognized, the additional incentives would resolve the conflict and reduce the negative arousal. Moreover, the newly identified incentive will boost the affective value of the chosen option. Thus, the climber will be even more motivated to reach the mountaintop as a result of having experienced the behavioral conflict.

The link between negatively arousing behavioral conflict and the search for positive incentives may be biologically hard-wired. Such a biological mechanism may make sense from an adaptive point of view. The production of positive affect to neutralize negative affect is instrumental in maintaining homeostasis (Solomon & Corbit, 1974). Moreover, as pointed out by some animal researchers, the mechanism to boost motivation under repeated failures to obtain reward may be highly adaptive for foraging animals (Clement et al., 2010). In fact, uncertainty in reward anticipation is known to increase the appetitive conditioning to cues associated with the reward (Anselme, Robinson, & Berridge, 2013), hence increasing the motivation to seek the reward. The same reasoning could undoubtedly apply to hunters and gatherers and perhaps to modern humans who face fierce competition in business and other professional circles, although this latter point remains speculative. The mechanism of searching for positive incentives in goals that are blocked may also be learned. As some researchers point out (Harmon-Jones et al., 2009), action may typically be more adaptive than inaction as a strategy to deal with behavioral conflict. If so, most people are rewarded more by searching for positive incentives in pertinent goals. They may therefore acquire this mechanism as an effective way to handle behavioral conflict. For our purposes, the origin of the mechanism is less important than the mechanism itself.

During the active search for positive incentives in one response option to choose and pursue, there will be coordination between memory search for relevant previous experience or prospective plans and attention directed to one of the options. In all likelihood, retrieval of some initial bit of information that makes one of the options slightly more attractive would foster a shift of attention toward the option, which in turn would encourage further search of relevant information in memory. This close interaction between memory search and attention will lead to the identification of additional incentives in the option (Shimojo, Simion, Shimojo, & Scheier, 2003; Simion & Shimojo, 2006). Once these positive incentives are identified in one of the decision options, they will allow a choice to be made, thereby reducing the initial behavioral conflict.

Consistent with the hypothesis that behavioral conflict motivates an active search for incentives linked to a response option to select and pursue, previous work shows that when one's goal is thwarted, the person is motivated to more vigorously pursue the goal (Brehm, 1966). More generally, people may become more engaged in a goal when it is blocked (Higgins, 2006). These effects are likely to be mediated by the search for incentives for blocked goals. Another analogous process has been discussed by opponent process theory (Solomon & Corbit, 1974). The theory argues that when negative affect (e.g., dissonance) occurs, it automatically recruits a slow-growing positive affect so as to maintain affective homeostasis. The biosocial model is consistent with opponent process theory insofar as both theories assume that the initial negative affect is sufficient to build up positive affect. Whereas opponent process theory merely postulates this contingency, the biosocial model assumes that it is mediated by an active search for positive incentives. Unlike the biosocial model, opponent process theory further assumes an analogous process for positive affect, insisting that initial positive affect is sufficient to produce negative affect that is suited to maintain homeostasis. This premise of opponent process theory may be questionable, insofar as, contrary to the theory, people often savor positive affect (Speer, Bhanji, & Delgado, 2014) and even try to build upon it (Fredrickson & Losada, 2005). Altogether, there is a solid basis to hypothesize that once negatively arousing behavioral conflict (dissonance as implemented in dACC and aINS) is activated, it automatically fosters an active search for positive incentives linked to a response option to select and pursue.

Specific mechanisms involved in identification of positive incentives and subsequent response selection (i.e., decision) are illustrated in Figure 5. The figure also notes the specific brain anatomy that supports these decision mechanisms. Researchers have suggested that the ventral striatum (vSTR), including the nucleus accumbens (Nacc), is particularly responsive to cues previously associated with rewards (i.e., incentives) (see Figure 2; Knutson & Cooper, 2005; Shenhav & Buckner, 2014). When such incentive cues are identified in one of the available options (e.g., the rock CD is very suitable for the upcoming occasion, or the growing expectation of a fabulous view from the summit), they will cause an increase of activity of dopaminergic (DA) neurons in the midbrain area (Bromberg-Martin & Hikosaka, 2009; Watanabe, Lauwereyns, & Hikosaka, 2003). This midbrain

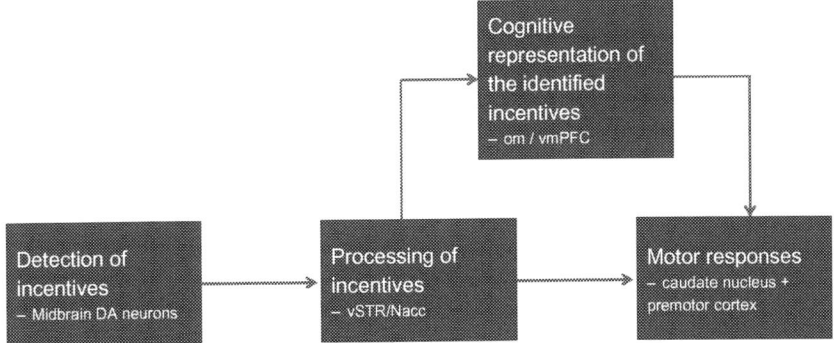

Figure 5 Incentive processing and response selection. When cues linked to previously rewarded experiences (called incentives) are detected, dopamine neurons in the mid-brain area are activated. This activation spreads to the striatal reward-processing region. The incentive information is then transmitted to the premotor cortical area through the caudate nuclei for response selection. At the same time, the incentive information identified in the reward-processing region is also cognitively encoded and maintained in working memory. These cognitive operations are performed in the orbitomedial/ventromedial prefrontal cortex. The resulting cognitive representation of the incentive is then used to regulate, top-down, the response selection.

DA activation will then spread to the striatal reward-processing region (vSTR/Nacc), where the incentive information is further processed.[3]

At this stage of processing, the activation of the reward-processing area is only transitory and, by itself, offers neither any motor plan (approach behavior toward the source of the positive incentive) nor any cognitive representations of the incentives. These more elaborate operations are carried out in subsequent processing steps, which involve both bottom-up and top-down pathways through which the incentive information is used to control response selection (Frank & Claus, 2006).

First, the incentive information may spread bottom-up through the caudate nuclei to the premotor cortex (Figure 2). Through this pathway,

---

[3] Although DA neurons are linked closely to reward processing, it is a mistake to confine them only to reward processing (Salamone & Correa, 2012). For example, the DA reward function highlighted in the current discussion is likely to coexist hand in hand with DA's role in enhancing glucocorticoid receptors in the prefrontal cortex, which are linked to "stress" responses (Butts, Weinberg, Young, & Phillips, 2011). It is therefore possible that dissonance produces a stress, which in turn increases prefrontal DA concentrations. This pathway may also have downstream consequences such as compromised executive functions. This pathway may be relatively slow-growing and, thus, may prove to be more relevant in cases involving dissonance-related distress of the sort that is long lasting as when individuals are torn apart over days or weeks over the decision they made. These cases are beyond the scope of the current discussion. However, they are obviously important and should be addressed in future work.

the response is directly controlled by the incentive information. Selection of the stimulus that carries the positive incentives that have been identified will be strongly primed. Second, it may also be cognitively represented, thus likely experienced subjectively (Brosch & Sander, 2013). The key site to cognitively represent positive incentives includes the orbital/ventral medial prefrontal cortex (om/vmPFC) (Elliott, Dolan, & Frith, 2000; Figure 2). A cognitive representation of the incentives that emerges may be combined with other, more context-specific cognitions about the impinging social situation. The resulting contextualized understanding of the incentive will be used to direct the response selection (Frank & Claus, 2006). For example, the response tendency toward the option with the identified incentives (generated through the bottom-up pathway involving the caudate) may be tempered or facilitated, depending on how appropriate such an action might be given the specific context in which the decision is being made.

3.3 Testing the Decision Mechanism

Evidence for the decision mechanism above comes from the Kitayama et al. (2013) study discussed earlier and another similar study by Jarcho et al. (2011). In both studies, participants rated decision options (CDs in Kitayama et al., and names and paintings in Jarcho et al.) both before and after choosing one option from each of many pairs of options. Kitayama et al. observed that after the choices, clear choice justification was observed. That is, right before the choices, there were no differences in liking for CDs that were to be chosen and those that were to be rejected. However, right after the choices, the chosen CDs were rated as significantly more likable than the rejected CDs. In the Jarcho et al. (2011) study, the researchers only used data from approximately 60% of participants who showed a reliable choice justification effect.

Importantly, both studies scanned participants while they made choices and tested whether any brain areas showed in-choice activations that predicted a greater justification effect. The two studies revealed two converging findings. First, in both studies, in-choice activity in a part of the sub-cortical reward-processing area (the vSTR, including the Nacc), was reliably related to postchoice preference change. The particular region identified in the Kitayama et al. (2013) study, shown in Figure 6A, was Nacc, which is part of the vSTR (Knutson & Cooper, 2005). Jarcho et al. (2011) also found the in-choice activity in the vicinity of vSTR predicted subsequent preference change. As noted previously, these regions are strongly associated

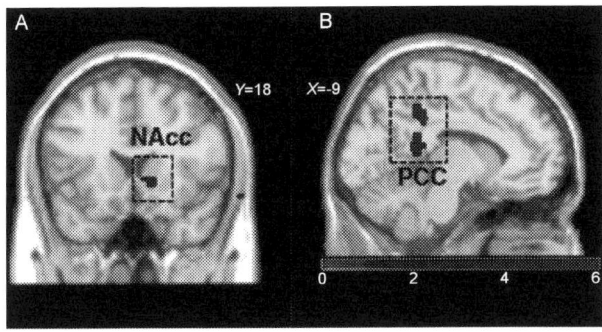

Figure 6 In-choice activation of the two areas of the brain predicted postchoice increase of preference for chosen options in the free-choice fMRI study by Kitayama et al. (2013). (A) Nucleus accumbens (Nacc) and (B) posterior cingulate cortex (PCC). *Reprinted from Kitayama et al. (2013) with permission from Elsevier.*

with anticipated reward and, thus, are thought to show incentive processing (Berridge, Robinson, & Aldridge, 2009; Knutson & Cooper, 2005; O'Doherty, Deichmann, Critchley, & Dolan, 2002; Shenhav & Buckner, 2014). Kitayama et al. interpreted this finding as indicating that on some choice trials, the decision maker successfully identified positive features, or incentives, associated with one of the options, which led to an increased preference for the option and, thus, allowed her to choose it. When the increased preference was assessed at a later point, the preference was correlated with the preceding Nacc activity. This evidence is consistent with the claim of the biosocial model that decision-consistent affective information is already activated at the precognitive level during choice, before a choice is actually made. It is this affective information that would enable one to make the choice. This information is generated so as to reduce behavioral conflict and used to guide the choice.

Both Jarcho et al. (2011) and Kitayama et al. (2013) also found that postchoice preference change was predicted by in-choice activity of the posterior cingulate cortex and adjacent precuneus (PCC/Pcu). PCC/Pcu is linked to autobiographic memory (van der Meer, Costafreda, & Aleman, 2010). Thus, this evidence is consistent with the hypothesis that the decision maker searches in memory for information that makes certain features more positive. Often, this information is self-relevant and thus episodic, as in the example above where the decision maker thinks about his plan to host a party next week and interprets one of the CDs in light of this plan. Thus, the more intensely memory is searched for such information (as shown by the PCC/Pcu activation), the more likely it will be for the decision maker to find a positive distinctive feature that would enable her to make a clear choice.[4]

As discussed previously, in the fMRI study on induced compliance by van Veen and colleagues (2009), while reading and responding to the stimulus sentences relevant to the first "boring phase" of the study, participants in the dissonance condition showed increased activity in both dACC and aINS. Importantly, in this study, the participants in the dissonance condition also showed increased activation in the midbrain area (see Figure 4). Because the midbrain area has high concentration of dopamine neurons, which respond to reward processing, it is possible that this activation signaled the hypothesized search for positive, rewarding experiences in the seemingly "boring" study the participants completed.

Three additional fMRI studies have utilized a free-choice paradigm similar to the one by Kitayama et al. (2013) and Jarcho et al. (2011), but examined neural activation during the prechoice and postchoice rating tasks, instead of in-choice neural activation. First, Izuma and colleagues (2010) had Japanese participants complete a similar free-choice paradigm with food options (Izuma et al., 2010). The researchers found a significant postchoice decrease of liking for rejected food options, but there was no postchoice increase of liking for chosen food options. This postchoice decrease of liking for rejected food options was mirrored in a corresponding decrease of vSTR activation for the rejected food options. Again, there was no effect for the chosen food options. Unfortunately, this study suffered from one idiosyncratic procedural aspect: Participants were explicitly reminded whether they had chosen each food option when they rated it for the second time after the choice. The results might therefore have reflected responses to this reminder rather than any representations of the pertinent food options that might be altered by the choice. The same confound existed in another imaging study by Qin et al. (2011). Hence, for our purposes, implications of these studies are uncertain.

---

[4] In the Kitayama et al. study, the Nacc and the PCC/Pcu were the only two areas that were related to postchoice preference change. In the Jarcho et al. study, however, two additional areas showed similar relations with postchoice preference change: the medial prefrontal cortex (mPFC) and the inferior frontal gyrus (IFG). Some caution is due, because the findings were not replicated in the Kitayama et al. study. Nevertheless, it is instructive that mPFC is also involved in self-relevant information processing, including episodic memory (Addis, Wong, & Schacter, 2007). Furthermore, IFG is often involved in emotion regulation. As Jarcho et al. argued, it is possible that IFG was implicated in downregulating negative affect associated with difficult decisions. In support of this analysis, Jarcho et al. found a reliable connectivity between IFG and aINS, such that strong IFG activity was linked to attenuated aINS activity.

Fortunately, the Sharot, De Martino, & Dolan (2009) study did not have any of such interpretive problems. The researchers asked British participants to rate how much they would enjoy many vacation destinations, make hypothetical choices between two vacation destinations, then rate the vacation destinations again. The researchers observed that preference ratings for chosen options increased, and those for rejected options decreased, after the choice. Moreover, they observed a postchoice increase in activation of the caudate nucleus for chosen (vs. rejected) options. The caudate nucleus is part of the brain area serving reward processing and action control, located between the vSTR and the premotor cortex, above vSTR, but below the premotor cortex (see Figure 2). It is thought to relay the reward information processed in vSTR to the premotor cortex. Moreover, this postchoice increase of caudate activation for chosen vacation destinations correlated with a comparable increase of self-reported preferences of the destinations. In light of the processing model in Figure 5, we may assume that affective information identified during choice (a function supposedly carried out in vSTR/Nacc) was transferred upward to the caudate region so as to control motor output, both actuarial and imaginary.

3.4 Effort Justification

One typical decision conflict occurs when a rewarding action is costly, as when arriving at a mountaintop on foot (rather than, say, transported to the top by a helicopter). The climber will be eager to reach every ridge, only to realize that there is (at least) one more to go before finally arriving at the mountaintop. This negative "prediction error" (the signal indicating the outcome is worse than expected) discourages the climber, thus providing a potent source of conflict with the effort he has expended to make it to the top. Another example involves initiation rituals that are required for one to join a special social club (Aronson & Mills, 1959; Atkinson & Whitehouse, 2011; Gerard & Mathewson, 1966). The attractive goal (joining the club) initiates an approach tendency, which is often interrupted and disrupted by difficulties and obstacles (hard, often painful, work), thereby resulting in a strong behavioral conflict. According to the biosocial model, when facing such a conflict, dACC is activated, which entails an activation of aINS. In combination, activation of this dissonance complex (dACC + aINS) prompts a search for additional positive incentives associated with the rewarding goal that is being pursued (reaching the mountaintop or joining the social club in the examples above). The incentive value of the goal should become even greater than before. This is exactly what a classic dissonance study by

Aronson and Mills (1959) found. Individuals showed elevated levels of commitment to a social club when they were required to go through a severe (vs. light) initiation ritual in order to join the club. This phenomenon, traditionally called effort justification, has since been replicated (Axsom & Cooper, 1985; Gerard & Mathewson, 1966).

Aronson and Mills (1959) interpreted their effort justification finding in terms of reduction of cognitive dissonance as originally formulated by Festinger (1957). That is, a belief that one is undergoing painful action (effort) is inconsistent with another belief that joining the club is not valuable. To resolve this cognitive inconsistency, individuals supposedly changed the belief that was more amenable to change, namely the evaluation of the club itself. Thus, the actor is said to justify the effort she expended to achieve her original goal by increasing the value of the goal. According to this interpretation, however, there must be cognitive beliefs to begin with. Moreover, the evaluation of the club must be more amenable to change than the evaluation of the pain associated with the effort. Our formulation requires neither of these assumptions. It holds that there is a conflict between the go tendency associated with the attractive club and the no-go tendency associated with painful effort. Because this conflict detected at dACC is negatively arousing, due to dACC's connections with aINS, individuals look for additional incentives in the goal at issue. For this reason, the club—the most salient incentive that is available in the situation—becomes even more rewarding and is evaluated more positively.

Effects similar to effort justification have been observed in a series of behavioral economics studies on the so-called "sunk-cost fallacy." According to this phenomenon, once individuals invest resources (e.g., time, effort, and money) on a certain decision option, they find it extremely hard to forego the investment, even when the pursuit of the initial option is no longer profitable and thus not desirable. The failure to forego the investment is considered irrational because all it does is to lead to further loss of resources (Cunha & Caldieraro, 2009). Although this phenomenon can be mediated by sophisticated cognitive inferences (e.g., mental accounting), as typically assumed in the current judgment and decision-making literature (Thaler, 1999), we propose that it is also likely to involve a precognitive affective mechanism, such that initial investment in an option is inherently conflict-prone and, thus, motivates the decision maker to identity positive incentives in the action itself.

3.5 Animal Dissonance

Both the dissonance complex that is activated in effort justification (dACC and aINS) and the affective processing involved in the reduction of dissonance (vSTR/Nacc) are not unique to humans. In fact, these brain structures are shared with nonhuman animals including other mammals (e.g., rodents and monkeys) and birds. It should therefore not come as a surprise that these nonhuman animals exhibit analogous effects.

Much of the research on "effort justification" in animals involves requiring animals to repeat a certain set of behaviors in order to receive a food reward. For example, in one experiment, starlings were trained to repeat flying 1 m in the air from perch to perch, and once they repeated it the required number of times, they were allowed to press a key to obtain a food reward (Kacelnik & Marsh, 2002). On some trials, the animal had to fly in the air only four times before they received a food reward (low effort condition), and on other trials, they had to fly 12 times to receive the same food reward (high effort condition). The keys were color-coded such that the key was in one color (e.g., green) on the high effort trials but another color (e.g., blue) on the low effort trials. In a test trial, the birds were given a choice between the two-colored keys to obtain food. The birds were reliably more likely to choose the key associated with high effort.

In a paper aptly titled "'Work ethic' in pigeons," Clement and colleagues have shown nearly identical effects (Clement et al., 2010). In the low effort condition, pigeons were trained to press a center key just one time, and then they could choose to press one of two color-coded keys. The pigeons learned that the red key yielded a food reward, whereas the yellow key yielded no food. The high effort condition was identical, except that the pigeons had to press the center key 20 times before choosing between two color-coded keys (blue and green). After the training sessions, the pigeons were given a choice between the key that yielded a food reward in the low effort condition and the key that yielded a food reward in the high effort condition. Importantly, the pigeons received the same amount of food in both conditions, so any difference in choice rates should have been due to level of effort rather than initial value of the reward. Once again, the birds preferred the keys associated with high effort.

The research on starlings and pigeons measured choices between options associated with high or low effort, but did not directly measure preference for the rewarding food itself. A recent study used rats and sought to go a step further by measuring palatability of a sucrose solution used as reward (Lydall et al., 2010). To measure palatability, the researchers performed a micro-structural analysis of licking during ingestion. Rats typically repeat a lick in clusters that are separated by pauses. It has been demonstrated that rats licks more within each cluster when consuming higher concentration sucrose solutions (Spector, Klumpp, & Kaplan, 1998). Thus, the number of licks within each cluster is a reliable measure of palatability. As may be predicted by the hypothesis that effort required to obtain food increases the palatability of the food, rats showed a reliably larger number of licks per cluster when consuming the same sucrose solution following 50 lever presses (high effort condition) than following 10 lever presses (low effort condition). In a separate condition, the researchers found an analogous, but less strong, effect of a delayed delivery of the sucrose solution, with the number of licks per cluster increasing as a function of the delay. It appears that the delay itself presented an obstacle to the goal of sucrose consumption.

In explaining these animal findings, a perceptual contrast mechanism has been proposed. That is, the same reward may appear more palatable when presented while the animal undergoes a negative internal state (Zentall, 2010). The biosocial model agrees with this point of view in general outline. In addition, however, it offers a specific affective mechanism by which this contrast effect may come about. When a delay occurs in the delivery of a reward, there arise a negative reward prediction error, which disrupts the approach behavior. The resulting behavioral conflict is negatively arousing, and, as a result, the animal seeks additional incentives in the reward being pursued.

3.6 Learning from Addiction

Building on the analysis of animal dissonance, the biosocial model suggests a close link between dissonance and addiction. For example, consider chronic gamblers in Vegas or any of numerous pachinko parlors in Tokyo. Among these individuals, the prospect of winning exists hand in hand with repeated losses. The gamblers are said to be addicted to gambles because they cannot stop gambling despite the fact that they repeatedly suffer monetary losses. However, the biosocial model suggests that the excessive attraction they exhibit toward the act of gambling may have an important origin in this very fact. That is, when the prospect of winning is combined with repeated failures to win, the combination produces acute behavioral conflict. As argued earlier, this negatively arousing state initiates an active search for positive incentives linked to an option to select and pursue. In all likelihood, then, positive affect will follow the conflict between the prospect of winning and the reality of repeated loss, and this affect will be conditioned to all cues associated with the goal of winning. These cues include slot machines, noise they generate, as well as neon signs and ambient lighting that often exist in Vegas and Atlantic City. The same mechanism may account for other forms of addiction, such as smoking, eating sweets, and reckless driving, to name just a few. For many smokers, for example, anticipated sensory pleasure stemming from a puff of a cigarette is strongly conditioned to otherwise neutral cues, such as the smell of coffee.

Flagel and colleagues have shown that conditioning of strongly appetitive motivational state to cues associated with a valued goal state (e.g., food) can easily be established in rodents (Flagel et al., 2010). Analogous conditioning has been demonstrated with pigeons (Zentall & Laude, 2013). In terms of neurophysiological mechanisms, these conditionings among non-human animals and the gambling and other forms of addiction in humans are analogous (Tomie, 1996). In fact, as shown by Flagel et al. (2010), among some sizable subgroup of rodents, the conditioning is so pronounced that they end up licking the response lever even when no food is forthcoming. Robinson and colleagues have called these animals "sign trackers," because they are attracted to cues predicting rewards rather than to the rewards themselves. The "sign trackers" are distinguished from "goal trackers," who are attracted only to rewards when they are presented (Robinson & Berridge, 2001). More recent work show that uncertainty associated with reward delivery (which likely produces a greater response conflict) increases sign-tracking behaviors in rodents (Anselme et al., 2013). The animals appear to be addicted in the sense of exhibiting excessive attraction to goal-related cues (the lever) under conditions of uncertainty or even extremely low probability of achieving the goal itself. As may be predicted, the sign-tracking rodents are much more susceptible to addiction than their goal tracking counterparts. Consistent with the biosocial model, it has been argued that this "sign-tracking" behavior is mediated by dopaminergic reward-processing pathways (Robinson & Berridge, 2001).[5]

---

[5] Human evidence on this point is limited. Moreover, where evidence exists, it is inconsistent. Whereas some studies show increased reward processing for problem gamblers relative to healthy controls (Oberg, Christie, & Tata, 2011), others show blunted reward processing among such individuals (Balodis et al., 2012). On the basis of the biosocial model, we might speculate that the results can diverge depending on whether increased motivational salience is conditioned to a gamble itself (which would increase reward processing within the gamble) or to cues associated with the gamble such as slot machines and ambient lighting (which could diminish reward processing within the gamble).

There is a lot to learn from the addiction research discussed here. This literature suggests that addiction and affective decision making share one important component in common, namely, the search for positive incentives to counter negative affect generated by delayed reward, denied views from the mountaintop, and perhaps normatively prohibited pleasures of smoking or drinking. Admittedly, addiction to illicit drugs is typically both more acute and intense than dissonance. Notably, certain illicit drugs, most notably cocaine, are likely to produce both pleasure and aversion (Ettenberg, 2004). Paradoxically, this aversion may produce behavioral conflict with the appetitive tendency, which may augment the pleasure associated with it.

Aside from obvious cases of addiction, affective conditioning and motivational cravings that result from such conditioning is quite commonplace across many domains of life and may be applicable to more mundane practices of social life. Humans are said to be symbolic animals (Lakoff & Johnson, 2003), meaning that we are deeply attached to, and strongly motivated by, symbols of significance. It may not be too far-fetched to suggest that we track symbols of our society and culture as eagerly and vigorously as Robinson's sign-tracking rodents lick the levers of their cages.

3.7 Ego-Depletion

Over the last two decades, many psychologists have been fascinated by self-control and the failure thereof (Heckhausen & Schulz, 1995; Kross, Ayduk, & Mischel, 2005; Mischel, Shoda, & Rodriguez, 1989). One influential analysis utilizes a metaphor of self-regulation as being based on a limited resource pool—the pool of capacities that can be translated into "willpower" (Baumeister et al., 2007). As the primary proponents of the theory argue, "the exertion of self-control … depend[s] on a limited resource." Thus, "just as a muscle gets tired from exertion, acts of self-control cause short-term impairments in subsequent self-control, even on unrelated tasks (Baumeister et al., 2007, p. 351)." This phenomenon has been called "ego-depletion." The theoretical framework proposed to account for the effect is intuitive and indeed has proven to be highly generative of empirical work over the last two decades. A large number of studies show that once working on a first, relatively taxing task, individuals show reduced performance in subsequent tasks even when the latter are unrelated to the first task. It appears then that the self-regulatory resource was depleted after the first task, with little left for the subsequent tasks. However, as argued by critics of the theory, there is no solid evidence for the presence of such a limited resource pool that is thought to be analogous to a muscle (Inzlicht & Schmeichel, 2012). Moreover, evidence is emerging that the depletion effect depends much on how individuals construe the nature of the situation in which they work (Job, Dweck, & Walton, 2010), calling into question the existence, let alone the involvement, of anything like a limited resource pool for self-control.

In an important effort toward clarifying mechanisms underlying the depletion effect, Inzlicht and Schmeichel (2012) presented a potential motivational mechanism for it. As these researchers argue, "initial acts of self-control shift people's motivation away from further restraint and toward gratification (p. 453)." The reason for this motivational shift is thought to involve specific construals on what is expected on them as experimental participants. According to Inzlicht and Schmeichel (2012), "when participants … work hard, … [they] may feel that they have done their part for the experiment, that they have fully met their commitment to the study, and are in fact 'owed' a break." This "self-indulgence" reduces the individuals' motivation to work on tasks administered in the study, thereby shifting their attention to gratification of potentially available pleasures. It is possible that higher-order inferences regarding the nature of obligations as an experimental subject may well be involved at least under certain circumstances. Moreover, at least in such cases, "self-indulgence" may be an accurate description of how subjects feel vis-à-vis the tasks required in the study.

It is not clear, however, whether specific construals such as obligations to the experimenter or owing a break are always involved in all of the numerous studies that show the depletion effect. The biosocial model offers a more parsimonious account of how the motivational shift can happen after working on a self-control task. When individuals work on a self-control task, the task by definition is boring and/or demanding. There is a temptation of quitting the task while completing it. This behavioral conflict is likely to automatically produce (by virtue of the link from ACC to reward-processing regions involving vSTR or Nacc) a search for positive incentives. Indeed, depleted individuals are strongly attracted to seemingly irrelevant cues for pleasure (Schmeichel, Harmon-Jones, & Harmon-Jones, 2010). The search for positive incentives may well distract the individuals from the focal task, especially when the task itself is not attractive. Under such conditions, it will shift the individuals' motivation away from the task. Instead, they will be strongly attracted toward potentially pleasurable activities (e.g., eating chocolate-chip cookies or impulsive buying) when an opportunity to engage in such activities is offered (Vohs & Faber, 2007). In other words, the mechanism of incentive search may be responsible for the shift of motivation toward gratification. That is to say, whereas Inzlicht and Schmeichel (2012) assume that motivational shift (which is caused by certain cognitive appraisals [e.g., "I did enough for this study", "I deserve a break"]) lead to attention to extraneous incentives, the biosocial model hypothesizes that behavioral conflict inherent in demanding/boring tasks sensitizes the actor to extraneous incentives, which in turn diminishes the motivation to work on the task at hand.

So far, the ego-depletion literature is isolated from the volume of research on effort justification. At first glance, the two phenomena do not hang together: In the effort justification effect, engagement in a boring or demanding task leads to increased attraction of the task, whereas in the depletion effect, engagement in a seemingly identical task leads to decreased attraction of the task. Given the limited resource account for the depletion effect, effort justification is an oxymoron: Why is it that people who are depleted after working on a boring task become more attracted to it? From the dissonance theory perspective, the depletion effect is a mystery: Why is it that people who feel convinced of the increased value of a task after expending effort on it end up faltering in it?

The biosocial model provides a simple explanation for both phenomena. They tap on the same fundamental affective and motivational dynamic and, yet, apparent effects are diametrically opposite because very different types of incentives are made salient in the respective situations. When positive incentives are inherent in the task at hand as when one expends effort to reach a mountaintop or when one works on a seemingly boring study for science, potently positive incentives are attached to the task (e.g., a view from the mountaintop or progress in science). Under such conditions, the search for positive incentives initiated by behavioral conflict inherent in the boring task increases the attraction of the task (effort justification). However, if no obvious positive incentives are available in the task and/or if clearly appealing positive incentives are available outside of the task, the search for positive incentives initiated by the behavioral conflict will be directed at the irrelevant incentives, leading to a loss of motivation to work on the initial task (depletion effect).

The same analysis provides an alternative interpretation for the result in the $20 condition of the classic induced-compliance study by Festinger and Carlsmith (1959). Recall that, in this study, subjects were asked to make a counter-attitudinal statement for either a small or large amount of incentive (i.e., $1 or $20). In accordance with cognitive dissonance theory, the researchers argued that the belief that one was making a counter-attitudinal statement with insufficient justification (i.e., the $1, rather than $20 condition) was dissonance arousing and, as a consequence, rationalization (as revealed in an attitude change in the direction of the statement) occurred in the $1 condition, but not in the $20 condition. This analysis rests on the assumption that the knowledge that one is getting $20 for the act provides a cognitive justification for it. It is compatibility of cognitive beliefs or the absence thereof that counts.

The biosocial model provides an alternative perspective. That is, making a counter-attitudinal statement produces negatively arousing behavioral conflict, which leads to a search for positive incentives. This search results in identification of something positive in events or objects involved in the statement, unless there are obvious extraneous incentives (such as the $20 offer). A key test of this reasoning would be to present a large extraneous incentive that is unrelated to the act itself. Whereas the traditional dissonance explanation would predict strong rationalization (because the incentive cannot be used to justify the act), the biosocial model would predict little or no rationalization (because this incentive terminates the search for positive incentives). For example, subjects in the $1 condition may be shown to engage in impulsive buying like Vohs and Faber's (2007) ego-depleted subjects did. Under such conditions, however, no rationalization of a conflict-producing behavior (i.e., the traditional dissonance effect) should occur. To the best of our knowledge, such an experiment has yet to be done.

An important strength of the biosocial model analysis of the depletion effect is its parsimony. There is no need to refer to higher-order construals of, say, obligations as an experimental subject or a desire for self-indulgence. Instead, the single, and simple, principle of behavioral conflict initiating an active search for positive incentives accounts for the assortment of relevant experimental results. Moreover, the biosocial model allows us to recognize that the depletion effect and the effort justification effect are very similar, tapping into the same fundamental affective and motivational dynamics. It further specifies the conditions in which one or the other effect is more likely to ensue. By so doing, it enables us to understand how the depletion effect may be related to other phenomena that might initially appear distinct, including other dissonance effects and addiction. Above and beyond these benefits, the biosocial model is based on known brain mechanisms. Importantly, it does not require any extraneous conceptual baggage such as a limited resource pool for self-control.

Altogether, the biosocial model goes beyond the Inzlicht and Schmeichel (2012) and specifies the affective and motivational brain mechanisms for the motivational shift that is evident in depletion effects. One important future direction could be to test the depletion effect among rodents and birds. The biosocial model would be refuted in favor of more cognitive accounts if these nonhuman animals failed to show similar effects.

4. TOP-DOWN REGULATION

So far, we have argued that dissonance arousal and reduction are affective and motivational in nature. The core of dissonance effects (as well as other related effects such as ego-depletion and addiction) involves a fundamental link from detection of behavioral conflict to a search for positive incentives. Cognition is secondary and only optionally involved. This, of course, does not mean that cognitions are irrelevant. They are likely to come into play in numerous different ways. They may even prove to be powerful in both impact and consequence. First and foremost, cognitions such as beliefs and values can be a source of significant behavioral conflicts, as when one's value of egalitarianism causes dissonance if the person is led to act in racially or sexually prejudiced fashion (Amodio et al., 2004). Second, the biosocial model also holds that higher-order cognitions sometimes regulate the system of conflict detection and, thus, modulate the magnitude of dissonance. It is this second possibility to which we now turn.

4.1 Brain Mechanisms

Imagine you are making a decision that has immediate consequences on your life. For example, you might be choosing between two cars because you need one quite soon to start commuting to your new job. You may be much more careful than usual this time, because you have to take into account various parameters including distance to the job, road conditions, and general professional expectations at the job. These cognitions will prompt you to "tighten" the belt of your thinking and planning. What this means, in neuroscience terminology, would be that you upregulate the sensitivity of your conflict detection system so as to minimize any errors in calculation. More specifically, the person will use her cognitive understanding of the situation to regulate her own psychological system of conflict detection located in dACC. One regulatory region that is neurally connected with dACC is the dorsolateral prefrontal cortex (dlPFC) (Paus & Alamancos, 2001; Richeson et al., 2003). Thus, when higher-order cognitions about one's need and desire to act are activated, these cognitions may engage dlPFC, which may in turn activate dACC. This regulatory pathway is called "top-down" because it is regulated by higher-order goals. These goals influence a neocortical regulatory region of the brain (dlPFC), which exercises its control over a cortical region (dACC) and, by so doing, regulates certain subcortical reward-processing mechanisms (vSTR/Nacc).[6]

Existing evidence suggests that such a top-down regulation of dACC through dlPFC may occur especially when active, appetitive actions are required by the current goals. Moreover, in this top-down regulation of action, it is the left rather than right dlPFC that plays an important role. Initial evidence for this assumption comes from neurophysiological research on depression. Typically, depression is characterized by the absence of desires for appetitive tendencies of approach. Depression may then be associated with an impairment of the ability to regulate one's appetitive behaviors. Davidson and colleagues have shown that depression is often associated with right-lateralized prefrontal activation or decreased activation of the left prefrontal cortex that includes dlPFC (Davidson et al., 2002). One interpretation of this well-documented association is that depression involves an impairment of the left dlPFC function to regulate appetitive, approach-oriented behaviors. In support of this analysis, several studies have shown that repeated magnetic stimulations of the left dlPFC often leads to a reduction of depressive symptoms that are resistant to antidepressive drugs (George et al., 1997). Paus and Alamancos (2001) showed that repetitive transcranical magnetic stimulation of the left dlPFC resulted in increased cerebral blood flow in the ACC area and, on the basis of this finding, reasoned that the stimulation of the left dlPFC may compensate the impaired ability of dACC. According to Paus and Alamancos (2001), one important function of the left dlPFC is to sensitize dACC, and the increased dACC function is thought to be necessary to carry out effective appetitive behaviors.

Altogether, we may hypothesize that when individuals are prepared to execute certain actions, their left dlPFC is engaged to exercise top-down control over dACC and to sensitize the individuals to behavioral conflicts. In the present context, this means that when individuals are prepared to

---

[6] Bear in mind that the higher-order goals themselves may be recruited by certain subcortical processing, such as the one implicated when one is identifying which goals may be most rewarding or dangerous. The subcortical processing in this case, however, is providing input to the higher-order regulatory processes.

execute certain actions, their conflict detection system may be sensitized so that the individuals are more likely to take note of and recognize existing conflicts in their decisions and behaviors, resulting in a greater magnitude of any dissonance that is induced (see the upper left corner of Figure 1).

4.2 Action Orientation

Preparedness for action has been referred to as action (vs. state) orientation (Kuhl, 1992) or, equivalently, implemental (vs. deliberate) mindset (Gollwitzer, Heckhausen, & Steller, 1990). Kuhl (1992) conceptualized the distinction as a relatively stable dispositional variable. Action-oriented people are thought to implement and execute their behavioral intentions more effectively. They tend to be more impulsive and behaviorally active. In contrast, state-oriented people exhibit a myriad of effects (e.g., rumination, deliberation, and anxiety) that impair their ability to implement actions. They are characterized by inability or unwillingness to pursue action with any vigor and, instead, tend to be more deliberative and even contemplative. The same dimension can vary as a function of situational demands and temporary goals (Gollwitzer et al., 1990; Kuhl, 1981). In fact, numerous studies have tested the implications of temporary activation of action versus state orientations for various behavioral outcomes, including dissonance and dissonance reduction (Harmon-Jones et al., 2009).

According to the biosocial model (Figure 1), when action orientation is evoked, and thus the left dlPFC is engaged, it will upregulate dACC, thereby sensitizing the decision maker to existing decision conflicts. It may be anticipated that action orientation should amplify dissonance and, thus, dissonance-motivated attitude change. Beckmann and Kuhl (1984) measured action versus state orientation with a self-report scale and examined whether this dispositional action orientation would moderate a choice justification effect (Beckmann & Kuhl, 1984). Participants were asked to rate the attractiveness of 16 different apartments both before and after making a hypothetical renting decision. As in numerous free-choice dissonance experiments, the preference for a chosen apartment increased after the choice. However, this choice justification effect was reliably larger for those high in dispositional action orientation.

Analogous effects have been obtained when action (vs. state) orientations are induced experimentally via priming procedures. In one such experiment, Harmon-Jones and Harmon-Jones (2002) had participants rate various aerobics exercises and then either make an easy choice (between a highly rated exercise and a lowly rated exercise) or a difficult choice (between two similarly rated exercises). Following the choice, participants were instructed to either list seven things that they do in a typical day (control condition) or seven things that they could do to improve their performance of the exercise (action-oriented condition). As predicted, the researchers found that participants increased their preference for the chosen option and decreased their preference for the rejected option following a difficult, but not an easy, choice. Importantly, this effect was larger for the individuals primed with an action orientation than for those in the control group. Note that, in this experiment, action orientation was induced after the choice. Hence, this orientation increased the choice justification effect after, rather than during, the choice. The biosocial model accommodates a finding like this by hypothesizing that the decision mechanism that leads to choice justification can be recursively engaged (Figure 1). We will return to this point later in the current article.

The biosocial model holds that when action orientation is induced, it will engage the left dlPFC, which sensitizes dACC, thereby increasing sensitivity to potential conflicts in the decision. Evidence for this assumption comes from a series of studies by Harmon-Jones et al. (2008). In one study, the researchers found that priming action orientation led to both increased left frontal EEG asymmetry and increased choice-induced dissonance (Harmon-Jones & Harmon-Jones, 2002). Recall that the activation of the left dlPFC is reflected in the left frontal EEG asymmetry (Sutton & Davidson, 1997). Hence, this evidence strongly suggests that the left dlPFC activity may significantly modulate the dissonance effect.

Critically, the researchers directly manipulated the left frontal EEG asymmetry using neurofeedback training (Allen, Harmon-Jones, & Cavender, 2001) and tested whether this experimentally manipulated left frontal EEG asymmetry would be related to choice-induced dissonance. The study consisted of three sessions (spread across 3 days) where the participant was given direct feedback in the form of auditory signals to indicate whether their relative left frontal EEG asymmetry was moving in the desired direction (Harmon-Jones et al., 2008). Half of the participants were given training to increase their left frontal EEG asymmetry, whereas the other half were given training to decrease their left frontal EEG asymmetry. Participants initially received 2 days of neurofeedback training. On the third day, they rated their preference for psychology experiments, chose between two equally preferred options, received their third session of neurofeedback training, and then rated the options again. The results showed a powerful

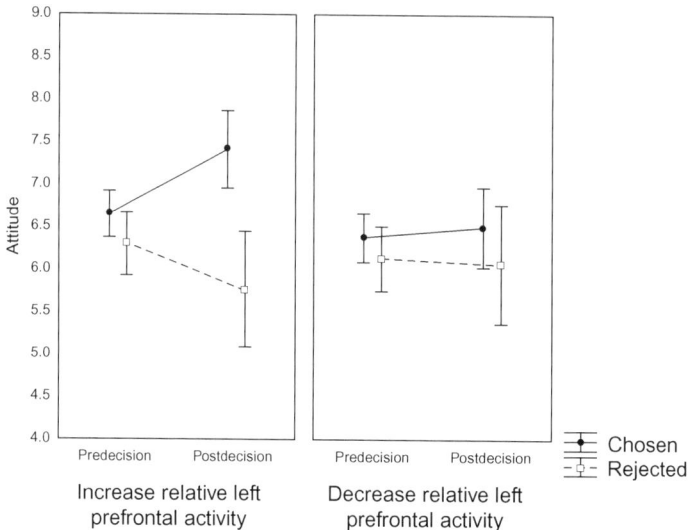

Figure 7 When the left frontal EEG asymmetry is increased via neurofeedback, a clear justification effect is observed (the right panel). That is, preferences for chosen and rejected items spread after choice, but this effect is eliminated when the left frontal EEG asymmetry is decreased via neurofeedback (the left panel). *Reprinted from Harmon-Jones et al. (2008) with permission from APA.*

effect of neurofeedback. As shown in Figure 7, individuals who had been trained to increase their left frontal cortical activation showed a clear choice justification effect. In contrast, this effect disappeared for those who had been trained to decrease their left frontal cortical activation. The finding suggests that the left dlPFC causes choice-induced dissonance to increase. This is consistent with the hypothesis that the activation of the left dlPFC activates dACC, which sensitizes the decision maker to potential decision conflicts.

4.3 Arousal or Reduction?

Harmon-Jones and colleagues (2008, 2009) have explained their findings in terms of their action-based model of dissonance, which postulates that decision conflict impedes an effective execution of an action. Thus, when action orientation is enhanced, the conflict becomes especially aversive, thereby strongly motivating the decision maker to resolve the conflict. In other words, the reason why the decision maker would try to resolve the decision conflict is to achieve the goal of executing effective actions. It would follow, then, that in the absence of any immediate need or desire for action execution, the dissonance effect should dissipate or at least should become weaker. Action orientation is thus held to modulate dissonance reduction.

The biosocial model holds that when action orientation is induced, it sensitizes the conflict detection system as implemented in dACC. Thus, when oriented toward action, individuals will be especially sensitized to available decision conflicts. Once the conflicts are registered, they cause negative arousal, which motivates the decision maker to find positive features in one of the available decision options. When action orientation is weak and/or a contrasting state of state orientation is dominant, the sensitivity of the dACC conflict detection system is lowered. Under such conditions, the decision maker may not take note of existing decision conflicts. Hence, there will be no dissonance effect either. These implications of the biosocial model are consistent with the action-based hypothesis, with a few points of possible disagreement.

To begin, the action-based model implies that it is the effort to reduce dissonance that is modulated by action versus state orientation. Conflicts inherent in a choice supposedly produce the dissonance regardless of whether action orientation has been induced or not. Thus, state-oriented people do not feel motivated to reduce the dissonance that has been induced by the conflicts. In contrast, the biosocial model implies that action or state orientation influences the dACC sensitivity and, thus, it modulates the magnitude of dissonance itself. Indeed, the biosocial model suggests that as long as strong behavioral conflicts are detected, they are likely to activate negative arousal, thereby motivating the decision maker to look for positive features unique to one of decision options. This prediction may be tested with neuroimaging methods, with the activation of dACC and aINS as an index of dissonance arousal (see Figure 3).

Another potential point of disagreement concerns the relative weight the two analyses place on action orientation. The biosocial model acknowledges that action orientation is one factor that increases the sensitivity of dACC. However, it also suggests that there are many other factors that modulate the sensitivity of dACC. Some regulate the sensitivity of dACC through top-down regulatory pathways, including the one mediated by the left dlPFC. These factors include action orientation. But there may be other top-down factors that regulate the magnitude of dissonance. For example, social situations vary in the latitude of normatively permissible behaviors. Thus, some settings, such as funerals and libraries, are much narrower in the latitude of tolerance and, thus, more tight than others, such as public parks and rock concerts (Gelfand et al., 2011). More careful top-down monitoring of one's behavior may be called for in tight social situations. We may then anticipate that individuals should experience greater dissonance in tight rather than loose situations, net of action orientation. At this point, we are unaware of any data speaking to this prediction. Nor do we know whether the effect of situational tightness might also be mediated by the left dlPFC. Future work should address this and other factors that regulate the sensitivity of dACC through top-down pathways.

The biosocial model also assumes that in addition to the top-down factors discussed in this section, there likely exist many significant factors that regulate the sensitivity of dACC bottom-up, through different neural pathways (see the lower left corner of Figure 1). These pathways are likely to be just as important as the top-down pathways, including the one mobilized by action orientation. We now turn to the bottom-up regulatory pathways of dissonance.

5. BOTTOM-UP REGULATION

5.1 Brain Mechanisms

The dACC functions may be regulated, bottom-up, by cues signaling either safety or threat. When individuals are reassured of their safety, they can relax, because there is no need to be vigilant for any potential contingencies in the environment. Thus, safety cues downregulate dACC, thereby reducing the magnitude of behavioral conflict (i.e., dissonance). In contrast, when the individuals face difficulties, risks, and potential dangers, they will be threatened. Such threat cues will mobilize neural mechanisms that enable them to be vigilant for any potential environmental contingencies that pose a threat. Threat cues upregulate dACC, thereby increasing the magnitude of behavioral conflict (i.e., dissonance).

The regulatory path illustrated above is called "bottom-up" because the cues of safety or threat are detected in subcortical regions (as shown below) and take control over a cortical region (dACC). It should be born in mind that these cues themselves may often require substantial neocortical processing, such as when one is exposed to religious symbols or one's sense of the self is affirmed as we shall see below. However, it still remains the case that the primary source of regulation is located in the subcortical regions; thus, the regulatory pathway itself is directed upward from these regions.

Previous work suggests certain plausible brain mechanisms for the bottom-up regulation of the dACC function. In particular, safety cues may downregulate dACC through subcortical dopaminergic (DA) pathways. These pathways originate in specific midbrain areas (the substantia nigra and the ventral tegmental area). DA neurons of these regions are strongly activated by positive incentive cues. This DA burst is likely to spread to the striatal reward-processing region as noted earlier (see Section 3.2). More importantly in the present context, it can also spread to dACC. In this case, the DA burst in midbrain may be expected to decrease the dACC functions, because the connection between the DA pathway and the dACC is largely inhibitory (Bromberg-Martin & Hikosaka, 2009; Walsh & Anderson, 2012). This implies that positive incentive cues, especially those that are likely to result in relatively tonic increase of a positive state, may result in inhibition of the dACC sensitivity and, thus, to a reduced ability to recognize available conflicts in one's behavior and decisions. Although this analysis is speculative and must be examined further in future work, it provides a reasonable neural mechanism that depresses the ACC sensitivity as a function of relatively tonic, positive incentive cues including those signaling safety.

Often times, the world is capricious, full of unexpected happenstances. And, of course, people may also be frightened by the prospect of their own death. According to terror management theory (Greenberg, Solomon, & Pyszczynski, 1997), one cultural instrument humans invented to offer an assurance of eternal life and salvation is religion (Norenzayan & Shariff, 2008). If the hypothesis above is correct in that safety cues downregulate dACC function, religious ideations may be sufficient to cause a tonic deactivation of dACC, especially for those with religious faith. A series of ERP studies reported by Inzlicht and colleagues have provided initial support for this prediction (Inzlicht, McGregor, Hirsh, & Nash, 2009; Inzlicht & Tullett, 2010).

In this work, the researchers examined ERPs of Canadian participants, who worked on a standard color-naming Stroop task. The participants were shown a series of color words presented in a color that either matched or mismatched the semantic meaning of the word. They indicated the font color by pressing a colored response key while ignoring the semantic word meaning. When individuals make an error in a cognitive conflict task like this, their ERPs, especially those in the midline frontal area, show a notable negative-going spike nearly simultaneously with the initiation of the response. As noted earlier, this ERP component is called ERN (Gehring & Willoughby, 2004; Holroyd & Coles, 2002). ERN is thought to originate in dACC (Bush et al., 2000). It signals two types of conflict or error. First, it can signal response conflict between a response that has just been initiated and a correct response that is based on cognitive processing of the word meaning (Botvinick et al., 2004; Yeung, 2004). Second, it can also signal a negative reward prediction error (Walsh & Anderson, 2012), which occurs when the actual outcome (i.e., error) is worse than expected (i.e., correct response). The negative reward prediction error interrupts the behavior and, thus, can be seen as a go- versus no-go-type behavioral conflict. Both of these computations have been localized to dACC or nearby regions. Thus, when the dACC sensitivity is reduced, the ERN magnitude should be decreased.

Data provided support for the above prediction. In their first set of experiments, Inzlicht et al. (2009) measured "religious zeal" by using a self-report scale (e.g., "I aspire to live and act according to my religious beliefs," "My religious beliefs are grounded in objective truth") and found that the ERN magnitude systematically decreased as a function of religious zeal. In their subsequent studies, the researchers primed positive religious ideations directly and tested whether individuals would manifest less ERN (Inzlicht & Tullett, 2010). As predicted, ERN was weaker in the religious priming condition for religious participants but not for atheist participants (who would not be expected to view religion as a safety cue).

Conversely, when safety cues are removed, when they are psychologically absent, or when the level of anxiety is increased, dACC function should be increased. There is increasing evidence that the ERN magnitude increases as a function of trait anxiety (Hajcak, 2012). Moreover, numerous studies have shown that avoidance-related motivational states influence ERN (Gehring & Willoughby, 2004; Holroyd & Coles, 2002). For example, when motivation is increased by monetary incentives or by the presence of another person evaluating the participant's performance, the ERN magnitude is increased (Boksem, Tops, Wester, Meijman, & Lorist, 2006; Hajcak, Moser, Holroyd, & Simons, 2006).

Pertinent neural pathways by which anxiety or certain other threats upregulate the dACC function are largely unknown. One possible pathway implicates the amygdala. Impinging threats are likely to sensitize ACC (Öhman, 2005) via the amygdala, which is known to respond strongly to threat cues (Nader, Schafe, & Le Doux, 2000; Öhman, 2005). It is possible that the amygdala activation directly sensitizes the dACC. Much caution is justified here, because the amygdala responds to rewards as well as fears or threats, subserving motivational functions that are far more fine-grained and nuanced than previous theorizing implied (Robinson, Warlow, & Berridge, 2014).

In addition to the direct link from the amygdala to ACC, anxiety or fear detected at the amygdala may influence ACC through an indirect route. As noted above, dACC is linked through inhibitory connections to the dopaminergic (DA) reward pathway, which originates in the midbrain. The firing rates of the midbrain DA neurons are likely to decrease upon the detection of a threat cue (Bromberg-Martin & Hikosaka, 2009; Frank & Claus, 2006). The decreased activation of the DA pathway, in turn, may be expected to disinhibit the ACC because, as noted, the connection of the DA pathway to the ACC tends to be inhibitory (Walsh & Anderson, 2012). In this way, threat cues may increase dACC sensitivity.

5.2 Generalized Other and dACC Sensitivity: A Cultural Variation

Some signals of safety such as religion may be universally available across cultures (Norenzayan & Gervais, 2012). Likewise, some signals of threat such as loss of monetary reward may be universal. However, many cues of both safety and threat may also be inherently entrenched in divergent cultural practices and meanings. Effects of such cues may be highly variable across cultures. One such cue may involve images of what George Mead called the "generalized other" (Mead, 1934).

It has been proposed that cultures vary systematically in terms of the model of the self that is shared and authenticated therein (Kitayama & Uskul, 2011; Markus & Kitayama, 1991). In Eastern cultures (especially East Asian cultures), the self is assumed to be interdependent. According to this model of the self, one's behavior is guided and organized by others' expectations and obligations to them. For these individuals, evaluations by others are so important that when interacting with others, they are very likely to worry about these evaluations. In fact, Asians typically attend closely to their potential shortcomings and negative features (Kitayama, Markus, Matsumoto, & Norasakkunkit, 1997) and, thus, tend to be more pessimistic (Chang & Asakawa, 2003) and higher in social anxiety (Okazaki, Liu, Longworth, & Minn, 2002). This pessimism enables the individuals to maintain positive evaluations in the eyes of the others (Heine, Kitayama, & Lehman, 2001). Once socialized in this interdependent cultural system, individuals may associate certain negative emotions such as worry, apprehension, and anxiety with an image of a "generalized other" (Mead, 1934). Accordingly, face cues may acquire the potential to upregulate the dACC functions.

In contrast, in Western cultures, especially European American cultures, the self is assumed to be independent. According to the independent model of the self, one's behavior is guided and organized by his or her internal attributes such as desires, attitudes, and preferences. These individuals tend to focus on positive aspects of themselves (Kitayama et al., 1997) and are thus optimistic (Taylor & Brown, 1988). As may be expected, European Americans tend to be relatively low in social anxiety (Okazaki, 2000) while showing markedly higher levels of general trust as compared to Asians (Yamagishi, Cook, & Watabe, 1998). Once socialized in this cultural context, individuals may acquire contrastingly positive associations with images of the generalized other. These images may then be accorded the potential to serve as safety cues and inhibit the dACC functions.

In a recent experiment, Park and Kitayama (2014) had both European American and Asian participants perform a speeded flanker task responding to the direction of a center arrow flanked by either congruent (same direction) or incongruent (opposite direction) arrows (Park & Kitayama, 2014). Right before the flanker was presented, a realistic face image that was both racially and emotionally neutral was presented very briefly for the average duration of 90 ms. As expected, the face priming changed the magnitude of the ERN. For Asians, the ERN was significantly larger in the face-priming condition as compared to control conditions where either an image of a house or a scrambled face was presented as a prime. This finding is consistent with the hypothesis that face priming sensitizes dACC. In contrast, face priming tended to decrease the magnitude of ERN for European Americans, suggesting that face priming desensitizes dACC. The pertinent waveforms are shown in Figure 8A and B for Asians and European Americans, respectively.

Note that in this experiment, the priming stimuli were presented for less than one-tenth of a second. Thus, although the primes were visible for the most part, they were very brief. Thus, it is unlikely that participants clearly registered them or exercised any effort to regulate their actions because of them (Cunningham et al., 2004). The pattern of data thus suggests that culture establishes quite divergent emotional conditionings to the generic face image, consistent with the hypothesis that the positive versus negative associations the face cues have for the two cultural groups of participants are due to the underlying dimension of interdependence (as opposed to independence). If this hypothesis is correct, the cultural difference may be explained by individual differences on this dimension. Figure 8C shows the magnitude of the face-priming effect on ERN as a function

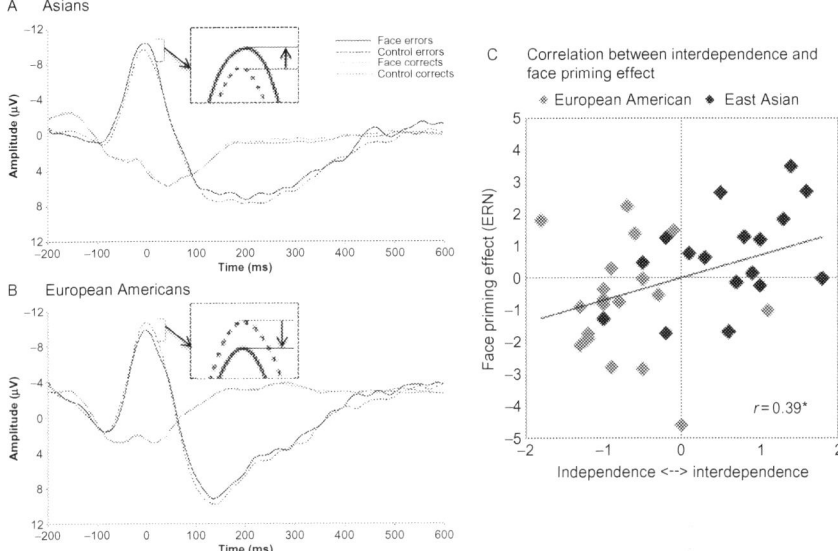

Figure 8 ERN magnitude as a function of culture and face priming. (A) Wave forms for Asians. The ERN peak is higher in the face-priming condition than in the control conditions. (B) Wave forms for European Americans. The ERN peak is lower in the face-priming condition than in the control condition. (C) The face-priming effect is predicted by interdependent (vs. independent) self-construal. *Reprinted from Park and Kitayama (2014) with permission from Oxford University Press.*

of interdependent self-construal. As can be seen, as one's level of interdependence becomes higher, the face-priming effect on ERN becomes more positive. The data are consistent with the hypothesis that Asians show a positive face-priming effect (with the face increasing the ERN magnitude) because they are relatively higher in interdependence, whereas European Americans show a negative face-priming effect (with the face decreasing the ERN magnitude) because they are relatively independent.

Another paradigm suitable in testing error processing involves a gambling task. Hitokoto, Glazer, and Kitayama (2014) presented their participants with two boxes on the computer screen and asked them to choose one to obtain monetary points. Right after the choice, feedback was delivered regarding whether they had gained or lost certain points. This gamble was repeated a number of times. When the gamble was presented on each trial, a priming stimulus (either face or scrambled face) was presented very briefly, for 90 ms, between the two boxes. The goal was to determine whether the face priming would also modulate ERP error signals. In a gambling task like this, approximately 270 ms after the feedback, there emerges a negative deflection of ERP around the frontal central scalp location when the outcome is negative and, thus, worse than expected. This signal is called feedback-related negativity (FRN) and is analogous to ERN in that it is an index of the detection of a negative reward prediction error (Gehring, 2002; Gehring & Willoughby, 2004; Miltner, Braun, & Coles, 1997).

Hitokoto et al. tested whether the magnitude of FRN would be moderated by face priming, with an expectation that the FRN magnitude would increase as a function of face priming for Asians, but it should decrease as a function of face priming for European Americans. This, in fact, was the case with one caveat. In this study, two different groups of Asians were tested, Asian Americans (i.e., individuals with Asian heritage who had been born and brought up in the United States) and Asian sojourners (i.e., those with Asian heritage who had been born and brought up in Asia and who came to the United States relatively recently). As shown in Figure 9, the face-priming effect on FRN was positive for Asian Americans, but negative for European Americans, as predicted. Interestingly, the pattern for Asian sojourners was more similar to the one for European Americans

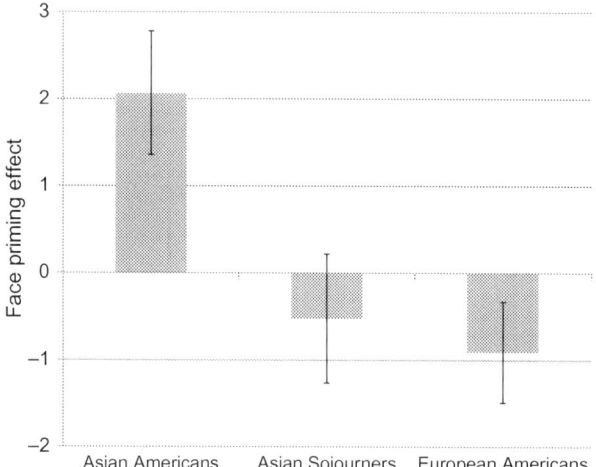

Figure 9 Magnitude of FRN (feedback contingent negativity on loss vs. win trials) in the face priming (as compared to scramble face control) condition in a gambling paradigm. For Asian Americans, face priming significantly increased the magnitude of FRN (the magnitude of negativity on loss vs. win trials), whereas for European Americans face priming tended to decrease it. This effect achieved statistical significance once trials with bursts of alpha wave were excluded. Unexpectedly, Asian sojourners showed a pattern that is no different from the European American pattern. *Taken from Hitokoto et al. (2014).*

than for Asian Americans. This finding must first be replicated before being taken seriously. Tentatively, we may speculate that Asians who chose to come to the United States for college (and then chose to participate in a neuroimaging study under certain recruitment procedures and conditions) might be self-selected to be more independent than may be typical among Asians.[7]

5.3 Culture, Face Priming, and Dissonance

The ERP studies discussed earlier by both Inzlicht and colleagues on the effect of religion priming (Inzlicht & Tullett, 2010) and by Kitayama and colleagues on the face priming (Hitokoto et al., 2014; Park & Kitayama, 2014) offer some significant implications for the biosocial model, because the ERP signals tested in these studies (ERN and FRN/FRP) are thought to originate in dACC and serve as reliable indices of the dACC sensitivity. To the extent that dissonance effects are also mediated by the ACC sensitivity, there should be comparable effects of priming on the magnitude of dissonance effects.

In a series of cross-cultural free-choice dissonance studies, Kitayama and colleagues have provided substantial evidence for this hypothesis (Imada & Kitayama, 2010; Kimel et al., 2014; Kitayama et al., 2004). In a typical free-choice dissonance study, participants are asked to rate several choice options both before and after they make a choice between two of the options. The two options happened to be options that were rated similarly during the first prechoice rating period. Numerous studies conducted in North America have found that after the choice, attraction to the chosen CD increases and attraction to the rejected CD decreases (e.g., Harmon-Jones et al., 2009). As noted earlier, Kitayama et al. (2013) provided the first neuroimaging evidence indicating that a difficult choice like this produces a conflict as indicated by dACC + aINS activation, which in turn prompts the chooser to find positive distinctive features in one of the options. Once these positive distinctive features have been identified (as indicated by the Nacc activity), the chooser will make a clear choice (see Figures 1 and 5). After the choice,

---

[7] The aforementioned study by Park and Kitayama (2014) also tested Asian sojourners and found their pattern to be contrastingly different from the pattern for European Americans (Figure 8C). Moreover, cross-cultural dissonance studies available in the literature (to be discussed in Section 5.3) tested Asians in Asia, Asian Americans, and Asian sojourners and found patterns that are, for the most part, very similar to one another, although no study directly compared Asian Americans and Asian sojourners within a single study as in the Hitokoto et al. (2014) study.

the chosen CDs become more attractive because of this newly identified positive information associated with it.

Importantly, an earlier study had shown that under this standard free-choice situation, Asians do not show the choice justification effect (Heine & Lehman, 1997). The two ERP face-priming studies (Hitokoto et al., 2014; Park & Kitayama, 2014) suggest why this might be the case. In the absence of any watching faces, the dACC of Asians might not be sufficiently activated. Perhaps, due to anxiety associated with images of others, the absence of such others may serve as a potent cue for safety. Importantly, Asians should show a reliable choice-justification effect once they are exposed to a face cue while making a choice. Conversely, European Americans should show the choice-justification effect in the absence of any face cues, but they might not show it once they are exposed to face cues (signaling safety) during choice. In one study (Kitayama et al., 2004), both Asian and European American participants rated 10 popular music CDs both before and after making a choice between two CDs that had initially been rated as nearly equally liked. A poster (seemingly prepared for a conference presentation) was inconspicuously displayed on the wall in front of half of the participants (Figure 10A). The poster showed several schematic faces that appeared to be "watching" the participants. The remaining half of the participants were not exposed to this face poster.

As predicted, there was a significant face × culture interaction, which is illustrated in Figure 10B. Replicating the earlier study by Heine and Lehman (1997), Asians did not show any justification effect (i.e., increased liking for

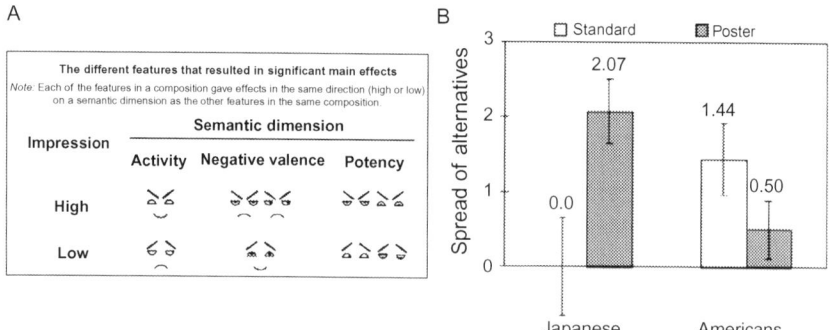

Figure 10 Effects of face-priming on choice justification. (A) Face poster used. (B) Japanese showed a justification effect only in the face-priming condition. But European Americans showed it only in the no-priming condition. *Reprinted from Kitayama et al. (2004), copyright © (2004) with permission of SAGE Publications.*

the chosen CD and decreased liking for the rejected CD) in the no-poster condition. However, once they were exposed to the face cues, these participants showed a highly significant choice justification effect. The finding is consistent with the hypothesis that Asians associated anxiety and worry with face cues. Moreover, they appear to take the absence of face cues as signaling safety. This finding is also consistent with the biosocial model, suggesting that the face cues sensitized dACC, initiating the decision mechanism that assigns positive affect to the chosen CD. Equally importantly, European Americans showed a reliable justification effect in the absence of the face cues, replicating numerous previous studies. However, this effect became weaker in the face-priming condition. The reduced justification effect in the face (vs. control) condition has since been replicated (Imada & Kitayama, 2010; Kimel et al., 2014). The finding suggests that European Americans associate a positive incentive of safety with an image of the generalized other. The face cues therefore desensitize dACC, leading to reduced conflict detection and choice justification.

In a subsequent study, Imada and Kitayama (2010, Study 2) showed that for the face-priming effect to occur, it is critical that face representations must be activated when exposed to the prime. In this study, Asian and European Americans were tested in a free-choice dissonance paradigm. Instead of the face poster, the researchers used a letter-size sheet of paper on which three dots were printed in either a triangular formation or a reversed triangular formation (see Figure 11A). This sheet was inconspicuously placed in front of the participants. After the free-choice procedure, the experimenter took up the sheet and asked the participants to complete a picture by using the three dots. As shown in Figure 11B, some participants drew a face by using the three dots, whereas some others drew some other picture. Conceptually replicating the Kitayama et al. (2004) study, the choice justification effect was significantly greater for Asians who drew a face than those who did not. Conversely, the effect was significantly greater for European Americans who did not draw a face than those who did (Figure 11C).

In both the Kitayama et al. (2004) study and the Imada and Kitayama (2010) study, face-priming pictures were presented throughout the experimental procedure. A recent study tried to sharpen the analysis by examining the critical time window in which the face-priming effect would be maximal. According to the biosocial model, the face cues are considered to modulate dACC sensitivity, which initiates the decision mechanism that produces positive affect assigned to an option to be chosen. This process can be complete before a decision is made, although the process

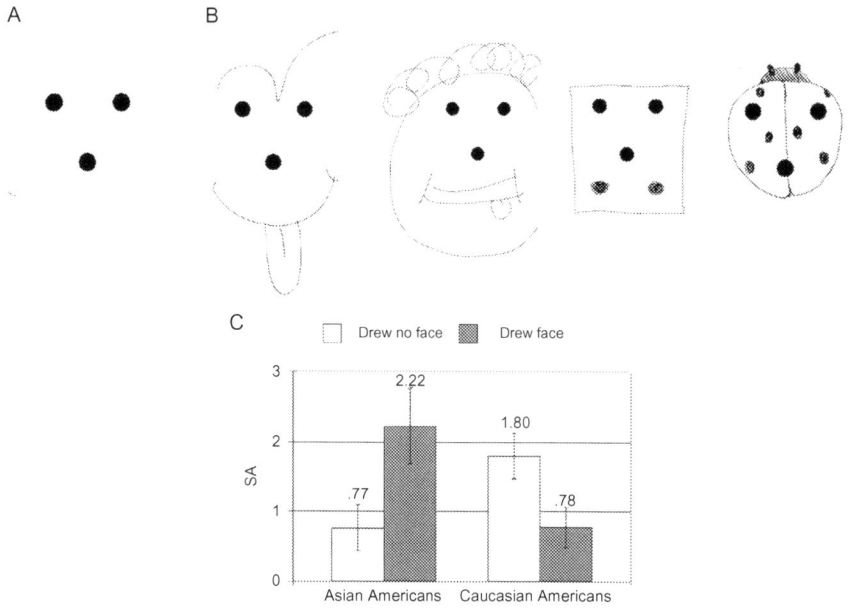

Figure 11 Face-priming effect in choice justification. (A) A three-dot configuration placed in front of participants. (B) Sample drawings using the three-dot configurations. Note some are faces, whereas the others have nothing to do with face. (C) For Asians, those who drew a face showed a greater justification effect, whereas for European Americans, those who drew a face showed a weaker justification effect. *Reprinted from Imada and Kitayama (2010) with permission from Guilford Press.*

may sometimes be recursively engaged. This analysis implies that the face-priming effect observed in the two studies discussed above should be more pronounced when participants are exposed to face cues while they make a choice rather than after the choice.

To examine this issue, Imada and Kitayama (2010, Study 1) used the original face-priming procedure of Kitayama et al. (2004). Unlike in the Kitayama et al. (2004) study, however, right after making a choice on one desk, participants were asked to move to another desk in the same room. The experimenter casually told them to do so because she had to clean up the first desk for another session. The face poster was placed in front of either the first desk or the second desk. Thus, the participants were exposed to the face poster either while making a choice or after the choice. As predicted by the biosocial model, Asians showed a significantly larger choice justification effect when they were exposed to the face poster while they made a choice than when they were exposed to it after the choice. In contrast, European Americans showed a completely reversed pattern, with the choice justification effect significantly weaker when they were exposed to the poster during the choice than afterward.

The same analysis can be extended to explain cultural differences in dissonance effects as a function of the choice being made for the self versus for a close other. When individuals make a choice for themselves in a private setting, no subjective representation of the generalized other is actively available. Under such conditions, European Americans tend to show a much larger justification effect than do Asians. However, when the individuals make a choice for a close other in a public setting, images of others watching the choice (including the other person for whom the choice is being made) become highly salient. It may be expected, then, that under such conditions, Asians will show a choice justification effect more strongly than do European Americans. A series of studies by Hoshino-Browne and colleagues has confirmed these predictions (Hoshino-Browne et al., 2005). This Asian effect appears to be mediated by their self being relatively interdependent. In a recent series of studies, Kimel, Grossmann, and Kitayama (2012) show that European Americans also show this effect when primed with interdependent orientations.

Taken together, the cumulative evidence reviewed in this section shows that for Asians, face priming upregulates the ACC sensitivity and, as a consequence, increases the attractiveness of the chosen options. In contrast, for European Americans, face priming downregulates dissonance and, as a consequence, decreases the attractiveness of the chosen options. Moreover, the fMRI evidence reviewed earlier indicates that the change in attractiveness is likely to be anchored in the corresponding change in activity in the striatal reward-processing areas (Jarcho et al., 2011; Kitayama et al., 2013). It is important to bear in mind, however, these areas are involved not only in "liking," but also in the motivational striving of "wanting"; moreover, these two aspects of reward processing are distinct, overlapping only partially (Berridge, 2012; Berridge et al., 2009). Accordingly, it is of interest to determine whether the culturally variable choice effect observed in the studies reviewed here could be extended to motivational inclinations toward chosen goals.

Another recent study investigated this possibility by having both European Americans and Koreans choose one of three tests measuring different aspects of IQ (fluid IQ, creativity, and analytic IQ) (Na & Kitayama, 2012). One-third of the participants made this choice with the face poster hung in front of them, whereas another one-third did so without any such poster. The remaining third did not make this choice, but the experimenter simply assigned one of the tests to work on. After these manipulations,

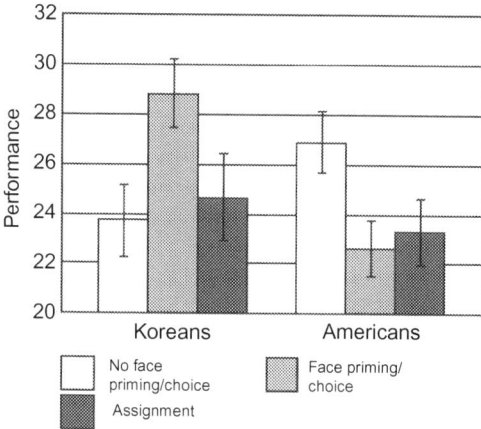

Figure 12 Face-priming effect on task performance. Koreans worked hardest when they had chosen the task in front of a face poster, but European Americans worked hardest when they had chosen the task in the absence of any face poster. *Reprinted from Na and Kitayama (2012) with permission from Elsevier.*

the participants moved to a separate individual booth and worked on the chosen/assigned test. Unbeknownst to the participants, they worked on an identical set of remote association questions. The researchers measured how many questions they solved within 5 min. The results are summarized in Figure 12. As can be seen, Koreans solved more questions in the face priming/choice condition than in either the no face priming/choice condition or the assignment condition. This result demonstrates that after making a choice in the presence of face priming, Asians are not only attracted to the chosen goal (as shown in the dissonance studies discussed earliear) but also motivated strongly to achieve the goal. That is, the incentive value of the chosen goal has been increased, as predicted by the hypothesis that faces serve as a threat cue for these individuals. In contrast, European Americans solved more questions in the no face priming/choice condition than in the face priming/choice condition or in the assignment condition. This shows that for European Americans the incentive-increasing effect of choice is diminished by face priming, as predicted by the hypothesis that faces serve as a safety cue for these individuals.

5.4 Self-Affirmation, Mortality Salience, and Other Bottom-Up Factors

The current analysis implies that all cues signaling safety should down-regulate dACC functions, thereby reducing the ability of the decision maker to recognize existing decision conflicts and thus reducing dissonance effects. By extending this logic, the biosocial model provides a comprehensive framework in which to understand effects of self-affirmation (Sherman & Cohen, 2006; Steele, 1988) and mortality salience (Greenberg et al., 1997).

Self-affirmation occurs when certain positive features of the self such as moral integrity and competence are confirmed and reinforced. Cognitions required to achieve this state of affirmation may be called affirmation resources. People with sufficient affirmation resources are considered resilient, resulting in less defensive reactions when facing potentially threatening events (Sherman & Cohen, 2006). They become more resilient when they are reminded of available affirmation resources, such as high values they possess or high competence or ability of the self (Creswell et al., 2005). The biosocial model suggests that when the self is affirmed, the subcortical DA reward pathway is activated, which in turn inhibits dACC.[8] Under these conditions, people will be relatively more oblivious to existing behavioral conflicts, thereby ceasing to show dissonance effects. Numerous studies have confirmed this general prediction (Heine & Lehman, 1997; Steele, Spencer, & Lynch, 1993). The affirmed individuals may also be less defensive because they are relatively oblivious to potential conflicts or errors they may commit.

One important caveat must be noted. Exactly what information serves as an affirmation resource depends on a myriad of contextual factors including personality, situation, and broader sociocultural context. For example, confirming one's own personal values may be highly affirming to those who hold an independent sense of the self, but not to those who hold a more interdependent sense of the self. In support of this possibility, evidence indicates that choice justification is readily eliminated when one's personal values are confirmed for European Americans (who tend to hold an independent sense of the self), but this manipulation does not seem to work for Asians (who tend to hold an interdependent sense of the self). Instead, for Asians, it is confirmation of group values (e.g., values shared by family members) that tend to have an equivalent self-affirming effect (Hoshino-Browne et al., 2005).

Moreover, every society and culture offers many other cues signaling safety. Familiarity and banality of daily life, in and by itself, may signal safety

---

[8] Self-affirmation can have multiple effects. Thus, in addition to activating the midbrain DA pathway (thus, downregulating dACC), it might also motivate people to work hard on competence tasks because it enhances a general sense of self-competence. Self-affirmed individuals may then engage a top-down regulatory control to upregulate dACC (Legault, Al-Khindi, & Inzlicht, 2012). Thus, the net effect of self-affirmation on dACC sensitivity may depend on the relative strength of the two effects. This top-down factor, however, is unlikely to be relevant in many dissonance situations where no cognitive competence is at issue.

(Zajonc, 1968). Or the mere absence of potential threats (e.g., other watching others for Asians) may serve as a safety cue (as argued earlier). Likewise, certain religious rituals involving symbolic cleansing or secular practices intended to improve hygiene may also function in similar fashion. Recent work shows that an opportunity to wash one's hands was sufficient to "wash away" a dissonance effect (Lee & Schwarz, 2010), consistent with the notion that washing hands is an effective cue signaling safety, thus down-regulating dACC, which reduces the dissonance effect.

Currently, there is little direct evidence pertaining to the neural pathways activated by self-affirming information (or for that matter any cues signaling safety) to alleviate the dissonance effects. As noted earlier, animal studies show that such positive incentive cues activate the midbrain DA neurons, which in turn downregulate dACC (Bromberg-Martin & Hikosaka, 2009). It stands to reason that individuals who are affirmed and/or relaxing in safety may show greater DA activation, which then downregulates regions including dACC. In principle, it is now in our reach to perform a critical test of the hypothesized neural pathway with available neuroimaging methods.

Another major source of dACC sensitivity is mortality salience. When mortality is made salient, people are assumed to be frightened. Although this fear is held to be unconscious insofar as it is exceedingly difficult to pin it down on the basis of subjective self-reports, it is likely to instigate the threat detection system of the brain that most likely includes the amygdala. This activation of threat may well decrease midbrain DA activity. In combination, mortality salience is likely to upregulate dACC sensitivity, thereby amplifying associated effects including error processing as revealed in ERN or FRN and dissonance reduction. As in the case of self-affirmation, this prediction by terror management theory, particularly the one pertaining to the dissonance effect, has received strong empirical support (Friedman & Arndt, 2005; Greenberg et al., 1997; Jonas, Schulz-Hardt, & Frey, 2005). At the same time, as is also true in the case of self-affirmation, the specific conditions in which this fear is instigated may depend on a number of contextual variables. For example, individualists may be more responsive to a thought of death of their personal self, but collectivists may be more responsive to a thought of death of their group (Kashima, Halloran, Yuki, & Kashima, 2004).

One benefit of an encompassing theoretical framework like the one proposed here is to highlight a common underlying mechanism that cuts across disparate, seemingly independent phenomena such as self-affirmation and mortality salience. Self-affirmation is one particular way to highlight the safety of the self, whereas mortality salience is one particular way to highlight an excruciating threat to the self. At the level of brain mechanisms involving dACC sensitivity, these two phenomena can be seen as representing the opposite ends of a theoretical continuum defined by the degree of sensitivity of the dACC-based conflict detection system. In principle, there may be many other variables that influence this system. The biosocial model then may serve as a valuable heuristic tool for discovering new moderating variables of dissonance and related phenomena.

6. RECURSIVE LOOP
6.1 Aversive Consequences

The biosocial model implies that behavioral conflict (i.e., dissonance) is inherent in difficult decisions. Often, the conflict is aroused and resolved by the time a decision is made. In fact, this conflict itself constitutes an important part of the mechanism for decision making. However, once a decision is made, this decision may become a source of additional conflict, consistent with the notion of postdecisional dissonance. For example, the decision may go against a prevailing norm of the situation. This may alert the person to regulate her behavior more carefully, which could engage the left dlPFC to increase the sensitivity of dACC. Alternatively, the person may recognize potential aversive consequences of the decision, in which case the decision may become a cue for self-threat, mobilizing the bottom-up regulatory pathway to increase the dACC sensitivity.

Given the biosocial model, the renewed effort to resolve behavioral conflict is likely to direct the decision maker's attention to other available positive incentives associated with the decision, insofar as this incentive information is likely to reduce the behavioral conflict and negative arousal associated with it, and enable her to resurrect her original decision. In short, this recursive loop of dissonance arousal and reduction may further amplify the justification effect. This is exactly what Cooper and Fazio (1984) demonstrated and featured in their New Look perspective on dissonance.

6.2 Misattribution

The dissonance arousal before an initial decision can be quite brief and transitory. Once aroused, it can dissipate quickly when positive incentives are identified in one of the decision options. The negative arousal is coded in terms of transitory activation of aINS. Although it powerfully regulates attention involved in the search for positive incentives, it may also be too brief to surpass the threshold for conscious awareness. For all practical purposes, the negative arousal of dissonance may be subliminal. However, once the recursive loop of dissonance is engaged, the negative arousal may repeat itself and; moreover, the recursive loop may involve more deliberate, slow-growing psychological processes. Hence, the negative arousal of dissonance may be subjectively experienced.

Once the aINS activation reaches the conscious threshold, this activation itself may become the target of cognitive interpretations. It is possible that the decision maker correctly interprets the negative arousal as resulting from her decision conflict. However, there may be other environmental cues (e.g., a noisy room) that may reasonably explain why one might be feeling the negative arousal. Under these conditions, the decision maker may mis-attribute her negative arousal to the environmental cues. To the extent that such misattribution occurs, the decision maker will no longer experience any need to reduce it. The justification effect may dissipate accordingly. A large number of studies conducted by Zanna, Cooper, and many others during the 1970s provided convincing evidence for the potent effect of experimentally manipulated misattribution cues (Zanna & Cooper, 1974; see Cooper & Fazio, 1984, for a review).

6.3 Split Brain

The biosocial model holds that the conscious, interpretive aspects of disso-nance arousal and experience, which are mediated by the recursive loop of Figure 1, are functionally separate and independent of the subcortical mech-anism of dissonance we have identified. Intriguing evidence for this assump-tion comes from research on split-brain patients (Gazzaniga, 2013; Wolman, 2012). In the 1940s, to treat severe forms of epilepsy, the corpus callosum (which connects the two cortical hemispheres) was sometimes surgically dis-sected. The surgery helped contain the seizure to one side of the brain. In the 1950s, a small group of researchers led by Roger Sperry investigated neuro-psychological characteristics of these split-brain patients. One conclusion from this body of work is that the two hemispheres have very different func-tions (Gazzaniga, 2013). In large part, the left hemisphere, but not the right hemisphere, is responsible for verbal, linguistic, and interpretive capacities. Among split-brain patients, subcortical mechanisms (which retain the neu-rological unity) are capable of automatically executing certain simple responses that are requested, whereas the left hemisphere is required to inter-pret what they have done and why they have done so.

One dramatic demonstration of this point comes from a patient called P.S. (Ledoux, Wilson, & Gazzaniga, 1977). In one study, for example, P.S. was flashed one picture to one visual field (so that it is projected on the contralateral hemisphere) and asked to point to the same one from several pictures that were placed in front of him. He had no problem in carrying this out. Now imagine that two pictures are shown, with a chicken claw flashed on the right visual field (projected on the left hemisphere) and a snow scene on the left visual field (projected on the right hemisphere). Under such a condition, P.S.'s left and right hands (controlled by the contralateral hemispheres) pointed to the pictures of chicken and snow shovel, respectively. This is exactly what one would expect if each hemisphere independently responded to what it saw. Of importance for our purpose, when P.S. was asked why he did what he did, he immediately came up with a narrative that seemed reasonable, "The chicken claw goes with the chicken, and you need a shovel to clean out the chicken shed" (Gazzaniga, 2013, p. 13). The observation is consistent with a view that separate from whatever processing modules are required in the production of automatic matching responses, there exists an interpretive module, supposedly localized in the left, verbal hemisphere, which uses one's own automatically generated responses as cues and interprets them within a coherent narrative. By so doing, split-brain patients like P.S. manage to maintain the unitary sense of the self even though much of their mind is physically split into two halves. Earlier on, we noted a demonstration of a free-choice dissonance effect among amnesic patients (Lieberman et al., 2001). It is possible that what is missing in these patients is a failure in retrospective story making (which involves episodic recollection of previous experiences), with all other dissonance machineries kept intact.

It is evident, then, that some significant portion of the higher-order system of interpretation and story making, supposedly localized in the left "verbal" hemisphere, is functionally separate and independent of the rest of the psychological mechanisms that automatically carry out various functions including dissonance and other forms of affective decision making. Thus, the specific precognitive neural network of affective decision making operates independently of the conscious, deliberate looping mechanisms. The latter are important and powerful; yet, they are only secondary to the core neural mechanism of affective decision making we have identified. Thus, as Zajonc (1980) put it, "preferences [often] need no inferences (page 151)."

7. CONCLUSIONS

7.1 Evaluating the Biosocial Model

In the present paper, we drew on recent advances in both neuroscience and animal behavior and proposed that when people face a conflict between two competing behaviors such as approach versus avoidance and go versus no-go, they develop a new affective disposition. This newly emerging affect enables one to select a response while forming the basis for an elaborate cognition that justifies the selected response. This model, called the biosocial model, reconceptualized dissonance as affective (rather than cognitive). It explains both how decisions are made and how the decisions that are made are subsequently rationalized. Moreover, by postulating both top-down and bottom-up regulatory pathways, the model integrates all major moderating factors of dissonance, including action orientation, self-affirmation, mortality salience, and culture. Equally important, the model provides a coherent framework to understand a disparate set of affective and motivational phenomena, including animal behaviors that mimic effort justification, addiction, and ego-depletion. Furthermore, the model suggests why humans are affectively and motivationally attached to symbols of culture. The mechanism stipulated by the biosocial model may be one significant biological preadaptation for symbolic culture.

The model is grounded in known brain mechanisms. Although, at this point, not all details are supported by existing data, they are testable with currently available neuroimaging methods such as EEG and fMRI. By specifying the underlying brain mechanisms, the model makes it possible to locate the mechanisms of affective decision making within a broader, expanding theoretical framework of affective, cognitive, and social neuroscience (Lieberman, 2007). Moreover, the model is also socioculturally open. In particular, the regulatory pathways are likely affected by sociocultural learning and conditioning. Numerous sociocultural inputs, including action versus state orientation, religion, self-affirmation, and images of the Meadian generalized other, can systematically modulate the basic decision-making mechanics in a highly systematic fashion. Thus, the model can be legitimately called "biosocial." It can illuminate, not only the underlying neural mechanisms, but also the nature of sociocultural reinforcement contingencies that shape these mechanisms.

7.2 How Cognitive is Cognitive Dissonance?

As noted earlier, dissonance has long been considered cognitive in the sense that inconsistencies among beliefs are considered to define dissonance. This perspective was instrumental in establishing cognitive theories in social psychology during the 1950s and 1960s, thereby paving the way to the productive era of social cognition research in the 1970s and 1980s (Fiske & Taylor,

2013). The biosocial model, in contrast, suggests that the conflict at issue is not purely cognitive. It is much more behavioral, such as conflict between approach and avoidance or between go-response and no-go response. This consideration may shed some new light on the question of why not all cognitive beliefs lend themselves to dissonance. Some beliefs give rise to behavioral tendencies more readily or more vigorously than others, and according to the biosocial model, only those cognitions with direct implications for behavior lead to dissonance.

For example, in most contemporary secular societies, knowledge that the earth rotates around the sun is completely disconnected from behavioral reality. Thus, even though it clearly contradicts everything else people experience about the relationship between the earth and the sun, this conflict does not produce dissonance. Imagine, however, what might have happened to someone who practiced science at the dawn of Modern Europe like Galileo Galilei did in seventieth century Italy. With his commitment to the then-emerging science, the belief about the rotation of the earth would have carried entirely different behavioral implications. Galileo must have felt tempted, and perhaps obligated in the name of science, to express a view that was entirely incompatible with, and thus heretical to, a central dogma of the prevailing moral authority of the time, the Catholic Church. He must have been torn apart by dissonance (which, we should add, must have made his commitment to science even firmer than ever). This example illustrates why cognitions are important only to the extent that they have power to mobilize potent behavioral responses. Otherwise, cognitions are irrelevant vis-à-vis dissonance, and accordingly, the role they have in dissonance is inevitably secondary.

7.3 Future Directions

The biosocial model offers some important directions for future research. First, it is important to test specific neural mechanisms and pathways involved in certain key social psychological processes, such as action orientation, self-affirmation, and mortality salience. The biosocial model is specific enough to guide and direct such research in a systematic fashion. For example, self-affirmation should downregulate dACC through the midbrain DA pathway. Whether this is valid or not is consequential to cognition, emotion, and behavior in many social situations. Hence, empirically addressing this and other related questions is important for the future expansion and elaboration of social psychological theories.

Second, the biosocial model opens the door to an uncharted terrain of social genomics (Cole, 2009; Kim & Sasaki, 2014). For example, dissonance is fundamentally affective and motivational. Moreover, much of the striatal affective mechanism that is placed at the core of the dissonance process is innervated strongly by dopamine (DA) neurons (Berridge & Robinson, 2003). Accordingly, there is every reason to believe that some DA system genes are involved in modulating the functioning of core mechanisms of dissonance. One gene that is often consequential in DA-related processes such as reward processing and reinforcement learning is the dopamine D4 receptor gene, *DRD4* (Kitayama, King, et al., 2014). This gene, however, is linked to other genes that are relevant to the DA system including other DA receptor genes such as *DRD2* and *DRD3*, DA transporter genes (e.g., *DAT1*), as well as those involved in dopamine clearance (*COMT*, *MAOA*, and *MAOB*) (Saez, Set, & Hsu, 2014). By explicating the functions of these genes for neural processing and behavior, either alone or in combination, it may become possible to triangulate the nature of relevant neural mechanisms in greater detail.

In closing this paper, we wish to point out that the affective mechanisms articulated by the biosocial model are likely to play fundamental roles in maintaining human society and culture. To be a cultural member is to be conditioned, affectively and motivationally, to a system of signs established in a particular, geographically, religiously, and historically constituted group. In this sense, humans may all prove to be Robinson's "sign trackers" to varying degrees. The underlying biology of reward processing may be crucial in generating a motivation for people to commit themselves to their traditions, religions, nations, and other signs of their culture. From this point of view, it should not come as a surprise that certain DA system genes are closely associated with the acquisition of cultural worldviews (Kitayama, King, et al., 2014). The biosocial model, then, may be pointing to new avenues of research in cultural psychology and beyond by bringing to the foreground hitherto neglected issues and questions about the biological basis of culture and society.

ACKNOWLEDGMENTS

We thank Nobuhiro Abe, Kent Berridge, Keisei Izuma, Hazel Markus, Richard Nisbett, Terry Robinson, and members of the University of Michigan Culture and Cognition Lab for their helpful comments on an earlier draft. Research reported here was supported by grants from National Science Foundation (BCS 0717982 and SES 1325881) and National Institute for Aging (5RO129509-02).

REFERENCES

Addis, D. R., Wong, A. T., & Schacter, D. L. (2007). Remembering the past and imagining the future: Common and distinct neural substrates during event construction and elaboration. *Neuropsychologia, 45*(7), 1363–1377.

Agam, Y., Hämäläinen, M. S., Lee, A. K. C., Dyckman, K. A., Friedman, J. S., Isom, M., et al. (2011). Multimodal neuroimaging dissociates hemodynamic and electrophysiological correlates of error processing. *Proceedings of the National Academy of Sciences of the United States of America, 108*(42), 17556–17561.

Allen, J. J. B., Harmon-Jones, E., & Cavender, J. H. (2001). Manipulation of frontal EEG asymmetry through biofeedback alters self-reported emotional responses and facial EMG. *Psychophysiology, 38*(4), 685–693.

Amiez, C., Joseph, J. P., & Procyk, E. (2006). Reward encoding in the monkey anterior cingulate cortex. *Cerebral Cortex, 16*, 1040–1055.

Amodio, D. M., Harmon-Jones, E., Devine, P. G., Curtin, J. J., Hartley, S. L., & Covert, A. E. (2004). Neural signals for the detection of unintentional race bias. *Psychological Science, 15*, 88–93.

Anselme, P., Robinson, M. J. F., & Berridge, K. C. (2013). Reward uncertainty enhances incentive salience attribution as sign-tracking. *Behavioural Brain Research, 238*, 53–61.

Aronson, E. (1969). The theory of cognitive dissonance: A current perspective. *Advances in Experimental Social Psychology, 4*, 1–35.

Aronson, E., & Mills, J. (1959). The effect of severity of initiation on liking for a group. *Journal of Abnormal and Social Psychology, 59*, 177–181.

Atkinson, Q. D., & Whitehouse, H. (2011). The cultural morphospace of ritual form. *Evolution and Human Behavior, 32*(1), 50–62.

Axsom, D., & Cooper, J. (1985). Cognitive dissonance and psychotherapy: The role of effort justification in inducing weight loss. *Journal of Experimental Social Psychology, 21*, 149–160.

Balodis, I. M., Kober, H., Worhunsky, P. D., Stevens, M. C., Pearlson, G. D., & Potenza, M. N. (2012). Diminished frontostriatal activity during processing of monetary rewards and losses in pathological gambling. *Biological Psychiatry, 71*(8), 749–757.

Baumeister, R. F., Vohs, K. D., & Tice, D. M. (2007). The strength model of self-control. *Current Directions in Psychological Science, 16*(6), 351–355.

Beckmann, J., & Kuhl, J. (1984). Altering information to gain action control: Functional aspects of human information processing in decision making. *Journal of Research in Personality, 18*, 224–237.

Bem, D. J. (1967). Self-perception: An alternative interpretation of cognitive dissonance phenomena. *Psychological Review, 74*(3), 183–200.

Berridge, K. C. (2012). From prediction error to incentive salience: Mesolimbic computation of reward motivation. *European Journal of Neuroscience, 35*(7), 1124–1143.

Berridge, K. C., & Robinson, T. E. (1995). The mind of an addicted brain: Neural sensitization of wanting versus liking. *Current Directions in Psychological Science, 4*(3), 71–76.

Berridge, K. C., & Robinson, T. E. (2003). Parsing reward. *Trends in Neurosciences, 26*(9), 507–513.

Berridge, K. C., Robinson, T. E., & Aldridge, J. W. (2009). Dissecting components of reward: "Liking", "wanting", and learning. *Current Opinion in Pharmacology, 9*(1), 65–73.

Boksem, M. A. S., Tops, M., Wester, A. E., Meijman, T. F., & Lorist, M. M. (2006). Error-related ERP components and individual differences in punishment and reward sensitivity. *Brain Research, 1101*(1), 92–101.

Botvinick, M. M., Cohen, J. D., & Carter, C. S. (2004). Conflict monitoring and anterior cingulate cortex: An update. *Trends in Cognitive Sciences, 8*(12), 539–546.

Brehm, J. W. (1956). Postdecision changes in the desirability of alternatives. *Journal of Abnormal and Social Psychology, 52*(3), 384–389.

Brehm, J. W. (1966). *A theory of psychological reactance*. San Diego, CA: Academic Press.

Bromberg-Martin, E. S., & Hikosaka, O. (2009). Midbrain dopamine neurons signal preference for advance information about upcoming rewards. *Neuron, 63*, 119–126.

Brosch, T., & Sander, D. (2013). Neurocognitive mechanisms underlying value-based decision-making: From core values to economic value. *Frontiers in Human Neuroscience, 7*.

Bush, G., Luu, P., & Posner, M. I. (2000). Cognitive and emotional influences in anterior cingulate cortex. *Trends in Cognitive Sciences, 4*(6), 215–222.

Butts, K. A., Weinberg, J., Young, A. H., & Phillips, A. G. (2011). Glucocorticoid receptors in the prefrontal cortex regulate stress-evoked dopamine efflux and aspects of executive function. *Proceedings of the National Academy of Sciences of the United States of America, 108*(45), 18459–18464.

Carter, C. S., & van Veen, V. (2007). Anterior cingulate cortex and conflict detection: An update of theory and data. *Cognitive, Affective, & Behavioral Neuroscience, 7*(4), 367–379.

Chang, E. C., & Asakawa, K. (2003). Cultural variations on optimistic and pessimistic bias for self versus a sibling: Is there evidence for self-enhancement in the West and for self-criticism in the East when the referent group is specified? *Journal of Personality and Social Psychology, 84*(3), 569–581.

Chen, M. K., & Risen, J. L. (2010). How choice affects and reflects preferences: Revisiting the free-choice paradigm. *Journal of Personality and Social Psychology, 99*(4), 573–594.

Chua, H. F., Gonzalez, R., Taylor, S. F., Welsh, R. C., & Liberzon, I. (2009). Decision-related loss: Regret and disappointment. *NeuroImage, 47*(4), 2031–2040.

Clement, T. C., Feltus, J. R., Kaiser, D. H., & Zentall, T. R. (2010). "Work ethic" in pigeons: Reward value is directly related to the effort or time required to obtain the reward. *Psychonomic Bulletin and Review, 7*(1), 100–106.

Cole, S. W. (2009). Social regulation of human gene expression. *Current Directions in Psychological Science, 18*(3), 132–137.

Cooper, J., & Fazio, R. H. (1984). A new look at dissonance theory. *Advances in Experimental Social Psychology, 17*, 229–266.

Creswell, J. D., Welch, W. T., Taylor, S. E., Sherman, D. K., Gruenewald, T. L., & Mann, T. (2005). Affirmation of personal values buffers neuroendocrine and psychological stress responses. *Psychological Science, 16*(11), 846–851.

Croyle, R. T., & Cooper, J. (1983). Dissonance arousal: Physiological evidence. *Journal of Personality and Social Psychology, 45*, 782–791.

Cunha, M., Jr., & Caldieraro, F. (2009). Sunk-cost effects on purely behavioral investments. *Cognitive Science, 33*(1), 105–113.

Cunningham, W. A., Johnson, M. K., Raye, C. L., Gatenby, J. C., Gore, J. C., & Banaji, M. R. (2004). Separable neural components in the processing of black and white faces. *Psychological Science, 15*(12), 806–813.

Damasio, A., & Carvalho, G. B. (2013). The nature of feelings: Evolutionary and neurobiological origins. *Nature Reviews. Neuroscience, 14*(2), 143–152.

Davidson, R. J., Lewis, D. A., Alloy, L. B., Amaral, D. G., Bush, G., Cohen, J. D., et al. (2002). Neural and behavioral substrates of mood and mood regulation. *Biological Psychiatry, 52*(6), 478–502.

Egan, L. C., Bloom, P., & Santos, L. R. (2010). Choice-induced preferences in the absence of choice: Evidence from a blind two choice paradigm with young children and capuchin monkeys. *Journal of Experimental Social Psychology, 46*(1), 204–207.

Eisenberger, N. I., & Lieberman, M. D. (2004). Why rejection hurts: A common neural alarm system for physical and social pain. *Trends in Cognitive Sciences, 8*(7), 294–300.

Elkin, R. A., & Leippe, M. R. (1986). Physiological arousal, dissonance, and attitude change: Evidence for a dissonance-arousal link and a "don't remind me" effect. *Journal of Personality and Social Psychology, 51*, 55–65.

Elliot, A. J., & Devine, P. G. (1994). On the motivational nature of cognitive dissonance: Dissonance as psychological discomfort. *Journal of Personality and Social Psychology*, 67(3), 382–394.

Elliott, R., Dolan, R. J., & Frith, C. D. (2000). Dissociable functions in the medial and lateral orbitofrontal cortex: Evidence from human neuroimaging studies. *Cerebral Cortex*, 10, 308–317.

Ettenberg, A. (2004). Opponent process properties of self-administered cocaine. *Neuroscience & Biobehavioral Reviews*, 27(8), 721–728.

Festinger, L. (1957). *A theory of cognitive dissonance*. Stanford, CA: Stanford University Press.

Festinger, L., & Carlsmith, J. M. (1959). Cognitive consequences of forced compliance. *Journal of Abnormal and Social Psychology*, 58, 203–210.

Fiske, S. T., & Taylor, S. E. (2013). *Social cognition*. London: Save Publications.

Flagel, S. B., Clark, J. J., Robinson, T. E., Mayo, L., Czuj, A., Willuhn, I., et al. (2010). A selective role for dopamine in stimulus—Reward learning. *Nature*, 469(7328), 53–57.

Frank, M. J., & Claus, E. D. (2006). Anatomy of a decision: Striato-orbitofrontal interactions in reinforcement learning, decision making, and reversal. *Psychological Review*, 113(2), 300–326.

Fredrickson, B. L., & Losada, M. F. (2005). Positive affect and the complex dynamics of human flourishing. *American Psychologist*, 60(7), 678–686.

Friedman, R. S., & Arndt, J. (2005). Reexploring the connection between terror management theory and dissonance theory. *Personality and Social Psychology Bulletin*, 31(9), 1217–1225.

Gazzaniga, M. S. (2013). Shifting gears: Seeking new approaches for mind/brain mechanisms. *Annual Review of Psychology*, 64, 1–20.

Gehring, W. J. (2002). The medial frontal cortex and the rapid processing of monetary gains and losses. *Science*, 295(5563), 2279–2282.

Gehring, W. J., & Willoughby, A. R. (2004). Are all medial frontal negativities created equal? Toward a richer empirical basis for theories of action monitoring. In M. Ullsperger, & M. Falkenstein (Eds.), *Errors, conflicts, and the brain. Current opinions on performance monitoring* (pp. 14–20). Leipzig: Max Planck Institute of Cognitive Neuroscience.

Gelfand, M. J., Raver, J. L., Nishii, L., Leslie, L. M., Lun, J., Lim, B. C., et al. (2011). Differences between tight and loose cultures: A 33-Nation Study. *Science*, 332(6033), 1100–1104.

George, M. S., Wassermann, E. M., Kimbrell, T. A., Little, J. T., Williams, W. E., Danielson, A. L., et al. (1997). Mood improvement following daily left prefrontal repetitive transcranial magnetic stimulation in patients with depression: A placebo-controlled crossover trial. *American Journal of Psychiatry*, 154, 1752–1756.

Gerard, H. B., & Mathewson, G. C. (1966). The effects of severity of initiation on liking for a group: A replication. *Journal of Experimental Social Psychology*, 2, 278–287.

Gollwitzer, P. M., Heckhausen, H., & Steller, B. (1990). Deliberative and implemental mind-sets: Cognitive tuning toward congruous thoughts and information. *Journal of Personality and Social Psychology*, 59(6), 1119–1127.

Greenberg, J., Solomon, S., & Pyszczynski, T. (1997). Terror management theory of self-esteem and cultural worldviews: Empirical assessments and conceptual refinements. *Advances in Experimental Social Psychology*, 29, 61–139.

Hajcak, G. (2012). What we've learned from mistakes. *Current Directions in Psychological Science*, 21(2), 101–106.

Hajcak, G., Moser, J. S., Holroyd, C. B., & Simons, R. F. (2006). The feedback-related negativity reflects the binary evaluation of good versus bad outcomes. *Biological Psychology*, 71(2), 148–154.

Han, S., Fan, Y., Xu, X., Qin, J., Wu, B., Wang, X., et al. (2009). Empathic neural responses to others' pain are modulated by emotional contexts. *Human Brain Mapping*, *30*(10), 3227–3237.

Harmon-Jones, E., Amodio, D. M., & Harmon-Jones, C. (2009). Action-based model of dissonance: A review, integration, and expansion of conceptions of cognitive conflict. *Advances in Experimental Social Psychology*, *41*, 119–166.

Harmon-Jones, E., & Harmon-Jones, C. (2002). Testing the action-based model of cognitive dissonance: The effect of action orientation on postdecisional attitudes. *Personality and Social Psychology Bulletin*, *28*(6), 711–723.

Harmon-Jones, E., & Harmon-Jones, C. (2008). Action-based model of dissonance: A review of behavioral, anterior cingulate, and prefrontal cortical mechanisms. *Social and Personality Psychology Compass*, *2*(3), 1518–1538.

Harmon-Jones, E., Harmon-Jones, C., Fearn, M., Sigelman, J. D., & Johnson, P. (2008). Left frontal cortical activation and spreading of alternatives: Tests of the action-based model of dissonance. *Journal of Personality and Social Psychology*, *94*(1), 1–15.

Harmon-Jones, E., & Mills, J. (Eds.). (1999). *Cognitive dissonance: Progress on a pivotal theory in social psychology*. Washington, DC, USA: American Psychological Association.

Heckhausen, J., & Schulz, R. (1995). A life-span theory of control. *Psychological Review*, *102*(2), 284–304.

Heine, S. J., & Lehman, D. R. (1997). Culture, dissonance, and self-affirmation. *Personality and Social Psychology Bulletin*, *23*, 389–400.

Heine, S. J., Kitayama, S., & Lehman, D. R. (2001). Divergent consequences of success and failure in Japan and North America: An investigation of self-improving motivations and malleable selves. *Journal of Personality and Social Psychology*, *81*(4), 599–615.

Higgins, E. T. (2006). Value from hedonic experience and engagement. *Psychological Review*, *113*(3), 439–460.

Hillman, K. L., & Bilkey, D. K. (2012). Neural encoding of competitive effort in the anterior cingulate cortex. *Nature Neuroscience*, *15*(9), 1290–1297.

Hitokoto, H., Glazer, J., & Kitayama, S. (2014). *Are you more motivated when watched? Feedback-related potentials vary with culture and face priming*. Unpublished manuscript, University of Michigan.

Holroyd, C. B., & Coles, M. G. H. (2002). The neural basis of human error processing: Reinforcement learning, dopamine, and the error-related negativity. *Psychological Review*, *109*(4), 679–709.

Hoshino-Browne, E., Zanna, A. S., Spencer, S. J., Zanna, M. P., Kitayama, S., & Lackenbauer, S. (2005). On the cultural guises of cognitive dissonance: The case of Easterners and Westerners. *Journal of Personality and Social Psychology*, *89*(3), 294–310.

Imada, T., & Kitayama, S. (2010). Social eyes and choice justification: Culture and dissonance revisited. *Social Cognition*, *28*(5), 589–608.

Immordino-Yang, M. H., Yang, X.-F., & Damasio, H. (2014). Correlations between social-emotional feelings and anterior insula activity are independent from visceral states but influenced by culture. *Frontiers in Human Neuroscience*, *8*.

Inzlicht, M., McGregor, I., Hirsh, J. B., & Nash, K. (2009). Neural markers of religious conviction. *Psychological Science*, *20*(2), 385–392.

Inzlicht, M., & Schmeichel, B. J. (2012). What is ego depletion? Toward a mechanistic revision of the resource model of self-control. *Perspectives on Psychological Science*, *7*(5), 450–463.

Inzlicht, M., & Tullett, A. M. (2010). Reflecting on God: Religious primes can reduce neurophysiological response to errors. *Psychological Science*, *21*(8), 1184–1190.

Izuma, K., & Adolphs, R. (2013). Social manipulation of preference in the human brain. *Neuron*, *78*, 563–573.

Izuma, K., Matsumoto, M., Murayama, K., Samejima, K., Sadato, N., & Matsumoto, K. (2010). Neural correlates of cognitive dissonance and choice-induced preference change. *Proceedings of the National Academy of Sciences of the United States of America,, 107*(51), 22014–22019.

Izuma, K., Matsumoto, M., Murayama, K., Samejima, K., Norihiro, S., & Matsumoto, K. (2013). Neural correlates of cognitive dissonance and decision conflict. *Advances in Cognitive Neurodynamics*, 623–628.

Izuma, K., & Murayama, K. (2013). Choice-induced preference change in the free-choice paradigm: A critical methodological review. *Frontiers in Psychology, 4*, 1–12.

Jarcho, J. M., Berkman, E. T., & Lieberman, M. D. (2011). The neural basis of rationalization: Cognitive dissonance reduction during decision-making. *Social Cognitive and Affective Neuroscience, 6*(4), 460–467.

Job, V., Dweck, C. S., & Walton, G. M. (2010). Ego depletion—Is it all in your head?: Implicit theories about willpower affect self-regulation. *Psychological Science, 21*(11), 1686–1693.

Jonas, E., Schulz-Hardt, S., & Frey, D. (2005). Giving advice or making decisions in someone else's place: The influence of impression, defense, and accuracy motivation on the search for new information. *Personality and Social Psychology Bulletin, 31*(7), 977–990.

Kacelnik, A., & Marsh, B. (2002). Cost can increase preference in starlings. *Animal Behaviour, 63*(2), 245–250.

Kashima, E. S., Halloran, M., Yuki, M., & Kashima, Y. (2004). The effects of personal and collective mortality salience on individualism: Comparing Australians and Japanese with higher and lower self-esteem. *Journal of Experimental Social Psychology, 40*, 384–392.

Kennerley, S. W., Walton, M. E., Behrens, T. E. J., Buckley, M. J., & Rushworth, M. F. S. (2006). Optimal decision making and the anterior cingulate cortex. *Nature Neuroscience, 9*(7), 940–947.

Kim, H. S., & Sasaki, J. Y. (2014). Cultural neuroscience: Biology of the mind in cultural contexts. *Annual Review of Psychology, 65*(1), 487–514.

Kimel, S. Y., Grossmann, I., & Kitayama, S. (2012). When gift-giving produces dissonance: Effects of subliminal affiliation priming on choices for one's self versus close others. *Journal of Experimental Social Psychology, 48*(5), 1221–1224.

Kimel, S. Y., Lopez-Duran, N., & Kitayama, S. (2014). Physiological correlates of choice-induced dissonance: An exploration of HPA-axis responses. *Journal of Behavioral Decision Making*.

Kitayama, S., Chua, H. F., Tompson, S., & Han, S. (2013). Neural mechanisms of dissonance: An fMRI investigation of choice justification. *NeuroImage, 69*, 206–212.

Kitayama, S., King, A., Yoon, C., Tompson, S., Huff, S., & Liberzon, I. (2014). The dopamine D4 receptor gene (DRD4) moderates cultural difference in independent versus interdependent social orientation. *Psychological Science, 25*(6), 1169–1177.

Kitayama, S., Markus, H. R., Matsumoto, H., & Norasakkunkit, V. (1997). Individual and collective processes in the construction of the self: Self-enhancement in the United States and self-criticism in Japan. *Journal of Personality and Social Psychology, 72*(6), 1245–1267.

Kitayama, S., Snibbe, A. C., Markus, H. R., & Suzuki, T. (2004). Is there any "free" choice? Self and dissonance in two cultures. *Psychological Science, 15*, 527–533.

Kitayama, S., Tompson, S., & Chua, H. F. (2014). Cultural neuroscience of choice justification. In J. Forgas, & E. Harmon-Jones (Eds.), *Control within: Motivation and its regulation* (pp. 313–330).New York: Psychology Press, Sydney Symposium.

Kitayama, S., & Uskul, A. K. (2011). Culture, mind, and the brain: Current evidence and future directions. *Annual Review of Psychology, 62*(1), 419–449.

Knox, R. E., & Inkster, J. A. (1968). Postdecision dissonance at post time. *Journal of Personality and Social Psychology, 8*(4), 319–323.

Knutson, B., & Cooper, J. C. (2005). Functional magnetic resonance imaging of reward prediction. *Current Opinion in Neurology*, *18*(4), 411.

Kross, E., Ayduk, O., & Mischel, W. (2005). When asking "why" does not hurt distinguishing rumination from reflective processing of negative emotions. *Psychological Science*, *16*(9), 709–715.

Kuhl, J. (1981). Motivational and functional helplessness: The moderating effect of state versus action orientation. *Journal of Personality and Social Psychology*, *40*(1), 155–170.

Kuhl, J. (1992). A theory of self-regulation: Action versus state orientation, self-discrimination, and some applications. *Applied Psychology*, *41*(2), 97–129.

Lakoff, G., & Johnson, M. (2003). *Metaphors we live by*. Chicago: University of Chicago Press.

Lawrence, D. H., & Festinger, L. (1962). *Deterrents and reinforcement: The psychology of insufficient reward*. Palo Alto, CA: Stanford University Press.

Ledoux, J. E., Wilson, D. H., & Gazzaniga, M. S. (1977). A divided mind: Observations on the conscious properties of the separated hemispheres. *Annals of Neurology*, *2*(5), 417–421.

Lee, S. W. S., & Schwarz, N. (2010). Washing away postdecisional dissonance. *Science*, *328*(5979), 709.

Legault, L., Al-Khindi, T., & Inzlicht, M. (2012). Preserving integrity in the face of performance threat: Self-affirmation enhances neurophysiological responsiveness to errors. *Psychological Science*, *23*(12), 1455–1460.

Lewin, K. (1947). Frontiers in group dynamics: II. Channels of group life; social planning and action research. *Human Relations*, *1*(2), 143–153.

Lieberman, M. D. (2007). Social cognitive neuroscience: A review of core processes. *Annual Review of Psychology*, *58*, 259–289.

Lieberman, M. D., Ochsner, K. N., Gilbert, D. T., & Schacter, D. L. (2001). Do amnesics exhibit cognitive dissonance reduction? The role of explicit memory and attention in attitude change. *Psychological Science*, *12*(2), 135–140.

Losch, M. E., & Cacioppo, J. T. (1990). Cognitive dissonance may enhance sympathetic tonus, but attitudes are changed to reduce negative affect rather than arousal. *Journal of Experimental Social Psychology*, *26*(4), 289–304.

Lydall, E. S., Gilmour, G., & Dwyer, D. M. (2010). Rats place greater value on rewards produced by high effort: An animal analogue of the "effort justification" effect. *Journal of Experimental Social Psychology*, *46*(6), 1134–1137.

Markus, H. R., & Kitayama, S. (1991). Culture and the self: Implications for cognition, emotion, and motivation. *Psychological Review*, *98*(2), 224–253.

Mead, G. H. (1934). *Mind, self, and society: From the standpoint of a social behaviorist*. Chicago: University of Chicago Press.

Miltner, W. H. R., Braun, C. H., & Coles, M. G. H. (1997). Event-related brain potentials following incorrect feedback in a time-estimation task: Evidence for a "generic" neural system for error detection. *Journal of Cognitive Neuroscience*, *9*(6), 788–798.

Mischel, W., Shoda, Y., & Rodriguez, M. (1989). Delay of gratification in children. *Science*, *244*(4907), 933–938.

Na, J., & Kitayama, S. (2012). Will people work hard on a task they choose? Social-eyes priming in different cultural contexts. *Journal of Experimental Social Psychology*, *48*(1), 284–290.

Nader, K., Schafe, G. E., & Le Doux, J. E. (2000). Fear memories require protein synthesis in the amygdala for reconsolidation after retrieval. *Nature*, *406*(6797), 722–726.

Norenzayan, A., & Gervais, W. (2012). The cultural evolution of religion. In E. Slingerland, & M. Collard (Eds.), *Creating consilience: Integrating science and the humanities* (pp. 243–265). Oxford: Oxford University Press.

Norenzayan, A., & Shariff, A. F. (2008). The origin and evolution of religious prosociality. *Science*, *322*(5898), 58–62.

Oberg, S. A. K., Christie, G. J., & Tata, M. S. (2011). Problem gamblers exhibit reward hypersensitivity in medial frontal cortex during gambling. *Neuropsychologia, 49*(13), 3768–3775.

O'Doherty, J. P., Deichmann, R., Critchley, H. D., & Dolan, R. J. (2002). Neural responses during anticipation of a primary taste reward. *Neuron, 33*(5), 815–826.

Öhman, A. (2005). The role of the amygdala in human fear: Automatic detection of threat. *Psychoneuroendocrinology, 30*(10), 953–958.

Okazaki, S. (2000). Asian American and white American differences on affective distress symptoms: Do symptom reports differ across reporting methods? *Journal of Cross-Cultural Psychology, 31*(5), 603–625.

Okazaki, S., Liu, J. F., Longworth, S. L., & Minn, J. Y. (2002). Asian American-White American differences in expressions of social anxiety: A replication and extension. *Cultural Diversity & Ethnic Minority Psychology, 8*(3), 234–247.

Park, J., & Kitayama, S. (2014). Interdependent selves show face-induced facilitation of error processing: cultural neuroscience of self-threat. *Social Cognitive and Affective Neuroscience, 9*(2), 201–208.

Paus, T., & Alamancos, M. C. (2001). Cortico-cortical connectivity of the human mid-dorsolateral frontal cortex and its modulation by repetitive transcranial magnetic stimulation. *European Journal of Neuroscience, 14*, 1405–1411.

Qin, J., Kimel, S., Kitayama, S., Wang, X., Yang, X., & Han, S. (2011). How choice modifies preference: Neural correlates of choice justification. *NeuroImage, 55*(1), 240–246.

Richeson, J. A., Baird, A. A., Gordon, H. L., Heatherton, T. F., Wyland, C. L., Trawalter, S., et al. (2003). An fMRI investigation of the impact of interracial contact on executive function. *Nature Neuroscience, 6*(12), 1323–1328.

Robinson, T. E., & Berridge, K. C. (2001). Incentive-sensitization and addiction. *Addiction, 96*, 103–114.

Robinson, M. J. F., Warlow, S. M., & Berridge, K. C. (2014). Optogenetic excitation of central amygdala amplifies and narrows incentive motivation to pursue one reward above another. *Journal of Neuroscience, 34*(50), 16567–16580.

Saez, I., Set, E., & Hsu, M. (2014). From genes to behavior: Placing cognitive models in the context of biological pathways. *Frontiers in Neuroscience, 8*, Article 336, 1–10.

Salamone, J. D., & Correa, M. (2012). The mysterious motivational functions of mesolimbic dopamine. *Neuron, 76*(3), 470–485.

Schachter, S. (1964). The interaction of cognitive and physiological determinants of emotional state. *Advances in Experimental Social Psychology, 1*, 49–80.

Schmeichel, B. J., Harmon-Jones, C., & Harmon-Jones, E. (2010). Exercising self-control increases approach motivation. *Journal of Personality and Social Psychology, 99*(1), 162–173.

Sharot, T., De Martino, B., & Dolan, R. J. (2009). How choice reveals and shapes expected hedonic outcome. *The Journal of Neuroscience, 29*(12), 3760–3765.

Sharot, T., Fleming, S. M., Yu, X., Koster, R., & Dolan, R. J. (2012). Is choice-induced preference change long lasting? *Psychological Science, 23*(10), 1123–1129.

Shenhav, A., & Buckner, R. L. (2014). Neural correlates of dueling affective reactions to win-win choices. *Proceedings of the National Academy of Sciences, 111*(30), 10978–10983.

Shenhav, A., Straccia, M. A., Cohen, J. D., & Botvinick, M. M. (2014). Anterior cingulate engagement in a foraging context reflects choice difficulty, not foraging value. *Nature Neuroscience, 17*(9), 1249–1254.

Sherman, D. K., & Cohen, G. L. (2006). The psychology of self-defense: Self-affirmation theory. *Advances in Experimental Social Psychology, 38*, 183–242.

Shimojo, S., Simion, C., Shimojo, E., & Scheier, C. (2003). Gaze bias both reflects and influences preference. *Nature Neuroscience, 6*(12), 1317–1322.

Shultz, T. R., & Lepper, M. R. (1996). Cognitive dissonance reduction as constraint satisfaction. *Psychological Review, 103*(2), 219–240.

Simion, C., & Shimojo, S. (2006). Early interactions between orienting, visual sampling and decision making in facial preference. *Vision Research, 46*, 3331–3335.

Simon, D., Krawczyk, D. C., & Holyoak, K. J. (2004). *Construction of preferences by constraint satisfaction.*

Singer, T. (2004). Empathy for pain involves the affective but not sensory components of pain. *Science, 303*(5661), 1157–1162.

Singer, T., Critchley, H. D., & Preuschoff, K. (2009). A common role of insula in feelings, empathy and uncertainty. *Trends in Cognitive Sciences, 13*(8), 334–340.

Solomon, R. L., & Corbit, J. D. (1974). An opponent-process theory of motivation: I. Temporal dynamics of affect. *Psychological Review, 81*(2), 119–145.

Spector, A. C., Klumpp, P. A., & Kaplan, J. M. (1998). Analytical issues in the evaluation of food deprivation and sucrose concentration effects on the microstructure of licking behavior in the rat. *Behavioral Neuroscience, 112*(3), 678–694.

Speer, M. E., Bhanji, J. P., & Delgado, M. R. (2014). Savoring the past: Positive memories evoke value representations in the striatum. *Neuron, 84*(4), 847–856.

Steele, C. M. (1988). The psychology of self-affirmation: Sustaining the integrity of the self. *Advances in Experimental Social Psychology, 21*, 261–302.

Steele, C. M., Spencer, S. J., & Lynch, M. (1993). Self-image resilience and dissonance: The role of affirmational resources. *Journal of Personality and Social Psychology, 64*(6), 885–896.

Stone, J., & Cooper, J. (2001). A self-standards model of cognitive dissonance. *Journal of Experimental Social Psychology, 37*(3), 228–243.

Sutton, S. K., & Davidson, R. J. (1997). Prefrontal brain asymmetry: A biological substrate of the behavioral approach and inhibition systems. *Psychological Science, 8*(3), 204–210.

Taylor, S. E., & Brown, J. D. (1988). Illusion and well-being: A social psychological perspective on mental health. *Psychological Bulletin, 103*(2), 193–210.

Thaler, R. H. (1999). Mental accounting matters. *Journal of Behavioral Decision Making, 12*(3), 183–206.

Tomie, A. (1996). Locating reward cue at response manipulandum (CAM) induces symptoms of drug abuse. *Neuroscience & Biobehavioral Reviews, 20*(3), 505–535.

van der Meer, L., Costafreda, S., & Aleman, A. (2010). Self-reflection and the brain: A theoretical review and meta-analysis of neuroimaging studies with implications for schizophrenia. *Neuroscience Letters, 34*, 935–946.

van Veen, V., Krug, M. K., Schooler, J. W., & Carter, C. S. (2009). Neural activity predicts attitude change in cognitive dissonance. *Nature Neuroscience, 12*(11), 1469–1474.

Vohs, K. D., & Faber, R. J. (2007). Spent resources: Self-regulatory resource availability affects impulse buying. *Journal of Consumer Research, 33*(4), 537–547.

Walsh, M. M., & Anderson, J. R. (2012). Learning from experience: Event-related potential correlates of reward processing, neural adaptation, and behavioral choice. *Neuroscience & Biobehavioral Reviews, 36*(8), 1870–1884.

Watanabe, K., Lauwereyns, J., & Hikosaka, O. (2003). Neural correlates of rewarded and unrewarded eye movements in the primate caudate nucleus. *The Journal of Neuroscience, 23*, 10052–10056.

Wolman, D. (2012). A tale of two halves. *Nature, 483*, 260–263.

Xu, X., Zuo, X., Wang, X., & Han, S. (2009). Do you feel my pain? Racial group membership modulates empathic neural responses. *Journal of Neuroscience, 29*(26), 8525–8529.

Yamagishi, T., Cook, K. S., & Watabe, M. (1998). Uncertainty, trust, and commitment formation in the United States and Japan. *American Journal of Sociology, 104*(1), 165–194.

Yeung, N. (2004). Independent coding of reward magnitude and valence in the human brain. *Journal of Neuroscience, 24*(28), 6258–6264.

Zajonc, R. B. (1968). Attitudinal effects of mere exposure. *Journal of Personality and Social Psychology, 9*(2, Pt. 2), 1–27.

Zajonc, R. B. (1980). Feeling and thinking: Preferences need no inferences. *American Psychologist, 35*(2), 151–175.

Zajonc, R. B., & Markus, H. (1984). Affect and cognition: The hard interface. In C. E. Izard, J. Kagan, & R. B. Zajonc (Eds.), *Emotions, cognition, and behavior* (pp. 73–102). New York: Cambridge University Press.

Zanna, M. P., & Cooper, J. (1974). Dissonance and the pill: An attribution approach to studying the arousal properties of dissonance. *Journal of Personality and Social Psychology, 29*(5), 703–709.

Zentall, T. R. (2010). Justification of effort by humans and pigeons: Cognitive dissonance or contrast? *Current Directions in Psychological Science, 19*(5), 296–300.

Zentall, T. R., & Laude, J. R. (2013). Do pigeons gamble? I wouldn't bet against it. *Current Directions in Psychological Science, 22*(4), 271–277.

CHAPTER THREE

Detecting and Experiencing Prejudice: New Answers to Old Questions

Manuela Barreto*,†,1, Naomi Ellemers‡
*Department of Psychology, University of Exeter, Exeter, United Kingdom
†Lisbon University Institute (CIS-ISCTE/IUL), Lisbon, Portugal
‡Institute of Psychology, Leiden University, Leiden, The Netherlands
1Corresponding author: e-mail address: m.barreto@exeter.ac.uk

Contents

Advances in Experimental Social Psychology, Volume 52
ISSN 0065-2601
http://dx.doi.org/10.1016/bs.aesp.2015.02.001

Abstract

This contribution reviews the state of the art of research on the effects of prejudice on its targets. We structure this review around ongoing debates and core questions that have been guiding this field of research and how these are addressed by recent evidence. We address five central themes that have characterized research on the way prejudice emerges in modern societies, and the impact this has on its targets. First, we examine whether members of devalued groups tend to over- or underestimate the extent to which they are targeted by discrimination. Second, we assess the self-protective and harmful effects of perceived discrimination on well-being. Third, we consider whether concealable stigmas are less problematic than visible stigmas. Fourth, we examine whether individual success is helpful or harmful for the disadvantaged group. Finally, as a fifth theme, we review evidence of the social costs of confronting prejudice and highlight the more neglected social benefits of confrontation. The research evidence we present in this way aims to resolve a number of common misunderstandings regarding the presence and implications of prejudice in modern societies.

Whether prejudice still exists, how this can be detected, and what the implications of this might be represent questions of long-standing interest in academic as well as public debates. Over the years, empirical evidence aiming to shed more light on these issues has accumulated. Nevertheless, the answers remain elusive. One reason is that—as is the case for many issues in the social sciences—results of studies carried out reflect, at least in part, beliefs and political debates that are salient at a given point in time, and yield different results in different national, cultural, and historical contexts (e.g., Ceci, Ginther, Kahn, & Williams, 2014; Miller, Eagly, & Linn, 2014). Hence, it is not always self-evident how evidence from such studies provides cumulative insights, or whether "inconclusive" results primarily document changes over time and across contexts. As a result, the multitude of efforts pertaining to this domain of inquiry has not inevitably resulted in the emergence of clear and consistent answers to these questions. Nevertheless, with ongoing changes in the social fabric relating to globalization, migration, and inequality, the questions remain as relevant and challenging as ever.

In this contribution, we review the state of the art of research on the detection and effects of prejudice on their targets. We address core debates, recurrent questions, and frequent misconceptions relating to this field of research and show how empirical research conducted by ourselves and other researchers informs these issues. Our overarching aim in doing this is to address and hopefully resolve a number of common misunderstandings regarding the way prejudice is experienced in modern societies, with a particular focus on the impact this has on its targets. We thus follow up on prior literature reviews addressing some of these issues (Crocker & Major, 1989; Major, Quinton, & McCoy, 2002; Schmitt & Branscombe, 2002), advancing their insights by including additional evidence that has become available since, elaborating on areas not covered by those papers, and structuring this review around a number of key debates and questions in the field.

The first issue we address relates to the *detection* of prejudice and discrimination. There is by now clear consensus that prejudicial views and discriminatory treatment can take different forms, some of which are easier to detect than others. Nevertheless, there is less agreement as to whether members of devalued groups tend to downplay or exaggerate the extent to which they encounter discrimination, or when and why they are most likely to do so. We review evidence from experimental studies in which the objective presence versus absence of discrimination could be kept equal, as this allowed researchers to isolate the cognitive and motivational factors that play a role in prejudice recognition.

We follow up on this discussion by considering whether perceptions of discriminatory treatment can help protect individual *well-being*, or are more likely to be harmful instead. In this area of inquiry, a multitude of studies has been recently carried out and both types of effects have been documented. Reviewing this work allows us to identify relevant moderators that may help understand and predict the systematic nature of these different patterns of results.

We then move on to examine whether the experience of prejudice and discrimination, as well as its implications, depends on the *nature* of the stigma under consideration. Specifically, we compare the situation of those for whom their devalued identity is immediately apparent, as it is implicated in some visible characteristic or bodily feature (such as gender or race), to the experience of those who have the choice whether or not to reveal their stigmatized identity (e.g., relating to their health status, social background, or sexual preferences). At first sight, having a concealable stigma would seem to be less challenging, and a common view is that suffering in such cases results from the choice to reveal or "flaunt" one's stigmatized identity. We present recent evidence suggesting the situation is not that straightforward, as there are important costs to hiding, as well as significant benefits associated with revealing a stigmatized identity.

We continue our consideration of ways in which individuals can cope with a stigmatized identity by addressing the pursuit of *individual advancement* as a further topic of interest. Here we consider implications of the view that current outcomes and relations in contemporary societies reflect the achievement and merits of individuals, instead of being codetermined by their membership in social groups. Specifically, we examine how the success of individuals who can be seen to represent a devalued group reflects on others sharing the same identity, and define the conditions under which their personal successes either undermine or benefit group-level advancement.

We conclude our review by considering how people may benefit or suffer from *confronting* prejudice. In this final section, we extend existing insights that have revealed that those who claim to have suffered discrimination are likely to incur considerable social costs. Countering the widespread conclusion that targets of discrimination fare better when they do not protest their unequal treatment, we highlight existing findings for the benefits of confrontation. In addition, we review more recent evidence that reveals how these negative implications of confronting prejudice might be curbed, reminding us of the ways in which such initiatives may contribute to the achievement of social equality.

By addressing these five issues in turn, this review considers the different phases in the process of detecting, experiencing, and countering prejudice and discrimination (see also Barreto, 2014). On the one hand, these multiple aspects covered in this review attest to the complex and multifaceted nature of the processes involved. At the same time, organizing the relevant evidence around these different issues and concerns, and identifying the types of processes involved at each stage, helps uncover the systematic and predictable nature of the variety of effects that have been documented. We conclude this review by noting how combining the different insights that emerge at each level can help us develop a deeper understanding of how people detect and experience the prejudice to which they are exposed. In doing so, we also consider the ways in which this can inform attempts to mitigate the negative impact of discrimination in practice.

1. DO MEMBERS OF DEVALUED GROUPS OVER- OR UNDERESTIMATE THE EXTENT TO WHICH THEY ARE TARGETED BY DISCRIMINATION?

A commonly held view is that members of underprivileged groups in society are hypersensitive to the possibility of discriminatory treatment.

They are believed to overestimate the occurrence of discrimination, and to complain of unequal treatment even when there is no reason to do so. Yet, empirical research shows that detecting discriminatory treatment is not self-evident, particularly given that prejudice and discrimination are rarely blatantly expressed (e.g., Barreto & Ellemers, 2005a, 2005b). Indeed, contemporary societies uphold strong egalitarian values, which are inconsistent with overt expressions of prejudice (see Barreto & Ellemers, 2013 for a recent review). As such, people who hold prejudiced attitudes are unlikely to express them openly but can do so, instead, in more subtle ways. Subtle expressions of bias range from the use of biased language (e.g., describing the ideal candidate for a specific job in purely masculine terms, Stout & Dasgupta, 2011), to assumptions based on stereotypes (e.g., assuming that a judge is necessarily white, Czopp & Monteith, 2003, or that women are necessarily emotional in work contexts, Cihangir, Barreto, & Ellemers, 2010), to paternalistic behaviors (e.g., introducing restrictions on women's activities in order to protect them, Moya, Glick, Expósito, de Lemus, & Hart, 2007), among others.

As a result of this ambiguity, discrimination claims can be easily questioned. Indeed, individuals do not always agree whether specific events involve discriminatory treatment. For example, those who identify with groups that tend to be targeted by prejudice are more likely to perceive prejudice against devalued groups than members of groups that do not tend to be targeted by prejudice (e.g., Johnson, Simmons, Trawalter, Ferguson, & Reed, 2003). In addition, even when people acknowledge that their group is commonly a target of discrimination, they may or not be aware of being personally discriminated against. This tendency for people to report less discrimination against themselves personally than against the average member of their group has been observed in a variety of social groups and designated the "personal–group discrimination discrepancy" (Crosby, 1982; Taylor, Wright, Moghaddam, & Lalonde, 1990).

Early research on this topic attempted to explain this discrepancy by establishing whether members of devalued groups are overly vigilant about discrimination targeting the group as a whole (artificially inflating ratings of group discrimination), or whether, alternatively, they tend to minimize the extent to which discrimination targets them personally. Current approaches emphasize the possibility that these discrepancies in perceptions of prejudicial treatment can be explained by cognitive and motivational factors that may affect perceptions of personal and group prejudice, and do so differently among members of different groups (Adams, Tormala, &

O'Brien, 2006). Empirical research, however, does not necessarily provide clear evidence as to whether prejudice perceptions under- or overestimate its actual occurrence. Indeed, the methodological characteristics of the great majority of studies in this area (e.g., correlational studies or studies where discrimination is plausible but not certain) make it hard to ascertain what would exactly qualify as overly vigilant responses or as an underestimation of exposure to prejudice. In addition, in the past, the tendency to under- or overestimate discriminatory treatment has often been indirectly inferred from the *effects* of such perceptions. For example, negative effects of perceptions of discrimination on well-being have led to the inference that individuals should be motivated to minimize such perceptions so as to minimize threat (e.g., Schmitt & Branscombe, 2002). By contrast, the finding that perceptions of discrimination can also play a protective role has often led to the inference that, at times, individuals may be motivated to perceive themselves as targets of prejudice, potentially resulting in the overestimation of such experiences (Major et al., 2002).

Recent research has started to examine this issue in a more direct and systematic fashion, for example, by keeping exposure to prejudice or discrimination constant and varying a range of factors that affect the extent to which it is detected when it occurs. Below, we examine this research and discuss what it implies regarding devalued group members' tendency to over- or underestimate discriminatory treatment.

1.1 Base-Rate Expectations and Information Availability

People are generally motivated to think of the world as an equal and just place, and strongly endorse individual mobility ideologies (Ellemers & Van Laar, 2010; see also Lerner, 1980). In fact, individuals tend to avoid expressing explicitly biased judgments, and even try to control relatively implicit biases, especially when the moral implications of doing so are made salient (Van Nunspeet, Derks, Ellemers, & Nieuwenhuis, 2015; Van Nunspeet, Ellemers, Derks, & Nieuwenhuis, 2014). Yet, systematic differences in important societal outcomes remain—for instance between men and women in pay levels and career progress—that cannot be explained by legitimate causes for such differences, such as level of education or nature of employment (for an overview, see Ellemers, 2014). Nevertheless, members of advantaged groups as well as members of groups that suffer disadvantage often prefer not to interpret this as indicative of group-based discrimination. Instead, they persist in the belief that individual merit is the decisive explanatory variable for such differences (Stephens & Levine, 2011). Hence, they attribute diverging outcomes of themselves and others to differences in genetic make-up, diverging individual abilities, or personal choices, even if there is no evidence for such systematic differences, for instance between men and women in math ability (e.g., Ceci et al., 2014), leadership ambitions (Hyde, 2014), or "hard wired" behavioral tendencies (Fine, 2013). An important consequence of these meritocracy beliefs is that people have a strong tendency to expect to be treated fairly and equally, and this in itself can be an impediment to their ability and willingness to acknowledge instances of prejudice or discrimination, even when this causes them personal disadvantage (see Barreto, Ellemers, Cihangir, & Stroebe, 2009 for a more elaborate discussion of this issue).

Indeed, paradoxically, a first factor that makes it more difficult to detect prejudicial treatment is the ostensible presence of anti-discrimination measures. People's awareness that equal opportunity measures are in place, for instance in their work organization, makes them less vigilant for the possibility of bias, and the visible presence of members of undervalued groups (even if this is only a small minority) only makes this worse (Kaiser et al., 2013). This so-called paradox of equality can even cause individuals to display *more* bias, for instance leading managers to recommend more bonuses and promotions for men than for equally qualified women, when their organization more explicitly values and promotes an individual merit system (Castilla & Benard, 2010). What, then, are valid cues to detect unequal treatment, if the presence of anti-discrimination policies in itself does not imply fair treatment and can even elicit bias?

The general assumption is that people are able to recognize discrimination when it occurs. In fact, this is also reflected in legal definitions, assuming that discrimination claims can be evaluated on the basis of evidence that individuals are treated differently due to their group membership, despite equal abilities or qualifications (see also Rudman, Glick, & Phelan, 2008). In reality, however, the situation is almost never that clear. Those who are rejected in procedures for job vacancies or promotions often have only their own experience to go by. People need to actively search for aggregate information to be able to decide whether or not bias is likely. However, indicators of individual abilities are often ambiguous or incomparable, or information that would make it possible to systematically compare the way members of different groups are treated is simply not available (Crosby, Clayton, Alksnis, & Hemker, 1986).

Even if there is clear evidence of group-based disadvantage, individual group members do not necessarily detect its occurrence unless they also personally suffer from it (Stroebe, Ellemers, Barreto, & Mummendey, 2009). When individuals are themselves recipients of negative outcomes, they are more attentive to cues to discrimination (such as the disadvantage of the ingroup as a whole) so as to deflect personal responsibility for the negative outcome and thereby protect their sense of competence (Crocker & Major, 1989). If individuals do not receive a negative outcome, however, they do not have this motivation and may, instead, fail to realize that the group as a whole is disadvantaged. We examined this in two studies where individual outcomes were evaluated in the presence versus absence of information about group disadvantage (Experiment 1) or where individual and group outcomes were congruent versus incongruent (Experiment 2). Female participants in both studies took part in a bogus selection procedure during which they were interviewed by a male interviewer. Participants knew that they were not applying for any concrete job, but were told that they were likely to experience similar procedures when applying for jobs in the future. In both experiments, half of the participants were told that, if the interview had been for a real job, the interviewer would have recommended that they would be accepted, whereas the remaining participants were told the interviewer would have recommended rejection. All participants then received some information about how prior applicants had done. In Experiment 1, orthogonally to the acceptance/rejection manipulation, half of the participants saw that the interviewer had accepted 4% of the female candidates and 60% of the male candidates; the remaining participants did not receive this information about group disadvantage. In Experiment 2, we modified this design slightly by providing all participants with information about group outcomes, but varying whether the group was said to be advantaged or disadvantaged, in addition to again orthogonally manipulating whether participants themselves had been personally rejected or accepted. As such, in Experiment 2, we varied whether personal and group outcomes were congruent or incongruent.

Among other variables, we assessed the extent to which participants attributed their own outcome to group-based disadvantage and the extent to which they perceived the selection procedure, up to that point, to be fair or legitimate. The results of both studies showed that participants attributed their outcome to group-based disadvantage only when they were personally rejected and their group was clearly disadvantaged. Importantly, participants

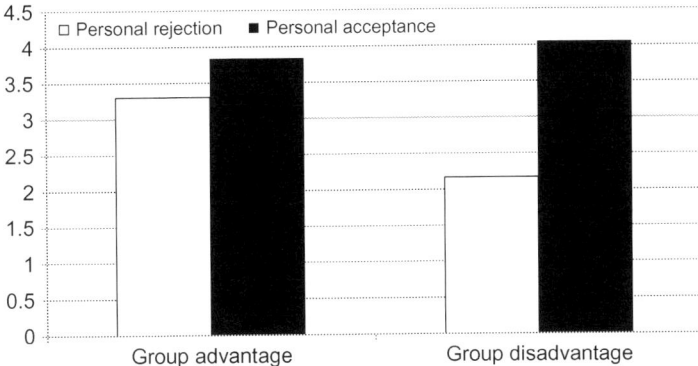

Figure 1 Perceived legitimacy of the system as a function of personal outcome (rejection vs. acceptance) and information about group outcomes (advantage vs. disadvantage). Scale range: 1–7; higher scores indicate more legitimacy. Only the third bar from the left differs significantly from all others. *Adapted from Stroebe, Dovidio, Barreto, Ellemers, and John (2011), Experiment 2.*

only questioned the legitimacy of the selection procedure when they had information about group disadvantage *and* they had been personally rejected, but not when they had been personally accepted (see Figure 1).

These results suggest that personal rejection does not lead to enhanced attributions to discrimination if there is no evidence that the group has received discriminatory treatment. Likewise, when members of one's group are systematically disadvantaged, this will not be seen as evidence of discrimination by individuals who have been individually successful. As a result, only when they have personally experienced unwarranted rejection *and* there is evidence that members of one's group are treated less favorably than members of other groups do they conclude that members of their group are discriminated against. Thus, in cases where one of these conditions is not met, people will be inclined to underestimate rather than overestimate the occurrence of bias. Importantly, however, there are conditions that favor the detection of bias. Below we will consider some of the conditions that either facilitate or impede the detection of bias.

1.2 Typicality of Prejudiced Events

People tend to think of prejudice as being characterized by intentional displays of hostility that members of advantaged groups direct toward members of disadvantaged groups. However, this "prototype" of what prejudice is only covers some of the ways in which group-based unequal treatment appears (e.g., Inman & Baron, 1996; see Barreto, 2014 for a review). In fact, prejudice can take many shapes and forms. Prejudicial expectations can be positive, at least at the surface, can be endorsed by those who are the target of such expectations, and can lead to differential treatment even when this is not intended.

Blatant, "old-fashioned" forms of discrimination are easy to recognize. This is the case, for instance, when an employer refuses to promote women because they "lack leadership skills," or when migrant workers are not hired because "they are lazy." However, most people nowadays are aware that such blatant sexist or racist statements can be legally sanctioned, or at least are considered to be "politically incorrect." As a result, even those who hold prejudicial views have learned to express these in more veiled and subtle ways. For instance, rather than explicitly calling into question the leadership abilities of women, people may do this more implicitly: Emphasizing that men and women receive equal advancement opportunities at work, while observing that relatively few women hold leadership positions, implies that this must somehow be due to women's deficient leadership abilities, career ambitions, or personal life choices. Such "denial of discrimination" has been identified as a form of "modern" sexism (Swim, Aikin, Hall, & Hunter, 1995; Swim & Cohen, 1997), or "neo-sexism" (Tougas, Brown, Beaton, & Joly, 1995), which, though differently expressed, relates to more old-fashioned sexist and blatantly discriminatory views. Likewise, prejudicial views toward migrants in Europe and Americans from African descent nowadays tend to be expressed in more subtle and implicit ways (Dovidio & Gaertner, 1986; Pettigrew & Meertens, 1995).

Importantly, however, when asked to evaluate these "modern" expressions of discrimination, the targets of such views are unlikely to recognize them as expressing prejudice (Barreto & Ellemers, 2005a; Ellemers & Barreto, 2009a). In one set of studies, we examined this by presenting participants with items from the old-fashioned or the modern sexism scales and describing these either as opinions held by the general public (Experiment 1) or as opinions held by a potential future supervisor (Experiments 2 and 3). Modern sexist "opinions" expressed a denial that gender discrimination still exists whereas hostile sexist "opinions" expressed an explicit belief in the inferiority of women. In all three studies, hostile sexism was clearly recognized as sexism (means between 5.16 and 5.72, across the three studies, on

7-point Likert-type scales). Modern sexism was perceived as significantly less sexist than hostile sexism in all studies, in some cases clearly below the scale mid-point, suggesting that it was not perceived as sexist at all (means between 2.93 and 3.93 across the three studies). This had important implications for the extent to which participants expressed a desire to protest against these opinions, with significantly greater intentions to protest, and actual protest behaviors, against hostile than against modern sexism. These results indicate that the movement toward more subtle and implicit expressions of bias contributes to the tendency to underreport versus over-report prejudice. The finding that people are unlikely to protest against modern types of prejudice also perpetuates their existence, since, by remaining unchallenged, these forms of prejudice remain unrecognized as such.

Another development in the way prejudicial views are expressed relates to the way in which perceived differences between groups are characterized. At first sight, such expressions may seem harmless, for instance because they are presented in a positive form, masked as humor (LaFrance & Woodzicka, 1998) or even flattery (Cihangir et al., 2010). Nevertheless, to the extent that (a) such humor implicitly supports gender role differentiation or questions their change (sexist jokes), (b) flattery focuses on irrelevant characteristics (appearance in a professional context), or (c) praise makes low expectations explicit, they still implicitly convey and maintain biased views. Indeed, instead of focusing on the negative expectations they have about the task abilities of women ("hostile" sexism), people may choose to emphasize the positive qualities that (allegedly) characterize women, for instance in the relational or moral domain ("benevolent" sexism; Glick & Fiske, 1996). At first consideration, such positive statements might not seem objectionable. Nevertheless, benevolent sexist views are not harmless: They are most likely to be observed in contexts characterized by gender inequality (Glick et al., 2000) and have been linked to negative attitudes toward women, for instance when they are victims of rape or domestic violence (Glick, Sakalli-Ugurlu, Ferreira, & Souza, 2002). Thus, the absence of explicitly negative views does not imply equal treatment. Indeed, it has been established that whereas white Americans have become less likely to express negative attitudes toward black Americans over the years, they have remained just as likely to display racial bias in (simulated) personnel selection decisions (Dovidio & Gaertner, 2000). Thus, the decreased expression of negative attitudes or expectations by no means implies that discriminatory treatment is a thing of the past.

When discriminatory treatment is masked with positive views, however, it is less likely to be detected. For instance, women are generally disinclined to perceive benevolent sexist views as indicating discrimination, and in fact report they like the individuals expressing such views (Barreto & Ellemers, 2005b; Kilianski & Rudman, 1998; Swim, Mallett, Russo-Devosa, & Stangor, 2005). At the same time, exposure to benevolent sexist views— and the failure to detect this as a form of discrimination—elicits stereotype-confirming responses among women. For instance, women who are exposed to benevolent sexism are more likely to describe themselves in relational terms, and less inclined to emphasize their task abilities, compared to women who are exposed to hostile sexist views or control conditions. Further, women who anticipate a task interaction with an individual endorsing benevolent sexism are less likely to express leadership ambitions (Barreto, Ellemers, Piebinga, & Moya, 2010). Thus, on the one hand, the absence of negative views does not prevent the occurrence of biased treatment, as we have seen above. On the other hand, stereotypical views that seem to emphasize positive group-based qualities cause targets to focus on their ability to demonstrate these positive qualities, instead of challenging the stereotypical expectations to which they are exposed. This is another mechanism through which contemporary expressions of bias induce people to accommodate to stereotypical views, rather than reporting group-based discrimination.

Finally, due to the "prototype" people have of what prejudice is, the common belief remains that people are able to evaluate members of their own group without bias. As a result, including representatives of disadvantaged groups in organizational or legal decision-making procedures is considered an effective strategy to prevent discriminatory treatment. Yet, to the extent that stereotypical expectations reflect social role relations (e.g., Eagly & Karau, 2002), they are likely to be widely shared by members of disadvantaged as well as advantaged groups. This does not mean these views are valid or accurate, nor does it imply that members of disadvantaged groups will not discriminate against their own group. In fact, there is now convincing evidence that individuals who belong to disadvantaged groups, but who achieve individual success by overcoming group-based discrimination, are more likely—instead of less likely—than members of advantaged groups to discriminate against other members of their ingroup, as we will explain in more detail below (for a more detailed review, see Ellemers, Rink, Derks, & Ryan, 2012). However, unless expressions of bias are very blatant and unambiguous, they are less likely to be recognized as indicating discrimination when they are voiced or endorsed by members of the disadvantaged group (Baron, Burgess, & Kao, 1991; Barreto & Ellemers, 2005a). For example, in a study comparing responses to modern and to hostile sexism, we found that both male and female participants perceived any of these messages as more sexist when voiced by a male source than when it was voiced by a female source (Barreto & Ellemers, 2005a). As a paradoxical result, the inclusion of target group representatives in decision-making procedures (e.g., appointing African American judges or including senior women in selection committees) may not—in itself—constitute an effective way to prevent bias. In fact, when such target group representatives endorse (subtle) bias, it is *less* likely to be recognized as a form of discrimination. This is another reason why the occurrence of discrimination in modern societies is likely to be underestimated.

In sum, people generally are less likely to recognize modern (vs. old-fashioned) forms of prejudice, because these are more subtle (e.g., denial of discrimination), are framed in a seemingly positive way (e.g., humor, flattery), or are endorsed by members of the disadvantaged group. The prevalence of such less prototypical expressions of bias contributes to the likelihood that the occurrence of discrimination is underestimated, rather than overestimated.

1.3 Contextual Cues to Discrimination

Due to the implicit nature of many forms of bias, and the common conviction that equal opportunities can be warranted by formal guidelines, additional cues are needed to detect bias. As a counterpoint to our previous observation that people are less likely to detect implicit bias when this is expressed by members of the disadvantaged group, detection of prejudice is more likely when perpetrated by those who represent the advantaged group (Barreto & Ellemers, 2005a, 2005b). We have argued above that this offers a more prototypical representation of a discriminatory event, in which members of an advantaged group display bias against members of disadvantaged groups. However, more recent evidence suggests there may be additional processes that contribute to this effect, which involve informational salience relating to power asymmetries.

Indeed, recent evidence suggests that power attracts scrutiny, which can ensure that when the powerful express prejudice, this is more easily detected than when prejudice is expressed by powerless individuals. When social power differences are present, this implies that people have asymmetrical control over each other's resources and outcomes (Fiske & Berdahl, 2006). However, those who have power can interpret and use this asymmetrical control in different ways, some of which may result in behaviors that favor powerless individuals, whereas others may favor other individuals with power (for an overview of different approaches to and the implications of power, see Sassenberg, Ellemers, Scheepers, & Scholl, 2014). As a result, it is very important for subordinates to pay close attention to the communications and actions of those in power, so as to interpret and anticipate how they are likely to invest the control they have. By contrast, individuals low in power lack such resource control; hence, it may seem less important to interpret their actions or to detect their motives. As a result, expressions of prejudice should be relatively likely to be noticed, remembered, and detected when voiced by individuals in a position of power, whereas exposure to similarly prejudicial views may pass without notice when expressed by someone with low power.

Interestingly, research revealed that people generally expect those in power (e.g., supervisors at work) to feel responsible for equal treatment and are more likely to anticipate bias from those without power (e.g., their coworkers; Barreto, Ellemers, & Fiske, 2010). However, when female team members were actually exposed to a man expressing a preference to work with "guys," they were less able to recall the source of the biased statement when it had been voiced by another member of their team (i.e., a relatively low power individual) than when it had been expressed by a team leader (someone with high power). It is perhaps natural that people should care about the views of their coworkers in the team, particularly with regard to ascertaining who might deliver biased treatment in the work context. Moreover, it might be expected that this attentiveness would be enhanced in conditions of outcome dependency. However, this research did not find evidence that attention to biased statements was driven by outcome dependency. In fact, the increased attention to comments made by someone in power occurred regardless of whether or not individuals personally depended on that individual for their own outcomes (i.e., whether the source was the leader of their own team or of another team; Barreto, Ellemers, & Fiske, 2010). Thus, the results of this research suggest that the *perceptual salience* of those in power is the decisive factor in noting whether bias occurs. Importantly, people appear less inclined to notice and remember prejudicial treatment by someone in a low power position, even if this is likely to be relevant to the self in further team interactions (Barreto, Ellemers, & Fiske, 2010).

Prior work has demonstrated that powerful individuals are more likely to rely on stereotypes and engage in more global and abstract information processing (Fiske, 1993; Guinote, 2007). The evidence reviewed above suggests that this is relatively likely to be noticed and detected. Furthermore, this seems to be the case regardless of whether this powerful individual has power over the self or over others. Crucially, this suggests that the tendency to notice and remember bias does not rely on a self-interested motivation due to asymmetrical dependency relations (Fiske & Berdahl, 2006). It also speaks against the possibility that people are prone to overestimate the occurrence of perceived prejudice in order to explain negative outcomes they personally incur. Instead, the observed effects seem to be driven by the differential perceptual *salience* of behavior displayed by powerful versus powerless others, as a moderating factor that facilitates the detection of bias.

Importantly, this nuances the conclusion drawn above, namely that prejudicial views expressed by representatives of the advantaged group (e.g., men making negative comments about women) match the prototype of what discrimination is, which should facilitate the detection of bias. It seems that such intergroup power differentials may interact with interpersonal power relations, so that relatively explicit prejudicial comments by outgroup members may pass unnoticed and remain unchallenged as long as they are made by individuals who are seen as having relatively low power. Overall, people more frequently encounter and interact with others who have relatively low power (such as coworkers) than high power (e.g., supervisors). All else being equal, this implies that people are likely to underestimate the occurrence of bias occurring in the majority of their day-to-day interactions.

In addition to the position of those who express bias, the observations and responses of *others* present in the situation can also function as contextual cues that make it easier (or more difficult) to detect bias (see Major et al., 2002 for a review). In view of our discussion above, the added value of such social cues should be particularly salient when expressions of bias are subtle and ambiguous. This was examined in a series of studies in which female participants participated in a mock online job interview, where a male interviewer asked them about their appearance (Cihangir, Barreto, & Ellemers, 2014). While waiting for the interviewer's decision, candidates participated in a computer chat session with male or female confederates, who had ostensibly been exposed to the same procedure. The chat session revealed that other candidates either approved of the procedure and found the questions appropriate, or disapproved of the procedure and considered the questions inappropriate. Then participants learned the interviewer had rejected their application for the job.

After being exposed to views of others who questioned the validity of the selection procedure, participants were more likely to perceive discrimination and less inclined to attribute their rejection to personal shortcomings. After being informed that others had found the procedure appropriate, participants were less inclined to perceive discrimination and more likely to consider the rejection as indicating a lack of personal competence. The impact of the judgments of others on the tendency to perceive discrimination emerged regardless of whether others who had questioned or approved the procedure were men or women (Cihangir et al., 2014). This is relevant to our previous conclusion that those who are subjected to subtly biased treatment are relatively disinclined to perceive this as discrimination, especially if others around them see no problem with the relevant procedures. When others indicate doubt about the validity of such procedures, however, people are more likely to recognize being subjected to biased treatment. On the one hand, this resonates with our prior observation that the joint occurrence of personal rejection and group-level discrimination increases the likelihood that bias is recognized (Stroebe et al., 2009). On the other hand, the impact of procedural judgments on people's ability to acknowledge subtle bias seems to occur regardless of whether procedures are called into question by members of the advantaged group or of the disadvantaged group. An important implication of the findings of the Cihangir et al. (2014) study is, thus, that people are more likely to perceive (subtle) discrimination after their treatment has been questioned by others.

1.4 Individual Needs and Dispositions

So far, we have considered situational features and contextual cues as external factors that may either help or hinder individuals to recognize the occurrence of discrimination. In addition, there are a number of individual-level needs and dispositions that may impact on the likelihood that people perceive biased treatment as stemming from group-based discrimination.

First, we consider the effects of individual differences in beliefs about the properties of the social system. Above, we have argued that the widely shared conviction that differential outcomes reflect differences in individual merit reduce the likelihood that people perceive or recognize group-based discrimination (Barreto et al., 2009). Arguably, the extent to which this is the case should depend on their willingness to actually endorse such meritocracy beliefs. Indeed, research has shown that personal meritocracy beliefs impede the recognition of prejudice. For instance, the extent to which women personally endorse system justifying beliefs predicts their perceptions of pay entitlement (O'Brien, Major, & Gilbert, 2012). When individuals believe that women should earn less than men, they are less likely to perceive gender differences in pay levels as indicating discrimination. Likewise, a study among stay-at-home mothers established that individuals who viewed their current situation as resulting from personal choice were less inclined to perceive workplace barriers as indicating gender discrimination (Stephens & Levine, 2011). Conversely, individuals who think discrimination is widespread and believe it will occur on future occasions (i.e., perceive this as a pervasive phenomenon) are more likely to perceive unequal treatment as unfair and discriminatory (for an overview, see Jetten, Iyer, Branscombe, & Zhang, 2013).

Second, the nature of personal goals can modify information processing and hence impacts on individual differences in sensitivity to evidence of discrimination. Thus, although personal beliefs about characteristics of the social system affect the way outcome differences are *interpreted*, personal goals may facilitate or impede the likelihood that such outcome differences are even *observed*. This has been established in different ways.

A first example of such an effect was observed in a series of studies in which female research participants were subjected to a simulated job selection procedure and were rejected by a male interviewer (Stroebe, Barreto, & Ellemers, 2010). They then received the opportunity to select and read information about the qualifications and outcomes of other male and female participants, which would allow them to discover that the selection decisions were systematically gender biased. That is, participants were able to see a matrix on the computer screen, the cells of which corresponded to other participants. If they clicked through those cells, they would be able to see the other participants' characteristics (gender, age, study) and whether or not they had been selected. Since cells remained open as they were clicked, the more cells participants opened, the more they would be able to uncover that gender had played a role in the selection decisions. The experimental procedure was used to induce interpersonal differences in the self-relevance of such information, by leading participants to think that the domain under investigation was predictive of their future outcomes in a range of situations (Study 1) or by making them believe that they would need this information for future reference (Study 2).

In both cases, participants who were led to believe that it would be self-relevant to learn more about the way their outcomes compared to those of others were more likely to search the available information. In turn, the amount of information they sought predicted the likelihood that they realized that the procedure had been gender biased (Stroebe et al., 2010). Thus, this research reveals that the personal significance of specific performance or outcome domains can drive perceptions of prejudice, because individuals are more likely to search for information that might unveil prejudicial treatment when the domain is self-relevant than when it is not. Importantly, however, increased self-relevance enhanced information processing, but this only led to heightened perceptions of prejudice when prejudicial treatment had in fact been received. Indeed, we additionally varied whether or not the information contained in the matrix revealed discriminatory treatment and found that self-relevance led to increased information search but this only led to increased perceptions of prejudice when the matrix contained information about gender-biased evaluations. Thus, there was no evidence that domain self-relevance as such raises self-serving tendencies that might lead people to overestimate the occurrence of prejudicial treatment.

Another way in which personal goals can influence information processing and hence facilitate the detection of prejudice is through the self-regulatory strategies people adopt for goal achievement. In this context, a distinction can be made between individuals who focus on the achievement of ideal outcomes (promotion focus; Higgins, 1997) or on securing that obligations are met (prevention focus). The impact of such individual differences on processing of social information was examined (Ståhl, Van Laar, Ellemers, & Derks, 2012) by assessing people's chronic tendencies to focus on promotion or prevention goals (Study 1) and by inducing situational differences in the adoption of these self-regulation goals (Study 2). Participants in this research were first exposed to a prospective interaction partner, who was said to endorse prejudicial views. In a subsequent information processing test, individuals with a chronic or situational focus on promotion goals attended more to subtle cues of social acceptance rather than rejection. This was evident in their response times to facial expressions of happiness rather than contempt (Study 1) and to subliminally presented words indicating respect rather than prejudice (Study 2). In this research, a focus on prevention goals did not affect the way social information was processed. Importantly, research has also revealed that a focus on social acceptance can undermine perceptions of discriminatory treatment (Carvallo & Pelham, 2006). Hence, taken together, these results suggest that a personal focus on promotion goals leads people to attend to cues of social acceptance (rather than rejection), which may cause them to underestimate the occurrence of bias.

Finally, personal attitudes toward one's group membership and individual differences in the level of ingroup identification can enhance or impede perceptions of prejudice. Even though people can be categorized by others as interchangeable members of a particular social group, they are likely to differ from each other in the extent to which they internalize that specific group membership into their self-views (for an overview, see Barreto & Ellemers, 2003). Such differences in the salience of group-level identities relate to subjective beliefs about the inevitability of group membership due to the perceived permeability of group boundaries on the one hand and emotional self-importance of the group on the other (Ellemers, 2012; Ellemers & Jetten, 2013). Importantly, the tendency to adopt a group-level conception of the self also affects the likelihood that people perceive unequal outcomes as indicative of bias (Jetten et al., 2013). Accordingly, those who identify most strongly with their group are most likely to perceive ambiguous cues to unequal treatment as indicative of discrimination (Branscombe, Schmitt, & Harvey, 1999; Major, Quinton, & Schmader, 2003).

1.5 Conclusion

The evidence reviewed in this section leads us to conclude that members of devalued groups often fail to recognize the discrimination that targets them, due to just world beliefs and the fact that contemporary expressions of bias tend to be subtle and implicit. Additional contextual cues or enhanced personal motivation are needed for them to perceive group-based unequal treatment. This suggests that in the absence of such factors that facilitate prejudice recognition, members of devalued groups will tend to underestimate (rather than overestimate) the extent to which they are targeted by discrimination, even if this goes against their self-interest.

2. IS PERCEIVING DISCRIMINATORY TREATMENT SELF-PROTECTIVE OR HARMFUL TO INDIVIDUAL WELL-BEING?

Relating to the previous discussion is the notion that people might perceive themselves to be targets of discriminatory treatment to avoid facing any personal shortcomings that may account for their disappointing outcomes. Again, empirical evidence does not offer straightforward support for this commonly held view, even though a vast body of research has examined whether or not perceiving prejudice or discriminatory treatment has a negative impact on individual well-being.

Early work suggested that prejudice should have a strong negative impact on the psychological well-being of its targets (Allport, 1979; Goffman, 1963; Tajfel, 1981). Later reflections focused on the fact that when comparing the self-reported psychological well-being of members of stigmatized and nonstigmatized groups, very few differences were found, and those often indicated better well-being among members of some stigmatized groups than among members of groups that do not tend to be stigmatized (Crocker & Major, 1989; Twenge & Crocker, 2002). Over the years, research into whether or not perceiving prejudice or discriminatory treatment has a negative impact on individual well-being has accumulated, yielding seemingly inconclusive effects. Although some researchers found clear negative effects of prejudice on physical and psychological well-being, others demonstrated that perceiving oneself to be a target of prejudice can protect self-esteem (e.g., Major et al., 2002; Schmitt & Branscombe, 2002).

More recently, research has focused on reconciling these findings by identifying the individual and contextual factors that moderate these effects, and some of the mechanisms through which they occur (see also meta-analyses by Jones, Peddie, Gilrane, King, & Gray, 2013; Pascoe & Smart Richman, 2009; Schmitt, Branscombe, Postmes, & Garcia, 2014). These reviews concluded that the effects of perceptions of discrimination on well-being depend on a number of moderating factors. Below we review the state of the art in this area, identifying the factors that influence how discrimination affects well-being and elaborating on the mechanisms through which this occurs.

2.1 It Is Not Straightforward: Moderating Variables

Initial attempts to understand the effects of discrimination on well-being have tended to assume that these are driven by concerns that the application of group-based expectations leads to less favorable outcomes than people might expect to receive if they were judged on their individual merit alone (e.g., Crocker & Major, 1989; Major et al., 2002). More recent research, however, clarified that category-based treatment in itself may undermine well-being, regardless of whether this results in desired or undesired outcomes. That is, well-being is not merely affected by the disadvantage that often results from bias, but—more generally—by the neglect of individual preferences regarding the identity on the basis of which one would like to be treated (Barreto & Ellemers, 2002, 2003). For example, in one study, we asked a representative sample of the Dutch adult population to recount an episode in which they had been categorized by others. Participants described situations where categorization had led to either positive or negative expectations about the self. Positive categorizations were associated with more agreement and more positive emotions than negative categorization. However, positive categorizations were less easy to detect as overgeneralizations and this, in turn, resulted in lower self-confidence, revealing a detrimental effect of imposed categorizations even when they appear to be positive (Ellemers & Barreto, 2006).

A second set of studies further clarified this effect (Barreto, Ellemers, Scholten, & Smith, 2010). In three experiments, we examined participants' responses to contextually inappropriate categorizations, i.e., categorizations that were both irrelevant to the task at hand and inconsistent with participants' own preferences. Participants in these studies were asked to proofread a series of texts, which were on topics that had been thoroughly pretested to be stereotypically male, female, or neutral, but of equal attractiveness. Participants were asked which texts they would prefer to proofread and were then allocated two texts to work on, allegedly by another participant. In all studies, participants, who were all female, were given the stereotypically female texts to proofread, irrespective of the preference they had stated. In the first two studies, we simply examined how participants felt when this happened, as a function of whether this task assignment had been made without any explanation or explicitly because "you are a woman." Results showed that agreement with the categorical treatment was never high across all studies and conditions, although female participants expressed less agreement and more anger when this allocation was made with an explicit reference to gender. In addition, this categorical treatment hurts participants' well-being, since it elicited negative self-directed emotions, particularly when this task allocation was made without any explicit justification. A final study demonstrated that these effects emerge even when the categorization results in advantageous treatment. In this study, we varied whether participants were allocated stereotypically female texts that had been previously rated in a pilot test as either equally or *more attractive* than the male stereotypical and the neutral tasks. Despite the fact that, in this study, performing female stereotypical tasks would actually be more attractive, participants still rejected this categorization when it did not match their own stated preference, particularly when this was accompanied by the explicit reference to gender as the (contextually inappropriate) task allocation criterion. In addition, negative self-directed emotions were again revealed, especially when the categorization was not justified. In this study, we additionally measured personal state self-esteem and found parallel effects for this measure, i.e., negative effects of implicit and inappropriate categorizations on self-esteem, irrespective of whether or not this categorization actually gave participants an advantage in the form of more attractive task assignments.

Thus, on the one hand, exposure to prejudice can benefit well-being as it allows individuals to externalize the causes of their negative outcomes. Indeed, blaming others helps direct negative emotions away from the self and should be helpful as a self-protective strategy, at least in the short term. On the other hand, exposure to biased treatment also indicates lack of control over one's own fate or self-definition and implies that individual efforts or attributes are less likely to be acknowledged or rewarded. We now consider each of these possibilities in turn, aiming to identify the moderating variables that enhance the likelihood that beneficial or harmful effects for well-being emerge.

2.2 Externalization of Negative Affect

Factors that contribute to externalization of blame for unequal treatment (reviewed in the prior section) should also facilitate the occurrence of positive effects of discrimination for well-being. To the extent that it is more obvious that procedures are unfair, it is easier to blame others instead of the self for disappointing outcomes, and this should protect well-being. Indeed, this is exactly what was observed in research that compared how different types of prejudice affect individual well-being (Barreto & Ellemers, 2005a, 2005b). For example, in one study, we presented women with subtle or blatant sexist statements that allegedly represented societal attitudes. Subtle sexist statements were items from the modern sexism scale (denying the existence of discrimination), whereas blatant sexism consisted of items from the old-fashioned sexism scale (hostility toward women). Old-fashioned sexism was expected to be recognized as sexist and therefore to elicit anger. Denial of continued discrimination was expected to be more ambiguous, given that participants had no evidence against which to gauge the veracity of the claim that gender discrimination no longer affects women's social standing. At the same time, denying the existence of discrimination implies that existing gender inequalities are not caused by bias and raises the possibility that they may be caused, instead, by women's inadequacies. This, in turn, was expected to elicit anxiety, but not anger. As described in the prior section, we found that participants saw denial of gender discrimination as less sexist than hostility toward women. With regard to affective reactions, we found that whereas subtle expressions of prejudice elicited negative self-directed affect (such as anxiety and self-doubt), people responded to more blatant forms of prejudice by directing their negative affect toward the perpetrator (e.g., other-directed anger) (Barreto & Ellemers, 2005a, 2005b).

Additional research further confirmed that this shift in the focus of negative affective responses depends on the ability to realize that others—not the self—are to be blamed for unfavorable outcomes, and the perceived likelihood that this indeed is the primary cause for current events. The research we reviewed above revealed that the ability of female job applicants to recognize subtle bias as a form of gender discrimination is enhanced when others around them suggest this is the case, regardless of whether these others are men or women (Cihangir et al., 2014). However, this same research revealed that whether such perceptions of discrimination were beneficial or harmful for well-being depended on *who* had suggested this was the case. To examine this, in a first experiment (Cihangir et al., 2014; Experiment 1), we measured self-handicapping, i.e., provision of excuses in advance of a task ("I'm hungry," "I have not slept well last night"), which is regarded as an indicator of poor self-confidence (Rhodewalt, 1990). To gain further insight into this process, we also measured self-stereotyping (using an adapted version of the Bem sex roles inventory; Bem, 1974). In the second study (Cihangir et al., 2014; Experiment 2), we additionally measured state performance self-esteem, task performance, and the extent to which participants wished to protest about the selection procedure. Across both studies, the pattern was consistent: When other women had suggested discrimination might have played a role, this elicited dysfunctional responses, that is, it lowered performance-related self-esteem and exacerbated self-handicapping and self-stereotyping tendencies, compared to when no suggestion of sexism had been made (see Table 1; see also Adams, Garcia, Purdie-Vaughns, & Steele, 2006). However, when the suggestion that sexism might have played a role had been made by other males present, this effectively protected well-being, as it led job candidates to report increased self-esteem and to display less self-handicapping and less

Table 1 Affective and Behavioral Outcomes of a Suggestion of Sexism Made by Male or Female Sources

Suggestion of Sexism	Yes		No	
Gender of Source	Male ($N = 22$)	Female ($N = 23$)	Male ($N = 22$)	Female ($N = 23$)
Self-handicapping				
Experiment 1	2.44[b] (0.80)	2.95[a] (0.95)	2.99[a] (0.74)	2.46[b] (0.63)
Experiment 2	2.34[b] (0.63)	2.84[a,*] (1.02)	2.63[a,b] (0.89)	2.39[b,*] (0.86)
Performance self-esteem	5.63[a] (0.74)	5.00[c] (0.83)	5.27[b] (0.94)	5.43[b] (0.97)
Self-stereotyping				
Experiment 1	4.19[b,*] (0.48)	4.67[a,†] (0.81)	4.59[a,*] (0.58)	4.29[b,†] (0.59)
Experiment 2	4.21[b] (0.64)	4.75[a,*] (0.62)	4.47[a,b] (0.77)	4.44[b,*] (0.53)
Task performance	11.23[a] (2.33)	9.78[b] (2.54)	9.55[b] (2.46)	10.30[a,b] (1.94)
Filing complaint	15 (68.18%[a])	7 (30.44%[b,*])	9 (40.91%[b,*])	11 (47.83%[b])

Note: Standard deviations are reported in parentheses beside each mean. Scores range from 1 to 7 except for task performance (0–15) and protest (0-cell N or to 100%). Means with different superscripts within each row differ reliably from each other at $p < 0.05$. Means that share * or † differ from each other at $0.05 < p < 0.12$.
Adapted from Cihangir et al. (2014).

self-stereotyping (Cihangir et al., 2014). Positive effects of suggestions of sexism made by male (but not by female) sources also extended to better task performance and more protest about the treatment received. This suggests that the willingness of those who represent the perpetrator group to acknowledge biased treatment is an important precondition for the beneficial effects of perceiving discrimination. If, by contrast, perceptions of bias are only shared among those who suffer from it, this may even exacerbate negative effects on well-being. These results complement explanations focusing on the importance of awareness raising and social support, as they suggest that the perceived credibility of externalizing blame—granted, in these studies, by the support of members of the perpetrator's group—is an important precondition for such support to benefit individual well-being.

Such preconditions may also be set by *institutional* practices and guidelines to which people are exposed. As already mentioned, the institutional endorsement of nondiscriminatory practices has important effects on individuals' ability to detect discrimination (Castilla & Benard, 2010; Kaiser et al., 2013) and is likely to increase attributional uncertainty when discrimination does occur. Whether or not organizations are open to the possibility that discrimination occurs under ambiguous circumstances and tolerates uncertain attributions is an additional factor that affects how discrimination is experienced. This idea was examined by placing individuals in a setting in which uncertain attributions to discrimination were either seen as offering an opportunity for the organization to learn and develop, or were characterized as undermining trust and damaging for the organization. Comparing responses to subtle prejudice in these different contexts revealed that more negative self-directed affect was reported when uncertain claims of biased treatment were discouraged, whereas less self-blame was observed when individuals were led to believe that uncertain attributions would be tolerated in that context (Cihangir, Ellemers, & Barreto, in preparation; see also Barreto et al., 2009).

Thus, here too, as we have seen above (and countering common beliefs), it seems that people are disinclined to easily or automatically blame others for their own misfortunes as a standard response to protect their own well-being. Importantly, when they do so, it is not self-evident that this will be self-protective rather than increasing negative feelings about the self. Individuals only direct their negative emotional responses to discrimination toward others when unfair treatment is relatively identifiable because it is blatant, or when the possibility of unfair treatment is explicitly acknowledged by other individuals or institutional procedures.

2.3 Implications for the Self

Another class of moderating variables that has been examined encompasses conditions that increase the *implications* of discrimination for the self, either because of past experiences or because of likely future implications of their current experience. Past experiences that make individuals' self-views more resilient, or future prospects that offer scope for change and improvement, contribute to the emergence of positive well-being effects in response to biased treatment.

When people work together on joint tasks, differences in the extent to which their contributions are valued impact on the likelihood that they feel respected and fully included as a team member (Ellemers, Sleebos, Stam, & de Gilder, 2013). When people with a different background or another perspective on the task enter a new work context, they are generally expected to adapt to existing practices. Even when the reason to involve them is to seek novel approaches or to enhance creativity, existing team members are reluctant to adapt to the needs of newcomers or to accommodate to their work preferences (for an overview, see Rink, Kane, Ellemers, & Van der Vegt, 2013). Being in an environment dominated by outgroup members makes people think it is unlikely that their group's characteristics are valued (Derks, Van Laar, & Ellemers, 2006, 2007). The prospect of working with others who are different from them leads them to expect that their work preferences are unlikely to be validated by others (Rink & Ellemers, 2006), and to the extent that this puts them in a position of low power, this is likely to raise physiological threat (Scheepers, De Wit, Ellemers, & Sassenberg, 2012).

Thus, when members of devalued groups first gain access to work contexts or job levels in which they are underrepresented, or perform tasks that they are not (stereotypically) expected to be good at, there are a number of factors that elicit uncertainty and undermine feelings of self-esteem and efficacy. In turn, this uncertainty elicits maladaptive forms of physiological stress, as was established for instance among women during a car parking task (Derks, Scheepers, Van Laar, & Ellemers, 2011). Performing under such conditions tends to raise threat and a focus on preventing negative outcomes, which may temporarily result in performance enhancement, but over time induces cognitive depletion and impairs performance (Ståhl, Van Laar, & Ellemers, 2012).

As a result, individuals who are devalued because of their group membership—such as young Muslim women in the Netherlands—feel discouraged by the way they are treated and report reduced ambitions for education and work (Van Laar, Derks, & Ellemers, 2013; Van Laar, Derks, Ellemers, & Bleeker, 2010). Prior experiences that have this effect make people particularly vulnerable to the effects of subtle prejudice, which—due to its ambiguous nature—directs attention to the possibility of being personally inadequate. Indeed, research established that individual well-being is reduced under these circumstances as exposure to subtle prejudice or implicit stereotypes raises feelings of anxiety and uncertainty, and lowers task performance (Cihangir et al., 2010; Derks, Van Laar, & Ellemers, 2009). By contrast, people are more resilient to these negative effects of subtle discrimination when prior experiences help them buffer their self-esteem or induce them to affirm their self-worth (Cihangir et al., 2010; Derks et al., 2009).

Specifically, low self-esteem is a source of vulnerability in situations where individuals are unable to externalize blame, such as contexts where they encounter subtle discrimination. We examined this reasoning in two experiments where we manipulated participants' self-esteem and subsequently examined how they responded to rejection associated with subtle or blatant prejudice (Cihangir et al., 2010). Participants underwent a bogus job interview, which included gender-biased questions, indirectly referring to stereotypes about women (e.g., "Do you think it will be hard to combine your family with your career?"; "Do you often get emotional at work because of something you have not managed to do?"). After this interview, while participants waited for the interviewer's decision, self-esteem was manipulated by giving participants a general knowledge test that was either very difficult and impossible to solve within the allocated time (eliciting low self-esteem) or very easy and perfectly possible to complete with the time allocated (eliciting high self-esteem). At this point, participants were informed that the interviewer thought that they were not suitable for the position for which they had been interviewed. To manipulate ambiguity of discrimination, participants in the blatant (but not in the subtle) condition also read that the interviewer generally thought that women were not suitable for this kind of job and explicitly linked the participant's gender to their decision. In Experiment 1, we then measured both self-directed and other-directed negative emotions, reasoning that self-esteem should moderate effects only on *self-directed* emotions. Manipulation checks confirmed that both manipulations had been successful. More importantly, results showed that participants reported more negative self-directed emotions when they had encountered subtle discrimination, but only when they had low self-esteem, and not when their self-esteem was high (see Table 2). In addition, self-esteem did not moderate effects on negative other-directed emotions, which were higher in the blatant than in the subtle conditions. Responses in the blatant condition were unaffected by self-esteem.

A second experiment (Cihangir et al., 2010; Experiment 2) replicated these findings and extended them to measures of self-concern, self-stereotyping, and task performance. We found that low self-esteem made individuals vulnerable to subtle discrimination, in that individuals with low self-esteem expressed more negative self-directed emotions, more self-concern, and more self-stereotyping than individuals with high self-esteem when they encountered subtle discrimination. In addition, individuals with low self-esteem underperformed when they encountered subtle relative to blatant discrimination, whereas the task performance of individuals with high self-esteem was not affected by the way they were treated. Once more, no parallel effects of self-esteem were revealed when

Table 2 How Self-esteem Moderates Affective and Behavioral Outcomes of Subtle (but Not Blatant) Prejudice

Ambiguity of Sexism	Blatant		Subtle	
Self-esteem	Low	High	Low	High
Self-directed negative emotions				
Experiment 1	1.73^b (0.77)	1.79^b (0.73)	2.43^a (1.18)	1.80^b (0.89)
Experiment 2	2.51^a (0.59)	$2.77^{a,b}$ (0.93)	2.80^a (0.92)	2.39^b (0.76)
Self-concern	2.99^a (1.05)	$3.16^{a,b}$ (0.93)	3.33^a (1.15)	2.72^b (0.98)
Self-stereotyping	4.64^a (0.58)	$4.83^{a,b}$ (0.48)	4.94^a (0.60)	4.60^b (0.48)
Performance	11.76^a (2.28)	$11.17^{a,b}$ (3.02)	$10.80^{b,*}$ (2.27)	12.14 (2.62)

Note: Standard deviations are reported in parentheses beside each mean. Scores range from 1 to 7 except for task performance (0–15). Means with different superscripts within each row differ reliably from each other at $p < 0.05$.
Adapted from Cihangir et al. (2010).

participants encountered blatant discrimination, again demonstrating how the ability to externalize blame can be protective, even for individuals with low self-esteem.

Just as prior experiences may raise levels of uncertainty and make people more vulnerable to the effects of subtle discrimination, future prospects may have similar effects. It is generally more difficult to ignore or discount experiences with discrimination if these have more far-reaching implications for the self (see also Schmitt, Branscombe, & Postmes, 2003). As a result, exposure to prejudice is more damaging to well-being when the party holding such views has power over the self (Barreto, Ellemers, & Fiske, 2010), or when one expects to encounter it again in the future because one believes prejudice to be pervasive (Stroebe et al., 2011). Conversely, well-being effects are mitigated when low power individuals hold prejudicial views or when encountering prejudice seems an exceptional experience (Schmitt, Branscombe, et al., 2003; Schmitt, Ellemers, & Branscombe, 2003; Stroebe et al., 2011).

Thus, adding to prior work showing that exposure to implicit prejudice may lower task ability and performance outcomes (e.g., due to stereotype threat, for an overview see Schmader, Johns, & Forbes, 2008), we note that such motivation and performance deficits are complemented, or perhaps even preceded, by a number of mechanisms that reduce well-being and self-confidence and elicit self-defeating performance strategies.

2.4 Social Implications

As we have noted above, responses to prejudice and discrimination are not driven only by self-protective concerns or by the desire to explain away one's disappointing outcomes. Instead, people who acknowledge that bias persists may also suffer in terms of well-being out of concern for the broader social implications of this fact. Arguably, the well-being effects of such concerns should be intensified to the extent that prejudice against one's group is seen as more persistent and pervasive, both because this implies the self is more likely to suffer future discrimination and because the realization that bias persists undermines fundamental just world beliefs.

Evidence to this effect was observed in two studies where perceived pervasiveness of prejudice against one's group was manipulated (Stroebe et al., 2011). In the first experiment, participants imagined taking part in a selection procedure for a very attractive job. To give participants the opportunity to attribute a subsequent rejection to discrimination, the interviewer was described as politically conservative, holding traditional beliefs, and having selected 80% men and 20% women in prior selection procedures. We manipulated perceived pervasiveness of gender discrimination by providing participants with information about the likelihood of encountering someone like this particular interviewer in future job interview procedures (unlikely vs. likely). Participants then imagined that the interviewer had rated them as unsuitable for the job and completed manipulation checks, attributions to prejudice, and measures of well-being (emotions, self-esteem). Results revealed that well-being was protected when the prejudice participants encountered seemed rare, instead of pervasive. Specifically, when gender discrimination was perceived as pervasive, attributions to discrimination were significantly and negatively related to well-being. When, however, discrimination was perceived as rare, attributions to discrimination were unrelated to indicators of well-being.

This protective effect of perceiving discrimination as rare may emerge because this mitigates future consequences for the self. However, evidence suggests that the negative effects may emerge, at least in part, because of their broader societal implications, that is, because of the implications they have for one's beliefs in the world as a just place. In a second experiment (Stroebe et al., 2011; Experiment 2), after participants imagined receiving the negative feedback, a third of the participants were given the chance to affirm their belief in the world as a just place, whereas the remaining participants were not. Participants who had their beliefs in a just world affirmed read about a

victim of a tragic accident who was characterized as having brutally mur-
dered a young woman but had avoided a life prison sentence due to a tech-
nicality. A second third of the participants had their beliefs in a just world
threatened by hearing a similar story about a surgeon who had recently
miraculously saved the life of a young woman; a final set of participants
where in the control condition, where there was no mention of any accident
or victim. Results showed that when discrimination was perceived as
rare, attributions to discrimination were, as in the first study, unrelated to
negative affect (see Figure 2). However, when discrimination was perceived
to be pervasive, attributions to discrimination were negatively related to

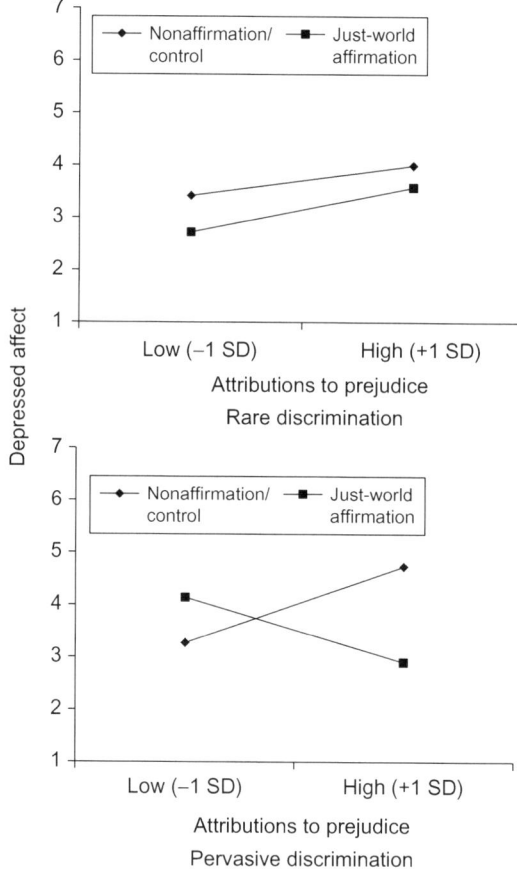

Figure 2 Depressed affect as a function of attributions to discrimination, perceived pervasiveness of discrimination, and opportunity to reaffirm beliefs in a just world. *From
Stroebe et al. (2011), Experiment 2, with permission.*

well-being—but only when participants had no chance to reaffirm their belief in the world as a just place. Indeed, even when research participants were led to believe that prejudice was pervasive (hence, they were likely to encounter it in the future), their well-being was protected when their just world beliefs were reasserted in another way (Stroebe et al., 2011). Taken together, this evidence speaks for the notion that the negative effects of experiencing discrimination for well-being stem at least in part from a consideration of the broader implications this has for one's beliefs about the world, not the self.

The important role that broader social arrangements have for individual well-being is further illustrated by studies that addressed physiological markers of dysfunctional (threat) versus functional (challenge) cardiovascular responses to stress (see also Blascovich & Tomaka, 1996). Here, we see that the prospect of continued social inequality elicits a physiological stress response, but the possibility of change in how the group is evaluated decreases these negative effects of devaluation. That is, the dysfunctional physiological stress typically experienced by members of groups with low social status is relieved by the prospect that the devalued standing of the group is unstable and might improve in the future (Scheepers & Ellemers, 2005). Likewise, the negative effects of group-based exclusion on physiological stress are alleviated when the possibility of future inclusion is made salient. This is the case, for instance, when individuals are challenged to meet the standard for inclusion, instead of pointing out how their group membership prevents them from gaining acceptance (Cihangir, Scheepers, Barreto, & Ellemers, 2013). Thus, exposure to prejudice has less negative effects on physical well-being when there is scope for future improvement.

In sum, when social implications are more severe and pervasive, this is more harmful for well-being. This is at least in part due to broader concerns about social justice and stability of existing social relations, instead of merely reflecting self-relevant considerations about the likelihood of encountering future disadvantage. Indeed, unless discrimination is quite blatant and explicit, people are unlikely to engage in efforts to redress it, such as through collective action (Ellemers & Barreto, 2009a).

2.5 The Role of Group Identification

A specific question that has arisen in this literature is whether identification with a devalued group is likely to function as a source of resilience or as a source of vulnerability to the effects of prejudice. It makes sense to assume that the more an individual identifies with a group that is devalued in society at large, the more negatively their well-being should be affected. In fact, this might be why one of the strategies members of devalued groups can use to achieve a positive identity is to reduce the extent to which they identify with this group (Ellemers, 1993). Research shows that identification can indeed constitute a source of vulnerability by increasing exposure to prejudice (Kaiser & Pratt-Hyatt, 2009), enhancing detection of ambiguous prejudice (Major et al., 2003; Operario & Fiske, 2001), promoting self-stereotyping and assimilation to prejudiced beliefs (Schmader, 2002), and intensifying the negative effects of prejudice on well-being (McCoy & Major, 2003; Sellers & Shelton, 2003).

More recently, evidence has also accumulated for the protective role of group identification and, importantly, for the mechanisms through which this occurs (e.g., Haslam, Jetten, Postmes, & Haslam, 2009; Jetten, Haslam, & Haslam, 2012). Individuals draw closer to their group when they encounter prejudice or discrimination (Branscombe et al., 1999; Jetten, Branscombe, Schmitt, & Spears, 2001; Knowles & Gardner, 2008), and this has been shown to protect self-esteem (Bourguignon, Seron, Yzerbyt, & Herman, 2006), prevent depression (Sani, Herrara, Wakefield, Boroch, & Gulyas, 2012), and reduce destructive behavior in response to exclusion (Stock, Gibbonds, Walsh, & Gerrard, 2011). Importantly, individuals only increase group identification after encountering prejudice if they are already highly identified with their group (McCoy & Major, 2003; Wann & Branscombe, 1990), clarifying that identification is better seen as a resource than as a coping strategy (Leach, Rodriguez Mosquera, Vliek, & Hirt, 2010). Recent knowledge regarding some of the mechanisms underlying this protective effect clarifies that group identification promotes social support seeking (Haslam, O'Brien, Jetten, Vormedal, & Penna, 2005) and exposure to a positive definition of the group from the "inside," which helps combat more external negative views (Crabtree, Haslam, Postmes, & Haslam, · 2010). Also, group identification attenuates depressive attribution styles, which are strongly responsible for depression symptoms (Cruwys, South, Greenaway, & Haslam, 2014).

2.6 Conclusions

In sum, the evidence reviewed in this section clarifies that the effects of discrimination on individual well-being systematically depend on factors that determine the concrete *implications* of discrimination for the (social) self. To the extent that moderating factors make it more likely that factors outside the self are to blame for unequal outcomes, they facilitate self-protective responses and benefit well-being. However, when the self is more strongly implicated, due to the accumulation of past or the anticipation of future experiences, when individuals consider broader group-level and social outcomes of discrimination, or when they do not have the opportunity to seek support from others like them, experiencing discrimination has quite negative effects on well-being.

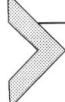

3. ARE CONCEALABLE STIGMAS LESS PROBLEMATIC THAN VISIBLE STIGMAS?

A third issue we address is whether those with socially devalued identities that are immediately apparent to others are more vulnerable than people who can conceal their devalued identity. Goffman (1963) theorized that individuals whose stigmatized identities are visible are *discredited* in the eyes of others, whereas individuals whose stigmatized identities are concealable are *discreditable*, that is, only discredited if they choose to reveal their identity to others. Examples of identities that are often both stigmatized and concealable are mental illness (Corrigan & Matthews, 2003; Link, 1987), physical illness (Cole, Kemeny, & Taylor, 1997), facial features (or disfigurement; Frable, Blackstone, & Scherbaum, 1990), and homosexual orientation (Croteau, 1996). It is important to note that identity concealment differs from individual mobility. Whereas individual mobility consists of "passing into" a more positively evaluated group, identity concealment consists of "passing as" a member of that group. By concealing a stigmatized identity, members of stigmatized groups do not necessarily leave the group, either physically or psychologically (Hebl, Tickle, & Heatherton, 2000). Although the more important a specific identity is to the self-concept, the less likely the individual is to hide that identity (Griffith & Hebl, 2002; Ragins, 2008), a person may have reasons to hide an identity that are unrelated to identification, such as to escape bodily harm (Clair, Beatty, & MacLean, 2005).

Concealing a socially stigmatized identity has clear benefits. Indeed, whereas people with visible social stigmas are often vulnerable to others' negative views of them, and the implications these may have, individuals with concealed stigmas are not so easily or frequently treated on the basis of their socially stigmatized identity (Farina, Gliha, Boudreau, Allen, & Sherman, 1971; Jones et al., 1984). As a consequence, those who belong to a socially stigmatized group that is not immediately apparent should be less worried about others having negative expectations of them (Barreto, Ellemers, & Banal, 2006) and, therefore, should also be less vulnerable to the effects of these negative expectations on their performance (Quinn, Kahng, & Crocker, 2004).

Individuals with concealable stigmas often hide these identities from others precisely because they anticipate such benefits of secrecy. We examined this in two experimental studies (Newheiser & Barreto, 2014, Studies 1a, $N = 49$, and 1b, $N = 105$). In the first experiment (Study 1a), participants indicated whether or not they had any of a range of concealable social stigmas and then imagined a social interaction in the workplace context where they had to decide whether they would hide or reveal this identity. As expected, the results showed that participants were more likely to indicate that they would hide, rather than reveal, their stigmatized identity in the imagined context. Participants in this study were also asked to indicate the extent to which they thought that each strategy (i.e., hiding or revealing) would have positive effects on their relationships at work. Participants reported believing that revealing their stigmatized identity would have negative effects on their work relationships, whereas hiding it would have no effect on their relationships at work. A second experiment (Study 1b) placed participants in the same situation, but then manipulated whether participants imagined hiding or revealing their identity to their coworkers. Participants in each condition then indicated how positive they anticipated their interaction with coworkers would be. Participants who imagined concealing their identity rated their interpersonal experience as more positive than participants who imagined revealing this identity. Participants in both conditions were subsequently asked what they would actually choose to do if they experienced this situation. In all conditions, participants stated a clear preference for hiding the stigmatized identity, relative to revealing it. These patterns were revealed also when we adjusted for general openness about the identity, identification with the concealable group, and perceived coworker bias against that identity. Taken together, these studies suggest that people expect that they would benefit from hiding, instead of revealing, a stigmatized identity and report a preference for keeping a stigmatized identity hidden during interpersonal interactions.

Despite the benefits anticipated, evidence has accumulated that the effects of this identity management strategy are not as positive as might be expected, even when balanced against the expectation that the consequences of revealing are likely to be quite severe (Quinn & Chaudoir,

2009). Indeed, research has revealed that stigmatized identities do not cease to be problematic just because they are out of the sight of others (see also Pachankis, 2007). Below, we review evidence for the effects of concealing stigmatized identities, highlighting some of the aspects that characterize the unique predicament of individuals with concealable identities.

3.1 Identity Concealment and Psychological Well-Being

Because the negative effects of stigmatization on well-being are typically associated with the negative group-based treatment received, and because this type of treatment is less frequent when stigma is concealed, individuals with concealable stigmas could be expected to endure fewer psychological costs than individuals with visible stigmas. However, individuals with concealable identities face a range of problems that are detrimental to their well-being, some of which are unique to concealable stigmas.

First, although they may not as easily incur the costs of being personally treated on the basis of their devalued group membership, individuals with concealable stigmas still suffer from the broader societal devaluation of their identity. Indeed, just like individuals with visible stigmas, individuals with concealable stigmas are highly aware of the poor regard others have for their identity (Quinn & Chaudoir, 2009). These negative views are often culturally prevalent and, in the case of acquired stigmas, often internalized before the stigmatized characteristic is acquired (e.g., Link, 1987). In addition, those who hide a stigmatized identity can actually be more easily exposed to disparaging remarks about their group, because others do not feel the need to monitor expressions of prejudice around them (Wahl, 1999). These disparaging views of one's social identity are, in themselves, damaging to well-being, even if individuals are not the direct target of group-based treatment as long as they conceal their identity (Schmitt & Branscombe, 2002).

Second, individuals with concealable stigmas must additionally contend with the burden of having to choose whether to hide or reveal their identity in each new encounter (Beals, Peplau, & Gable, 2009; Major & Gramzow, 1999; Pachankis, 2007). Indeed, choosing to hide or reveal a stigmatized identity is generally not a one-off "coming out" event, but an act that must be reconsidered and reenacted in each new situation. Having the choice of whether to reveal the stigmatized identity has some advantages, primarily because this allows individuals with social stigmas to choose to reveal their stigmatized identity only when they feel comfortable doing so (Kelly & McKillop, 1996). Often, individuals choose to conceal their stigmatized identity in public contexts, such as in the workplace, and to reveal it in private contexts, such as among friends and family (D'Augelli & Grossman, 2001; Goffman, 1959). The opposite also occurs, such as when homosexual individuals hide their sexuality from their family but not from their coworkers, or when individuals with HIV join public support groups (Pachankis, Goldfried, & Ramrattan, 2008). Individuals who decide to conceal their stigmatized identity in an initial social encounter may need to revisit this decision as the relationship progresses. This is a difficult dilemma that entails both revealing a devalued identity and acknowledging the initial deceit to someone who may have, in the meantime, become a significant other. The fact that individuals with concealable identities need to make deliberate decisions as to whether, when, and how they reveal their identity across multiple settings represents a significant psychological burden—a burden individuals with immediately visible stigmas, as well as nonstigmatized individuals, are spared.

Once they have made the decision to hide their identity, individuals with concealable stigmas also incur significant costs. Akin to what happens with other secrets, the more individuals attempt to keep an identity concealed, the more salient it becomes in their mind, so that whereas visible identities are more salient to observers, hidden identities can be more salient to the individual who hides it than identities that are not hidden (Smart & Wegner, 1999). In this regard, it is important to distinguish situations when the stigmatized identity is simply not known to others (as researched, for example, by Quinn et al., 2004) from active efforts made by individuals to misrepresent their identity ("passing," as researched, for example, by Major & Gramzow, 1999). Whereas the former situation might efficiently protect from stigmatization, individuals in such circumstances might be unaware that they are misrepresenting their identity, so this is unlikely to increase stigma salience. By contrast, actively passing is a strategy used to respond to stigmatization and involves a deliberate act of deceit. It is this active deceit that involves a persistent effort to maintain secrecy, which is associated with thought intrusion that, in turn, increases the salience of the stigmatized identity (Smart & Wegner, 1999).

Identity concealment is also associated with negative affect. For example, compared to revealing the stigmatized identity, hiding elicits self-concern (Santuzzi & Ruscher, 2002) and generalized psychological distress (Beals et al., 2009; Frable et al., 1990; Link, Mirotznik, & Cullen, 1991; Meyer, 2008). We examined this in two experimental studies ($N=145$ and $N=110$) where we induced a stigmatized identity and led participants to either hide or reveal this identity during a dyadic task with another participant (Barreto et al., 2006). Participants were asked to perform, in a dyad, a task associated with Art History, although they did not study this subject. Participants were then allegedly paired with a student who was the same gender and age as themselves, but who was either studying the same subject as themselves or studying Art History. In both cases, to ensure that participants' identity was devalued in all contexts, participants heard that their dyad partner had stated a preference to work with someone who studied Art History. At this point, we explained to participants that, unfortunately, we did not have enough Art History students present in the lab at that moment and introduced the manipulation of hiding versus revealing the stigmatized identity. In the hiding condition, we suggested to participants that they pretend that they were students of Art History, whereas in the reveal condition they received the suggestion to reveal their actual study major. In both cases, participants were asked to indicate whether they agreed with this suggestion, ensuring that although they did not self-select into conditions—essential for the examination of causal relations—participants still had some responsibility for the choice to either hide or reveal their identity, mirroring experiences with hiding or revealing stigma in real-life contexts. After indicating their agreement with this procedure, participants sent the corresponding information about themselves to their alleged partner, so they actually hid or revealed their stigmatized identity. In both experiments, participants then estimated how well their partner expected them to perform and indicated their performance-related self-confidence. In Experiment 2, participants additionally indicated the extent to which they felt guilt and shame and performed a simple task (i.e., listing the similarities and differences between two paintings).

As displayed in Table 3, the results showed that when participants hid the stigmatized identity, they estimated that their partner would have more positive expectations of them than when they revealed the stigmatized identity. Importantly, however, participants who hid their identity reported lower performance-related self-confidence than participants who revealed their real identity. Correlational analyses showed that whereas anticipated partner expectations and self-confidence were *positively* related when participants revealed their identity, these were, instead, *negatively* related when participants hid their identity. That is, although hiding may protect individuals from stereotypical expectations, it can actually lower their self-confidence, and it can do so to the extent that it increases perceived partner expectations. Experiment 2 clarified that these effects emerge because hiding elicits guilt

Table 3 Perceived Partner Expectations, Self-confidence, and Guilt/Shame as a Function of Hiding or Revealing a Stigmatized Identity

	Hide	Reveal
Experiment 1		
Perceived partner expectations	5.36 (1)	4.11 (1.02)
Self-confidence	3.96 (0.87)	4.22 (0.96)
Experiment 2		
Perceived partner expectations	5.36 (1.17)	4.14 (0.98)
Self-confidence	3.89 (0.92)	4.31 (0.92)
Guilt/shame	2.29 (1.27)	1.73 (1.05)

Note: Scores range from 1 to 7, with high values indicating higher expectations, higher self-confidence, and more guilt and shame. Standard deviations are presented in parentheses. All means differ significantly between columns.
From Barreto et al. (2006), with permission.

and shame, which, in turn, lower self-confidence. Indeed, as in Experiment 1, participants' self-confidence suffered when they hid their identity, and this was mediated by feelings of guilt and shame. Interestingly, Experiment 2 also revealed that, despite protecting from negative partner expectations, hiding did not improve individual performance. Indeed, task performance was unaffected by the manipulation of hiding/revealing, and it was positively correlated with partner expectations when participants revealed their identity, but only positively correlated with self-confidence when participants hid their identity, suggesting that improved partner expectations when hiding do not benefit performance. In both studies, we also varied whether or not the alleged interaction partner shared the group membership of the participant, but this factor did not interact with hiding versus revealing to predict any of the dependent measures—its only effect was that participants perceived the outgroup partner to have lower expectations of them than the ingroup partner, irrespective of whether they hid or revealed their identity.

Thus, despite expectations to the contrary, hiding a stigmatized identity can actually have negative effects. One might wonder whether these negative effects are absent when the need to hide the identity is greater, such as when one feels that revealing might make one vulnerable to specific threats. However, somewhat paradoxically, research shows that psychological distress is greater when individuals expect that revealing might be more consequential—even though this is exactly when hiding is more protective, it is also when individuals are more worried about being exposed (Quinn & Chaudoir, 2009). Also, greater psychological distress occurs when the concealed identity is more important to the self, as well as when it is more salient in the social environment (Quinn & Chaudoir, 2009).

These affective costs emerge from the increased salience of the stigmatized identity, when concealed, as well as from the inadequacy felt concerning the act of deceit involved in identity concealment. In addition, feelings of depression can emerge due to a cognitive separation between the private and the public self, elicited by the frequent adaptation of self-presentation to what is deemed acceptable in each context (Sedlovskaya et al., 2013). Finally, psychological distress among individuals with concealable stigmas might be worsened due to difficulties in accessing social support from similar others (Frable, Pratt, & Hoey, 1998), which further increases their sense of isolation and difference (Frable, 1993).

Identity concealment can also negatively affect physical health. Even though concealment might protect the physical health of those individuals who are particularly vulnerable to social rejection (Cole et al., 1997), it has detrimental health effects on others (Cole, Kemeny, Taylor, & Visscher, 1996). Furthermore, concealment has indirect negative health effects by making it harder to access valuable resources such as health care and social support (Chesney & Smith, 1999; Link et al., 1991; Major, Richards, Cooper, Cozzareli, & Zubek, 1998). For example, to ensure that their identity remains secret, a considerable percentage of individuals with mental health problems do not seek help—or, when they do, fail to comply with treatment prescriptions if doing so might risk outing their problem (Corrigan, 2004).

Taken together, the evidence reviewed in this section clarifies that individuals with concealable social stigmas contend with a series of predicaments that create psychological distress and damage their physical health. The question remains as to whether these costs are worth enduring. Because identity concealment primarily addresses the problem of social rejection, the answer to this question would seem to hinge on whether identity concealment successfully increases the social acceptance of individuals with a social stigma.

3.2 The Myth of Social Acceptance Through Identity Concealment

When individuals choose to hide a stigmatized identity, they tend to do so to increase the likelihood that they are accepted by others (Newheiser & Barreto, 2014, Experiments 1a and 1b). Indeed, social acceptance often hinges on initial impressions, which are colored by preexisting prejudices and expectations (Fiske & Taylor, 2013). These prejudices may even prevent interactions from taking place, such as when people avoid interacting with socially stigmatized individuals (Houston & Bull, 1994; Kleck & Strenta, 1980). Members of socially stigmatized groups anticipate these negative attitudes and often engage in strategies to combat them (Shelton, Richeson, & Salvatore, 2005), such as choosing to conceal the stigmatized identity when it is concealable (Goffman, 1963; Newheiser & Barreto, 2014, Studies 1a and 1b). In this sense, concealing a social stigma has the benefit of allowing stigmatized individuals to initiate interactions with nonstigmatized others that might otherwise not have been possible. Once members of stigmatized and nonstigmatized groups interact, however, social acceptance will depend on how they behave toward one another. At this stage, identity concealment may become problematic.

Identity concealment can damage social interactions for at least two reasons. First, it is accompanied by concerns about being exposed as untruthful (Ragins, Singh, & Cornwell, 2007) and with careful monitoring of one's behavior to avoid being "found out" (Frable et al., 1990). This motivates individuals to limit the amount of information they offer about themselves, so as not to risk revealing information that unmasks their deceit. This is damaging to social interactions because lack of self-disclosure is associated with awkward social interactions (Herek, 1996), and self-disclosure is critical for the development of intimacy in social relationships (e.g., Collins & Miller, 1994). Second, the act of deceit involved in identity concealment restricts the extent to which one experiences a sense of authenticity, or of being true to oneself (Major & Gramzow, 1999; Wood, Linley, Maltby, Baliousis, & Joseph, 2008). Indeed, identity concealment compromises one's self-image as moral (Barreto et al., 2006), and because morality plays a crucial role in self-definition (Schwartz, 1992; Van Lange & Sedikides, 1998), concealing a stigmatized identity is an obstacle to one's sense of authenticity.

To examine this reasoning, we carried out two experiments in which participants underwent a social interaction with a nonstigmatized individual while either hiding or revealing their stigmatized identity (Newheiser & Barreto, 2014, Experiments 2 and 3). First, we aimed to demonstrate that hiding a stigmatized identity from an interaction partner has negative social consequences and that this happens, in part, because hiding one's identity limits one's sense of authenticity and degree of self-disclosure. Participants were university students who were randomly assigned to either hide or reveal an identity that was experimentally devalued (i.e., a study major described as contextually low status). Participants were told that they would interact with another participant, and that they would be randomly assigned to the role of interviewer or interviewee. In reality, all participants performed the role of interviewee and interacted with a confederate (blind to the study design and hypotheses) who performed the role of interviewer. Participants were told that their alleged interaction partner had stated a preference to interact with a medical student (of the participants' age and gender) and ranked the participants' study major as the second-to-least preferred. As in Barreto et al. (2006), participants then received the suggestion that they should hide or reveal their identity during the interaction and were asked to express agreement with this suggest before proceeding.

Prior to the interaction, we measured the extent to which participants felt a sense of authenticity (e.g., "I worry that during the interaction I won't be able to be myself") and acceptance (e.g., "At this moment, I feel accepted"). The interaction was video recorded and subsequently coded by independent observers, who were blind to the study's design and hypotheses and unaware that the participant possessed a contextually devalued identity. Observers coded the extent to which the participant disclosed information about themselves (not limited to information about the devalued identity), evaluated the interaction (e.g., "overall, this interaction seemed pleasant"), and gave their opinion about the participant (e.g., "to what extent would you like to meet the participant?"). After making these ratings, external observers also measured the duration of the interaction and how long the participant and the confederate talked during the interaction.

As displayed in Table 4, results showed that participants who hid a stigmatized identity during the interaction reported greater authenticity concerns and a lower sense of acceptance than participants who revealed a stigmatized identity. We also observed that authenticity concerns mediated the effect of hiding versus revealing on participants' sense of acceptance. Thus, although revealing a stigmatized identity is expected to reduce social acceptance, our results indicate that, instead, individuals *feel less accepted* when they hide than when they reveal a stigmatized identity, due to authenticity concerns.

We subsequently examined the impact that hiding or revealing a social stigma might have for the actual social interaction. Interactions were significantly shorter when participants hid their identity than when they revealed their identity (see Table 4). Participants also talked less when they hid than when they revealed their identity, but confederates talked a similar amount

Table 4 Participant and Observer Ratings as a Function of Hiding Versus Revealing a Stigmatized Identity

	Hide	Reveal
Participants' ratings		
Expected authenticity	4.28 (1.59)	2.39 (1.12)
Expected acceptance	4.02 (0.97)	4.72 (1.08)
Observers' ratings		
Self-disclosure	3.35 (0.81)	3.96 (1.32)
Evaluation of participant	4.16 (0.69)	4.57 (0.90)
Evaluation of interaction	4.04 (0.76)	4.48 (0.78)
Duration of interaction	172 s (51 s)	212 s (81 s)
Participant talk time	68 s (44 s)	104 s (72 s)

Note. Scores range from 1 to 7, with high values indicating higher authenticity, acceptance, and more positive observer ratings, with the exception of time measurements, which are made in seconds. Standard deviations are presented in parentheses. All means differ significantly between columns, with the exception of evaluation of participant, for which means are marginally significantly different.
From Newheiser and Barreto (2014), Experiment 2, with permission.

across both conditions (an average of 51 s, SD = 10 s). The total interaction time was almost perfectly correlated with the amount of time participants talked, but not significantly correlated with the amount of time confederates talked ($r(46) = 0.99$, $p < 0.001$). That is, consistent with the idea that hiding a stigmatized identity curbs self-disclosure, participants who hid their identity talked less during the interaction, and this led to shorter interactions, compared to participants who revealed their identity.

Observers also rated participants who were hiding their identity as disclosing less about themselves than participants who revealed their identity. In addition, observers had a (marginally significant) less positive impression of participants who hid their identity, compared to participants who revealed, and a less positive impression of the interactions involving participants who were hiding their identity than of the interactions involving participants who revealed their stigmatized identity. In addition, observers' ratings of participants' self-disclosure mediated their impression of the participant and their impression of the interaction (see Figure 3). In sum, ironically, although individuals hide stigmatized identities to increase their feelings of belonging and the extent to which they are actually accepted, our results show that participants who hid their identity not only experienced a weaker

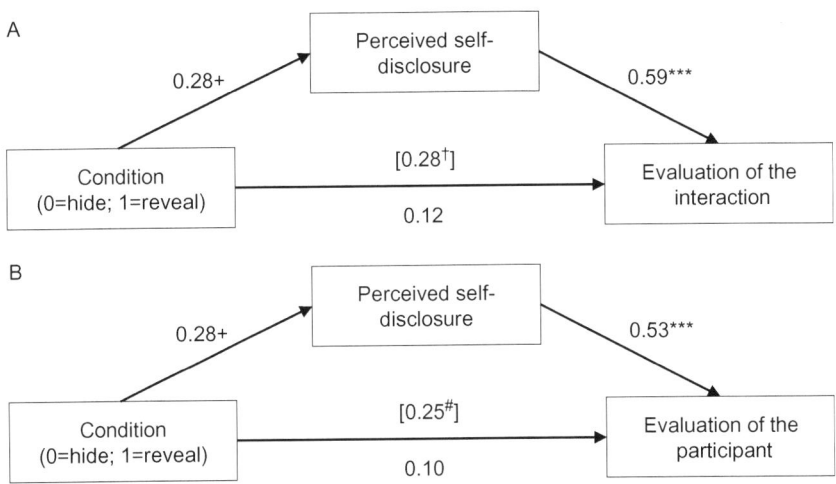

Figure 3 The effect of hiding versus revealing a contextually stigmatized identity during a social interaction on external observers' evaluations of (A) the interaction and (B) the participant, mediated by perceived self-disclosure. Standardized coefficients: $^{\#}p = 0.085$, $^{\dagger}p = 0.056$, $^{+}p = 0.057$, $^{***}p < 0.001$. *From Newheiser and Barreto (2014), Experiment 2, with permission.*

sense of belonging, but were also less positively evaluated, talked less, and had less positive interactions than participants who revealed their identity.

A subsequent study examined these processes with a culturally devalued identity: a history of mental illness (Newheiser & Barreto, 2014, Experiment 3). Revealing a history of mental illness is highly threatening and severely stigmatizing (Link, 1987; Sibicky & Dovidio, 1986). As such, it is possible that hiding is a more effective strategy in social interactions involving this identity than we have so far revealed for experimentally created stigmas, although research showing that the severity of the expected consequences of revealing does not reduce the negative effects of hiding led us to expect similar effects to those we obtained with experimental stigmas. In addition, this time, in line with the idea that the dynamics of interpersonal interactions cannot be fully understood without taking into account the interdependent perspectives of all interaction partners, we focused on the interaction partners' perceptions of the social interaction, rather than on the impressions of external observers. We employed a similar method as in the prior study, but whereas Experiment 2 used confederates as interaction partners (guaranteeing that interaction partners behaved in a standardized manner across conditions), we now examined face-to-face interactions between a nonstigmatized and a stigmatized participant (and, consequently, analyses treat dyads as the unit of analysis). The stigmatized participant either hid or revealed their identity, whereas nonstigmatized participants did not receive such instructions. We sought to examine whether hiding would limit stigmatized participants' feelings of authenticity and whether this would, in turn, impair their partner's interaction experience. Authenticity was, this time, measured after the interaction, and the partner's experience of the interaction was gauged by assessing the extent to which the nonstigmatized partner experienced intimacy with their stigmatized partner during the interaction.

As in the prior studies (Newheiser & Barreto, 2014, Experiments 1a and 1b), stigmatized participants revealed more negative expectations about the interaction when they expected to reveal than when they expected to hide their identity. However, in line with Experiment 2, stigmatized participants felt less authentic during the interaction when they hid, rather than revealed, their identity. As expected, nonstigmatized participants felt equally authentic across conditions. When it came to experiences of intimacy and adjusting for both participants' negative expectations and authenticity concerns— since these worked in opposite directions across the two conditions— nonstigmatized participants experienced less intimacy with their partner during the interaction when their stigmatized partner hid, rather than revealed, their identity (see Figure 4). Intimacy did not vary across conditions for stigmatized participants.

This research suggests that hiding a stigmatized social identity can lead those who hide to behave in ways that prevent them from reaping its potential to secure social inclusion. The question becomes whether there are circumstances under which hiding a stigmatized identity is less detrimental to social interactions. We examined this possibility in an experimental study in which participants without a social stigma interacted with stigmatized participants who hid their stigmatized identity in different ways (Newheiser, Barreto, Ellemers, Derks, & Scheepers, in press).

Hiding a stigmatized identity involves both preventing exposure as stigmatized and promoting a more positive image of oneself (Goffman, 1963). When seeking to hide a stigmatized identity, one may focus primarily on either of these aspects of concealment (Barreto & Ellemers, 2003, 2009; Shih, Young, & Bucher, 2013). The costs of concealment appear to be particularly related to efforts to prevent exposure, raising the question of whether those who hide can incur less negative effects of hiding stigma by focusing on the act of positive self-presentation. A focus on preventing exposure seems akin to a prevention focus, as theorized by regulatory focus

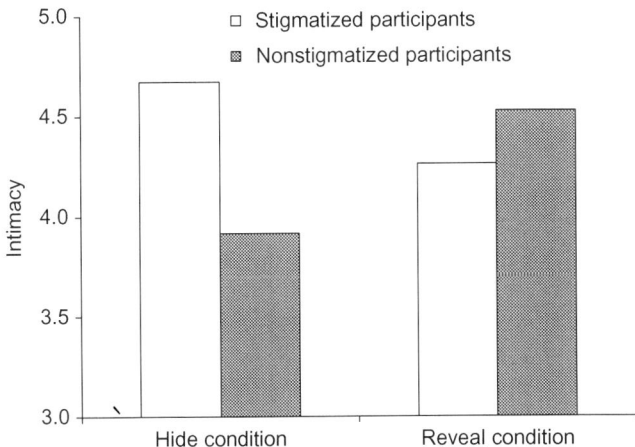

Figure 4 The effect of a stigmatized interaction partner's hiding versus revealing their stigmatized identity on stigmatized and nonstigmatized participants' intimacy with their interaction partner, adjusting for participants' negative expectations prior to and authenticity during the interaction. Scale range: 1–7; higher scores indicate more intimacy. *From Newheiser and Barreto (2014), Experiment 3, with permission.*

theory (Higgins, 1997, 1998), under which people primarily seek to secure the absence of negative outcomes. By contrast, a focus on promoting a more positive image of oneself is similar to a promotion focus, under which people primarily seek to secure the presence of positive outcomes. Framing social relationships in prevention or promotion terms can affect social perfor-mance. For example, social performance is enhanced when relationships are viewed as opportunities (akin to promotion focus) rather than risks (akin to prevention focus; Anthony, Wood, & Holmes, 2007). We examined whether framing social interactions as opportunities rather than risks can improve the social performance of individuals who conceal a stigmatized identity (Newheiser et al., in press). That is, individuals who conceal a devalued identity may typically focus on preventing exposure as stigmatized, a possibility that may help explain why concealment might impair intimacy-building during social interactions (Newheiser & Barreto, 2014). However, promotion focus may alleviate the negative interpersonal consequences of hiding a devalued identity, because it allows one to concentrate on the opportunities the interaction provides to attain positive outcomes (Higgins, 1997; see also Miller & Myers, 1998).

To examine this, we recruited participants for a study on analytical per-formance in dyads. We experimentally manipulated stigma by providing bogus information about the analytical abilities of students of the same study major as the participant: stigmatized participants were described as the second-to-worst performers, while nonstigmatized participants were described as the second-to-best. In addition, we again told stigmatized participants that their partner had stated a preference to work with students of other majors and had indicated the participants' own study major as their second-to-last preference. At this point, stigmatized participants received the suggestion that they hide their identity and were randomly assigned to a prevention focus, promotion focus, or control condition. Instructions in the Prevention and Promotion Focus conditions first stated that because students from participants' own discipline do not perform well on the analytical task, their partner might have low expectations about their performance. This statement was included to explain the purpose of concealing the devalued identity (i.e., to reduce these negative expectations).

In the Prevention Focus condition ($N=20$ dyads), stigmatized participants received the following information: "To prevent your partner from having low expectations for you and to prevent your interaction from not being optimal, it is important that you avoid making a negative impression on your partner. To achieve this, we suggest that you avoid revealing your study major when you talk with your partner and that you conceal information that may result in a negative impression. This way you can prevent your partner from thinking negatively about you, and can conceal the fact that you are a [stigmatized discipline] student." Each sentence was focused on precluding the negative outcome (a hallmark of prevention focus) of revealing the identity. In the Promotion Focus condition ($N=23$ dyads), instead, the focus was on achieving the positive outcome of hiding the identity (positive expectations, a positive impression), in line with promotion goals. In the Control condition ($N=20$ dyads), we did not explicitly mention negative expectations in order not to strengthen the prevention focus that may be induced by stigma (Oyserman, Uskul, Yoder, Nesse, & Williams, 2007). Instead, in the Control condition, stigmatized participants read: "Given previous research showing that students from your discipline do not perform well on this task, your partner may have certain expectations regarding your performance. In order to take those expectations and their possible effects into account, we suggest that you do not reveal your study major but rather conceal it while talking with your partner." Thus, in the control condition, neither positive nor negative outcomes were emphasized.

Importantly, nonstigmatized participants did not receive instructions about regulatory focus or their own identities. At this point, dyads composed of one stigmatized and one nonstigmatized participant were brought together in a separate room to get acquainted with one another. Interactions were unstructured, could focus on any topic and last as long as participants wanted, and were videotaped. Participants tended to discuss topics one would expect from previously unacquainted students (e.g., student life, hobbies). Interaction duration did not vary across conditions and lasted on average around 6 min.

After the interaction, both stigmatized and nonstigmatized participants indicated their perceived interaction positivity (e.g., "The interaction was awkward"). Videotaped interactions were coded by external observers blind to the study design and hypotheses. Separate cameras were focused on each of the dyad members, and they were coded individually. We assessed the extent to which participants appeared to be hiding information (e.g., "To what extent did the participant seem to be hiding information?"), as well as participants' perceived engagement with the interaction (e.g., "To what extent did the participant seem engaged in the conversation?").

Analyses were again conducted with dyad as the unit of analysis. Results showed that regulatory focus did not affect stigmatized participants' ratings of interaction positivity, but they did affect nonstigmatized participants' judgments. Nonstigmatized participants rated the interaction as more positive in the promotion focus condition than in the prevention or control conditions (Table 5, top panel). External observers rated stigmatized participants as hiding more information than nonstigmatized participants and stigmatized participants as hiding less information in the promotion than in the prevention or control conditions (Table 5, bottom panel). Finally, all participants—that is, both stigmatized and nonstigmatized participants—were judged as more engaged in the interaction when the stigmatized participant had received promotion rather than prevention or control instructions.

In sum, stigmatized individuals who hide their identity can show enhanced social performance if they approach social interactions with a promotion focus (i.e., as an opportunity to make a positive impression) rather than a prevention focus (i.e., as a risk of exposure). More research is needed to provide evidence for the precise mechanisms underlying these processes, as well as to identify further conditions under which socially stigmatized individuals who feel the need to hide their identity might do so without the costs typically associated with this strategy.

Table 5 Positivity of the Interaction (Rated by Participants) and Perceived Extend of Hiding (Rated by Observers) as a Function of Regulatory Focus

Positivity of the Interaction (Participants)		*M* (SD)
Stigmatized participants	Promotion condition	4.22 (1.42)
	Prevention condition	4.48 (1.31)
	Control condition	4.69 (1.25)
Nonstigmatized participants	Promotion condition	4.90[a] (1.35)
	Prevention condition	4.37[b] (1.59)
	Control condition	3.99[b] (1.24)
Extent of Hiding Information (Observers)		*M* (SD)
Stigmatized participants	Promotion condition	2.94[b] (0.99)
	Prevention condition	3.43[a] (0.95)
	Control condition	3.66[a] (1.03)
Nonstigmatized participants	Promotion condition	2.64[b] (0.81)
	Prevention condition	2.78[b] (1.07)
	Control condition	2.50[b] (0.63)

Note. Scores range from 1 to 7, with high values indicating more positivity and more perceived hiding of information. Standard deviations are presented in parentheses. Within each measure, means with different subscripts differ at $p < 0.05$.
Adapted from Newheiser et al. (in press).

3.3 Conclusions

Concealable stigmas are problematic in many ways. Although concealable stigmas allow individuals to control when they reveal their stigma to others, this choice is often made on the basis of false expectations. Individuals with a stigmatized identity expect that concealing their identity will protect their well-being and promote positive relationships with others, but evidence suggests that this is not the case. It would appear important both to continue creating contexts where stigmatized individuals feel comfortable revealing their identity and to continue developing our understanding of when hiding might be associated with the benefits that it is expected to have.

4. IS INDIVIDUAL SUCCESS HELPFUL OR HARMFUL FOR THE DISADVANTAGED GROUP?

Individual success among members of groups that are otherwise disadvantaged is often perceived as incompatible with group loyalty. For example, members of disadvantaged groups often perceive other ingroup members who attain economic success and gain residence in more privileged areas as disloyal to the group (Postmes & Branscombe, 2002). This is problematic because disadvantaged groups have much to gain from their more successful group members. Indeed, the success of members of disadvantaged groups can, in itself, disconfirm negative stereotypes and expectations about the disadvantaged group, thereby contributing to the improvement of the group's status in the eyes of outgroup (Hewstone, 1989) and ingroup members (Dasgupta & Asgari, 2004). In addition, successful members of disadvantaged groups can function as powerful role models and mentors to other members of the disadvantaged group who also seek success, improving their aspirations and performance in domains where they are typically negatively stereotyped (Lockwood & Kunda, 1997; Marx & Roman, 2002).

However, this potential for successful members of disadvantaged groups to benefit their group is often not realized. First, instead of their success disproving negative stereotypes and expectations, successful group members are often subtyped by observers as unrepresentative of the group, which contributes to stereotype maintenance (see Richards & Hewstone, 2001 for a review). In addition, the potential of successful members of the disadvantaged group to function as role models is likely to be thwarted when they are perceived as disloyal to the group, because this creates psychological distance between more and less successful group members, which inhibits being a role model or a mentor (Postmes & Branscombe, 2002). The sections that follow elaborate on these and other conditions under which disadvantaged groups are (un)likely to benefit from the individual success of their members.

4.1 Coping with Multiple Identities

When members of disadvantaged groups pursue individual success, they often encounter the problem that self-preferred identities do not necessarily align with the way one is viewed by others (Barreto & Ellemers, 2003; Ellemers & Jetten, 2013). Because success is relatively infrequent among members of disadvantaged groups, successful individuals who belong to disadvantaged groups often constitute a numerical minority, among a majority of individuals who represent a more advantaged group (Kanter, 1977). This renders their disadvantaged group membership (if visible) highly salient to others (Fiske & Taylor, 2013), even if this is not necessarily how they prefer to see themselves in this context. The resulting discrepancy between preferred self-views and treatment by others is a potential source of tension and distress (Barreto & Ellemers, 2003). This is the case, for instance, when members of disadvantaged groups enter domains where they are underrepresented (e.g., women in managerial positions): although their identity as a member of the disadvantaged group may be salient to others (e.g., gender), their own sense of identity might, instead, be more strongly based on belongingness to the group they have newly entered (e.g., manager).

One way to resolve this state of affairs is to try to bring in line external treatment with preferred self-views. For instance, successful members of disadvantaged groups may lower their identification with the disadvantaged group (Ellemers, 1993) or seek other ways to affirm their preferred identity if it is not recognized by others (Barreto & Ellemers, 2002). They may do this is by publicly favoring the desired group to demonstrate one's suitability as a proper group member (Noel, Wann, & Branscombe, 1995; see also Ellemers & Jetten, 2013). Unfortunately, such displays of bias in favor of the aspired group are easily interpreted as signs of disloyalty to the group of origin (Van Laar, Bleeker, Ellemers, & Meijer, 2014). Thus, when trying to succeed against the odds, individuals are placed in a double bind. They must emphasize how they are different from other members of their group to overcome bias and realize their personal ambitions. However, by doing this, they easily forfeit the support of others like them, instead of being seen as leading the way (Ellemers et al., 2012).

After having succeeded to achieve their desired position, members of the disadvantaged group find themselves in a minority position, which not only curbs their opportunities for further development but also limits the likelihood that they are seen as attractive role models. First, this minority position enhances the discrepancy between internal and externally imposed identities as outlined above, which can be damaging to self-views (Barreto, Ellemers, Scholten, et al., 2010). In addition, the perceptual salience associated with being in a numerical minority activates social stereotypes associated with the minority group (Inzlicht & Ben-Zeev, 2000). Although these stereotypes may not refer to the category that is most important for the successful individual, the awareness that these stereotypes are salient to others is sufficient to impair individual performance (Derks et al., 2009; Steele & Aronson, 1995; see Schmader, Hall, & Croft, 2014 for a recent review). Additionally, the high status positions offered to members of disadvantaged groups tend to offer less favorable conditions, making failure more likely, as has been extensively documented for women in leadership positions (Ellemers et al., 2012). At the same time, the salience of their minority status makes any performance deficiencies highly visible. Because the effectiveness of role models for improving aspirations and performance of disadvantaged individuals relies on their visible success, this constitutes a significant obstacle to the extent to which they can be helpful to the group.

Another obstacle to the extent to which successful members of a disadvantaged group can benefit their group is that individuals who are personally successful—when their group is not—often fail to perceive discrimination against their group as a whole (Stroebe et al., 2009; see also Derks, Ellemers, Van Laar, & de Groot, 2011). Because the self-relevance of a particular outcome is crucial in motivating the search for information that might uncover discriminatory treatment (Stroebe et al., 2010), if individuals are not personally rejected, they can easily remain unaware that others in their group are targets of discrimination, which constitutes an additional reason why they may fail to display solidarity toward less fortunate group members.

4.2 Achieving Success Against the Odds

Individual success is often seen as a first step—or even the royal road—toward broader change in relations between social groups (Duguid, 2011). However, there is by now overwhelming evidence that such change will not be realized as long as broader group-based expectations remain in place (for an overview, see Ellemers et al., 2012). As long as individual successes are regarded (also by those who succeed) as exceptions to stereotypical expectations, they will tend to legitimate and stabilize existing differences between groups, instead of changing them. This has been examined quite extensively among women aiming to achieve career success in male-dominated work contexts. For instance, Ellemers, Van den Heuvel, De Gilder, Maass, and Bonvini (2004) examined this by comparing self-reported career ambitions of junior male and female academics (PhD students), with the way they were perceived by more senior male and female faculty (full professors). Results obtained in the Netherlands and Italy consistently revealed no reliable differences in self-reported career commitment, nor were objective differences visible in the academic performance of male and female PhD students. If anything, female postgraduate students tended to report being more committed to their career than male students; this difference was not significant in Study 1 (the Netherlands), but was statistically reliable in Study 2 (Italy). Male faculty members accordingly perceived male and female PhD students to be equally committed to advancement in their academic careers. However, perceptions of female professors revealed that they judged female PhD students to be significantly less committed to their career than male students. Thus, female faculty members were most inclined to underestimate the career ambitions of more junior academics. Whereas this so-called Queen Bee effect has been cited as indicating that women are to blame for holding back other women (Sheppard & Aquino, 2013), Ellemers et al. (2004) conducted additional analyses which established that the tendency of senior academics to underestimate the ambitions of more junior scholars did not represent such a generic tendency. When distinguishing between different age cohorts, it became evident that the Queen Bee response was most clearly visible among the older generation of female professors. These were the individuals who were most likely to have encountered gender bias in their own careers and who presented themselves as different from other women to overcome this.

Further research among senior women in a range of different organizations confirmed that the tendency to distance the self from other members of one's group is used as a strategy to achieve individual success when encountering prejudicial expectations (Derks, Ellemers, et al., 2011), in particular by those who do not see their gender identity as relevant in a professional context. Women who reported low gender identification at the start of their career and encountered gender discrimination during their career described themselves in highly masculine terms. The discrepancy between their self-views and the discriminatory treatment they received also caused them to emphasize differences between themselves and other women and to endorse stereotypical views of those other women. This pattern was not observed for low gender-identified women who had not encountered gender discrimination in their careers, nor for women who reported high gender identification, regardless of their own career experiences (Derks, Ellemers, et al., 2011).

A follow-up study, in which senior women in the police were induced to consider career experiences in which they had experienced gender bias or to consider how they had been evaluated in terms of their personal qualifications, revealed converging results (Derks, Van Laar, Ellemers, & De Groot, 2011). That is, when senior police women who were disinclined to identity with their gender group were prompted to consider their experiences with gender bias, they indicated highly masculine self-descriptions, engaged in ingroup distancing, and indicated gender discrimination was no longer a problem. When low gender-identified women considered their experiences with being evaluated in terms of their personal qualifications, they did not display these "Queen Bee" responses. Senior police women who were strongly gender identified responded differently when prompted to think of their experiences with gender bias. This made them more inclined to endorse equal opportunity programs in the police force and increased their willingness to make an effort to help other women advance (Derks, Van Laar, et al., 2011). Thus, this research again confirms that "Queen Bee" responses do not represent a generic inclination of women being competitive toward each other. Instead, it is a consequence of the self-group distancing strategy followed by women who are disinclined to identify with their gender group, yet are treated on the basis of their gender at work. In other words, past experiences with gender discrimination caused these women to emphasize their own ambitions and commitment to their career as a way to convince others they should not just be considered as representatives of their gender group. As a by-effect of the way they coped with the gender bias they encountered, these women simultaneously considered junior women to be relatively less motivated and ambitious (Derks, Van Laar, et al., 2011).

Thus, the tendency of successful individuals to distance the self from other group members reflects the discrepancy between preferred self-views and treatment by others and stems from attempts to individually escape group-based discrimination, in order to succeed against the odds. Indeed, similar self-distancing responses to cope with negative group-based expectations were observed among Hindustani workers in the Netherlands. When individuals who reported low ethnic identification were confronted with ethnic bias at work, they were more inclined to self-present in terms of stereotypically Dutch features and reported negative affect toward other members of their group (Derks, Van Laar, Ellemers, & Raghoe, 2014).

4.3 Becoming a Mentor or Role Model

Taken together, this evidence suggests that successful members of disadvantaged groups often fail to benefit their group, despite their potential to do so. First, their minority position in the advantaged group makes it more difficult for them to demonstrate their ability to perform well. Additionally, their desire to overcome any prejudice they encounter causes them to distance themselves from other group members and to underestimate their fellow members' potential instead of helping them advance. Finally, their own successes make it less likely that either they or those around them realize that other members of their group continue to suffer disadvantage. For all these reasons, success often remains associated with the advantaged group, perpetuating social inequalities.

Importantly, however, individual success is not *necessarily* accompanied by dis-identification and disaffection from the group. Indeed, individual success is not the same as individual mobility, as conceptualized within social identity theory (Tajfel & Turner, 1979). Whereas individual mobility necessarily involves psychological distancing from the ingroup, members of disadvantaged groups can be individually successful while remaining psychologically committed to their group. Research suggests that when this happens, individual success can indeed be beneficial for the disadvantaged group. Specifically, individuals who are successful but remain highly identified with their group show strong ingroup loyalty (Derks, Ellemers, et al., 2011; Derks, Van Laar, et al., 2011). Importantly, successful individuals are less likely to dis-identify with their group when their new social environment values the areas in which their group excels (Van Laar et al., 2010). This is the case, for instance, when ethnic minority representatives are recruited by companies who wish to cater to a more diverse group of clients, or when women are sought out for leadership positions because of their social–emotional skills. Even though the drawback of such developments is that stereotypical expectations of the group's characteristic features or abilities are maintained, the advantage is in the fact that these are now more explicitly seen as being of *value* in a professional context. As a result, in cases such as these, the success of individual group representatives can make it easier for other group members to envision ways to achieve professional success as well. Additionally, the disadvantaged group can prevent successful individuals from turning away from the group when they refrain from considering behavioral adaptations people make (e.g., in their way of speech, dress, or lifestyle) to achieve professional success as a sign of disloyalty. Indeed, when the group explicitly endorses and supports individual advancement efforts, and does not question people's sense of emotional involvement in the group when they make behavioral changes, individuals are less likely to turn away from the group, which makes it easier for others who follow to do the same (Van Laar et al., 2014). Remaining identified with the group thus seems to be an important requirement for others to regard the successful individual as a role model. Indeed, successful members of devalued groups can only function as positive role models when they are seen as characteristic for the group they represent (Asgari, Dasgupta, & Stout, 2012).

4.4 Conclusions

In sum, a range of cognitive and motivational processes may prevent successful members of disadvantaged groups from helping the disadvantaged group to improve its status, or from assisting other group members to achieve similar levels of success. Research shows that successful group members can provide this type of help, but this hinges on maintaining a strong psychological connection to the disadvantaged group. Doing so is not self-evident, as revealed by the research reviewed in this section. The challenge for future research, therefore, is to elaborate on the conditions under which this is likely to happen and investigate different ways to achieve it.

5. IS CONFRONTING PREJUDICE SOCIALLY COSTLY OR SOCIALLY BENEFICIAL?

Confronting prejudice is an assertive form of coping that involves directly addressing the source of prejudice to express displeasure at, or disagreement with, the treatment received (Shelton, Richeson, Salvatore, & Hill, 2006). Individuals confront on behalf of their group when they express their belief that a particular prejudiced view inaccurately reflects the group. Alternatively, individuals can confront on behalf of themselves alone, such as when they state that they are different from the typical ingroup member (e.g., Becker, Barreto, Kahn, & de Oliveira Laux, 2014; Garcia, Schmitt, Branscombe, & Ellemers, 2010).

Research in this area has revealed that confronting prejudice is accompanied by social costs, that is, negative evaluations by those who witness the confrontation (see Kaiser & Major, 2006 for a review). This finding is highly salient in the literature and has strongly influenced current understandings of how individuals cope with prejudice. However, these theoretical developments have paid less attention to the finding that confrontation also has clear social benefits. In this section, we aim to provide a more complete view of the social effects of confrontation by reviewing evidence for both the social costs and the social benefits of confronting prejudice, as well as the factors that modify how confrontation is evaluated.

5.1 The Infrequency of Confrontation

The idea that confrontation might have social costs was raised to explain the finding that targets of prejudice or discrimination rarely confront it (Kaiser & Major, 2006). When asked in private, or when asked to respond to a hypothetical situation, individuals often indicate that if they were to face prejudice, they would readily confront the perpetrator (Shelton & Stewart, 2004; Swim & Hyers, 1999; Woodzicka & LaFrance, 2001). However, in reality, these estimated responses are not often borne out in public behavior. A striking example is provided by Fitzgerald, Swan, and Fischer (1995), who showed that even though 65% of female participants indicated that they would confront sexism in a particular scenario, when they encountered that situation in reality, in a separate study, none of the participants confronted the sexist treatment.

Subsequent research uncovered that concerns about how others might react to confrontation—that is, the anticipated social costs of confronting—play a crucial role in motivating targets of prejudice to refrain from confronting. Indeed, targets are less likely to confront prejudice when they expect more social costs to accrue from confrontation (Shelton & Stewart, 2004), and they prefer to retaliate indirectly, rather than to directly confront (Lee, Soto, Swim, & Bernstein, 2012). Research also suggests that targets of prejudice expect different social costs from confronting in the presence of different audiences. For example, individuals make fewer attributions of the negative outcomes they receive to discrimination in front of an audience made out of members of the perpetrator's group than in front of an ingroup audience, presumably because the latter might be less likely to respond negatively to these attributions (Stangor, Van Allen, Swim, & Sechrist, 2002). People seem particularly concerned about making public attributions to discrimination for their own outcomes and are more likely to publicly attribute a negative outcome to discrimination if this outcome pertains to another individual than if it pertains to themselves (Sechrist, Swim, & Stangor, 2004). This suggests that there is something specific about making attributions to discrimination for one's own outcomes that individuals expect might render them particularly vulnerable to social sanction. As a result of these concerns about the social costs of confrontation, individuals are less likely to blame biased behavior (from specific individuals) than biased institutions or policies for negative outcomes (Sechrist & Delmar, 2006).

This research strongly suggests that individuals anticipate social costs for confronting prejudice or discrimination and that their concern about these costs helps explain why confrontation is not more prevalent. However, these findings beg the question of whether or not these concerns are justified. That is, do people really frown upon individuals who claim to be targets of discrimination or who confront perpetrators for expressing prejudice? And do these social costs vary in the ways people expect them to vary, with, for example, greater costs accruing from outgroup than from ingroup evaluations?

5.2 The Social Costs of Confrontation

Individuals who report being a target of prejudice or discrimination in the workplace often suffer interpersonal and institutional retaliation (Bergman,

Langhout, Palmieri, Cortina, & Fitzgerald, 2002; Feagin & Sikes, 1994; Fitzgerald et al., 1995; Stockdale, 1998). Experimental research has shown that those who claim to be a target of prejudice, or who confront prejudice perpetrators, are seen as oversensitive or as complainers, irrespective of the likelihood that this claim was in fact justified (e.g., Dodd, Giuliano, Boutell, & Moran, 2001; Kaiser & Miller, 2001). It thus appears that claiming to have received discriminatory treatment is indeed accompanied by social costs, as anticipated by targets.

The social costs of confrontation are more pronounced when the specific issue being confronted is subject to stronger social regulation. For example, individuals more readily confront racism than they confront sexism, reflecting the fact that social norms against racism are stronger than social norms against sexism (Czopp & Monteith, 2003; Steentjes, Kurz, Barreto, & Morton, 2014). Confrontation is also accompanied by heavier social costs when individuals confront on behalf of themselves than when they confront on behalf of others (Czopp & Monteith, 2003). This is in line with what individuals appear to expect, claiming discriminatory treatment more frequently on behalf of others than on behalf of themselves (Sechrist et al., 2004). However, not all expectations are borne out. For example, whereas confrontation is more negatively evaluated by members of the outgroup than by ingroup members (Dodd et al., 2001), as targets appear to expect, confronters can also be derogated by members of their own group (Garcia, Reser, Amo, Redersdorff, & Branscombe, 2005).

Research has also clarified why claims of discriminatory treatment are associated with social costs. Attributing a negative outcome to discrimination threatens fundamental beliefs in a just world, according to which negative outcomes should be attributed to lack of deservingness, not to unfair treatment (Kaiser, Dyrenforth, & Hagiwara, 2006). Threats to beliefs in a just world, such as discriminatory treatment, are highly aversive and actively avoided (Lerner, 1980). Individuals will do what they can to avert these threats, going so far as to blame victims, if that helps maintain the view that the world is a just place. Claiming to be a target of discrimination threatens this belief and can thus motivate derogation of the claimant (Kaiser et al., 2006). In addition, targets who claim discriminatory treatment can be seen as avoiding personal responsibility for the negative outcome they received. In contexts dominated by strong beliefs in merit, avoidance of personal responsibility is strongly sanctioned and can damage the reputation of the target and of the target's group as a whole. This might explain why individuals who attribute others' outcomes to discrimination incur fewer social costs than individuals who attribute their own outcomes to discrimination, because only the latter can be considered to be avoiding their personal responsibility for the negative outcome. This might also explain why confronters can also be derogated by members of their own group, who might endorse beliefs in a just world as much as members of the perpetrator's group (Jost, Banaji, & Nosek, 2004).

5.3 The Social Benefits of Confrontation

Since being uncovered, the social costs of confrontation documented in the research reviewed above have become well known in the field, are commonly cited, and are often used to make a variety of theoretical inferences (see Kaiser & Major, 2006 for a more detailed review). This research has been very valuable, for example, in clarifying that the fear of social costs might explain why individuals often fail to confront when they encounter prejudice. However, despite supporting evidence, less emphasis has been placed on the fact that confrontation also has important *social benefits*.

It is clear that confrontation has personal (or intrapsychic) benefits, such as increasing feelings of closure (Hyers, 2007), self-esteem (Crosby, 1993; Gervais, Hillard, & Vescio, 2010), and empowerment (Haslett & Lipman, 1997). This would appear relatively easy to integrate with the finding that confrontation has social costs, given that these costs and benefits occur on different spheres of experience. Perhaps harder to integrate, however, is evidence that confrontation also has social benefits, that is, that confrontation can have benefits in the social sphere. Two kinds of evidence demonstrate these social benefits: First, confronting prejudice seems to be an important prejudice reduction strategy, benefiting social relations between members of different groups, potentially including between the perpetrator and the target. Second, confronters are not always negatively evaluated, and even when they are negatively evaluated, this is often restricted to some specific impression domains, while at the same time they are positively evaluated in others.

Regarding the first point, it is important to stress the value of confrontation as a prejudice reduction strategy and a mechanism for social change. Confrontation can motivate perpetrators to avoid making prejudiced remarks (Czopp, Monteith, & Mark, 2006). It can elicit apologies from perpetrators, who can become motivated to compensate the victim for the prejudice expressed, which, in turn, might result in a more positive interaction than if they had not been confronted (Mallett & Wagner, 2011). In addition, whereas people tend to disapprove of those who protest against biased treatment when this is seen as rare, this is not the case when discrimination is seen as pervasive. These different perceptions of the pervasiveness of discrimination might stem from actual differences in the incidence and visibility of discriminatory treatment (e.g., of women in strongly male-dominated jobs). However, they may also reflect differences in the inclination to acknowledge and perceive that subtle and implicit displays of bias persist and represent systematic occurrences of unequal treatment (Schmitt, Ellemers, et al., 2003). Such differential awareness of the continued pervasiveness of biased treatment and systematic discrimination may stem from individual differences in past exposure to discrimination, from differences in knowledge or information availability regarding its prevalence, or from social influence attempts from others who may either emphasize or downplay the incidence of bias.

When discrimination is believed to be pervasive, confronting prejudice is seen as more appropriate and desirable than failing to protest against unfair treatment (Garcia et al., 2010). Indeed, when prejudice is confronted, it is perceived as more problematic compared to when individuals fail to clearly express their displeasure to perpetrators, causing bias to pass undetected (e.g., Henry & Meltzoff, 1998; Hunter & McClelland, 1991). Confrontation also has positive effects on others: It reduces prejudice in observers and it increases the likelihood that they will also confront, either at that same moment or in the future (Blanchard, Crandall, Brigham, & Vaughn, 1994; Rasinski & Czopp, 2010). Importantly, the prospect of prejudice reduction appears to motivate confrontation. Indeed, individuals are more likely to confront when they are optimistic that confrontation is likely to change the prejudicial views of the perpetrator (Rattan & Dweck, 2010; see also Kaiser, Major, & McCoy, 2004 for effects of general optimism).

Regarding the second point, that is, that confronters are not only or always negatively evaluated, research documenting the social costs of claiming discriminatory treatment has also specified a range of positive effects that have been less frequently acknowledged. For example, in their original work on this topic, Kaiser and Miller (2001) showed that although individuals who attributed a negative outcome to discrimination were seen as more oversensitive than individuals who attributed the negative outcome to poor performance, the former were, at the same time, also seen as more honest or true to themselves. Given the importance of morality in impression formation (Wojciszke, 2005), this might be taken to suggest that those who claim discriminatory treatment might have had a significant social benefit. In addition, Dodd et al. (2001) showed that women who confronted sexism were less liked but more respected than women who did not confront sexism. Given that respect is closely linked to social status (Fiske, Xu, Cuddy, & Glick, 1999), this again suggests that confronters may accrue significant social benefits. Importantly, recent research demonstrates that women might be aware of this trade-off between being liked and being respected when choosing whether or not to confront. Specifically, women only refrain from confronting when their goal for the specific interaction is to be liked, but they are more likely to choose to confront when their goal is, instead, to be respected (Mallett & Melchiori, 2014). Taken together, this reexamination of evidence from early work on the social costs of attributions to discrimination suggests that confrontation can be simultaneously associated with costs and benefits, and the extent to which this might constrain coping responses is likely to depend on the particular goal individuals have in a specific context.

Besides revealing simultaneous social costs and benefits of confrontation, research has also uncovered that individual and situational factors can affect how confronters are evaluated. For example, confronters are more positively evaluated by highly identified than by weakly identified ingroup members, presumably because prejudice is more self-relevant for the former, who therefore see a greater need for confrontation (Kaiser, Hagiwara, Malahy, & Wilkins, 2009). At times, group members may place so much value on ensuring that the prejudicial treatment does not pass unnoticed that they may approve of forms of confrontation that could appear particularly costly in terms of the group's reputation as oversensitive. We examined this in a study where men and women evaluated a female target who confronted sexism aggressively (expressing displeasure and slapping the perpetrator in the face) or nonaggressively (merely expressing displeasure), or who did not confront at all in a scenario participants were asked to read (Becker & Barreto, 2014). Participants were asked to what extent they perceived each reaction as threatening for men and for women (e.g., "To what extent do you think that the woman's reaction harms the image of men [women] as a group?"), their impression of the target (along warmth and competence attributes), their feelings toward the target (e.g., hostility, anger), and the extent to which they supported the target's response (e.g., "how much do you agree with the woman's reaction?"). Gender identification was assessed before participants read the scenario and again at the end of the study.

The results showed that how the female target was evaluated depended on the precise nature of her behavior, as well as on participants' gender identification. Participants indicated that nonaggressive confrontations were the

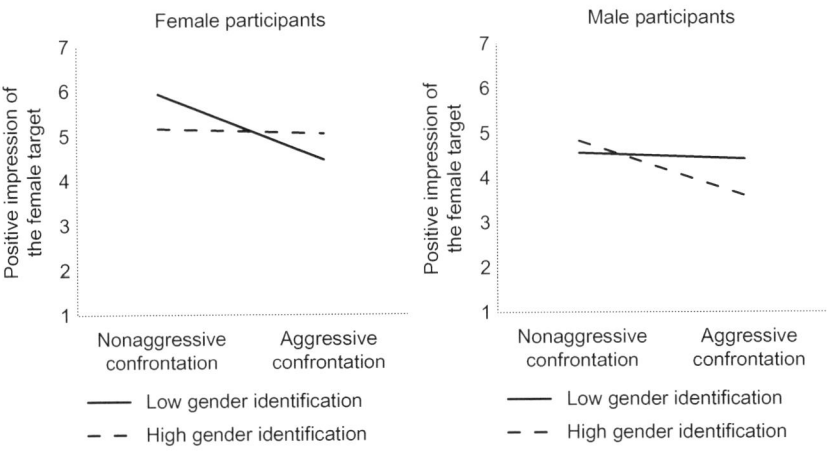

Figure 5 Positive impression of the female target as a function of her behavior among female and male participants. *Adapted from Becker and Barreto (2014), Figure 1.*

least threatening for women, with aggressive confrontation being judged as equally threatening as no confrontation—indeed, female participants revealed a tendency to perceive no confrontation as more threatening to women than aggressive confrontation. Evaluations of the target mirrored this perceived threat: overall, participants tended to evaluate the female target who confronted nonaggressively more positively than the aggressive confronter and the no confronter. However, these evaluations also largely depended on participants' gender and their gender identification (see Figure 5 for an example). For women, weak identifiers showed generally more negative responses toward the female target who confronted aggressively than toward the target who responded nonaggressively, whereas high identifiers tended not to differentiate between these two targets. For men, on the other hand, it was high identifiers who differentiated between the aggressive and the nonaggressive confronters, showing greater negativity toward the former.

Results also revealed that reading about an ingroup member who confronted sexism aggressively led weakly identified women to further distance themselves from the group, relative to when they read about a nonaggressive target, whereas highly identified women maintained their level of identification irrespective of the target's reaction (see Figure 6). Men did not show such a tendency—although, interestingly, there was a nonsignificant tendency for weakly identified men to increase their gender identification when

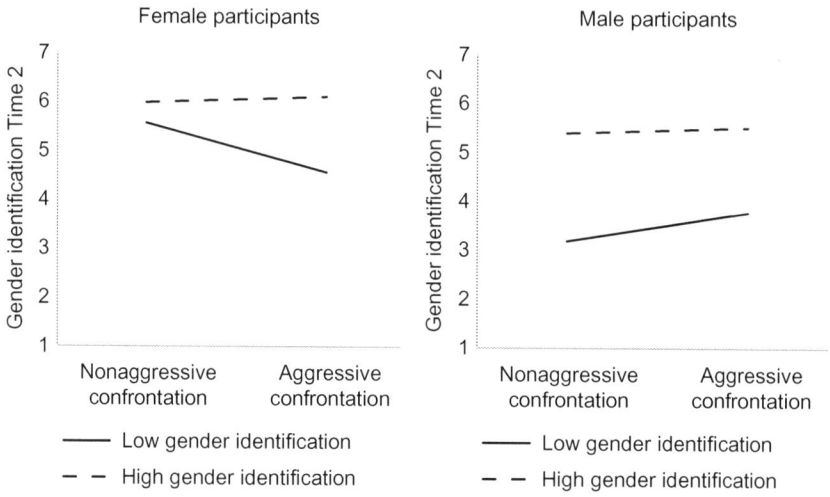

Figure 6 Gender identification at Time 2 as a function of the target's behavior among female and male participants. *Adapted from Becker and Barreto (2014), Figure 2.*

reading about a female target who confronted a male sexist perpetrator aggressively. In sum, this study shows that whether confronters incur social costs depends on the precise nature of their confrontation and the extent to which their audience identifies with the group targeted by prejudice. The study also stresses that confrontation can be costly for the group too, if it alienates its less identified members and mobilizes weakly identified outgroup members.

Ingroup members are particularly positive about ingroup confronters when they believe that discrimination against their group is pervasive, relative to when they believe that discrimination is rare (Garcia et al., 2010; Kahn, Barreto, Kaiser, & Rego, in press). This was examined in a study by Garcia et al. (2010), assessing how people who differed in the extent to which they thought gender discrimination was pervasive evaluated a female lawyer who was passed over for promotion at her law firm, despite being clearly better qualified than her male contestant. Research participants were asked to respond to different scenarios, one in which the female lawyer complained that her superior individual qualifications had not been taken into account, one in which she complained that the law firm did not fairly consider the abilities of women, and one in which she indicated disagreement with the outcome but decided not to complain. Research participants received one of these three scenarios and were asked to report their emotional responses toward the female lawyer (anger), their evaluation of her as a person, and the appropriateness of her response. They were also asked to rate the unfairness of the decision that had been made. For all these dependent variables, participants' responses to the action taken by the female lawyer depended on how pervasive they thought gender discrimination to be, despite the fact that they all considered the decision that had been made to be equally unfair and discriminatory. Specifically, those who thought of gender discrimination as being pervasive expressed most anger against the female lawyer when she decided *not* to protest the way she had been treated. Additionally, those who considered discrimination to be pervasive were more inclined to like the female lawyer when she protested against her treatment than when she refrained from doing so, and saw either form of protest as more appropriate than no protest as a response to the way she had been treated. Mediation analyses further revealed that the tendency to report anger and dislike toward the target was mediated by the perceived appropriateness of the response displayed by female lawyer, in view of the perceived pervasiveness of gender discrimination (Garcia et al., 2010). Thus, results of this study showed that individuals who considered gender discrimination to be a pervasive problem in society thought that any form of protest constitutes a more appropriate response to the treatment the female lawyer had received than no protest. Because individuals who considered discrimination to be pervasive approved of the appropriateness of protest in response to the treatment received, they refrained from expressing anger or dislike toward the complainant.

A separate set of studies replicated this pattern and demonstrated that it is reversed when confronters are evaluated by members of the perpetrator's group (Kahn et al., in press; Experiment 1). This may be because the perceived pervasiveness of sexism has very different implications for men and for women. For women, perceiving sexism as pervasive might award the motivation needed to support confrontation of what might otherwise appear to be a relatively unimportant statement or behavior that does not justify the costs that might be accrued through confrontation. For men, perceiving sexism as pervasive implies that confrontations might be encountered more frequently and that social change, if it is to occur, might be more drastic than when sexism is believed to be rare. In fact, perceiving sexism to be rare allows men to project an egalitarian image by supporting confrontations of sexism, without loss of social advantage. To examine this reasoning, we provided male and female participants with information regarding the pervasiveness of sexism (rare vs. pervasive, as in Garcia et al., 2010) and subsequently asked them to respond to a scenario of a female target who either confronted or did not confront sexism. The pattern of responses obtained for women was similar to that revealed by Garcia et al. (2010): women were more supportive of confrontation by female targets when they perceived sexism to be pervasive than when they perceived sexism to be rare. However, we found the reverse pattern for men: men were less supportive of female confronters of sexism when they were made aware of the pervasiveness of discrimination against women than when they believed that discrimination against women was rare.

A subsequent study replicated these findings and revealed that this pattern was modified when participants were initially self-affirmed (Kahn et al., in press; Experiment 2). Self-affirmation theory proposes that individuals can protect their self-image from threat by affirming an unrelated aspect of their identity (Steele, 1988; for a review, see Sherman & Cohen, 2006). As such, by examining effects of self-affirmation, it is possible to shed light on the specific threats driving participants' responses. In our study, self-affirmation affected female participants' support for confrontation only when sexism was rare. That is, women who believed sexism was rare were more supportive of confrontation when they were self-affirmed than when they were not, but their support when sexism was pervasive remained high across self-affirmation conditions. This suggests that women who were not self-affirmed experienced a threat that dampened their support in the rare conditions—possibly the threat of appearing oversensitive. Men's responses were also affected by self-affirmation only in the rare conditions, where they reported greater support for confrontation when *not* self-affirmed than when self-affirmed. Self-affirmation did not affect men's responses when they believed that sexism was pervasive—this remained relatively low in all conditions. This suggests that men who were not self-affirmed experienced a threat that heightened support in the rare conditions—possibly the threat of appearing sexist.

Internalized norms or ideologies, and their match with what is confronted, can also affect whether confrontation is positively or negatively evaluated. For example, women who score low on benevolent sexism are more likely than women high in benevolent sexism to express positive attitudes toward another woman who confronts a sexist decision (Kahn, Barreto, & Kaiser, in preparation). However, women low in benevolent sexism are actually less likely than women high in benevolent sexism to express positive attitudes toward a woman who confronts a decision supporting traditional gender roles, suggesting that evaluations of the confronter do not necessarily hinge on the assertive act of confrontation in itself, but on the specific goal of this behavior (Kahn et al., in preparation). Importantly, internalized ideologies have also been shown to motivate confrontation, which is more likely when it does not conflict with these ideologies. For example, women who endorsed traditional gender norms prescribing submission were more likely to remain silent in the face of sexist remarks (Swim, Eyssell, Quinlivan, & Ferguson, 2010).

5.4 Conclusions

Taken together, the evidence reviewed in this section clarifies that confronting prejudice can have both social costs and social benefits, sometimes simultaneously and sometimes in different contexts. It also clarifies that people appear to be reasonably aware of both the potential costs and the potential benefits of confrontation, for example, choosing to confront when they seek to be respected, but refraining from doing so when they primarily seek to be liked. This more complete analysis of the costs and benefits of confrontation therefore advances our understanding of when and why individuals are likely to confront. People appear to confront prejudice when they expect confrontation's social benefits to accrue (e.g., when they are optimistic about thereby improving the perpetrator's attitudes, Rattan & Dweck, 2010) and are more likely to do so when they perceive these benefits to be particularly important (e.g., when they perceive prejudice against their group to be pervasive, Kahn et al., in press, or self-relevant, Kaiser et al., 2009). Future research should more completely acknowledge these costs and benefits and the decision process involved when individuals consider whether or not to respond to prejudice by engaging in confrontation.

6. OVERALL CONCLUSIONS

We have reviewed work that illuminates various facets of how prejudice and discrimination are experienced in modern societies. This is an area of research that has been highly productive, with developments spanning traditional areas of enquiry as well as new areas that had been overlooked before. We therefore felt that it was now time to galvanize evidence to answer specific questions and address public or academic debates around the experience of disadvantage in modern societies. In doing so, we revisited old studies and cast their findings in a new light, such as highlighting findings that did not seem sufficiently striking to stick in our memory when they were first published, but which have become more important as our knowledge has progressed. But for the most part, we reviewed recent evidence from our labs, as well as recent work carried out by other experts in this field. Our aim was to move the field forward by identifying core answers we are now able to provide, as well as questions that remain to be answered.

This analysis has important implications for how we think about prejudice and its effects. The conclusions we draw all relate, in some way, to a central idea that modern societies are characterized by strong illusions of meritocracy, where apparent improvements often do not only hide but actually sustain social inequalities, and they do so through various processes (see also Barreto et al., 2009; Ellemers & Barreto, 2009b). Although some of these apparent improvements reflect genuine attempts at suppressing biases and might have some benefits in the short term, the evidence reviewed here suggests that they can backfire in unexpected ways or in their long-term effects.

First, we clarified that individuals tend to underestimate (rather than overestimate) the extent to which they encounter prejudice or discrimination. This is often due to lack of information needed to infer prejudicial treatment, but it can also emerge due to a range of cognitive and motivational processes that impair detection of discrimination. Beliefs in meritocracy are not only one of the core factors influencing this blindness to injustice, but are also, in turn, reinforced by the failure to detect discrimination.

Second, we showed that though blaming one's negative outcomes on discrimination may offer some protection, usually of one's sense of competence, this only occurs while individuals are able to maintain the belief that society is generally just and meritocratic. Inequalities thus remain unaddressed not only because they are undetected but also because the perception of unequal treatment may serve important psychological functions, such as the need to maintain the perilous illusion that society is perfectly meritocratic. In the long run, however, as these experiences are repeated, these beliefs are challenged. As discrimination comes to be perceived as more pervasive, it becomes most damaging to well-being, but it is also then that affective and behavioral responses start to raise the possibility of change, underlining the importance of personal experiences with discrimination in this process.

Our third focus was on the circumstances under which individual success can or cannot be helpful for a disadvantaged group. Again, the answer here is complex, but can be narrowed down to the idea that individual success can only benefit the group when it is not seen to demonstrate the legitimate and meritocratic nature of the social system. It is only when members of disadvantaged groups succeed while remaining aware of disadvantage that they can truly offer the group a helping hand and have their hand accepted by less successful members of the disadvantaged group.

We then discussed the unique problem of having a stigmatized identity that is concealable. The issue here is whether the opportunity to conceal a devalued identity offers individuals protection from the damaging effects of stigma. This is a misrepresentation held by the very individuals who use this strategy, who do so in the anticipation that it will offer them protection and ensure social acceptance. Unfortunately, this is not what evidence suggests. Even when the costs of revealing are great, individuals suffer from actively concealing a socially stigmatized identity. Thus, social stigma creates social inequalities in everyday lives, even when the stigmatized identity is not visible, and therefore in the absence of direct stigmatization. Recent research offers promising insights by identifying some circumstances under which this may be improved, but more work is needed in this area.

The final aspect we addressed was whether confrontation of prejudice is uniquely associated with social costs and, if not, why exactly confrontation remains so rare. The evidence here clarifies that confrontation is associated both with social costs and with social benefits, along slightly different domains, and that whether individuals choose to confront or not depends on the goals they prioritize in any given interaction (e.g., to be liked vs. to be respected). Future research might wish to elaborate on this finding to understand why confrontation tends to be so rare, despite its benefits and the importance of perceived competence and respect in modern societies. An intriguing possibility is that members of disadvantaged groups, who tend to be stereotyped as relatively incompetent but warm (Fiske, Cuddy, Glick, & Xu, 2002), might find it difficult to behave in ways that jeopardize positive evaluation in the very dimension in which they are seen as superior (i.e., warmth), even when this might function so as to enhance their social status by eliciting competence judgments.

Although this review was structured around separate questions, which were answered on the basis of different studies, some recurring themes emerge. The importance of beliefs in merit in exacerbating the negative effects of discrimination is a central theme, as already mentioned, and these beliefs are stronger when prejudice is subtle, when it is perceived as rare, and when group inequalities are perceived to be entirely justified. By contrast, perceiving discrimination has beneficial effects when individuals engage in a group-level analysis of the treatment they have received, thereby resorting to the group as a resource, when power holders (including members of the advantaged group) acknowledge discrimination, and when the contribution of each group is recognized, such as when a diversity climate is encouraged. Paradoxically, however, diversity measures can promote beliefs in meritocracy, by leading individuals and organizations to assume that group membership cannot continue to affect how individuals are treated (Kaiser et al., 2013). More research is needed, therefore, to specify how these assumptions can be curtailed in environments where diversity is encouraged and valued.

Aside from contributing to theory and research by advancing knowledge on the perception and experience of social disadvantage, our analysis has some practical implications. The finding that many discriminatory experiences remain undetected, even by targets themselves, further underlines the need to develop better procedures to monitor discrimination and its effects. Indeed, societal and organizational statistics regarding the prevalence of discrimination tend to rely on self-reports by targets themselves that do not take into account what scientific evidence suggests about detection of discrimination. Broad-scale social surveys, as well as smaller-scale workplace surveys, strongly underestimate discriminatory experiences by using old-fashioned measures of blatant prejudice or discrimination that require individuals to label their experiences as discriminatory, even though this can be done only in a minority of cases. In other cases, surveys ask participants to indicate the extent to which they feel they are treated differently from their peers, neglecting the fact that to respond to this question, individuals need to have access to information they often do not have. Although more sensitive measures have been developed (e.g., for sexual harassment, see Fitzgerald et al., 1995), they are rarely used in these broader contexts. More evidence-based procedures need to be encouraged, and it is the role of experts in this area to mobilize nonacademics to develop and implement such practices.

Given the multiple and ever-changing ways in which "difference" is expressed and experienced, it would also seem important to remain attentive to narratives of experiences, as well as to monitor broad patterns and distributions at a level in which aggregate information can be considered. In this context, it would also seem important for organizations to remain attentive and continue monitoring their procedures in an effort to uncover (unintended) biases. Nevertheless, given the pervasiveness and unconscious nature of these biases, we believe that it is unreasonable to expect that they might go away altogether any time soon, which we further believe underscores the need to use proactive (affirmative) actions to correct for disadvantage (Crosby, 2004). Such proactive measures would be unlikely to have the same detrimental effects found for measures aimed at reducing biases in recruitment and selection, because the problem identified with the latter is that they lead individuals and organizations to assume these biases no longer take place (Kaiser et al., 2013). Although bias reduction strategies should continue to be encouraged, organizations need to promote equality and diversity strategies while at the same time acknowledging that they are unlikely to completely eliminate bias and endorsing measures that successfully correct for this possibility.

Another implication of these findings, in our opinion, is that, to achieve equality in domains that are dominated by one specific social group, it is necessary to use measures that achieve this quite rapidly, overcoming as quickly as possible skewed or minority representations. Indeed, we reviewed evidence demonstrating that minority representations elicit a range of detrimental effects that result in underperformance and limit the extent to which members of disadvantaged groups who succeed can effectively benefit their group as a whole. Unsubstantial increases in the representation of disadvantaged groups are problematic also because they overload minority group members with the responsibility of representing their group and send discouraging signs of token representation (Barreto, Ellemers, & Palacios, 2004).

All in all, the knowledge accumulated in this area has provided some answers to old questions, but new questions continually emerge. This review highlighted some of these new questions, for example, with regard to gaining a deeper understanding of the experience of concealed identities and the conditions under which individuals might conceal their identity with truly protective effects. Another area for further inquiry is the somewhat paradoxical finding that confronting prejudicial statements or behavior has at least as many benefits as it has costs, but it is nevertheless a behavior that is rarely displayed. These two areas of research have in common their rare attention to the effectiveness of the strategies that members of devalued groups might use to cope with discrimination. Further research is clearly needed, in this and other areas, to continue improving our understanding of the experience of disadvantage in modern societies. We hope this review contributes to organizing our thoughts in preparation for these exciting next steps.

REFERENCES

Adams, G., Garcia, D., Purdie-Vaughns, V., & Steele, C. (2006). The detrimental effects of a suggestion of sexism in an instruction situation. *Journal of Experimental Social Psychology, 42*, 602–615.

Adams, G., Tormala, T. T., & O'Brien, L. T. (2006). The effect of self-affirmation on perceptions of racism. *Journal of Experimental Social Psychology, 42*, 616–626.

Allport, G. W. (1979). *The nature of prejudice.* Cambridge, MA: Perseus Books.

Anthony, D. B., Wood, J. V., & Holmes, J. G. (2007). Testing sociometer theory: Self-esteem and the importance of acceptance for social decision-making. *Journal of Experimental Social Psychology, 43*, 425–432.

Asgari, S., Dasgupta, N., & Stout, J. G. (2012). When do counterstereotypic ingroup members inspire vs. deflate? The effect of successful professional women on women's leadership self-concept. *Personality and Social Psychology Bulletin, 38*, 370–383.

Baron, R. S., Burgess, M. L., & Kao, C. F. (1991). Detecting and labeling prejudice: Do female perpetrators go undetected. *Personality and Social Psychology Bulletin, 17*, 115–123.

Barreto, M. (2014). Experiencing and coping with social stigma. In M. Mikulincer, P. R. Shaver, J. F. Dovidio, & J. A. Simpson (Eds.), *Group processes: Vol. 2. APA handbook of personality and social psychology* (pp. 473–506). Washington, DC: American Psychological Association.

Barreto, M., & Ellemers, N. (2002). The impact of respect vs. neglect of self-identities on identification and group loyalty. *Personality and Social Psychology Bulletin, 28*, 493–503.

Barreto, M., & Ellemers, N. (2003). The effects of being categorised: The interplay between internal and external social identities. *European Review of Social Psychology, 14*, 139–170.

Barreto, M., & Ellemers, N. (2005a). The perils of political correctness: Men's and women's responses to old-fashioned and modern sexist views. *Social Psychology Quarterly, 68*, 75–88.

Barreto, M., & Ellemers, N. (2005b). The burden of benevolent sexism: How it contributes to the maintenance of gender inequalities. *European Journal of Social Psychology, 35*, 633–642.

Barreto, M., & Ellemers, N. (2009). The paradox of social inclusion. In F. Butera & J. Levine (Eds.), *Coping with minority status: Responses to exclusion and inclusion* (pp. 269–292). New York: Cambridge University Press.

Barreto, M., & Ellemers, N. (2013). Sexism in contemporary societies: How it is expressed, perceived, confirmed, and resisted. In M. Ryan & N. Branscombe (Eds.), *The SAGE handbook of gender and psychology* (pp. 288–305). London, UK: Sage Publishers (chapter 18).

Barreto, M., Ellemers, N., & Banal, S. (2006). Working under cover: Performance-related self-confidence among members of contextually devalued groups who try to pass. *European Journal of Social Psychology, 36*, 337–352.

Barreto, M., Ellemers, N., Cihangir, S., & Stroebe, K. (2009). The self-fulfilling effects of contemporary sexism: How it affects women's well-being and behavior. In M. Barreto, M. Ryan, & M. Schmitt (Eds.), *The glass ceiling in the 21st century: Understanding barriers to gender inequality* (pp. 99–123). Washington, DC: American Psychological Association.

Barreto, M., Ellemers, N., & Fiske, S. T. (2010). "What did you say, and who do you think you are?": How power differences affect emotional reactions to prejudice. *Journal of Social Issues, 63*, 477–492.

Barreto, M., Ellemers, N., & Palacios, M. S. (2004). The backlash of token mobility: The impact of past group experiences on individual ambition and effort. *Personality and Social Psychology Bulletin, 30*, 1433–1445.

Barreto, M., Ellemers, N., Piebinga, L., & Moya, M. (2010). How nice of us and how dumb of me: The effect of exposure to benevolent sexism on women's task and relational self-descriptions. *Sex Roles, 62*, 532–544.

Barreto, M., Ellemers, N., Scholten, W., & Smith, H. (2010). To be or not to be: The impact of implicit versus explicit inappropriate social categorizations on the self. *British Journal of Social Psychology, 49*, 43–67.

Beals, K. P., Peplau, L. A., & Gable, S. L. (2009). Stigma management and well-being: The role of perceived social support, emotional processing, and suppression. *Personality and Social Psychology Bulletin, 35*, 867–879.

Becker, J., & Barreto, M. (2014). Ways to go: Men's and women's support for aggressive and non-aggressive confrontation of sexism as a function of gender identification. *Journal of Social Issues, 70*, 668–686.

Becker, J., Barreto, M., Kahn, K., & de Oliveira Laux, S. (2014). The collective value of 'me' (and its limitations): Towards a more nuanced understanding of individual and collective responses to prejudice. Manuscript under review.

Bem, S. L. (1974). The measurement of psychological androgyny. *Journal of Consulting and Clinical Psychology, 42*, 155–162.

Bergman, M. E., Langhout, R. D., Palmieri, P. A., Cortina, L. M., & Fitzgerald, L. F. (2002). The (un)reasonableness of reporting: Antecedents and consequences of reporting gender harassment. *Journal of Applied Psychology, 87*, 230–242.

Blanchard, F. A., Crandall, C. S., Brigham, J. C., & Vaughn, L. A. (1994). Condemning and condoning racism: A social-context approach to interracial settings. *Journal of Applied Psychology, 79*, 993–997.

Blascovich, J., & Tomaka, J. (1996). The biopsychosocial model of arousal regulation. In M. P. Zanna (Ed.), *Advances in experimental social psychology: Vol. 29* (pp. 1–51). New York: Academic Press.

Bourguignon, D., Seron, E., Yzerbyt, V., & Herman, G. (2006). Perceived group and personal discrimination: Differential effects on personal self-esteem. *European Journal of Social Psychology, 36*, 773–789.

Branscombe, N. R., Schmitt, M. T., & Harvey, R. D. (1999). Perceiving pervasive discrimination among African Americans: Implications for group identification and well-being. *Journal of Personality and Social Psychology, 77*, 135–149.

Carvallo, M., & Pelham, B. W. (2006). When fiends become friends: The need to belong and perceptions of personal and group discrimination. *Journal of Personality and Social Psychology, 90*, 94–108.

Castilla, E. J., & Benard, S. (2010). The paradox of meritocracy in organizations. *Administrative Science Quarterly, 55*, 543–576.

Ceci, S. J., Ginther, D. K., Kahn, S., & Williams, W. M. (2014). Women in academic science: A changing landscape. *Psychological Science in the Public Interest, 15*, 75–141.

Chesney, M. A., & Smith, A. W. (1999). Critical delays in HIV testing and care: The potential role of stigma. *The American Behavioral Scientist, 42*, 1162–1174.

Cihangir, S., Barreto, M., & Ellemers, N. (2010). The dark side of ambiguous discrimination: How state self-esteem moderates emotional and behavioral responses to ambiguous and unambiguous discrimination. *British Journal of Social Psychology, 49*, 155–174.

Cihangir, S., Barreto, M., & Ellemers, N. (2014). Men as allies against sexism: The positive effects of a suggestion of sexism by male (vs. female) sources. *Sage Open, 2014*, 1–12.

Cihangir, S., Ellemers, N., & Barreto, M. (in preparation). Better be sorry than safe: How social norms about uncertain attributions can induce self-defeating responses to subtle discrimination.

Cihangir, S., Scheepers, D. T., Barreto, M., & Ellemers, N. (2013). Responding to gender-based rejection: Objecting against negative and disproving positive intergroup differentiation. *Social Psychology and Personality Science, 4*, 151–158.

Clair, J. A., Beatty, J. E., & MacLean, T. L. (2005). Out of sight but not out of mind: Managing invisible social identities in the workplace. *Academy of Management Review, 30*, 78–95. http://dx.doi.org/10.5465/AMR.2005.15281431.

Cole, S. W., Kemeny, M. E., & Taylor, S. E. (1997). Social identity and physical health: Accelerated HIV progression in rejection sensitive gay men. *Journal of Personality and Social Psychology, 72*, 320–335.

Cole, S. W., Kemeny, M. E., Taylor, S. E., & Visscher, B. R. (1996). Elevated physical health risk among gay men who conceal their homosexual identity. *Health Psychology, 15*, 243–251.

Collins, N. L., & Miller, L. C. (1994). Self-disclosure and liking: A meta-analytic review. *Psychological Bulletin, 116*, 457–475.

Corrigan, P. (2004). How stigma interferes with mental health care. *American Psychologist, 59*, 614–625.

Corrigan, P. W., & Matthews, A. K. (2003). Stigma and disclosure: Implications for coming out of the closet. *Journal of Mental Health, 12*, 235–248.

Crabtree, J. W., Haslam, S. A., Postmes, T., & Haslam, C. (2010). Mental health support groups, stigma and self-esteem: Positive and negative implications of social identification. *Journal of Social Issues, 63*, 553–569.

Crocker, J., & Major, B. (1989). Social stigma and self-esteem: The self-protective properties of stigma. *Psychological Review, 96*, 608–630.

Crosby, F. J. (1982). *Relative deprivation and working women.* New York: Oxford University Press.

Crosby, F. J. (1993). Why complain? *Journal of Social Issues, 49*, 169–184.

Crosby, F. J. (2004). *Affirmative action is dead: Long live affirmative action.* New Haven, CT: Yale University Press.

Crosby, F., Clayton, S., Alksnis, O., & Hemker, K. (1986). Cognitive biases in the perception of discrimination: The importance of format. *Sex Roles, 14*, 637–646.

Croteau, J. M. (1996). Research on the work experiences of lesbian, gay, and bisexual people: An integrative review of methodological findings. *Journal of Vocational Behaviour, 48*, 195–209.

Cruwys, T., South, E. I., Greenaway, K. H., & Haslam, A. S. (2014). Social identity reduces depression by fostering positive attributions. *Social Psychological and Personality Science, 6*, 65–74. http://dx.doi.org/10.1177/1948550614543309.

Czopp, A. M., & Monteith, M. J. (2003). Confronting prejudice (literally): Reactions to confrontations of racial and gender bias. *Personality and Social Psychology Bulletin, 29*, 532–544.

Czopp, A. M., Monteith, M. J., & Mark, A. Y. (2006). Standing up for a change: Reducing bias through interpersonal confrontation. *Journal of Personality and Social Psychology, 90*, 784–803.

Dasgupta, N., & Asgari, S. (2004). Seeing is believing: Exposure to counterstereotypical women leaders and its effect on the malleability of automatic gender stereotyping. *Journal of Experimental Social Psychology, 40*, 642–658.

D'Augelli, A. R., & Grossman, A. H. (2001). Disclosure of sexual orientation, victimization, and mental health among lesbian, gay, and bisexual older adults. *Journal of Interpersonal Violence, 16*, 1008–1027.

Derks, B., Ellemers, N., Van Laar, C., & de Groot, K. (2011). Do sexist organizational cultures create the queen bee? *British Journal of Social Psychology, 50*, 519–535.

Derks, B., Scheepers, D., Van Laar, C., & Ellemers, N. (2011). The threat vs. challenge of car parking for women: How self- and group affirmation affect cardiovascular responses. *Journal of Experimental Social Psychology, 47*, 178–183.

Derks, B., Van Laar, C., & Ellemers, N. (2006). Striving for success in outgroup settings: Effects of contextually emphasizing ingroup dimensions on stigmatized group members' social identity and performance styles. *Personality and Social Psychology Bulletin, 32*, 576–588.

Derks, B., Van Laar, C., & Ellemers, N. (2007). Social creativity strikes back: Improving low status group members' motivation and performance by valuing ingroup dimensions. *European Journal of Social Psychology, 37*, 470–493.

Derks, B., Van Laar, C., & Ellemers, N. (2009). Working for the self or working for the group: How self- vs. group-affirmation affect collective behavior in low status groups. *Journal of Personality and Social Psychology, 96*, 183–202.

Derks, B., Van Laar, C., Ellemers, N., & De Groot, K. (2011). Gender bias primes elicit Queen Bee responses among senior police women. *Psychological Science, 22*, 1243–1249.

Derks, B., Van Laar, C., Ellemers, N., & Raghoe, G. (2014). Extending the Queen Bee effect: How Hindustani workers cope with disadvantage by distancing the self from the group. *Journal of Social Issues*. Manuscript under review.

Dodd, E. H., Giuliano, T. A., Boutell, J. M., & Moran, B. E. (2001). Respected or rejected: Perceptions of women who confront sexist remarks. *Sex Roles, 45*, 567–577.

Dovidio, J. F., & Gaertner, S. L. (1986). *Prejudice, discrimination, and racism: Historical trends and contemporary approaches*. San Diego, CA: Academic Press.

Dovidio, J. F., & Gaertner, S. L. (2000). Aversive racism and selection decisions: 1989 and 1999. *Psychological Science, 11*, 315–319.

Duguid, M. (2011). Female tokens in high-prestige work groups: Catalysts or inhibitors of group diversification? *Organizational Behavior and Human Decision Processes, 116*, 104–155.

Eagly, A. H., & Karau, S. J. (2002). Role congruity theory of prejudice toward female leaders. *Psychological Review, 109*, 573–598.

Ellemers, N. (1993). The influence of socio-structural variables on identity management strategies. *European Review of Social Psychology, 4*, 27–58.

Ellemers, N. (2012). The group self. *Science, 336*, 848–852.

Ellemers, N. (2014). Women at work: How organizational features impact career development. *Policy Insights from the Behavioral and Brain Sciences, 1*, 46–54.

Ellemers, N., & Barreto, M. (2006). Categorization in everyday life: The effects of positive and negative categorization on emotions and self-views. *European Journal of Social Psychology, 36*, 931–942.

Ellemers, N., & Barreto, M. (2009a). Collective action in modern times: How modern expressions of prejudice prevent collective action. *Journal of Social Issues, 65*, 749–768.

Ellemers, N., & Barreto, M. (2009b). Maintaining the illusion of meritocracy: How men and women interactively sustain gender inequality at work. In S. Demoulin, J. P. Leyens, & J. Dovidio (Eds.), *Intergroup misunderstandings: Impact of divergent social realities* (pp. 191–212). New York: Psychology Press.

Ellemers, N., & Jetten, J. (2013). The many ways to be marginal in a group. *Personality and Social Psychology Review, 17*, 3–21.

Ellemers, N., Rink, F., Derks, B., & Ryan, M. (2012). Women in high places: When and why promoting women into top positions can harm them individually or as a group (and how to prevent this). *Research in Organizational Behavior, 32*, 163–187.

Ellemers, N., Sleebos, E., Stam, D., & de Gilder, D. (2013). Feeling included and valued: How perceived respect affects positive team identity and willingness to invest in the team. *British Journal of Management, 24*, 21–37.

Ellemers, N., Van den Heuvel, H., De Gilder, D., Maass, A., & Bonvini, A. (2004). The underrepresentation of women in science: Differential commitment or the Queen-Bee syndrome? *British Journal of Social Psychology, 43*, 315–338.

Ellemers, N., & Van Laar, C. (2010). Individual mobility: The opportunities and challenges members of devalued groups encounter when trying to avoid group-based discrimination. In J. F. Dovidio, M. Hewstone, P. Glick, & V. Esses (Eds.), *Handbook of prejudice, stereotyping, and discrimination* (pp. 561–576). London: Sage.

Farina, A., Gliha, D., Boudreau, L., Allen, J., & Sherman, M. (1971). Mental illness and the impact of believing others know about It. *Journal of Abnormal Psychology, 77,* 1–5.

Feagin, J. R., & Sikes, M. P. (1994). *Living with racism: The black-middle class experience.* Boston: Beacon Press.

Fine, C. (2013). Neurosexism in functional neuroimaging: From scanner to pseudo-science to psyche. In M. K. Ryan & N. R. Branscombe (Eds.), *The SAGE handbook of gender and psychology* (pp. 45–60). London: Sage.

Fiske, S. T. (1993). Controlling other people: The impact of power on stereotyping. *American Psychologist, 48,* 621–628.

Fiske, S. T., & Berdahl, J. (2006). Social power. In A. W. Kruglanski & E. T. Higgins (Eds.), *Social psychology: Handbook of basic principles* (2nd ed., pp. 678–692). New York: Guilford.

Fiske, S. T., Cuddy, A. C., Glick, P., & Xu, J. (2002). A model of (often mixed) stereotype content: Competence and warmth respectively follow from perceived status and competition. *Journal of Personality and Social Psychology, 82,* 878–902.

Fiske, S. T., & Taylor, S. E. (2013). *Social cognition: From brains to culture.* London: Sage.

Fiske, S. T., Xu, J., Cuddy, A. C., & Glick, P. (1999). (Dis)respecting vs. (dis)liking: Status and interdependence predict ambivalent stereotypes of competence and warmth. *Journal of Social Issues, 55,* 473–489.

Fitzgerald, L. F., Swan, S., & Fischer, K. (1995). Why didn't she just report him? The psychological and legal implications of women's responses to sexual harassment. *Journal of Social Issues, 51,* 117–138.

Frable, D. E. S. (1993). Being and feeling unique: Statistical difference and psychological marginality. *Journal of Personality, 61,* 85–110.

Frable, D. E. S., Blackstone, T., & Scherbaum, C. (1990). Marginal and mindful: Deviants in social interactions. *Journal of Personality and Social Psychology, 59,* 140–149.

Frable, D. E. S., Pratt, L., & Hoey, S. (1998). Concealable stigmas and positive self-perceptions: Feeling better around similar others. *Journal of Personality and Social Psychology, 74,* 909–922.

Garcia, D. M., Reser, A. H., Amo, R. B., Redersdorff, S., & Branscombe, N. R. (2005). Perceivers' responses to in-group and out-group members who blame a negative outcome on discrimination. *Personality and Social Psychology Bulletin, 31,* 769–780.

Garcia, D. M., Schmitt, M. T., Branscombe, N. R., & Ellemers, N. (2010). Women's reactions to ingroup members who protest discriminatory treatment: The importance of beliefs about inequality and response appropriateness. *European Journal of Social Psychology, 40,* 733–745.

Gervais, S. J., Hillard, A. L., & Vescio, T. K. (2010). Confronting sexism: The role of relationship orientation and gender. *Sex Roles, 63,* 463–474.

Glick, P., & Fiske, S. T. (1996). The ambivalent sexism inventory: Differentiating hostile and benevolent sexism. *Journal of Personality and Social Psychology, 70,* 491–512.

Glick, P., Fiske, S. T., Mladinic, A., Saiz, J., Abrams, D., Masser, B., et al. (2000). Beyond prejudice as simple antipathy: Hostile and benevolent sexism across cultures. *Journal of Personality and Social Psychology, 79,* 763–775.

Glick, P., Sakalli-Ugurlu, N., Ferreira, M. C., & Souza, M. A. (2002). Ambivalent sexism and attitudes toward wife abuse in Turkey and Brazil. *Psychology of Women Quarterly, 26,* 292–297.

Goffman, E. (1959). *The presentation of self in everyday life.* New York: Anchor Books.

Goffman, E. (1963). *Stigma: Notes on the management of spoiled identity.* Englewood Cliffs, NJ: Prentice Hall.

Griffith, K. H., & Hebl, M. R. (2002). The disclosure dilemma for gay men and lesbians: "Coming out" at work. *Journal of Applied Psychology, 87,* 1191–1199.

Guinote, A. (2007). Power affects basic cognition: Increased attentional inhibition and flexibility. *Journal of Experimental Social Psychology, 43,* 685–697.

Haslam, S. A., Jetten, J., Postmes, T., & Haslam, C. (2009). Social identity, health and well-being: An emerging agenda for applied psychology. *Applied Psychology, 58,* 1–23 (Special Issue on 'Social Identity, Health and Well-being').

Haslam, S. A., O'Brien, A., Jetten, J., Vormedal, K., & Penna, S. (2005). Taking the strain: Social identity, social support and the experience of stress. *British Journal of Social Psychology, 44,* 355–370.

Haslett, B., & Lipman, S. (1997). Micro inequities: Up close and personal. In N. Benokraitis (Ed.), *Subtle sexism: Current practice and prospects for change.* Thousand Oaks, CA: Sage.

Hebl, M., Tickle, J., & Heatherton, T. F. (2000). Awkward moments. In T. F. Heatherton, R. E. Kleck, M. Hebl, & J. G. Hull (Eds.), *Stigma: Social psychological processes.* New York: Guilford.

Henry, J., & Meltzoff, J. (1998). Perceptions of sexual harassment as a function of target's response type and observer's sex. *Sex Roles, 39,* 253–271.

Herek, G. M. (1996). Why tell if you are not asked? Self-disclosure, intergroup contact, and heterosexuals' attitudes toward lesbians and gay men. In G. M. Herek, J. B. Jobe, & R. M. Carney (Eds.), *Out in force: Sexual orientation in the military* (pp. 197–225). Chicago, IL: University of Chicago Press.

Hewstone, M. (1989). Changing stereotypes with disconfirming information. In D. Bar-Tal, C. F. Graumann, A. W. Kruglanski, & W. Stroebe (Eds.), *Stereotypes and prejudice: Changing conceptions* (pp. 207–223). New York: Springer Verlag.

Higgins, E. T. (1997). Beyond pleasure and pain. *American Psychologist, 52,* 1280–1300.

Higgins, E. T. (1998). Regulatory focus as a motivational principle. In M. E. Zanna (Ed.), *Advances in experimental social psychology* (pp. 1–46). New York: Academic Press.

Houston, V., & Bull, R. (1994). Do people avoid sitting next to someone who is facially disfigured? *European Journal of Social Psychology, 24,* 279–284.

Hunter, C., & McClelland, K. (1991). Honoring accounts for sexual harassment. *Sex Roles, 24,* 725–752.

Hyde, J. S. (2014). Gender similarities and differences. *Annual Review of Psychology, 65,* 373–398.

Hyers, L. L. (2007). Resisting prejudice every day: Exploring women's assertive responses to anti-black racism, anti-semitism, heterosexism, and sexism. *Sex Roles, 56,* 1–12.

Inman, M. L., & Baron, R. S. (1996). Influence of prototypes on perceptions of prejudice. *Journal of Personality and Social Psychology, 70,* 727–739.

Inzlicht, M., & Ben-Zeev, T. (2000). A threatening intellectual environment: Why females are susceptible to experiencing problem-solving deficits in the presence of males. *Psychological Science, 11,* 365–371.

Jetten, J., Branscombe, N. R., Schmitt, M. T., & Spears, R. (2001). Rebels with a cause: Group identification as a response to perceived discrimination from the mainstream. *Personality and Social Psychology Bulletin, 27,* 1204–1213.

Jetten, J., Haslam, C., & Haslam, S. A. (2012). *The social cure: Identity, health, and well-being.* London: Psychology Press.

Jetten, J., Iyer, A., Branscombe, N. R., & Zhang, A. (2013). How the disadvantaged appraise group-based exclusion: The path from legitimacy to illegitimacy. *European Review of Social Psychology, 24,* 194–224.

Johnson, J. D., Simmons, C., Trawalter, S., Ferguson, T., & Reed, W. (2003). Variation in Black anti-White bias and target distancing cues: Factors that influence perceptions of 'ambiguously racist' behavior. *Personality and Social Psychology Bulletin, 29,* 609–622.

Jones, E., Farina, A., Hastorf, A., Markus, H., Miller, D., & Scott, R. (1984). *Social stigma: The psychology of marked relationships.* New York: Freeman.

Jones, K. P., Peddie, C. I., Gilrane, V. L., King, E. B., & Gray, A. L. (2013). Not so subtle: A meta-analytic investigation of the correlates of subtle and overt discrimination. *Journal of Management.* http://jom.sagepub.com/content/early/2013/10/11/0149206313506466.

Jost, J. T., Banaji, M., & Nosek, B. (2004). A decade of system justification theory: Accumulated evidence of conscious and unconscious bolstering of the status quo. *Political Psychology, 25*, 881–919.

Kahn, K. B., Barreto, M., & Kaiser, C. K. (in preparation). The effect of benevolent sexism on support for women who confront sexism.

Kahn, K. B., Barreto, M., Kaiser, C. K., & Rego, M. S. (in press). When do high and low status group members support confrontation? The role of perceived pervasiveness of prejudice. *British Journal of Social Psychology*.

Kaiser, C. R., Dyrenforth, P. S., & Hagiwara, N. (2006). Why are attributions to discrimination interpersonally costly? A test of system- and group-justifying motivations. *Personality and Social Psychology Bulletin, 32*, 1523–1536.

Kaiser, C. R., Hagiwara, N., Malahy, L. W., & Wilkins, C. (2009). Group identification moderates attitudes towards ingroup members who confront discrimination. *Journal of Experimental Social Psychology, 45*, 770–777.

Kaiser, C. R., & Major, B. (2006). A social psychological perspective on perceiving and reporting discrimination. *Law and Social Inquiry, 31*, 801–830.

Kaiser, C. R., Major, B., Jurcevic, I., Dover, T. L., Brady, L. M., & Shapiro, J. R. (2013). Presumed fair: Ironic effects of organizational diversity structures. *Journal of Personality and Social Psychology, 104*, 504–519.

Kaiser, C. R., Major, B., & McCoy, S. K. (2004). Expectations about the future and the emotional consequences of perceiving prejudice. *Personality and Social Psychology Bulletin, 30*, 173–184.

Kaiser, C., & Miller, C. (2001). Stop complaining! The social costs of making attributions to discrimination. *Personality and Social Psychology Bulletin, 27*, 254–263.

Kaiser, C. R., & Pratt-Hyatt, J. S. (2009). Distributing prejudice unequally: Do Whites direct their prejudice toward strongly identified minorities? *Journal of Personality and Social Psychology, 96*, 432–445.

Kanter, R. M. (1977). *Men and women of the corporation*. New York: Basic Books.

Kelly, A. E., & McKillop, K. J. (1996). Consequences of revealing personal secrets. *Psychological Bulletin, 120*, 450–465.

Kilianski, S. E., & Rudman, L. A. (1998). Wanting it both ways: Do women approve of benevolent sexism? *Sex Roles, 39*, 333–352.

Kleck, R. E., & Strenta, A. (1980). Perceptions of the impact of negatively valued physical characteristics on social interaction. *Journal of Personality and Social Psychology, 39*, 861–873.

Knowles, M. L., & Gardner, W. L. (2008). Benefits of membership: The activation and amplification of group identities in response to social rejection. *Personality and Social Psychology Bulletin, 34*, 1200–1213.

LaFrance, M., & Woodzicka, J. A. (1998). No laughing matter: Women's verbal and non-verbal reactions to sexist humor. In J. Swim & C. Stangor (Eds.), *Prejudice: The target's perspective* (pp. 61–80). San Diego, CA: Academic Press.

Leach, C. W., Rodriguez Mosquera, P. M., Vliek, M. L. W., & Hirt, E. (2010). Group devaluation and group identification. *Journal of Social Issues, 63*, 535–552.

Lee, E. A., Soto, J. A., Swim, J. K., & Bernstein, M. J. (2012). Bitter reproach or sweet revenge: Cultural differences in responses to racism. *Personality and Social Psychology Bulletin, 38*, 920–932.

Lerner, M. (1980). *The belief in a just world: A fundamental delusion*. New York: Plenum.

Link, B. G. (1987). Understanding labeling effects in the area of mental disorders: An assessment of the effects of expectations of rejection. *American Sociological Review, 52*, 96–112.

Link, B. G., Mirotznik, J., & Cullen, F. T. (1991). The effectiveness of stigma coping orientations: Can negative consequences of mental illness labeling be avoided? *Journal of Health and Social Behavior, 32*, 302–320.

Lockwood, P., & Kunda, Z. (1997). Superstars and me: Predicting the impact of role models on the self. *Journal of Personality and Social Psychology, 73*, 91–103.

Major, B., & Gramzow, R. H. (1999). Abortion as stigma: Cognitive and emotional implications of concealment. *Journal of Personality and Social Psychology, 77*, 735–745.

Major, B., Quinton, W. J., & McCoy, S. K. (2002). Antecedents and consequences of attributions to discrimination: Theoretical and empirical advances. In M. Zanna (Ed.), *Advances in experimental social psychology: Vol. 34* (pp. 251–330). New York: Academic Press.

Major, B., Quinton, W. J., & Schmader, T. (2003). Attributions to discrimination and self-esteem: Impact of group identification and situational ambiguity. *Journal of Experimental Social Psychology, 39*, 220–231.

Major, B., Richards, M. C., Cooper, M. L., Cozzareli, C., & Zubek, J. (1998). Personal resilience, cognitive appraisals, and coping: An integrative model of adjustment to abortion. *Journal of Personality and Social Psychology, 74*, 735–752.

Mallett, R. K., & Melchiori, K. J. (2014). Goal preference shapes confrontations of sexism. *Personality and Social Psychology Bulletin, 40*, 646–656.

Mallett, R. K., & Wagner, D. E. (2011). The unexpectedly positive consequences of confronting sexism. *Journal of Experimental Social Psychology, 47*, 215–220.

Marx, D. M., & Roman, J. S. (2002). Female role models: Protecting women's math performance. *Personality and Social Psychology Bulletin, 28*, 1183–1193.

McCoy, S. K., & Major, B. (2003). Group identification moderates emotional responses to perceived prejudice. *Personality and Social Psychology Bulletin, 29*, 1005–1017.

Meyer, I. H. (2008). Prejudice, social stress, and mental health in lesbian, gay, and bisexual populations: Conceptual issues and research evidence. *Psychological Bulletin, 129*, 674–697.

Miller, D. I., Eagly, A. H., & Linn, M. C. (2014). Women's representation in science predicts national gender-science stereotypes: Evidence from 66 nations. *Journal of Educational Psychology.* http://dx.doi.org/10.1037/edu0000005.

Miller, C. T., & Myers, A. M. (1998). Compensating for prejudice: How heavyweight people (and others) control outcomes despite prejudice. In J. K. Swim & C. Stangor (Eds.), *Prejudice: The target's perspective* (pp. 191–218). New York: Academic Press.

Moya, M., Glick, P., Expósito, F., de Lemus, S., & Hart, J. (2007). It's for your own good: Benevolent sexism and women's tolerance of paternalistic discrimination by intimate partners. *Personality and Social Psychology Bulletin, 33*, 1421–1434.

Newheiser, A.-K., & Barreto, M. (2014). Hidden costs of hiding stigma: Ironic interpersonal consequences of concealing a stigmatized identity in social interactions. *Journal of Experimental Social Psychology, 52*, 58–70.

Newheiser, A.-K., Barreto, M., Ellemers, N., Derks, B., & Scheepers, D. (in press). Is hiding a stigmatized identity during social interactions protective or detrimental? The moderating role of regulatory focus. *British Journal of Social Psychology.*

Noel, J. G., Wann, D. L., & Branscombe, N. R. (1995). Peripheral ingroup membership status and public negativity towards outgroups. *Journal of Personality and Social Psychology, 68*, 127–137.

O'Brien, L. T., Major, B. N., & Gilbert, P. N. (2012). Gender differences in entitlement: The roles of system justifying beliefs. *Basic and Applied Social Psychology, 34*, 136–145.

Operario, D., & Fiske, S. T. (2001). Ethnic identity moderates perceptions of prejudice: Judgments of personal versus group discrimination and subtle versus blatant bias. *Personality and Social Psychology Bulletin, 27*, 550–561.

Oyserman, D., Uskul, A., Yoder, N., Nesse, R., & Williams, D. (2007). Unfair treatment and self-regulatory focus. *Journal of Experimental Social Psychology, 43*, 505–512.

Pachankis, J. E. (2007). The psychological implications of concealing a stigma: A cognitive-affective-behavioral model. *Psychological Bulletin, 133*, 328–345.

Pachankis, J. E., Goldfried, M. R., & Ramrattan, M. E. (2008). Extension of the rejection-sensitivity construct to the interpersonal functioning of gay men. *Journal of Consulting and Clinical Psychology*, *76*, 306–317.

Pascoe, E. A., & Smart Richman, L. (2009). Perceived discrimination and health: A meta-analytic review. *Psychological Bulletin*, *135*, 531–554.

Pettigrew, T. F., & Meertens, R. W. (1995). Subtle and blatant prejudice in Western Europe. *European Journal of Social Psychology*, *25*, 57–75.

Postmes, T., & Branscombe, N. R. (2002). Influence of long-term racial environmental composition on subjective well-being in African Americans. *Journal of Personality and Social Psychology*, *83*, 735–751.

Quinn, D. M., & Chaudoir, S. R. (2009). Living with a concealable stigmatized identity: The impact of anticipated stigma, centrality, salience, and cultural stigma on psychological distress and health. *Journal of Personality and Social Psychology*, *97*, 634–651.

Quinn, D. M., Kahng, S. K., & Crocker, J. (2004). Discreditable: Stigma effects of revealing a mental illness history on test performance. *Personality and Social Psychology Bulletin*, *30*, 803–815.

Ragins, B. R. (2008). Disclosure disconnects: Antecedents and consequences of disclosing invisible stigmas across life domains. *Academy of Management Review*, *33*, 194–215.

Ragins, B. R., Singh, R., & Cornwell, J. M. (2007). Making the invisible visible: Fear and disclosure of sexual orientation at work. *Journal of Applied Psychology*, *92*, 1103–1118.

Rasinski, H. M., & Czopp, A. M. (2010). The effect of target status on witnesses' reactions to confrontations of bias. *Basic and Applied Social Psychology*, *32*, 8–16.

Rattan, A., & Dweck, C. S. (2010). Who confronts prejudice? The role of implicit theories in the motivation to confront prejudice. *Psychological Science*, *21*, 952–959.

Rhodewalt, F. (1990). Self-handicappers: Individual differences in the preference for antic-ipatory self-protective acts. In R. L. Higgins, C. R. Snyder, & S. Berglas (Eds.), *Self-handicapping: The paradox that isn't* (pp. 69–106). New York: Plenum Press.

Richards, Z., & Hewstone, M. (2001). Subtyping and subgrouping: Processes for the pre-vention and promotion of stereotype change. *Personality and Social Psychology Review*, *5*, 52–73.

Rink, F., & Ellemers, N. (2006). What can you expect? The influence of gender diversity in dyads on work goal expectancies and subsequent work commitment. *Group Processes and Intergroup Relations*, *9*, 577–588.

Rink, F., Kane, A. A., Ellemers, N., & Van der Vegt, G. (2013). Team receptivity to new-comers: Five decades of evidence and future research themes. *Academy of Management Annals*, *7*, 1–47.

Rudman, L. A., Glick, P., & Phelan, J. E. (2008). From the laboratory to the bench: Gender stereotyping research in the courtroom. In E. Borgida, & S. T. Fiske (Eds.), *Beyond common sense: Psychological science in the courtroom* (pp. 83–101). Oxford: Blackwell.

Sani, F., Herrara, M., Wakefield, J. R. H., Boroch, O., & Gulyas, C. (2012). Comparing social contact and group identification as predictors of mental health. *British Journal of Social Psychology*, *51*, 781–790.

Santuzzi, A. M., & Ruscher, J. B. (2002). Stigma salience and paranoid social cognition: Understanding variability in metaperceptions of prejudice among stigmatized targets. *Social Cognition*, *20*, 171–197.

Sassenberg, K., Ellemers, N., Scheepers, D., & Scholl, A. (2014). "Power corrupts" revisited: The role of construal of power as opportunity or responsibility. In J.-W. van Prooijen, & P. A. M. van Lange (Eds.), *Power, politics, and paranoia: Why people are suspicious about their leaders* (pp. 73–87). Cambridge, UK: Cambridge University Press.

Scheepers, D., De Wit, F., Ellemers, N., & Sassenberg, K. (2012). Social power makes the heart work more efficiently: Evidence from cardiovascular markers of challenge and threat. *Journal of Experimental Social Psychology*, *48*, 371–374.

Scheepers, D., & Ellemers, N. (2005). When the pressure is up: The assessment of social identity threat in low and high status groups. *Journal of Experimental Social Psychology, 41*, 192–200.

Schmader, T. (2002). Gender identification moderates the effects of stereotype threat on women's math performance. *Journal of Experimental Social Psychology, 38*, 194–201.

Schmader, T., Hall, H., & Croft, A. (2014). Stereotype threat in intergroup relations. In M. Mikulincer, P. R. Shaver, J. F. Dovidio, & J. A. Simpson (Eds.), *Group processes: Vol. 2. APA handbook of personality and social psychology* (pp. 447–471). Washington, DC: American Psychological Association.

Schmader, T., Johns, M., & Forbes, C. (2008). An integrated process model of stereotype threat effects on performance. *Psychological Review, 115*, 336–356.

Schmitt, M. T., & Branscombe, N. R. (2002). The meaning and consequences of perceived discrimination in disadvantaged and privileged social groups. *European Review of Social Psychology, 12*, 167–199.

Schmitt, M. T., Branscombe, N. R., & Postmes, T. (2003). Women's emotional responses to the pervasiveness of gender discrimination. *European Journal of Social Psychology, 33*, 297–312.

Schmitt, M. T., Branscombe, N. R., Postmes, T., & Garcia, A. (2014). The consequences of perceived discrimination for psychological well-being: A meta-analytic review. *Psychological Bulletin, 140*, 921–948.

Schmitt, M. T., Ellemers, N., & Branscombe, N. (2003). Perceiving and responding to gender discrimination at work. In A. Haslam, D. Van Knippenberg, M. Platow, & N. Ellemers (Eds.), *Social identity at work: Developing theory for organizational practice* (pp. 277–292). Philadelphia, PA: Psychology Press.

Schwartz, S. H. (1992). Universals in the content and structure of values: Theoretical advances and empirical tests in 20 countries. In M. Zanna (Ed.), *Advances in experimental social psychology: Vol. 25.* (pp. 1–65). New York: Academic Press.

Sechrist, G. B., & Delmar, C. (2006). When do men and women make attributions to gender discrimination? The role of discrimination source. *Sex Roles, 61*, 607–620.

Sechrist, G. B., Swim, J. K., & Stangor, C. (2004). When do the stigmatized make attributions to discrimination occurring to the self and others? The roles of self-presentation and need for control. *Journal of Personality and Social Psychology, 87*, 111–122.

Sedlovskaya, A., Purdie-Vaughns, V., Eibach, R. P., LaFrance, M., Romero-Canyas, R., & Camp, N. P. (2013). Internalizing the closet: Concealment heightens the cognitive distinction between public and private selves. *Journal of Personality and Social Psychology, 104*, 695–715.

Sellers, R. M., & Shelton, J. (2003). The role of racial identity in perceived racial discrimination. *Journal of Personality and Social Psychology, 84*, 1079–1092.

Shelton, J. N., Richeson, J. A., & Salvatore, J. (2005). Expecting to be the target of prejudice: Implications for interethnic interactions. *Personality and Social Psychology Bulletin, 31*, 1189–1202.

Shelton, J. N., Richeson, J. A., Salvatore, J., & Hill, D. M. (2006). Silence is not golden: The intrapersonal consequences of not confronting prejudice. In S. Levin, & C. Van Laar (Eds.), *Stigma and group inequality: Social psychological perspectives* (pp. 65–82). Mahwah, NJ: Erlbaum.

Shelton, J. N., & Stewart, R. E. (2004). Confronting perpetrators of prejudice: The inhibitory effects of social costs. *Psychology of Women Quarterly, 28*, 215–223.

Sheppard, L. D., & Aquino, K. (2013). Much ado about nothing? Observers' problematization of women's same-sex conflict at work. *Academy of Management Perspectives, 27*, 52–62.

Sherman, D. K., & Cohen, G. L. (2006). The psychology of self-defense: Self-affirmation theory. In M. P. Zanna (Ed.), *Advances in experimental social psychology: Vol. 38.* (pp. 183–242). San Diego, CA: Academic Press.

Shih, M., Young, M. J., & Bucher, A. (2013). Working to reduce the effects of discrimination: Identity management strategies in organizations. *American Psychologist, 68*, 145–157.

Sibicky, M., & Dovidio, J. F. (1986). Stigma of psychological therapy: Stereotypes, interpersonal reactions, and the self-fulfilling prophecy. *Journal of Counseling Psychology, 33*, 148–154.

Smart, L., & Wegner, D. M. (1999). Covering up what can't be seen: Concealable stigmas and mental control. *Journal of Personality and Social Psychology, 77*, 474–486.

Ståhl, T., Van Laar, C., & Ellemers, N. (2012). How stereotype threat affects cognitive performance under a prevention focus: Initial cognitive mobilization is followed by depletion. *Journal of Personality and Social Psychology, 102*, 1239–1251.

Ståhl, T., Van Laar, C., Ellemers, N., & Derks, B. (2012). Searching for acceptance: Prejudice expectations direct attention towards social acceptance cues when under a promotion focus. *Group Processes and Intergroup Relations, 15*, 523–538.

Stangor, C., Van Allen, K. L., Swim, J. K., & Sechrist, G. B. (2002). Reporting discrimination in public and private contexts. *Journal of Personality and Social Psychology, 82*, 69–74.

Steele, C. M. (1988). The psychology of self-affirmation: Sustaining the integrity of the self. In L. Berkowitz (Ed.), *Advances in experimental social psychology: Vol. 21.* (pp. 261–302). New York: Academic Press.

Steele, C. M., & Aronson, J. (1995). Stereotype threat and the intellectual performance of African Americans. *Journal of Personality and Social Psychology, 69*, 797–811.

Steentjes, K., Kurz, T., Barreto, M., & Morton, T. (2014). Social costs of confronting environmental disregard: Comparing normative processes around climate change and racial equality. Manuscript under revision.

Stephens, N. M., & Levine, C. S. (2011). Opting out or denying discrimination? How the framework of free choice in American society influences perceptions of gender inequality. *Psychological Science, 22*, 1231–1236.

Stock, M. L., Gibbonds, F. X., Walsh, L. A., & Gerrard, M. (2011). Racial identification, racial discrimination, and substance use vulnerability among African American young adults. *Personality and Social Psychology Bulletin, 37*, 1349–1361.

Stockdale, M. S. (1998). The direct and moderating influences of sexual harassment pervasiveness, coping strategies, and gender on work-related outcomes. *Psychology of Women Quarterly, 22*, 521–535.

Stout, J. G., & Dasgupta, N. (2011). When he doesn't mean you: Gender-exclusive language as ostracism for women. *Personality and Social Psychology Bulletin, 37*, 757–769.

Stroebe, K., Barreto, M., & Ellemers, N. (2010). When searching hurts: The role of information search in reactions to gender discrimination. *Sex Roles, 62*, 60–76.

Stroebe, K. E., Dovidio, J. F., Barreto, M., Ellemers, N., & John, M.-S. (2011). Is the world a just place? Countering the negative consequences of pervasive discrimination by affirming the world as just. *British Journal of Social Psychology, 50*, 484–500.

Stroebe, K., Ellemers, N., Barreto, M., & Mummendey, A. (2009). For better or for worse: The congruence of personal and group outcomes on targets' responses to discrimination. *European Journal of Social Psychology, 39*, 576–591.

Swim, J. K., Aikin, K. J., Hall, W. S., & Hunter, B. A. (1995). Sexism and racism: Old-fashioned and modern prejudices. *Journal of Personality and Social Psychology, 68*, 199–214.

Swim, J. K., & Cohen, L. L. (1997). Overt, covert, and subtle sexism: A comparison between the attitudes toward women and modern sexism scales. *Psychology of Women Quarterly, 21*, 103–118.

Swim, J. K., Eyssell, K. M., Quinlivan, E., & Ferguson, M. J. (2010). Self-silencing to sexism. *Journal of Social Issues, 63*, 493–507.

Swim, J. K., & Hyers, L. L. (1999). Excuse me—What did you just say?!: Women's public and private responses to sexist remarks. *Journal of Experimental Social Psychology, 35*, 68–88.

Swim, J. K., Mallett, R., Russo-Devosa, Y., & Stangor, C. (2005). Judgments of sexism: A comparison of the subtlety of sexism measures and sources of variability in judgments of sexism. *Psychology of Women Quarterly, 29*, 406–411.

Tajfel, H. (1981). *Human groups and social categories*. Cambridge: Cambridge University Press.

Tajfel, H., & Turner, J. T. (1979). An integrative theory of intergroup behaviour. In W. G. Austin, & S. Worchel (Eds.), *The social psychology of intergroup relations* (pp. 33–47). Monterey, CA: Brooks/Cole.

Taylor, D. M., Wright, S. C., Moghaddam, F. M., & Lalonde, R. N. (1990). The personal/group discrimination discrepancy: Perceiving my group, but not myself, to be a target for discrimination. *Personality and Social Psychology Bulletin, 21*, 254–262.

Tougas, F., Brown, R., Beaton, A. M., & Joly, S. (1995). Neosexism: Plus ça change, plus c'est pareil. *Personality and Social Psychology Bulletin, 21*, 842–849.

Twenge, J. M., & Crocker, J. (2002). Race and self-esteem: Meta-analyses comparing Whites, Blacks, Hispanics, Asians, and American Indians and comment on Gray-Little and Hafdahl (2000). *Psychological Bulletin, 128*, 371–408.

Van Laar, C., Bleeker, D., Ellemers, N., & Meijer, E. (2014). Ingroup and outgroup support for upward mobility: Divergent responses to ingroup identification in low status groups. *European Journal of Social Psychology, 44*, 563–577.

Van Laar, C., Derks, B., & Ellemers, N. (2013). Motivation for education and work in young Muslim women: The importance of value for ingroup domains. *Basic and Applied Social Psychology, 35*, 64–74.

Van Laar, C., Derks, B., Ellemers, N., & Bleeker, D. (2010). Valuing social identity: Consequences for motivation and performance in low status groups. *Journal of Social Issues, 66*, 602–617.

Van Lange, P. A. M., & Sedikides, C. (1998). Being more honest but not necessarily more intelligent than others: Generality and explanations for the Muhammad Ali effect. *European Journal of Social Psychology, 28*, 675–680.

Van Nunspeet, F., Derks, B., Ellemers, N., & Nieuwenhuis, S. (2015). Moral impression management: Evaluation by an in-group member during a moral IAT affects perceptual attention and conflict and response monitoring. *Social Psychological and Personality Science, 6*, 183–192.

Van Nunspeet, F., Ellemers, N., Derks, B., & Nieuwenhuis, S. (2014). Moral concerns increase attention and response monitoring during IAT performance: ERP evidence. *Social Cognitive and Affective Neuroscience, 9*, 141–149.

Wahl, O. F. (1999). Mental health consumers' experience of stigma. *Schizophrenia Bulletin, 25*, 467–478.

Wann, D. L., & Branscombe, N. R. (1990). Die-hard and fair-weather fans: Effects of identification on BIRGing and CORFing tendencies. *Journal of Sport and Social Issues, 14*, 103–117.

Wojciszke, B. (2005). Morality and competence in person- and self-perception. *European Review of Social Psychology, 16*, 155–188.

Wood, A. M., Linley, P. A., Maltby, J., Baliousis, M., & Joseph, S. (2008). The authentic personality: A theoretical and empirical conceptualization and the development of the Authenticity Scale. *Journal of Counseling Psychology, 55*, 385–399.

Woodzicka, J. A., & LaFrance, M. (2001). Real versus imagined gender harassment. *Journal of Social Issues, 57*, 15–30.

CHAPTER FOUR

The Motivated Gatekeeper of Our Minds: New Directions in Need for Closure Theory and Research

Arne Roets[*,1], Arie W. Kruglanski[†], Malgorzata Kossowska[‡], Antonio Pierro[§], Ying-yi Hong[¶]

*Ghent University, Department of Developmental, Personality, and Social Psychology, Ghent, Belgium
†University of Maryland, Department of Psychology, College Park, Maryland, USA
‡Jagiellonian University, Department of Psychology, Kraków, Poland
§University of Rome "La Sapienza", Department of Social and Developmental Psychology, Rome, Italy
¶Nanyang Technological University, Nanyang Business School, Singapore, Singapore
1Corresponding author: e-mail address: Arne.Roets@UGent.be

Contents

Abstract

For over three decades, the need for closure (NFC) construct has played a pivotal role in research programs addressing the motivational underpinnings of knowledge formation, judgment and decision making, and social and group cognition. In recent years, NFC research has entered a new phase with notable developments in both fundamental and applied research. The substantial progress in the domain of basic NFC research pertains to investigators' renewed interest in NFC's essentials, including its motivational nature, its role in the mobilization of task investment, the interplay between closure needs and abilities with implications for the measurement of NFC, its relation to cognitive depletion, its effects on memory phenomena, and its genetic and neural correlates. The second major development pertains to efforts to expand NFC research from the lab environment to real-world settings, including work on NFC effects on groups and organizations, its influence on the development and counteraction of prejudice, and its role in violent extremism. In this chapter, both developmental trends are discussed, highlighting their contributions to an advanced understanding of the motivational underpinnings of human cognition and behavior.

1. INTRODUCTION

The need for cognitive closure, a motivational construct at the cross roads of cognitive and social processes, has received a considerable amount of research attention over the past few decades. Introduced originally by Kruglanski (1980) in a *Psychological Review* article on lay epistemics (i.e., the processes whereby lay persons gain knowledge and understanding of the world), need for closure (NFC) theory has been applied to a wide variety of phenomena in the domains of social cognition (see Kruglanski & Webster, 1996) and of cognitively driven group dynamics (see Kruglanski, Pierro, Mannetti, & De Grada, 2006).

Major epistemic theorists (e.g., Kuhn, 1962; Lewin, 1951; Popper, 1934) maintain that the creation of human knowledge is a dynamic process in which cognitive frameworks are frozen, unfrozen, and refrozen (see also Kruglanski, 1989); theories about epistemic processes are no exception to this rule. Indeed, this has been the case with the NFC construct about which intensive research has continued unabated in the past several years. This work has yielded a rich crop of findings representing forays into previously unexplored territories, affording novel insights and enabling new theoretical elaborations. This chapter reviews these developments in research on the NFC as the motivated gatekeeper of the mind, and discusses their significance for understanding a broad range of phenomena in the domain of motivated cognition. To that end, our narrative is presented in three parts. In the first part, we revisit the NFC notion and describe its intellectual lineage, its properties, and its implications. In the second part, we review major novel lines of research that have tackled fundamental issues inherent in the NFC construct, including its motivational nature, the interplay between cognitive needs and abilities, its relation to cognitive depletion, its impact on memory, and its genetic and neurological bases. In the third part, we discuss and demonstrate the contribution of recent NFC findings to understanding significant real-world phenomena, including organizational behavior, the development, persistence, and reduction of prejudice, and the rise of violent extremism.

1.1 The NFC construct

Defined as the desire for "*an* answer on a given topic, *any* answer ... compared to confusion and ambiguity" (Kruglanski, 1990, p. 337), the NFC concept constitutes a core motivational construct of Kruglanski's theoretical framework of lay epistemics, a general theory about the process of knowledge formation (e.g., Kruglanski, 1980, 1989; Kruglanski, Dechesne, Orehek, & Pierro, 2009; Kruglanski, Orehek, Dechesne, & Pierro, 2010). NFC represents a motivational tendency whose magnitude is determined by the (perceived) benefits and costs of closure relative to the benefits and costs of lacking closure. A straightforward instigator of high NFC is time pressure that people experience routinely (e.g., Bukowski, von Hecker, & Kossowska, 2013; Kruglanski & Freund, 1983, Richter & Kruglanski, 1998; Roets & Van Hiel, 2011a); for example, failure to meet a deadline may carry a penalty, which induces a NFC intended to avoid it. Alternative mundane costs of lacking closure abound: because the attainment of closure eliminates the necessity for further information processing, various situations wherein information processing is difficult, laborious, or aversive can also foster a heightened desire for closure. For example, if the task at hand is dull or of low interest (e.g., Webster, 1993a), if performance is impeded by external stressors such as environmental noise (e.g., Kruglanski, Webster, & Klem, 1993), or if processing is felt to be laborious due to fatigue (e.g., Webster, Richter, & Kruglanski, 1996) or intoxication (e.g., Webster, 1993b), people may also experience an increased desire to reach closure (see Kruglanski, 2004; Kruglanski & Webster, 1996 for an overview).

Kruglanski and Webster (1996) portrayed the motivation toward closure as lying on a continuum with a high need to attain closure at one end and high need to avoid closure at the other end. For instance, in circumstances where information processing is experienced as intrinsically rewarding or of high interest (e.g., Webster, 1993b), or when the potential negative consequences of premature closure are especially salient because erroneous judgments are perceived as costly (e.g., Kruglanski & Freund, 1983), people are motivated to postpone or avoid closure.

In addition to transient states induced by situational determinants, the NFC also represents a dimension of stable individual differences (Webster & Kruglanski, 1994). Individuals high in dispositional NFC are characterized by a preference for order and for predictability, afforded by secure and stable knowledge that is constant across circumstances and unchallenged by exceptions. High NFC individuals also experience an urgent desire to reach swift and firm decisions, reflected in their need for decisiveness, and they feel discomfort with ambiguity, experiencing situations lacking closure as aversive. Finally, they are closed-minded, resistant to information inconsistent with their firm opinions, and reluctant to have their knowledge challenged.

To measure dispositional or "trait" NFC, Webster and Kruglanski (1994) developed the NFC scale, which was later revised by Roets and Van Hiel (2007). Both the original and the revised scale tap the five proposed expressions of NFC: preference for order, preference for predictability, (need for) decisiveness, aversion for ambiguity, and closed-mindedness. Various studies have shown consistently that the effects obtained with the individual difference measure converge with those obtained with the situational manipulations of NFC (e.g., see Roets, Van Hiel, Cornelis, & Soetens, 2008; Webster & Kruglanski, 1994). Such convergence supports the claim that motivation for closure is a *psychological mindset* with a variety of determinants including both momentary conditions and chronic personality tendencies, possibly with temperamental and genetic origins, as well as stemming from cultural norms and practices (see Kruglanski & Webster, 1996).

The construct of NFC fits within the long history of psychological research and theorizing on individuals' tendency toward closed- versus open-mindedness and shares features with related concepts such as intolerance of ambiguity (Eysenck, 1954; Frenkel-Brunswik, 1949), uncertainty orientation (Sorrentino & Short, 1986), openness to experience (McCrae & Costa, 1985), and need for cognition (Cacioppo & Petty, 1982). Yet, NFC is distinct from these alternative notions by dint of its explicitly motivational rather than cognitive or personality basis (for more elaborate arguments on this point, see Kruglanski, 2004; Kruglanski & Webster, 1996). Moreover, empirically, NFC yields relatively modest relations with these variables (usually $<|0.30|$) and, as we note at a later juncture, yields unique relations with third variables (see e.g., Cornelis & Van Hiel, 2006; Kruglanski & Webster, 1996; Onraet, Van Hiel, Roets, & Cornelis, 2011; Roets & Van Hiel, 2011b).

1.2 Behavioral consequences of NFC for judgment and decision making: Seizing and freezing

When the NFC is high (either because it is invoked by the situation or reflecting a dispositional trait), the absence of closure presents a deviation from a desired state, and therefore it is aversive and stressful. The most direct evidence for this assertion was recently provided by Roets and Van Hiel (2008, Study 1) who found that in a decision-making context, individuals high (but not low) in NFC showed higher levels of *distress* both in terms of increased systolic blood pressure and elevated heart rate during the task, and in terms of increased retrospectively reported distress. In a follow-up study (Roets & Van Hiel, 2008, Study 2) where closure was not readily attainable, high (but not low) NFC individuals showed a progressive increase of arousal assessed via a galvanic skin response, for as long as no conclusive solution was obtained.

Importantly, for high NFC individuals, the (aversive and stressful) absence of closure tends to "prompt activities aimed at the attainment of closure, [and] bias the individuals' choices and preferences toward closure-bound pursuits" (Kruglanski & Webster, 1996; p. 264); these appropriately affect information processing, knowledge formation, and decision making. Theoretically, elevated NFC was said to prompt two general proclivities, known as the urgency and the permanence tendencies (Kruglanski & Webster, 1996). The urgency tendency denotes an inclination to *seize* quickly on information that promises to bring about closure. Because immediate closure is desirable and any further postponement is felt to be bothersome, individuals with a high NFC may often leap to judgment on the basis of partial or inconclusive evidence.

The permanence tendency, in contrast, denotes the inclination to maintain closure by holding onto or *freezing* on the acquired knowledge. The freezing process strengthens the consolidation of such knowledge and immunizes it against contradictory information. Both "gatekeeping" tendencies serve to escape the aversive lack of closure, the first by terminating this state quickly and the second by keeping it from recurring.

One of the most straightforward consequences of the inclination to seize and freeze elicited by NFC pertains to the extent to which people sample information and generate hypotheses. Indeed, the desire to reach closure quickly, and to subsequently maintain closure, should lead people to consider less information when making judgments. In one of the early studies on NFC, Mayseless and Kruglanski (1987, Study 2) asked participants to identify a series of briefly presented, individual digits. Participants were permitted to request repeated tachistoscopic presentations of the digit to be identified. As expected, the extent of informational search (i.e., number of requested presentations) was highest in the need to avoid closure condition (induced by manipulation of the fear of invalidity), intermediate in the control condition, and lowest in the NFC condition (induced by instructions stressing the importance of forming unambiguous, clear-cut opinions, rather than the importance of being correct). This effect later was corroborated by Roets et al. (2008; see Figure 1) across different NFC manipulations (i.e., noise, time pressure, and fear of invalidity) and was further cross-validated with the dispositional measure of NFC (Roets et al., 2008; see also Roets & Van Hiel, 2006). The study by Roets et al. (2008) also showed that NFC differences in information sampling are most prominent under conditions where (epistemic) motivation is most relevant for behavior, i.e., in difficult, though not impossible tasks (see Wright & Kirby, 2001).

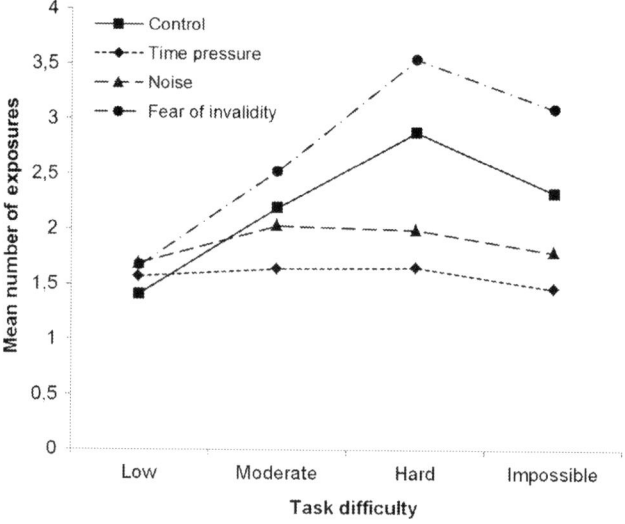

Figure 1 Mean number of exposures requested before attaining judgment on easy, moderate, hard, and impossible trials of the digit identification task for control, time pressure, noise, and fear for invalidity conditions. *Adapted from Roets et al. (2008, Study 2a).*

In another study, Mayseless and Kruglanski (1987, Study 3) presented participants with enlarged photographs of common objects, taken at unusual angles to mask their specific nature, and asked participants to list all conceivable hypotheses that came to mind regarding these objects' identity. Similar to the extent of information sampling, the number of generated hypotheses was the smallest in the high NFC condition, intermediate in the control condition, and largest in the need to avoid closure condition.

In addition to these basic effects, the NFC, through the instigation of seizing and freezing tendencies, has substantial effects on a number of classic phenomena in (social) psychology, discussed in Kruglanski and Webster's (1996) original review. The early studies on NFC by Kruglanski and Freund (1983) already demonstrated that high NFC (induced through time pressure) inflates impressional primacy effects (see also Freund, Kruglanski, & Shpitzajzen, 1985; Heaton & Kruglanski, 1991; Webster & Kruglanski, 1994; Webster et al., 1996), increases the tendency to base judgments on prevalent stereotypes (see also Dijksterhuis, van Knippenberg, Kruglanski, & Schaper, 1996; Jamieson & Zanna, 1989), and heightens assimilation of numerical estimates to anchor values (Kruglanski & Freund, 1983, Study 2). Other studies have demonstrated that NFC increases attributional biases (Webster, 1993a) and the effects of priming (e.g., Ford & Kruglanski, 1995). Each of these effects reflects an urgency-driven reliance on easily accessible, early information, and a permanence-driven disregard of later information: Anchors, primes, stereotypes, or other early or salient cues provide initial bases for judgment and as such are seized and frozen on under high NFC. Moreover, because repeated exposure is assumed to increase the perceived plausibility of an initial hunch, the strong reliance on such initial "information" under high NFC can also strengthen mere exposure effects, as demonstrated in a series of studies by Kruglanski, Freund, and Bar-Tal (1996).

The mechanisms of seizing and freezing also translate into interpersonal phenomena such as negotiation situations where high NFC individuals are shown to be more influenced by focal points (cf. a stronger adherence to anchor values) when setting limits and making concessions, and to rely more strongly on stereotypic perceptions of their opponents (DeDreu, Koole, & Oldersma, 1999). In addition, several studies examined NFC effects in intra- and intergroup contexts. Kruglanski et al. (2006) integrated these distinctly social NFC effects under the umbrella hypothesis of *group centrism*. Specifically, studies revealed that individuals under high NFC tend to prefer an autocratic group decision structure in which consensus and hence a stable, closure affording, shared reality is more likely, stemming from the disproportionate influence of the group's leaders (De Grada, Kruglanski, Mannetti, & Pierro, 1999; Pierro, Mannetti, De Grada, Livi, & Kruglanski, 2003). For example, Orehek et al. (2010) found that individuals with a high NFC preferred decisive, rigid political leaders over flexible, open-minded leaders whereas those with a low NFC exhibited just the opposite preference.

The group-centric tendency manifest under group members' high NFC also finds expression in pressure toward opinion uniformity, including a rejection of opinion deviates (Kruglanski & Webster, 1991), a distaste for diversity of membership (that connotes the possibility of divergence and dissensus), as well as aversion toward out-groups whose actions or opinions may threaten the in-group's world views (Pierro et al., 2003; Shah, Kruglanski, & Thompson, 1998). In the same vein, Livi, Kruglanski, Pierro, Mannetti, and Kenny (in press) found in three studies that groups composed of individuals high (vs. low) on NFC exhibited greater stability of group norms across different generations of group members. In summary, these studies show that, because groups provide shared knowledge that is therefore pervasive and readily accessible, high NFC individuals are eager to embrace the attendant epistemic security and to protect it from outside influences (i.e., out-groups) as well as from inside threats (i.e., newcomers and in-group deviants).

NFC theory postulates that the moment when a belief "crystallizes" and "turns from hesitant conjecture to a subjectively firm 'fact'" (Kruglanski & Webster, 1996, p. 266) represents the demarcation point that separates seizing from freezing tendencies. Nevertheless, a joint operation of both seizing and freezing tendencies often underlies the NFC effects. Indeed, most decision processes entail both pre- and postcrystallization stages, and seizing and freezing processes, although theoretically distinct and representing sequential phases, are strongly aligned because the motivation to quickly reach the desired state of closure (or, ending the aversive lack of closure) and the motivation to remain in this state (or, preventing the aversive lack of closure from recurring) are strongly intertwined. For example, the use of early cues to form judgments responsible for impressional primacy effects can be considered the result of the combination of an urgency-driven reliance on early information and a permanence-driven disregard of later information. Similarly, group centrism can be considered the result of reliance on easily accessible, shared in-group knowledge as well as derogation of new, "outside" information that threatens to upset one's sense of firm knowledge.

Nonetheless, the distinction between seizing and freezing can have important concrete implications as well. This was demonstrated by Kruglanski et al. (1993), who investigated the role of NFC in (resistance to) persuasion. In two experiments that used an experimental manipulation and a dispositional measure of NFC, respectively, they found that NFC can lead to both higher and lower susceptibility to persuasion, depending on the individual's position in the seizing–freezing sequence. In particular, when, based on earlier information, participants had already formed a definite opinion about the subject, participants high in NFC exhibited pronounced freezing on this opinion and were consequently less easily persuaded. However, if participants had not yet received enough information to form a definite opinion and therefore were still in the precrystallization phase, the position and arguments of the persuader actually provided the desired, readily available information to reach a definite opinion and, hence, closure. As a result, in these conditions, high levels of temporarily or stably present NFC facilitated adopting the persuader's opinion, increasing persuasibility.

In another early study by Kruglanski, Peri, and Zakai (1991), participants were asked to make a decision about the authorship of drawings based on a sample drawing. When participants had an initial hunch in which they had relatively high confidence (i.e., their opinion was already "crystallized"), participants under high NFC tended to search for *less* information than people under low NFC. Under these circumstances, freezing on the high-confidence hunch was an effective way to satisfy their NFC. However, when initial confidence was low, individuals under high (vs. low) NFC searched for *more* information in order to form an opinion and attain the desired closure.

Differential effects of seizing and freezing can also play an important role in the acculturation processes of immigrants. In particular, Kosic, Kruglanski, Pierro, and Mannetti (2004) examined the impact of NFC on the acculturation patterns of Croatian and Polish immigrant samples in Italy. Consistently across both samples and across different measures of acculturation, acculturation patterns were interactively determined by immigrants' NFC and the reference group in which they found themselves upon their arrival. Specifically, if the immigrants arrived in the host country (Italy in this case) together with other coethnics, higher levels of NFC were associated with a stronger tendency to adhere to the culture of origin (i.e., freezing effects) and thus decreased their tendency to assimilate to the host culture. By contrast, if on arrival they found themselves *without* other coethnics, higher levels of NFC augmented their tendency to embrace and adapt to the host culture and consequently reduced their adherence to the culture of origin. These findings indicate that in order to reduce the considerable uncertainty associated with arrival in a new country, high NFC immigrants may turn to whichever cultural reference framework is most capable of providing closure; in the company of coethnics, freezing on the culture of origin provides most immediate closure, whereas in the absence of the coethnic reference group, assimilation to the host country (seizing) provides closure best.

2. NEW DEVELOPMENTS IN NFC THEORY AND RESEARCH

The brief summary of the basic NFC effects on information processing and knowledge construction presented above corresponds to the core focus of the considerable body of research on NFC in the first two decades since its introduction (for more elaborate reviews, see Kruglanski, 2004; Kruglanski et al., 2010; Kruglanski et al., 2006; Kruglanski & Webster, 1996). However, in recent years, NFC-related work has entered a new phase, with notable progress in both basic and applied research. That phase is reflected in two major developments.

The first development pertains to investigators' renewed interest in the fundamentals of the NFC construct, yielding significant further insights into its core conceptual aspects, including the motivational nature of NFC and the interplay between closure needs and abilities; these also prompted advancements in the measurement of NFC as an individual difference variable, and inspired inquiries into the connection between capacity depletion and NFC, the role of NFC in memory phenomena, and the genetic and neural correlates of NFC.

The second major development in NFC research pertained to efforts to expand work on this construct from the lab environment to real-world settings, by studying the key role of NFC in tangible social issues, including significant NFC effects on groups and organizations, its influence on the development and counteraction of prejudice, and its role in political violence and extremism. These developments in both fundamental and applied NFC research are reviewed in the sections that follow.

2.1 NFC: Goal or motivational deficit?

Kruglanski and Webster (1996) proposed that the *need* for closure denotes a motivated tendency, a goal whose attainment gratifies the need in question (cf. Cohen, Stotland, & Wolfe's (1955) argument that a need is characterized by directing behavior toward a goal and causing tension when this goal is not attained). For instance, when uncertain about an ambiguous physical symptom, one's high NFC may prompt one to adopt the goal of finding an answer by consulting an expert (i.e., a medical doctor) presumed capable of providing closure on the subject, and quickly accepting ("seizing" on) whatever diagnosis the expert provides, thus gratifying the underlying need.

The bulk of empirically demonstrated NFC effects, such as the reduced amount of information gathering and hypothesis generation as well as the use of heuristics and readily available information, is consistent with the interpretation that it is the motivational *quest for closure* that produced them, yet an alternative interpretation might entail that they reveal an overall motivational deficit prompting a general reluctance to invest effort in judgments and decision making.[1]

Because in most prior studies the quickest ways to attain closure were also the least effortful, this research cannot decisively adjudicate the goal versus deficit interpretations of the NFC effects. Instead, the answer to this issue lies in responses of high NFC individuals in situations where attainment of closure is laborious and effortful. The question is whether under those circumstances, high NFC leads to increased or decreased mobilization of effort?

To address this issue, Roets and Van Hiel (2008, Study 2) used a categorization task in which participants were presented with a series of rectangles. The rectangles were embedded in a grid and defined by their height on the Y-axis and the position of a small vertical line within the rectangle on the X-axis. Participants' challenge was to discover the categorization rule using a trial-and-error strategy. The task only ended when participants correctly categorized 19 out of 20 successive trials, assumedly indicating they had found the correct decision rule. The results showed that under these circumstances, high NFC individuals exhibited higher and cumulative levels of distress, indicated by a substantial incline in galvanic skin conductance, as long as they had not discovered the decision rule (i.e., reached closure).

The observation that high (vs. low) NFC participants showed a cumulative increase in distress suggests that high NFC is unlikely to represent a *lack* of motivation. More direct evidence against this possibility was provided in a

---

[1] For example, one may argue that high levels of need for closure merely reflect low levels of need for cognition (Cacioppo & Petty, 1982), that is, a "deficit" in the extent to which one "engages in and enjoys thinking" (p. 1). However, as we already pointed out, several studies have shown that the negative correlation between need for cognition and need for closure is fairly modest, and that they yield distinct effects on third variables.

follow-up study by Richter, Baeriswyl, and Roets (2012), who used a similar categorization task to investigate the effect of task difficulty and NFC on engagement-related myocardial beta-adrenergic activity, a psycho-physiological indicator of task investment. The results confirmed that task difficulty effects on cardiac pre-ejection period (PEP) reactivity were moderated by NFC. Where difficulty was low, PEP reactivity (i.e., task engagement) was correspondingly low and independent of participants' NFC level. Where difficulty was high (i.e., closure was hard to achieve), participants with high NFC showed a corresponding increase in PEP reactivity, whereas this was not the case for those with low NFC. These findings clearly indicate that whereas low NFC participants disengaged when the task was more difficult, high NFC participants did not and actually increased their investment in the task to find the solution, and, hence, closure.

In this vein too, several behavioral studies demonstrated that the influence of NFC on information sampling depends on whether or not quick choices really provide closure. For example, Houghton and Grewal (2000) found that high NFC resulted in a less extensive information search in a consumer choice paradigm, but only when participants supposedly already had well-formed and accessible opinions on the product category because it was important to self. In a related study, Vermeir, Van Kenhove, and Hendrickx (2002) asked participants to choose between brands of unfamiliar products so that the reliance on prior knowledge was eliminated. They found that in these situations, high NFC individuals actually sought significantly more information *before* the point at which their (first) opinion was crystallized, but not thereafter. These finding are reminiscent of the results from the persuasion study by Kruglanski et al. (1993) and the drawings study by Kruglanski et al. (1991) described earlier.

Another study by Jaśko, Czernatowicz-Kukuczka, Kossowska, and Czarna (2013) examined the relation between NFC and decision making in an abstract and unfamiliar decision task. Participants were presented with a series of 5×5 matrices, each consisting of 25 gray boxes that turned either yellow or blue when clicked. The task was to decide which of those two colors prevailed on the board and participants could open as many boxes as they wanted before making this decision. After making their decision, the remaining boxes were uncovered, and participants received feedback about points earned (when they were correct) or lost (when they were incorrect). In the high anchor condition, participants read a statement that in this task, people on average open 24 boxes, whereas in the low anchor condition the information stated that people on average open 8 boxes.

In both conditions, participants were also informed that the average decision accuracy level achieved by others was 90%. The results revealed that when a low anchor was presented to participants, those high in NFC examined less information and spent less time on making a decision than individuals low in NFC. In the high anchor condition, the pattern of the results was reversed: high NFC participants searched for more information before making a decision and took longer to make the decision compared to low NFC participants. The authors argued that this anchoring effect occurred because the anchor information itself provides a readily available cue on which high NFC individuals could rely to reduce uncertainty. Additionally, the anchor may also be considered a group norm, to which high NFC individuals conform more strongly (see Kruglanski et al., 2006).

To sum up, various studies have shown that NFC is associated with limited information search, but only when there is an initial, satisfactory basis for closure, whether resulting from familiarity with a subject or sufficiently strong confidence in the initial guess. If high NFC individuals, however, lack a knowledge base on which they can relatively confidently rely, their efforts to sample information are equal or even exceed the efforts of low NFC individuals in their quest for a clear-cut answer. In light of these findings, it does not seem reasonable to view NFC effects as reflecting a cognitive or motivational deficit; rather, accumulating evidence attests to a motivational tendency, that is, a goal or a desire for "*an* answer on a given topic, *any* answer … compared to confusion and ambiguity" (Kruglanski, 1990, p. 337).

2.2 Need versus ability to achieve closure

Important recent advances in NFC research pertain to the distinction between the *need* for closure and the *ability* to achieve closure (AAC). As will be seen, this distinction is fundamental, because the two constructs: (a) are only weakly and usually negatively correlated, (b) yield different, and often opposite, main effects on relevant dependent variables, and (c) show occasional interaction effects with regard to some phenomena. Nonetheless, conflation of closure need and ability has been a recurrent issue in NFC research of the past decades.

A particularly salient expression of such confounding was rooted in psychometric problems with the original NFC scale (Kruglanski et al., 1993; Webster & Kruglanski, 1994). Specifically, Webster and Kruglanski (1994) conceptualized individual differences in NFC in terms of a unitary latent variable, which potentially manifests itself in various ways, that is, as a *preference for order*, a *preference for predictability*, *decisiveness*, *discomfort with ambiguity*, and *closed-mindedness*. These five different manifestations of the NFC were assumed to reflect a single underlying motivation; accordingly, the NFC scale was portrayed as a unidimensional measure with five facet subscales.

However, psychometric analyses (Neuberg, Judice, & West, 1997; see also Neuberg, West, Judice, & Thompson, 1997) showed that the *decisiveness* items had low and mostly negative correlations with the items of the other facets, and indicated a better fit for a two-factor model. In turn, the two-dimensional approach, and especially the interpretation of these dimensions as respectively representing the freezing and seizing tendencies, was questioned in regard to its lack of a theoretical (Kruglanski et al., 1997) and empirical (Roets, Van Hiel, & Cornelis, 2006) foundation. In subsequent research, disagreement about the underlying dimensionality and the lack of a shared understanding of the scale led researchers to apply and interpret the NFC scale at their own discretion, including one-dimensional (e.g., Golec & Federico, 2004) and multidimensional (e.g., Van Hiel, Pandelaere, & Duriez, 2004) reports, as well as applications in which the decisiveness subscale was omitted (e.g., Chirumbolo, Livi, Mannetti, Pierro, & Kruglanski, 2004). Some researchers even explicitly stated that the disagreement on how to measure NFC made them decide to omit the concept from their research, and focus on related concepts instead (Chaiken, Duckworth, & Darke, 1999).

A novel turn in this debate occurred when Roets and Van Hiel (2007) identified the multidimensionality issue to be the result of an unintended conflation of *need* and *ability* to achieve closure in the decisiveness items, following Mannetti, Pierro, Kruglanski, Taris, and Bezinovic's (2002) earlier hint concerning this possibility (see also the proposal by Bar-Tal, Kishon-Rabin, & Tabak, 1997 that epistemic needs and abilities should be treated as separate factors). Indeed, items from the original decisiveness scale, such as "When faced with a problem I usually see the one best solution very quickly," seem to refer to an ability to reach closure, rather than the motivation to reach closure, and might be responsible for the dimensionality issue with the original NFC scale.

Addressing this possibility, Roets and Van Hiel (2007) developed a new set of decisiveness items that were specifically tailored to measure epistemic *motivation* exclusively (i.e., the *need* for decisiveness), with items such as "When I am confronted with a problem, I'm dying to reach a solution very quickly." Their first experiment demonstrated that this revised set of items predicted the typical NFC seizing behavior in terms of judgmental latencies and extent of information processing (controlling for individual differences in ability), whereas the original decisiveness facet was not able to make these predictions. Moreover, Roets and Van Hiel's (2007) second experiment showed that response latencies predicted by the adapted need for decisiveness items were sensitive to experimentally induced manipulations of NFC. Specifically, in a dual-task paradigm, high scorers (compared to low scorers) on the adapted need for decisiveness scale responded more quickly on a decision-making task, but these differences disappeared when NFC was experimentally induced by lowering the importance of the decision task (hence increasing NFC through diminished concerns for accuracy). In contrast, scores on the original decisiveness *ability* facet scale showed no main effects or interaction with the NFC manipulation. Finally, the authors analyzed in two samples the psychometric properties of both the original and the adapted version of the NFC scale, showing that a reassembled NFC scale with the refined decisiveness items (tapping the *need* aspect of decisiveness) replacing the original items resolved the psychometric issues with the original scale and resulted in an unequivocally unidimensional *need* for closure scale. Also, the recently developed 15-item short version of the revised NFC scale (Roets & Van Hiel, 2011b; see Table 1) showed a straightforward unidimensional structure.

Subsequent research has further highlighted the importance of clearly demarcating individual differences in NFC from those in AAC; this was accomplished by showing the distinct relations of these two constructs with third variables, using the original decisiveness facet and/or Bar-Tal's (1994) Ability to Achieve Cognitive Structure (AACS) scale as measures of closure ability. For example, Roets and Van Hiel (2006) showed that whereas the revised decisiveness scale as well as the other facets yield strong relations of *need* for closure with prejudice and conservatism, no such relations are found with the *ability* to achieve closure (measured with the original decisiveness facet scale). In the same vein, Rubin, Paolini, and Crisp (2011) examined the relation between NFC and derogation of deviance in nonsocial stimuli. They presented participants with diagrams depicting two circles labeled "A circle" and "B circle." Inside each circle, there were six or seven category-consistent letters (e.g., "A" in circle A) and one category-inconsistent letter (e.g., "B" in circle A). Participants were asked to rate how much they liked or disliked a particular letter. Their findings showed that NFC was associated with greater liking for stimuli (letters "A" and "B") when they were located consistently with the assigned location of their

Table 1 Short version of the revised NFC scale

I do not like situations that are uncertain
I dislike questions which could be answered in many different ways
I find that a well-ordered life with regular hours suits my temperament
I feel uncomfortable when I do not understand the reason why an event occurred in my life
I feel irritated when one person disagrees with what everyone else in a group believes
I do not like to go into a situation without knowing what I can expect from it
When I have made a decision, I feel relieved
When I am confronted with a problem, I am dying to reach a solution very quickly
I would quickly become impatient and irritated if I would not find a solution to a problem immediately
I do not like to be with people who are capable of unexpected actions
I dislike it when a person's statement could mean many different things
I find that establishing a consistent routine enables me to enjoy life more
I enjoy having a clear and structured mode of life
I do not usually consult many different opinions before forming my own view
I dislike unpredictable situations

This scale is adapted from Roets and Van Hiel (2011b), based on the full revised NFC scale (Roets & Van Hiel, 2007), original scale by Webster and Kruglanski (1994).

relevant category (i.e., in the "A circle" and the "B circle," respectively), compared to letters at inconsistent locations (e.g., the letter "A" in the "B circle"). However, measures of the AAC (i.e., the original decisiveness scale as well as the AACS scale) showed no associations with location preference.

Moreover, closure needs and abilities may also have opposite effects on third variables. For example, Roets and Soetens (2010) showed that whereas closure *needs* were *positively* related to symptoms of psychopathology in a large nonclinical adult sample, the *ability* to achieve closure (measured by a combination of the original decisiveness scale and the AACS scale) showed strong *negative* relations with those symptoms. The authors proposed that in today's complex world, high NFC may lead to more distress in everyday life decision making (see Roets & Van Hiel, 2008), whereas low AAC may lead to feelings of frustration and helplessness, each contributing (independently) to decreased mental well-being.

In addition to the unique effects of closure needs (in contrast to abilities) and the opposite effects of closure needs and abilities, recent research has also uncovered intriguing interaction effects between the NFC and the ability to achieve it. In particular, it was found that for high NFC to yield substantial effects, in some instances, a considerable *ability* to achieve closure must be present as well. For example, Kossowska and Bar-Tal (2013a) showed that high NFC is associated strongly with heuristic information processing only among individuals with a high AAC. In particular, they found that NFC leads to both improved retrieval of schema-consistent information and higher filtering of schema-irrelevant and -inconsistent information, but only among individuals with a high AAC. For low-ability participants, high levels of NFC were associated with superior memory for schema inconsistent and irrelevant information (Study 1). Furthermore, these authors demonstrated that high levels of NFC are associated strongly with quick and simple decision making, but only among individuals who expect to be able to satisfy their epistemic needs. For people who expect to fail because of a low AAC, NFC tended to be associated with more complex and time-consuming decision making. Along similar lines, Kossowska and colleagues (Kossowska, Jaśko, & Bar-Tal, 2012; Kossowska, Jaśko, Bar-Tal, & Szastok, 2012) proposed that high levels of NFC in elderly respondents (see also, Cornelis, Van Hiel, Roets, & Kossowska, 2009; Sedek, Kossowska, & Rydzewska, 2014) do not always result in the same closure behavior found with young respondents (e.g., improved recall for consistent information), because the ability to achieve such closure may become insufficient with increased age.

Whereas the studies reviewed above treated the AAC as an individual difference variable (measured by a scale[2]), several studies have focused on situational manipulations that influence the *ability* to achieve closure as well. The results of these studies suggest that such situational interventions appropriately moderate the effects of NFC on different manifestations of heuristic processing. In particular, manipulations of positive mood or empowerment (Kossowska & Bar-Tal, 2013b; Kossowska, Jaśko, Bar-Tal, & Szastok, 2012, Study 2) increased participants' (perceived) *ability* to attain closure and, therefore, strengthened the positive association between NFC and heuristic

---

[2] Bar-Tal and Kossowska (2010) developed the Ability to Achieve Closure Scale, based on ability items from original Decisiveness scale and the Ability to Achieve Structure scale (Bar-Tal et al., 1997).

processing. Conversely, manipulations of self-image threat (Kossowska, Bukowski, & Guinote, 2013) or decreased cognitive control (Otten & Bar-Tal, 2002; Kossowska, Dragon, & Bukowski, 2015) lowered participants' ability to attain closure and, therefore, resulted in high NFC being associated with less, rather than more, heuristic processing.

To sum up, findings reviewed above suggest that inclusion of the AAC as an inherent component of the theory of lay epistemics may further elucidate our understanding of the use of epistemic seizing and freezing. This conclusion is consistent with the interpretation of NFC as a *goal*, for which the specific effects depend on the available *means* to that goal's pursuit (Kruglanski et al., 2002), which in turn is tapped by the *ability* to impose closure construct. Moreover, these studies support the idea that achieving closure via heuristic processing may not be merely the easy, default option that can be used in any situation or by any individual. Indeed, even though heuristic processing is typically considered to be the most efficient means of achieving certainty because it is relatively automatic and effort-free, some level of a specific (self-perceived) ability is apparently required for an individual to use it as a means to reach closure.

2.3 Motivation versus capacity depletion

In addition to the observation that NFC effects are different from and in some instances are moderated by the AAC, a more general issue that this brings up pertains to the interrelation between cognitive capacity and motivation as these both impact knowledge formation activities. In particular, although the NFC construct is essentially motivational in nature, the question of how epistemic motivation (i.e., NFC) is affected by cognitive capacity (i.e., cognitive resources) is fundamental to a complete understanding of people's knowledge formation processes.

In their original review, Kruglanski and Webster (1996) stated that "the relation between capacity and motivation allows for two separate possibilities: one in which the two are independent of each other and one in which they are causally related" (p. 280). The independence perspective assumes that capacity reduction as such has no motivational consequences whatsoever (even though it may be compensated for by motivational increments, see also Hockey, 1986). To illustrate this perspective, Kruglanski and Webster referred to a cycling metaphor in which "deflation of bicycle tires may be compensated for by enhanced pedaling effort even though it does not cause it" (p. 280). The causality perspective, on the other hand, assumes that depletion of cognitive capacity[3] induces a motivation to expend less effort on the requisite judgment because its rendition has now become more laborious. In other words, cognitive capacity depletion as such may induce a heightened NFC. In terms of the cycling metaphor, this would mean that due to the deflated tires, pedaling becomes so effortful that the cyclist is motivationally inclined to reduce his pedaling effort (and maybe to look for other less effortful ways to reach his target). Kruglanski and Webster (1996) implied the causality perspective to be the most probable one, although conclusive empirical evidence on that point was lacking at the time. Recently, however, several studies have specifically addressed this issue. Some such studies have focused on the effects of situational manipulations of NFC, others on the effects of individual differences in dispositional NFC; both types of research are reviewed in what follows.

2.3.1 Situational manipulations

The distinction between *motivation* and *cognitive capacity* is highly relevant to interpreting the effects of some popular ways of inducing NFC. The effects of experimentally induced NFC have been repeatedly cross-validated with converging effects of individual differences in dispositional NFC and vice versa (e.g., Chiu, Morris, Hong, & Melon, 2000; Roets et al., 2008; Webster & Kruglanski, 1994). Moreover, various NFC effects obtained with a particular manipulation have been replicated with other NFC manipulations (e.g., Roets et al., 2008). Yet, these cross-validations do not preclude the possibility that at least some NFC manipulations might not affect epistemic motivation exclusively, but also influence other key aspects of knowledge formation, in particular impacting cognitive capacity. Indeed, apart from constituting well-established manipulations of NFC, in the literature on human performance, noise and time pressure have usually been considered *stressors* that in and of themselves, without motivational mediation, impede attentional or cognitive performance (e.g., Ariely & Zakay, 2001; Hockey & Hamilton, 1983, Payne, Bettman, & Johnson, 1993).

Thus, in a study on the determinants of information processing extent, Roets et al. (2008) used Mayseless and Kruglanski's (1987) tachistoscope task, in which participants had to identify briefly presented, individual digits (allowing them to request for repeated presentations of each digit, until they felt "sure enough"). They found that in addition to their motivational effect

---

[3] It should be noted that cognitive capacity can be considered to be relative to the task demands. That is, relative cognitive capacity can be lowered by reducing cognitive capacity itself or by increasing the task demands; both interventions are assumed to yield similar effects.

on the extent of information sampling, both noise and time pressure also affected *performance* in the easy and moderately difficult versions of the task (Study 2a). Importantly, however, individual differences in dispositional NFC only showed the motivational effect on information sampling extent, but they did not influence performance (Study 2b). Together, these results suggest that noise and time pressure manipulations yielded a *dual effect* on both motivation and cognitive capacity. However, these findings do not provide straightforward answers to the issue of independence versus causality with respect to the relation between capacity and motivation. A recent follow-up study by Roets and Van Hiel (2011c) tackled this question more explicitly and yielded results supportive of the causality perspective. In that study, using the same tachistoscopic task as Roets et al. (2008), it was found that, compared to a control condition, inducing noise or time pressure resulted in an instant negative effect on performance (i.e., fewer correct identifications from the start) and a slightly delayed negative effect on the extent of information sampling (i.e., less information sampling later on). Furthermore, the impaired initial performance predicted the decline in investment over time, and the effects of noise or time pressure on investment decline were partially mediated through initial performance level. Importantly, because information sampling was affected by stressors only after— and proportionally to—the immediate effect on performance, it appears that the effects of the noise or time pressure manipulations on information sampling extent were not due to capacity reduction as such, but should be interpreted as the result of the capacity-engendered motivational reduction. To use Kruglanski and Webster's (1996) original cycling metaphor: deflation of tires (cf. capacity reduction) immediately reduced the cyclist's speed (cf. performance) even though the pedaling effort initially did not change; only after a few moments, the cyclist reduced his pedaling effort (cf. information sampling). Although tire deflation reduces the cyclist's ability to perform, in itself it does not determine the amount of effort the cyclist can put into pedaling (cf. noise does prevent people from sampling information). Yet the experience of reduced ability to perform changes the motivation of the cyclist, which ultimately affects the pedaling effort. Although these findings indicate that the effects of NFC on information sampling through noise and time pressure manipulations are indeed driven by motivation, the intricate interplay between motivation and cognitive capacity under these manipulations can complicate the interpretation of their effects and may sometimes require complex designs to demonstrate their exact nature. Therefore, we suggest that future research that uses these inductions cross-validate their effects with other manipulations or with a dispositional measure of NFC.

2.3.2 Individual differences

Converging evidence for the causality perspective also has emerged from research showing that individual differences in NFC are associated with identifiable individual differences in actual cognitive abilities. For example, Kossowska, Orehek, and Kruglanski (2010) demonstrated that individuals characterized by a high (vs. low) dispositional NFC also exhibit a slower working memory search (Study 1) and lower working memory capacity (Study 2; for similar results, see Kossowska, 2007a, Study 1, and Czernatowicz-Kukuczka, Jaśko, & Kossowska, 2014).

These findings suggest that less efficient control processes responsible for proper distribution of cognitive resources are associated with higher NFC. Kossowska and colleagues argued that when informational complexity by which individuals are surrounded exceeds their capacity to manage it (due to insufficient relative cognitive capacity), they are inclined to strive for simplification, predictability, and stability in their views. In other words: "need for closure [partly] arises out of long standing 'wired in' limitations in one's cognitive abilities" (Kossowska, 2007b, p. 1118). In line with this assertion, decreases in basic cognitive recourses (such as memory span and processing speed) associated with aging (e.g., Salthouse, 1996) have been proposed to create a need for a more "economic" use of available resources and higher levels of the NFC (Cornelis et al., 2009; see also Hess, 2001).

2.4 A foray into memory: Need for closure as basis of retrieval-induced forgetting

Nearly without exception, prior NFC research has focused on aspects of *judgment formation* targeting (a) the extent of information processing and hypothesis generation prior to *freezing*, (b) reliance on accessible stereotypes and easy heuristics en route to the crystallization of opinions, or (c) social preferences for consensus and uniformity that promise a stable judgmental environment or a firm shared reality. A novel line of research has examined NFC impact in the realm of *memory*. In this vein, studies by Kossowska and Bar-Tal (2013a) discussed earlier found that, given a sufficient AAC, high NFC individuals show improved retrieval of schema-consistent information and higher filtering of schema-irrelevant and -inconsistent information. Furthermore, recent research by Pica, Pierro, Bélanger, and Kruglanski (2013, 2014) focused on the improved capability that NFC may afford to center on a focal judgment of interest and keep at bay interfering cognitions. These properties may be of pivotal importance in the realm of *recall* specifically related to *retrieval* of desired items (e.g., a name of a person of interest) that may require the suppression of competing memories. An experimental setting expressly designed to study these phenomena is known as the *Retrieval Practice Paradigm* created to investigate what is known as *Retrieval-Induced Forgetting* (RIF; Anderson, 2003; Anderson, Bjork, & Bjork, 1994; Levy & Anderson, 2008).

In the retrieval practice paradigm, participants study and remember a set of category-exemplar pairs (usually eight categories, such as Fruits, Instruments, Colors, ..., with six items each: e.g., "Fruit-Apple" and "Fruit-Orange" in the category "Fruits"). Following the initial study phase, participants are asked to selectively retrieve half of the items of half of the categories (usually three items from a subset of four categories). The phase of selective retrieval is accomplished using cued stem tests (e.g., "Fruit-Ap___"). After a distraction task, participants are asked to recall all the exemplars of all the categories originally studied. Typically, subjects recall more retrieval-practice items (Rp+; e.g., "Fruit-Apple") and fewer non-practiced items from practice categories (Rp-; e.g., "Fruit-Orange"), as compared to items from nonpracticed categories (Nrp; e.g., "Color-White"). The improved recall of the practiced items (Rp+ > Nrp) is referred to as the *facilitation effect*. The latter, critical, effect of reduced recall of nonpracticed items in the practiced categories compared to recall of items from the nonpracticed categories (Nrp > Rp-) is referred to as *retrieval-induced forgetting*.

Whereas originally RIF has been treated as a "purely" cognitive effect (Anderson, 2003; Anderson et al., 1994; Levy & Anderson, 2008), there are good reasons to believe that it would also be impacted by motivational factors, particularly by the NFC. Under a heightened NFC, individuals tend to become impervious to information that could potentially undermine their targeted judgments and impressions (Kruglanski & Webster, 1996). There is a substantial body of evidence that retrieval of items from memory requires a focus on the class of items to be recalled and imperviousness to other items that could run interference with retrieval of the targeted items (Engle, Conway, Tuholski, & Shisler, 1995; Koessler, Engler, Riether, & Kissler, 2009; Roman, Soriano, Gomez-Ariza, & Bayo, 2009). Therefore, NFC could facilitate such selective focus, augmenting the RIF effect.

Several recent studies carried out within the *Retrieval Practice Paradigm* found support for the latter possibility. Specifically, Pica et al. (2013) found in two experiments that where suppression of interfering items was difficult (the amount of practice lent to the focal items was low), given the presence of adequate cognitive resources, RIF was positively affected by participants' NFC. In three subsequent studies, Pica et al. (2014) found strong NFC effects on RIF in a Retrieval Practice Paradigm couched in eyewitness scenarios: high NFC individuals were more prone than low NFC individuals to "forget" those particular pieces of information (e.g., items stolen from a house in a burglary case) whose retrieval was not privileged in the initial recall (Rp-). Intriguingly, this research (Pica et al., 2014, Study 3) also revealed that the NFC-induced suppression of interfering items allowed the implantation of false memories in places where the true items were suppressed (i.e., the "forgotten" evidence), a finding with obvious practical implications for real-life court environments. For example, early interrogations asking a witness to recall certain features about a suspect (e.g., color of his shirt) may not only hamper recall of other related features (e.g., color of his hat) in high NFC individuals during later interviews; it may also make them more susceptible for planted false memories about these related features (e.g., asking about the color of the suspect's cap in later interview may make the witness "remember" the suspect wearing a cap, rather than a hat).

2.5 Neural and genetic correlates

The dynamics of theory development in science are often shaped by novel discoveries in methods and concepts that enable a fresh look into basic theoretical constructs and a reexamination of prior postulates. Building on recent insights from neuroscience and behavioral genetics, several research programs have been initiated to explore the neurological and genetic correlates of the NFC. Although such approaches are new to NFC research, these cutting-edge programs have already yielded substantial insights into attentional control and regulatory processes associated with high levels of NFC, as well as into the genetic basis of cognitive and affective mechanisms underlying demonstrated NFC effects.

2.5.1 Neural correlates

Earlier behavioral studies have demonstrated that high NFC is related to an increased focus on a specific part of the cognitive field (i.e., on specific categories or concepts), suggesting that it affords superior cognitive selectivity and the ability to shut out irrelevant distractions and noise (Kossowska, 2007a, 2007b; Kruglanski & Webster, 1996; Pica et al., 2013, 2014). They also revealed that NFC reduces the incidence of uncertainty and conflict by privileging answers that successfully accommodate experience, representing a narrow goal pursuit that turns attention away from discrepancy and encourages rigid predictions that assimilate inconsistent observations. These psychological differences between high and low NFC individuals may map onto two widely studied (neuro)cognitive processes: *attentional control* (Lackner, Santesso, Dywan, Wade, & Segalowitz, 2013) and *conflict monitoring* (Botvinick, Braver, Barch, Carter, & Cohen, 2001).

Kossowska et al. (in press) investigated whether NFC is related to selective attention, as reflected in event-related potentials (ERPs) during a traditional color-naming Stroop task (1935) as well as a visual distractor task (VDT). In the latter task, a small letter against an emotional picture is presented in a random location on the screen. The required response is determined by a cue shown just before the picture. Both of the tasks pit competition between target and irrelevant features of the stimuli and require participants to respond to one dimension of a stimulus rather than another stronger, but conflicting, dimension. Therefore, these tasks require feature selection processes and allow to study early allocation of attention to the selected feature of the stimuli. The selective attentional control is usually indexed by N1 component[4] of the ERPs (Herrmann & Knight, 2001), with greater deviations in N1 indicating increased focus on attended stimuli and increased suppression of attentional response to unattended stimuli (Singhal, Doerfling, & Fowler, 2002). The results of this study revealed that higher NFC levels are related to higher N1 amplitude both in the Stroop task (bilaterally) and in the VDT (right hemisphere only, which is more strongly recruited when spatial attention is important). The latter effect is illustrated in Figure 2.

In addition, Kossowska, Czarnek, Wronka, Wyczesany, and Bukowski (2014) demonstrated that high (vs. low) NFC is related to the self-regulatory process of conflict monitoring, defined as a general mechanism for detecting when one's habitual response tendency is mismatched with responses required by the current situation (Yeung, Botvinick, & Cohen, 2004). Specifically, they found that low (vs. high) NFC is associated with significantly higher conflict-related neural activity when response inhibition was required. In their study, the electroencephalographic activity of the brain was recorded as participants completed a color-naming Stroop task

---

[4] This N1 component is a negative deflection in ERP on posterior scalp regions, which peaks between 140 and 250 ms after visual stimulus onset on posterior scalp regions (Mangun & Hillyard, 1988; Kappenman & Luck, 2011).

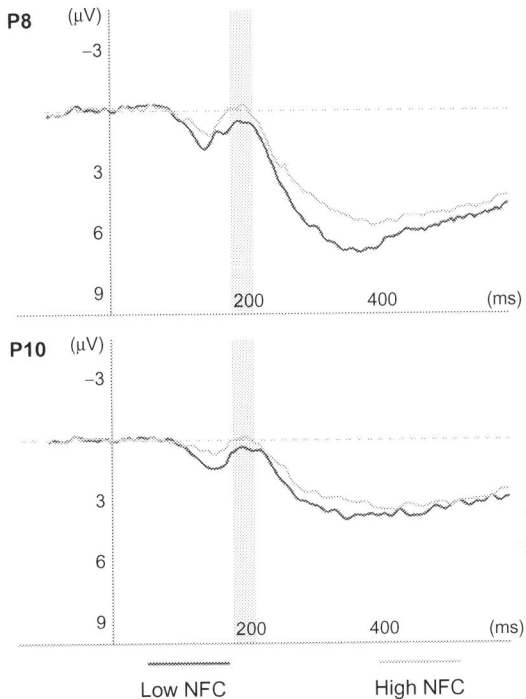

Figure 2 Stimulus-locked grand average ERPs recorded at right hemisphere parieto-occipital electrodes in VDT task in response to all trials for the low NFC (black lines) and high NFC (gray lines) group. Time windows of interest (N1 component; 180–210 ms poststimulus) are highlighted; time 0 indicates stimulus onset. *Adapted from Kossowska et al. (in press).*

(Stroop, 1935). Conflict-related anterior cingulate cortex (ACC[5]) activity was indexed by two ERP components: error-related negativity (ERN) and the N2 component.[6] In line with the hypothesis, low (vs. high) NFC was strongly and negatively correlated with ERN amplitudes (Figure 3), as well as with N2 amplitudes when participants performed incongruent (vs. congruent) trials in a Stroop task.

---

[5] Conflict monitoring has been associated with neurocognitive activity in the ACC (Botvinick et al., 2001; Carter et al., 1998).

[6] ERN is a medial–frontal potential that peaks within 100 ms of error commission in simple decision tasks (Falkenstein, Hohnsbein, Hoorman, & Blanke, 1990; Gehring, Goss, Coles, Meyer, & Donchin, 1993). Its amplitude depends critically on processing of target stimulus information (which underlies the ability to produce error-correcting responses). N2 is a component that typically peaks approximately 250 ms following a correct response in congruent and incongruent trials. Its amplitude depends primarily on processing of irrelevant stimulus information (which determines the level of incorrect response activation) (Yeung & Cohen, 2006).

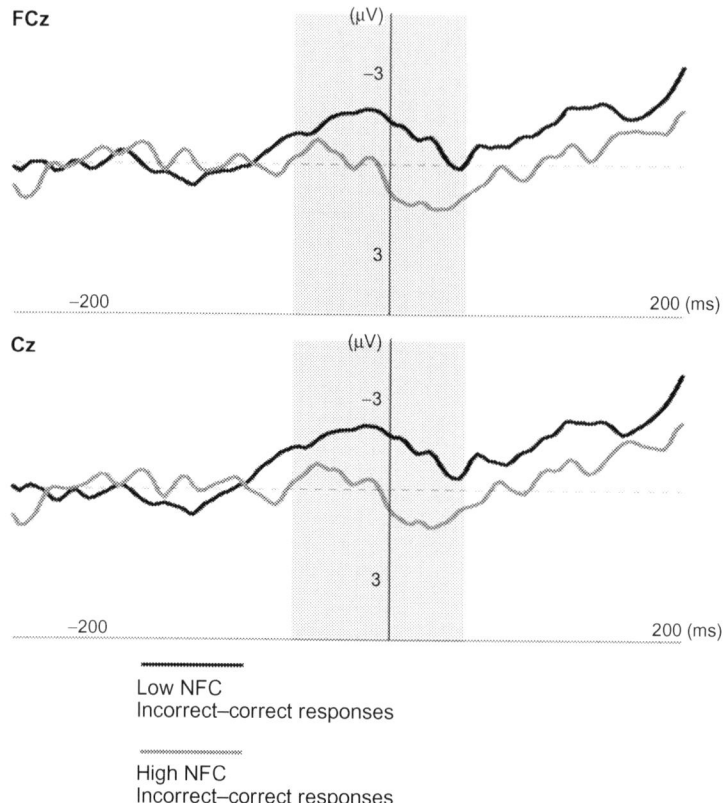

Figure 3 Response-locked grand average ERPs recorded at frontocentral (FCz, Cz) electrodes in Stroop task illustrating ERN component (ERP from incorrect responses minus ERP from correct responses; calculated for latency window −65 to 50 ms after motor response indicated on time 0). Black line represents responses obtained for low NFC group, and gray line shows responses measured for high NFC group. *Adapted from Kossowska et al. (2014).*

To summarize the results of these studies, greater NFC predicted higher neural activity when selection processes occurred (increased N1), while also predicting lower *conflict-related* activity (reflected in decreased ERN and N2 effect). These results may suggest that a speeded neural response to a distracting stimulus in high NFC individuals (i.e., disengaging attention from task-irrelevant information in the early stages of stimulus processing) appears to confer some advantage in acting as a bulwark against anxiety-producing uncertainty and minimizing the experience of error (Hajcak, 2012; Weinberg, Riesel, & Hajcak, 2012).

On the other hand, the greater selective focus on the target stimulus exhibited by high NFC individuals may exact a toll on flexibility due to higher freezing. Research by Viola, Tosoni, Kruglanski, Galati, and Mannetti (2014) used the flanker task (Eriksen & Eriksen, 1974) to investigate this hypothesis. In this task, participants are instructed to respond to a centrally presented target (e.g., letters or symbols) but have to disregard surrounding flanker stimuli, which can be congruent or incongruent with the target. Viola and colleagues found that high NFC individuals exhibited lesser cognitive flexibility, operationally defined as a reduced response time to incongruent (vs. congruent) relations between target and flanker stimuli if the preceding trial was incongruous (vs. congruous). Of particular interest, these differences were mediated by decreased corticocortical *connectivity* between the ACC and the dorsolateral prefrontal cortex (DLPFC) as assessed by fMRI. Such reduction of the functional connection between the ACC and DLPFC regions has previously been related to impairment of mechanisms for adaptation to behavioral conflict (Botvinick, Nystrom, Fissell, Carter, & Cohen, 1999; Kerns et al., 2004).

2.5.2 Genetic correlates

Recent research has also sought to examine the genetic underpinnings of NFC. In particular, Cheon, Livingston, Chiao, and Hong (2015) have focused on the genetic polymorphisms related to the affective and cognitive mechanisms that underlie NFC. In terms of affective mechanisms, we have already discussed how NFC is characterized by aversion and distress in the face of uncertainty and ambiguity, evidenced, for example, by the psychophysiological findings of Roets and Van Hiel (2008). Of special relevance to the genetic underpinnings of NFC, previous research has shown that possessing a short-allele (vs. long-allele) of the serotonin transporter gene (*5-HTTLPR*) is associated with greater emotional reactivity to uncertain, ambiguous, and unfamiliar situations (e.g., Drabant et al., 2012; Heinz et al., 2007). Hence, short-allele (vs. long-allele) carriers may also show higher levels of NFC.

In terms of cognitive mechanisms, NFC has been described as characterized by close-mindedness and rigid adherence to preexisting knowledge structures and expectations, thereby reflecting limited cognitive flexibility. Most relevant in this respect are the findings from previous research that possessing two Met-alleles (vs. two Val-alleles) of catechol-O-methyltransferase (*COMT*) polymorphism is associated with lower cognitive flexibility (Colzato, Waszak, Nieuwenhuis, Posthuma, & Hommel,

2010; Fallon, Williams-Gray, Barker, Owen, & Hampshire, 2013; Nolan, Bilder, Lachman, & Volavka, 2004). Hence, two Met-allele (vs. Val-allele) carriers may also show higher levels of NFC.

Both predictions were corroborated by the aforementioned work of Cheon et al. (2015) with a group of 116 Caucasian-American participants. Specifically, their results showed that (1) participants who possessed at least one short-allele (S/S or S/L) showed a higher NFC level than did those who possessed two L-alleles (L/L) of 5-HTTLPR, and (2) those who possessed two Met-alleles of COMT showed a higher NFC level than did those who possessed at least one Val-allele. Furthermore, the effects of 5-HTTLPR and COMT genotypes on NFC were found to be additive (rather than interactive), suggesting that these two genetic polymorphisms associated with affective and cognitive mechanisms, respectively, contribute to NFC independently. Of particular interest, the research by Cheon et al. (2015) further revealed that these genotypes, mediated through NFC, relate to social ideology and implicit racial prejudice as well. As such, this research is highly relevant to claims made at a further juncture in this review regarding the status of NFC as a fundamental basis of social attitudes and prejudice.

The findings reviewed above shed light on the affective and cognitive underpinnings of NFC and imply how fundamental epistemic motives may emerge from distinct biological pathways. Cheon et al.'s approach provides an innovative contribution to NFC research by using genetic markers as a vehicle to elucidate the biological (and associated psychological) mechanisms that underlie epistemic needs for closure, as well as the attitudinal consequences of such needs. That being said, it is important to understand that these results pertain to biogenetic mechanisms that probabilistically contribute to variations in epistemic needs, social attitudes, and ideologies, rather than defining these in a deterministic manner. Indeed, the study by Cheon et al. (2015) demonstrated that the motivational and attitudinal outcomes were predicted by *multiple* genetic mechanisms, and still other genes that contribute to discomfort with ambiguity/uncertainty or cognitive inflexibility may also play a role. Moreover, in addition to its genetic origins, dispositional NFC also depends on socialization and cultural norms (e.g., see Chiu et al., 2000; Dhont, Roets, & Van Hiel, 2013; Kruglanski & Webster, 1996), and social–environmental influences have been shown to moderate the pathways across genes and social cognition (e.g., see Cheon, Livingston, Hong, & Chiao, 2014).

2.6 Theoretical developments summary

Considerable recent research has contributed to a deeper understanding of fundamental aspects of the NFC construct. There is compelling evidence now that NFC constitutes a genuine motivational variable, that is, an authentic superordinate goal rather than a mere motivational deficit that curtails information processing. There also is evidence that understanding specific NFC effects requires taking into account the ability to impose closure and the habitual ways of reaching closure (e.g., via heuristics or extensive information processing). In short, the NFC constitutes a goal, whose particular cognitive and behavioral consequences depend on the perceived means to that goal's pursuit.

Progress has also been made in elucidating the relation between motivation and cognitive capacity in mediating NFC effects. It appears that both situational and developmental (i.e., age-related) restrictions in cognitive capacity may induce the NFC apart from the nonmotivational effects that capacity restrictions may impose. NFC research in the field of memory has revealed NFC to consistently moderate the suppression of interfering cognitions in the service of improved retrieval. Finally, there have been promising recent advances in understanding the neural and genetic underpinnings of the NFC, related to the situational and dispositional tendencies to exhibit this motivational tendency.

3. NFC EFFECTS IN REAL-WORLD SETTINGS

An important advance in the life of a theory is setting up bridges to real-life settings where its concepts are assumed to apply. As Lewin famously taught "there is nothing as practical as a good theory" (Lewin, 1947, p. 169). Thus, an important test of a theory's "goodness" is its real-world applicability. Recently, there has been growing research interest in the impact of NFC on real-life phenomena concerning significant social issues. The most substantial research programs in this surge of applied work pertain to NFC influences in *organizations*, its status as a *source of prejudice*, its role in *prejudice reduction*, and its relation with the development of *(violent) extremism*. We review these in turn.

3.1 NFC effects in organizational settings

Recent work has revealed a substantial influence of NFC on various key aspects of organizational dynamics. Most notably, these studies related

NFC to (1) attitudes toward *organizational change*, (2) organizational bases of *social power*, (3) preferences for *leader type*, (4) concerns with *leaders' fairness*, and (5) *organizational fit* effects.

3.1.1 Coping with organizational change

With recent surges in technological developments, increased channeling of venture capital into new projects, globalization trends, and companies' attempts to retain their competitive edge through mergers, downsizing, and restructuring, organizations today are facing more changes, at a more rapid pace, than ever before (Wamberg & Banas, 2000). Differences in the NFC are particularly relevant to the dialectics of permanence and change that these days constitute a central feature of life in organizations: Because of their desire for stability and permanence, individuals with high NFC in particular may feel uncomfortable with change and may be limited in their capability to cope with it.

Accordingly, Kruglanski, Pierro, Higgins, and Capozza (2007) tested the hypothesis that NFC is negatively related to individuals' ability to successfully cope with organizational change. This work included four studies conducted in various organizations in Italy, and employing contemporaneous (Studies 1, 2, and 3) as well as longitudinal designs (Study 4). The results showed that NFC was negatively related to a measure of coping with change in a variety of organizational settings and in diverse employee samples; these included nurses at a Roman hospital who had been subjected to extensive role changes (Study 1), employees of the Italian Postal Service which had recently been subjected to changes owing to a privatization of the sector (Study 2), and workers at the City of Rome whose organizational roles were undergoing alterations due to integration of various sections and an overall reorganization of incentive-systems (Study 3). In all these instances, different measures of coping with change were negatively related to NFC. Of particular importance, an interaction effect emerged between NFC and perceived organizational support for innovation and change within the organization, demonstrating that the relation between NFC and coping with change was less negative when perceived support of innovation and change was high, rather than low, embodying a group norm that high NFC individuals typically support (see Kruglanski et al., 2006). The fourth study in the Kruglanski et al. (2007) series employed a longitudinal design with measurements before and after the implementation of the organizational change in the Italian Postal Service System. Consistent with Studies 1–3, NFC was negatively related to positive expectancies about change, and to coping with change.

Furthermore, NFC scores were negatively related to work attitudes tapped in the second phase of the research (i.e., organizational commitment, job satisfaction), and these relations were mediated by coping with change scores.

3.1.2 Bases of social power in organizations

As discussed earlier, a number of studies examining NFC effects in group contexts (for an overview, see also Kruglanski et al., 2006) have pointed to the syndrome of *group centrism* under a heightened NFC, whereby (1) NFC augments the *desire for consensus* in groups, which (2) manifests itself in pressures toward uniformity, both of which promote (3) the emergence of an autocratic group structure.

Pierro, Kruglanski, and Raven (2012) hypothesized that these predilections of high NFC members should lead them to prefer what Raven, Schwarzwald, and Koslowsky (1998) called the "hard" bases of social power (including legitimate power, coercive power, and reward power) over "soft" power bases (including expert, informational, and referent power bases). According to Raven et al. (1998) the soft power bases allow recipients greater autonomy and are less controlling than the hard bases. Because autonomy may encourage extended deliberations in a group and retard the formation of consensus, high NFC group members should feel more comfortable with hard (vs. soft) power bases, given that the former are perceived as quicker means to opinion uniformity. This proposition was tested in three studies conducted in a variety of Italian organizations. The first and second study looked at the relation between supervisors' NFC and their preferred use of different (hard vs. soft) power tactics (measured via the Interpersonal Power Inventory usage scale, Raven et al., 1998; Schwarzwald, Koslowsky, & Ochana-Levin, 2004). Results of both studies confirmed that supervisors' NFC was positively related to their use of hard tactics and negatively related to their use of soft tactics. Notably, these relations remained stable controlling for other variables of obvious relevance to the exercise of power, such as participants' degree of authoritarian orientation (Adorno, Frenkel-Brunswik, Levinson, & Sanford, 1950; Altemeyer, 1998). The third study further elaborated on this issue and investigated the effects of a "fit" between subordinates' NFC and supervisors' power tactics on subordinates' job performance and effort investment, proposing that a correspondence between supervisors' and subordinates' shared normative reality may motivate subordinates and spur them to effort, leading to superior performance. Results of moderated regression analyses showed that subordinates' high (vs. low) NFC together with supervisors' use of hard tactics indeed predicted subordinates' improved job performance and effort investment, whereas subordinates' high (vs. low) NFC together with supervisors' use of soft tactics predicted inferior performance and reduced effort.

3.1.3 Leader prototypicality

A leader property of special relevance to followers' NFC is *prototypicality*, the degree to which a leader is perceived as similar to other group members, and hence the degree to which he or she is regarded as an embodiment of organizational identity. Specifically, stronger group centrism of high (vs. low) NFC individuals should lead them to be particularly attuned to prototypical versus nonprototypical leaders. Pierro, Cicero, Bonaiuto, van Knippenberg, and Kruglanski (2005) asked employees in three Italian companies to complete the NFC scale and a measure of perceived leader prototypicality. The results corroborated the hypothesis that high (vs. low) NFC individuals exhibit a substantially greater preference for, and satisfaction with, prototypical (vs. non prototypical) leaders; these effects were reflected in higher perceived leadership effectiveness, higher job satisfaction, higher self-rated performance, and lower turnover intentions. Notably, these findings complement and extend the social identity analyses of leadership effectiveness (Hogg, 2001); specifically, they support the proposition that people with high (vs. low) NFC are more attuned to group members who typify the group (hence are the prime exemplars of the group's consensual reality) and support their leadership status within the organization.

3.1.4 Procedural fairness

A dominant theme in fairness research is that (procedural) fairness fulfills an important uncertainty-reducing function (Lind, 2001; Van den Bos & Lind, 2002). Relatedly, procedural fairness conveys the extent to which the authority figures can be *trusted*, because it introduces constraints that remove anxieties about possible exploitation of subordinates by their superiors (Leventhal, 1980; Lind, 2001; Lind & Van den Bos, 2002; Tyler, 1997). Factors, like NFC, that represent concern with uncertainty reduction, should therefore moderate the reliance on leader's procedural fairness as perceived evidence of leadership effectiveness. In particular, the relation between perceived leader procedural fairness and leadership effectiveness should be stronger for followers high in NFC. Based on this reasoning, Pierro, Giacomantonio, Kruglanski, and van Knippenberg (2014) investigated the moderating role of NFC in the relations between procedural fairness and a variety of indicators reflecting different aspects of leadership effectiveness.

Two separate survey studies, conducted in a sample of bank employees (Study 1) and workers at a social security institution and an engineered environmental solutions company (Study 2), corroborated the predicted interactions between leader procedural fairness and NFC on indicators of leadership effectiveness. In particular, Pierro and colleagues (2014) found that especially for employees high in NFC, leaders perceived as high in procedural fairness yielded positive effects on team identification, job satisfaction, effort investment, and performance (both self- and supervisor-rated).

Additional evidence for the role of NFC in the relation between leader procedural fairness and indicators of leadership effectiveness was provided by Giacomantonio, Pierro, and Kruglanski (2011) in a survey study conducted on a sample of public employees. Consistent with research reported above, the results of this study showed that in leader–employee conflicts, perceived fairness of the leader promoted employees' use of a solution-oriented conflict handling style (as opposed to a nonconfrontational or control style), and this effect was stronger for employees high (vs. low) in NFC. In other words, because of its uncertainty-reducing properties, procedural fairness in leaders yields a more constructive (i.e., more effective) approach to conflict resolution for employees high in dispositional NFC.

3.1.5 Need for closure fit effects on performance in organizations

A central function of groups to their members is epistemic in nature, as they afford a shared reality to their members (see Kruglanski et al., 2006). On the one hand, the firmer a group's shared reality, the more attractive it should appear to individuals high in NFC, and the less attractive it should appear to those low in NFC, who avoid closure and are repelled by a rigid consensus admitting little or no doubt. On the other hand, whether the shared reality of a group is firm or not depends on whether its members hold cognitive firmness at a particular premium, which in turn is reflected in members' aggregated level of NFC. Thus, individuals whose NFC levels are similar to those of their fellow group members (and, hence, of the group as a whole) may be expected to function better and yield better organizational performance than individuals in groups who are mismatched in the NFC of their members. A recent study by Pierro, Sheveland, Livi, and Kruglanski (in press) provided support for this assertion, showing that NFC measured on the aggregate group level moderated the relation between individual-level NFC and individual-level performance. In particular, high NFC individuals performed better in workgroups in which the other members were also high in NFC, whereas low NFC individuals performed better in workgroups with lower levels of aggregate NFC (see Figure 4).

Furthermore, high NFC individuals identified themselves more with their work team when the remaining members of the team were also high in NFC, whereas low NFC individuals identified themselves more with the work team when the remaining members of the team were also low in NFC (see Figure 5). Finally, in line with the fit hypothesis, employees' levels of self-reported identification with their workgroups partially mediated the impact of the person–group NFC fit on performance.

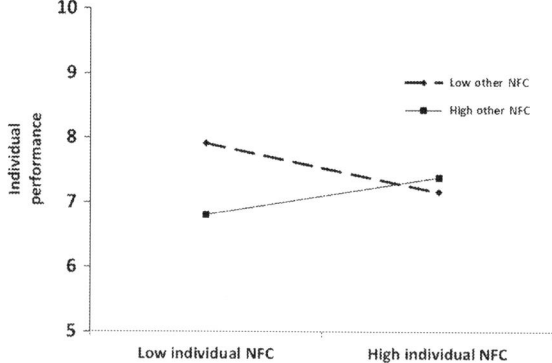

Figure 4 Individual-level performance as a function of individual and other members' need for closure. *Adapted from Pierro et al. (in press).*

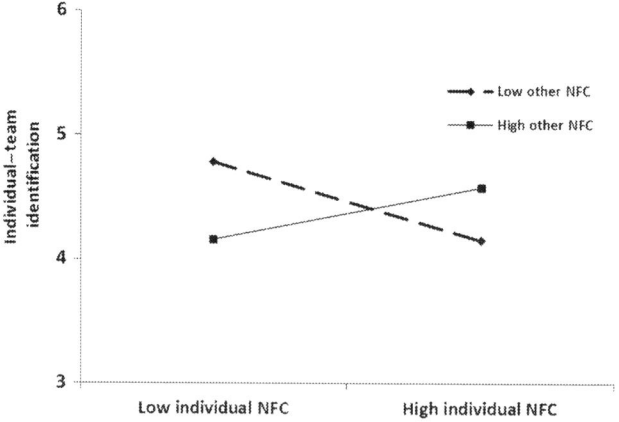

Figure 5 Individual-level team identification as a function of individual and other members' need for closure. *Adapted from Pierro et al. (in press).*

3.1.6 Summary

NFC has a substantial influence on various key aspects of organizational dynamics. In an era when organizational change has been moving at an unprecedented speed and to an unprecedented extent, the finding that NFC reduces employees' ability to cope with change is of high practical relevance, as is the finding that this effect can be attenuated when the organizational climate is supportive of change (Kruglanski et al., 2007). Moreover, the recent work on NFC in organizational settings has advanced our understanding of leadership styles and practices and their effect on employees, showing that NFC encourages the emergence of an autocratic, "hard powered" leadership structure in organizations (Pierro et al., 2012) and guides employees' preferences for and satisfaction with prototypical leaders (Pierro et al., 2005). Furthermore, because procedural fairness reduces uncertainty, high NFC employees do better if they have leaders who are perceived as high in procedural fairness (Pierro et al., 2014), which eliminates uncertainty as to outcomes and assuages attendant anxiety. Finally, organizational NFC studies have drawn attention to the importance of *leader–follower* and *individual–group* fit in NFC and its role in enabling optimal organizational functioning. In particular, a match between subordinates' NFC and supervisor power tactics (Pierro et al., 2012), or between individual and group NFC (Pierro et al., in press), enhances performance, whereas a mismatch reduces it.[7]

3.2 NFC and prejudice

3.2.1 NFC as the source of prejudice

As Kruglanski and Webster (1996) noted, knowledge-construction processes are suffused with social significance, not in the least because social entities such as social groups or categories are often the objects of knowledge-construction endeavors. Therefore, the way we perceive and "know" others should be subject to the same NFC-related effects as is nonsocial knowledge formation. In this vein, several recent studies have examined how NFC affects the way people see groups, in particular NFC effects on group stereotyping and prejudice. Specifically, Roets and Van Hiel (2011d) pointed out that, although NFC theory originates from a research tradition outside the prejudice literature, the NFC shows a striking similarity

---

[7] In two related studies conducted with Chinese government employees, Guan, Deng, Bond, Chen, and Chan (2010) found that NFC moderated—and, more specifically, augmented—both the positive relation between person-job fit and job satisfaction and the negative relation between person-job fit and turnover intention.

with characteristics of the "prejudice-prone personality" described by Allport (1954) in his seminal work on "The nature of prejudice," whereby "a person's prejudice is unlikely to be merely a specific attitude to a specific group; it is more likely to be a reflection of his whole habit of thinking about the world" (p. 170). Allport further argued that this way of thinking is shaped by motivated cognition and explicitly proposed that prejudice-prone individuals prefer a clearly structured world and have a particular need for order, especially social order. They also feel uncertain and uncomfortable in the face of ambiguity or a lack of clear answers and fail to see all relevant sides to a problem. As such, Allport's description of the motivated way of thinking by the prejudiced individual bears an uncanny similarity to the core concepts from NFC theory, as illustrated in Table 2.

Table 2 Fit between Allport's (1954) motivated cognitive style and need for closure

Prejudice-prone motivated cognitive style (Allport)	Need for closure (Kruglanski)
	Two underlying tendencies
"Urge for quick and definite answers" (p. 403)	Urgency tendency (seizing)
"Cling to past solutions… more given to perseveration" (p. 402)	Permanence tendency (freezing)
	NFC subscales
"Like order, especially social order" (p. 404)	Preference for order (e.g., "I like to have a place for everything and everything in its place")
"Feel more secure when they know the answers" (p. 402) and "Latch onto what is familiar" (p. 403)	Preference for predictability (e.g., "I don't like to go into a situation without knowing what I can expect")
"Afraid to say 'I don't know'" (p. 402) and "Better not to hesitate" (p. 403)	Need for decisiveness (e.g., "When I'm confronted with a problem, I'm dying to reach a solution very quickly")
"Cannot tolerate ambiguity" (p. 175, see also p. 401)	Discomfort with ambiguity (e.g., "I dislike it when a person's statement could mean many different things")
"Narrow-minded" and "Fail to see all relevant sides to his problem" (p. 402)	Closed-mindedness (e.g., "I do not usually consult many different opinions before forming my own view")

Adapted from Roets and Van Hiel (2011d).

Consistent with this parallelism, a number of studies have shown dispositional NFC to be strongly related to various measures of blatant, subtle, and modern forms of racial prejudice (e.g., Onraet et al., 2011; Roets & Van Hiel, 2006, 2011a; Van Hiel et al., 2004) and even to implicit measures of racism (Cunningham, Nezlek, & Banaji, 2004). Moreover, NFC has also been linked to other targets of prejudice, for example, groups based on sexual orientation or identity (Brandt & Reyna, 2010; Tebbe & Moradi, 2012). Recently, Roets, Van Hiel, and Dhont (2012) used Glick and Fiske's (1996, 1999) Ambivalent Sexism Inventory and Ambivalence toward Men Inventory scales to measure sexism toward women and men, respectively, and investigated these measures' relations with NFC. These studies found that NFC predicted sexism toward both women and men among both male and female respondents, demonstrating that NFC strongly relates to all gender-based prejudices, and actually has a substantially greater predictive power than even the actual gender of respondents! Of greatest interest, high NFC is not only linked to greater stereotypes and prejudiced attitudes toward members of the opposite sex, but toward one's own gender group as well (Roets et al., 2012). This finding indicates that, at least for some social categories, the effects of NFC on prejudice may go beyond simple in-group favoritism and out-group derogation.

To understand the relations between NFC and prejudice, it is crucial to recognize the ways in which high NFC individuals seek to satisfy their need for quick, easy, firm, and stable knowledge about the social world. Specifically, to meet their desire for closure in the social environment, people typically resort to *essentialist categorizations* and *authoritarian ideologies*, which represent some of the most powerful, proximal determinants of stereotyping and prejudice (see Roets & Van Hiel, 2011d).

3.2.1.1 Social categorization and essentialism

Categorization is widely recognized as a necessary process in the construction and organization of social knowledge. Indeed, Allport (1954) already stated that "Categorical thinking is a natural and inevitable tendency of the human mind" (p. 171), because (social) categorization allows people to bring structure to the (social) world and cope with its complexity. Moreover, for social categories to be useful in everyday life, people have to believe them to be meaningful beyond the level of artificial constructions. In particular, they have to believe that a social category captures a collective "essence" of some sort: a fundamental core that defines the group and expresses the common identity of its members, rendering them all fundamentally alike and allowing inferences to be drawn about them based on their category membership (see Gelman, 2003; Haslam & Levy, 2006; Medin, 1989). According to Allport, the "belief in essence" (p. 174) of social groups is characteristic of the prejudiced personality. This contention has been supported by various studies showing, for example, that a belief in essence of race predicted greater stereotyping of Blacks (Tadmor, Chao, Hong, & Polzer, 2013), a greater tendency to use race as the basis of categorization, and a greater sensitivity to race-related facial features in social categorization (Chao, Hong, & Chiu, 2013).

From the NFC perspective, allocation of individuals to essentialized social categories constitutes a useful manner to make quick, easy, and stable inferences about persons. Over the years, several studies have provided indirect evidence for a relation between NFC and essentialism. For example, Dijksterhuis et al. (1996) found that high NFC individuals perceive target groups as more homogeneous compared to low NFC individuals, whereas Kruglanski and Mayseless (1988) demonstrated that people high in NFC use substantially less case-specific or individuating information, focusing instead on group membership information when making social judgments about individuals. Moreover, Keller (2005) reported a positive relation between scores on an abridged version of the NFC scale and a measure of biological determinism, which can be considered an expression of essentialist thinking (see also Rangel & Keller, 2011).

More direct evidence for the essentialism hypothesis was provided in a series of recent studies by Roets and Van Hiel (2011a), who explicitly tested the relation between dispositional NFC and essentialist thinking about race, revealing strong correlations (up to $r = 0.50$) in various student and adult samples. Additionally, they demonstrated that NFC, experimentally induced by means of time pressure (vs. evaluation apprehension), increases essentialist thinking, even for fictitious ethnic groups (see Figure 6), and that endorsement of essentialist ideas about racial groups is responsible for a substantial part of the relation between NFC and racial prejudice, in various student and adult samples.

3.2.1.2 Socio-ideological attitudes

Jost, Glaser, Kruglanski, and Sulloway (2003) proposed that people adopt ideological belief systems in part because they promise to satisfy their deeper psychological needs and motives. Indeed, research over the past decade has consistently demonstrated that individual differences in NFC are strongly related to conservatism and Right-Wing Authoritarianism

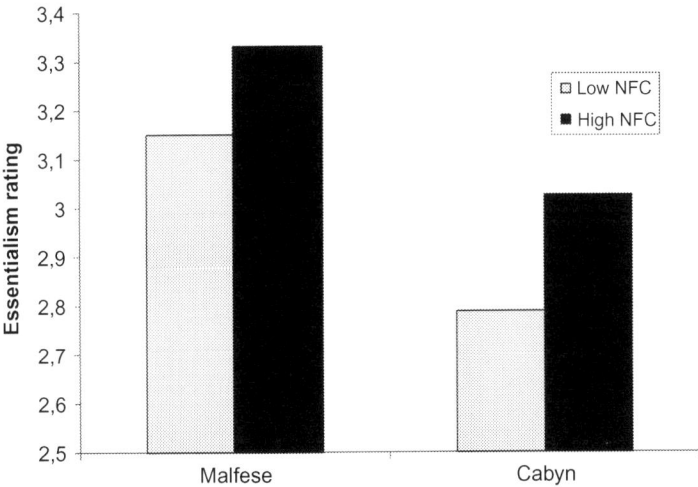

Figure 6 Essentialism ratings for two fictitious ethnic groups (the Malfese and the Cabyn) under high and low NFC manipulations (i.e., time pressure vs. feedback). *Adapted from Roets and Van Hiel (2011a, Study 2).*

(RWA; e.g., Cornelis et al., 2009; Dhont et al., 2013; Golec de Zavala & Van Bergh, 2007; Jost et al., 2003; Kossowska & Van Hiel, 2003; Kruglanski et al., 2006; Onraet et al., 2011; Roets et al., 2006; Van Hiel et al., 2004). Moreover, the assumption that NFC underlies authoritarian ideology is further supported by studies showing that situationally induced NFC also leads to typical expressions of authoritarianism, such as the derogation of opinion deviants (Kruglanski & Webster, 1991), the formation of and preference for autocratic group structures with centralized authority (Pierro et al., 2003), and an increased need for conformity and consensus (Kruglanski et al., 1993).

Various researchers have proposed models in which social–ideological attitudes mediate the impact of NFC on prejudice. Studies by Cunningham et al. (2004), Onraet et al. (2011), Roets and Van Hiel (2006), and Van Hiel et al. (2004) have demonstrated that elevated endorsement of *authoritarian attitudes* largely explains high NFC individuals' increased levels of blatant, subtle, and even implicit racism. Such models have typically revealed substantial mediation effects through RWA (Altemeyer, 1981, 1998) and to a lesser degree through Social Dominance Orientation (SDO; Pratto, Sidanius, Stallworth, & Malle, 1994).

Roets et al. (2012) demonstrated that mediation through socio-ideological attitudes also accounts for gender-based prejudice. Notably, although hostile and benevolent forms of sexism were differently related to RWA and SDO, the overall relation between NFC and sexism was again primarily mediated by RWA. Moreover, Dhont et al. (2013) recently found NFC in parents and their children to be concordant and, most importantly, that the intergenerational transmission of dispositional NFC underlies the transmission of authoritarianism and racism from parents to their children. The authors interpreted the intergenerational transmission primarily in terms of socialization processes, although genetics may also play a role. Indeed, the work by Cheon et al. (2015) suggested that the genetic polymorphisms underlying differences in NFC also predicted ideology and implicit racism (as measured by an Implicit Association Test) indirectly through NFC. Further research is warranted to illuminate the role of genetics in this important domain.

Although, in line with Jost et al. (2003), a host of studies have shown strong relations between NFC and *traditional* worldviews, this connection is not absolute. Indeed, Golec de Zavala and Van Bergh (2007) have demonstrated that NFC may also lie at the basis of other worldviews "whose content differs on the surface, but which share certain important formal and structural characteristics (p. 589)." In particular, these authors argued that although *traditional* worldviews are "based on belief in a single unshakeable truth of a transcendental, nonhuman character, not susceptible to rational verification or evaluation" (p. 590), whereas *modern* worldviews consider truth as "verifiable and legitimized by rational scientific means, rather than guaranteed by some transcendental reality" (p. 590), both worldviews define values as absolute rather than relative, and truth as definite rather than indeterminate. As such they are—as far as NFC is concerned—functionally similar, but both at odds with postmodern worldviews, which are existential or relativistic and cast "doubts on the existence of an objective truth that is independent of social and historical context" (p. 591). Accordingly, Golec de Zavala and Van Bergh (2007) found that although NFC was most strongly related to traditional worldviews, it also showed a substantial positive relation with modernism (whereas the relation with postmodernism was negative). Moreover, although NFC was overall positively related to conservative ideology, this relation resulted from two opposite indirect effects: a strong positive indirect effect through traditionalism and a weaker, negative indirect effect through modernism.

In a later study, Golec de Zavala, Cislak, and Wesolowska (2010) found that NFC was positively related to preference for aggressive actions against the out-group only when participants also identified themselves as conservative. Furthermore, in their second study, they found positive relations between NFC, political conservatism, perceived out-group threat, and out-group hostility, but high NFC individuals showed higher hostility toward the out-group only if they identified themselves as conservative and perceived the out-group as threatening.

Overall, the studies by Golec de Zavala and colleagues suggest that although NFC is generally associated with traditionalist ideologies giving raise to negative out-group attitudes, other worldviews (e.g., modernism) may also satisfy an individual's NFC, in which case, negative out-group attitudes are not consequential.

3.2.2 NFC-based prejudice reduction
Whereas numerous studies have focused on the positive relation between NFC and prejudice, findings from three recent research programs have suggested that the prejudice of high NFC individuals is neither inevitable nor irreversible. The first research program examined the possibility of changing (i.e., lowering) individuals' prejudice levels via changing their *level of NFC*. The second program investigated how reducing individuals' *ability* to meet their closure needs may reduce prejudice. Finally, the third program has explored the possibility of reducing prejudice through leveraging high NFC individuals' increased susceptibility to the positive effect of intergroup contact. These three programs are examined now in turn.

3.2.2.1 Reduction of NFC and prejudice through multicultural experiences
The possibility, documented in prior research, of situationally increasing or decreasing NFC opens up a way of reducing stereotyping and prejudice via the lowering of NFC (e.g., see Kruglanski & Freund, 1983). Unfortunately, given the transient nature of these effects, manipulating NFC offers little opportunity for an enduring prejudice reduction. Yet, recent research on the effects of multiculturalism has revealed a promising avenue that holds the possibility of creating a long-term impact on NFC and prejudice.

Tadmor, Hong, Chao, Wiruchnipawan, and Wang (2012) investigated the impact of exposure to multiculturalism on prejudice, through reduced levels of NFC. Although previous research has suggested that subtle exposure to culture mixing may increase individuals' levels of NFC (Morris, Mok, & Mor, 2011), Tadmor and colleagues argued that when immersed in an unfamiliar multicultural environment, reliance on automatic processes and schemas formed by socialization within one's own familiar culture becomes insufficient. Further, as multicultural experiences accumulate, so does the new information that is distinct, inconsistent, or even contradictory to internalized schemas of the relevant culture. As a result, scripts and knowledge structures no longer provide sufficient guidance on how to act, nor do they afford a sense of predictability. Crucially, in these circumstances, people are "armed with little knowledge and much uncertainty" (Tadmor et al., 2012, p. 753); this leads them to become "epistemically unfrozen" and ready to adopt new information in order to achieve the desired closure (cf. the differential effects of NFC on persuasion depending on the confidence in existing knowledge, see Kruglanski et al., 1993). Tadmor and colleagues proposed that reliance on existing knowledge structures, including stereotypes and prejudiced perception, will therefore be reduced when immersed in multicultural contexts. In a series of cross-sectional and experimental studies, they were indeed able to demonstrate that exposure to and/or experiences of multiculturalism led to a reduction in stereotype endorsement (Studies 1, 4, and 6), symbolic racism (Study 5), and discriminatory hiring decisions (Study 2). Moreover, experimental exposure to multicultural experiences caused a reduction in NFC (Studies 3 and 6), and the ameliorative effects of multicultural experiences on intergroup bias were fully mediated by lower levels of NFC (Studies 4, 5, and 6). Additionally, these studies showed that effects of exposure to multiculturalism on stereotyping and prejudice, through reduced levels of NFC, were not limited to attitudes toward the ethnic/cultural groups directly involved in the multicultural experience, but also generalized to other ethnic groups and other, unrelated, stereotyped groups, such as homosexuals. The latter findings further support the claim by Roets and Van Hiel (2011d) that NFC reflects Allport's (1954) idea of the *prejudiced personality*.

3.2.2.2 Inability to achieve closure

A second way whereby prejudice in high NFC individuals may be reduced has been suggested by a research program on the interaction between the NFC and the ability to achieve it. As noted earlier, Kossowska and Bar-Tal (2013a) showed in a series of studies that the degree to which high NFC individuals exhibit various closure-bound behaviors depends on their (perceived) AAC. Most relevant for the relation between NFC and prejudice is the study in which the authors investigated the interaction between NFC and AAC on stereotype-based impression formation (Study 3). Specifically, Kossowska and Bar-Tal argued that although individuals with high NFC are more motivated to use stereotypical thinking, when they are also low on AAC, they will be less able to freeze the epistemic process sufficiently to avoid inconsistent information, or to form one-sided and unambiguous categorizations. In their study, participants read a short description of a woman who was either portrayed in a traditional or a nontraditional role and were subsequently asked to rate the target on stereotypical dimensions of competence and warmth (see Fiske, Cuddy, & Glick, 2006). NFC and AAC were measured as dispositional variables and exhibited a significant interaction effect in line with the researchers' expectations: the target woman in the traditional role condition was rated as higher in warmth and lower in competence, whereas the woman in the nontraditional role was rated as less warm and more competent by high NFC respondents, but only when their AAC was also high. When AAC was low, high NFC respondents actually formed less stereotypic impressions.

In another set of studies, Kossowska et al. (2015) demonstrated that participants with high levels of NFC but low AAC actually exhibited positive attitudes toward a negatively stereotyped out-group (Gypsies). In this study, participants' perception of their AAC was experimentally lowered using a computerized version of a concept formation task, which was originally developed as the Informational Helplessness Training procedure (Sedek & Kofta, 1990). In the helplessness condition (low AAC), participants were requested to complete six tasks that were, in fact, unsolvable, whereas in the control condition, participants were given tasks that were solvable. The authors argued that, in the low AAC condition, high NFC participants lost confidence in their ability to make effective use of their schemas (negative stereotype of Gypsies in this case), which led to deeper processing of information inconsistent with the negative stereotype (i.e., positive information). As a result, the inability of low AAC individuals to use only one-sided and unequivocal descriptions of Gypsies may have facilitated more positive attitudes toward the out-group.

3.2.2.3 Intergroup contact

Arguably, the intergroup contact hypothesis formalized by Allport (1954) has been the single most influential scientific framework concerned with prejudice reduction (see Pettigrew & Tropp, 2006, 2008). Pettigrew and Tropp's (2006) recent meta-analysis of 515 studies confirmed that intergroup contact typically reduces intergroup prejudice (mean effect size, $r = -0.21$) and that the optimal contact conditions proposed by Allport (equal status, intergroup cooperation, the pursuit of common goals, and the presence of institutional support) are facilitating rather than necessary requirements for the effects.

Recently, Dhont, Roets, and Van Hiel (2011) investigated whether intergroup contact is also effective for high NFC individuals. Of interest, Allport (1954) himself argued against this being the case, assuming that people with a "prejudiced personality" (i.e., individuals high in NFC) are simply too rigid to change. However, in their studies, Dhont et al. (2011) found that not only was intergroup contact effective for high NFC individuals, but people high in dispositional NFC were actually *more* susceptible to the positive effects of intergroup contact on prejudice reduction than were low NFC scorers. This finding emerged not only in each of their cross-sectional studies but also in a field experiment (Study 3), lending particular credence to these findings. The latter, real-life intervention study showed that Belgian high school students, *especially* those high in NFC, who went on a 1-week, intense-contact school trip to Morocco, subsequently exhibited substantially less negative out-group attitudes than a control group that was not involved in the program (see Figure 7).

Finally, Dhont et al. (2011) proposed that the reduction of intergroup anxiety is an important mediator through which the effect of intergroup contact on various forms of prejudice in high NFC individuals operates. Indeed, intergroup contact has been shown to diminish intergroup anxiety, which consequently reduces prejudice (e.g., Brown & Hewstone, 2005; Pettigrew & Tropp, 2008). Based on the findings of Studies 4 and 5, the

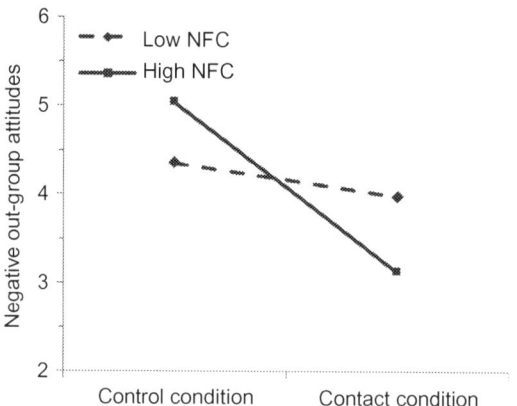

Figure 7 Effect of intergroup contact on negative attitudes toward the out-group under high (+1 SD) and low (−1 SD) dispositional NFC. *Adapted from Dhont et al. (2011, Study 3).*

authors concluded that people high in NFC—who feel most averse and fearful toward the unfamiliar, the ambiguous, and the unpredictable—benefit the most from the anxiety-reducing effects of positive intergroup contact.

Further insight into this process may accrue from research described earlier on genetic polymorphisms linking a short-allele (S-allele) of the serotonin transporter gene (5-HTTLPR) to higher NFC scores (Cheon et al., 2015). As it turns out, the same S-allele has also been associated with a higher susceptibility to particular environmental influences because of heightened emotional reactivity (Belsky & Pluess, 2009; Uher et al., 2011). Thus, positive environmental cues of intergroup contact may bring greater intergroup contact benefits to high NFC participants because of their genetic susceptibility to such influences. Similarly, negative intergroup contact may be expected to have stronger negative effects on intergroup attitudes of high (vs. low) NFC individuals, as was already shown for individuals scoring high on RWA (Dhont & Van Hiel, 2009), which, through NFC, is also linked to the 5-HTTLPR short-allele genotype (Cheon et al., 2015; see also Cheon et al., 2014).

In addition to reduced anxiety by increased familiarity with the out-group, the high salience of the positive information obtained by positive contact may also contribute to the more prominent effects of intergroup contact for high NFC individuals. In particular, positive information may replace negative information from earlier socialization as the most salient and easily accessible information, which then will be used (i.e., *seized upon*) by high NFC individuals when making judgments about the out-group. Indeed, the latter mechanism could explain why, in most of the studies by Dhont et al. (2011), the combination of high NFC and high contact actually yielded the lowest levels of prejudice.

3.2.3 Summary

NFC-based research on prejudice and prejudice reduction extends Allport's (1954) seminal insights into the nature of prejudice and its psychological bases. A growing body of evidence suggests that, in fact, NFC constitutes the specific aspect of personality, alluded to by Allport, that accounts for essentialist thinking, particular socio-ideological attitudes, and, consequently, the tendency to internalize stereotypes and display prejudices. Notably, other related constructs such as experiential openness and need for cognition do not show this striking theoretical convergence, and neither do they yield such strong and unique effects (e.g., Cornelis & Van Hiel, 2006; Onraet et al., 2011; Roets & Van Hiel, 2011d). However, NFC theory and research also suggest that negativity to an out-group is not an *inevitable* consequence of this "motivated way of thinking." For example, although high NFC individuals seek definite knowledge, the latter may also be conferred by schemas and structures that have no negative implications toward out-groups (e.g., the modernist world view). Finally, and of considerable practical importance, NFC theory suggests ways of reducing prejudice, be it through reducing the level of NFC, reducing confidence in one's AAC, reducing uncertainty-based intergroup anxiety, and/or refreezing attitudes on positive schemas. In this regard, it should be noted that such interventions have different applicability when aiming to reduce prejudice in high NFC individuals. Exposure to multiculturalism in order to lower NFC, or exposure to intergroup contact to reduce in-group anxiety and instigate refreezing on positive schemas may be used "chronically" to engender long-lasting attitude change. Yet, interventions based on the reduction of people's AAC in order to curb the use of stereotypes when judging people may be more suitable for specific, acute situations, such as job interviews. Given the potentially negative "side effects" of low AACS on mental well-being mentioned earlier (see Roets & Soetens, 2010), it seems that long-lasting reduction of AAC should be avoided.

3.3 NFC and violent extremism

Akin to the impact of NFC on social categorization and group centrism, recent work has examined NFC effects on extremism and political violence. In situations of real-life intergroup conflict, where determination and swift action are of the essence whereas ambivalence and indecision are an unaffordable luxury, NFC-based group centrism may greatly amplify social categorization and foster strong adherence to in-group narratives that portray the in-group as right and the out-group as wrong. This may encourage extreme anti-out-group attitudes that delegitimize out-group perspectives and justify aggression and violence against the out-group. Moreover, this research program also advances Oppression–Humiliation theories of terrorism (e.g., Juergensmeyer, 2000), by proposing that under (perceived) humiliation, NFC increases as a response to self-uncertainty and loss of personal significance, which in turn may lead to violent extremism. Three sets of studies examined these notions in real-world contexts (mostly) characterized by violent intergroup conflict.

3.3.1 Need for closure, group glorification/victimization, and extremism

Dugas et al. (2015) carried out five studies looking at the relation between NFC and aspects of group centrism that may lead to intergroup violence mediated by glorification of the in-group and the perception of it being unjustly victimized by the out-group. In the first two studies, conducted in Palestine's West Bank (Study 1) and in the United States (Study 2), respectively, NFC was shown to lead to a greater sense of moral license to engage in violence against a (deliberately unspecified) *out-group*, mediated by an increase in the in-group's perceived victimhood. The next two studies replicated the identical mediation pattern among Catholic students in Northern Ireland (Study 3) and Jewish-Israelis (Study 4), showing greater moral licensing to engage in violence against Irish Protestants and Palestinians, respectively. Finally, Study 5, with Jewish-Israelis, experimentally heightened (vs. reduced) NFC; this promoted greater moral license and more extreme moral decisions against members of the out-group on the part of high (vs. low) NFC participants, and the effects were again mediated by in-group glorification and its perceived victimhood.

3.3.2 Need for closure, in-group narrative, and extremism

Two recent studies examined the relation between participants' NFC, their embracing of the *in-group narrative* (extolling the group's virtues and its unjust victimhood), and the consequent support for aggression and violence against the adversarial out-group (Schori-Eyal, Halperin, Bar-Tal, Porat, & Kruglanski, 2015). These processes were examined in Israeli participants within the context of the Israeli-Palestinian conflict, one of the most enduring and intractable conflicts in the world today. Bruner (1990) defined collective narratives as "social constructions that coherently interrelate a sequence of historical and current events; they are accounts of a community's collective experiences, embodied in its belief system and represent the collective's symbolically constructed shared identity" (p. 76). In the context of an intractable intergroup conflict exemplified by the Israeli-Palestinian feud, an in-group narrative typically paints the in-group as just, moral and unfairly treated by the out-group (Bar-Tal, 2013; Haidt & Graham, 2007; Hammack, 2011a, 2011b). The present studies embraced the foregoing conceptual definition of "in-group narrative" and assessed it empirically.

The first study investigated the relation between NFC and support for violence against the Palestinian out-group, mediated by commitment to the group narrative. As expected, NFC was negatively related to support for compromise, willingness to forgive the Palestinians, and reconciliation. Conversely, respondents' NFC was positively related to support for moral license to employ "all means necessary" in defense of the in-group. Also as hypothesized, these relations were mediated by endorsement of the *group narrative*, measured indirectly via participants' (dis)agreement with items that affirm the legitimacy of alternative narratives likely to be at odds with the common, in-group enhancing, narrative. Specifically, participants were asked to report about the extent to which (1) they would like to read books or articles about the history of the Palestinian people; (2) they would like to get more information about the Israeli-Palestinian conflict from foreign sources, presenting unfamiliar aspects, (3) soldiers who witness forbidden behavior toward Palestinian civilians should expose the information to the media, and (4) if the Israel Defense Forces commit forbidden acts in the Occupied Territories, the Israeli media should report it.

The second study assessed participants' conflict-related attitudes at three points in time: (1) in January 2012, during a period devoid of major hostilities between Israelis and Palestinians, (2) during a military operation that Israel conducted in the Gaza strip in November 2012, and (3) in July 2013, shortly following the announcement that Israeli-Palestinians negotiations are about to resume but prior to the commencement of actual negotiations. The three waves of data collection represented a unique opportunity to test the hypothesized model at the peak of dramatic political events, as well as revisiting the same participants while the conflict-engendered tension ebbed and flowed. The methodology also enabled the examination of concrete, event-specific manifestations of both militant and conciliatory tendencies as a function of participants' NFC and their commitment to the in-group narrative. Across all three waves of this research, NFC was positively associated with support for aggression against the out-group and negatively associated with support for compromise (both to end the escalation and as part of impending peace negotiations). Importantly, this relation was mediated by commitment to the in-group narrative, this time measured directly via items such as "the history of the conflict we grew up with is the most accurate one, relative to the history as told by the Palestinians" and "many things that we learned about the conflict have been shown to be wrong" (reverse scored).

3.3.3 Humiliation, need for closure, and radicalism

Whereas the first two sets of studies described above demonstrated the relation between NFC and extremism and explained mechanisms behind this relation, a third set of studies examined how intergroup conflict situations can heighten the individual's actual level of NFC. In three studies, Kruglanski et al. (2015) tested the hypothesis that feeling humiliated, excluded, or discriminated against brings about a loss of personal significance (see Kruglanski et al., 2013), which instills self-uncertainty and doubt about one's self worth. Such situations may be ubiquitous in conditions of intergroup conflict in which personal suffering in hands of the enemy, or losses inflicted on one's group (casualties, defeats) combine to produce powerful feelings of lost significance.[8] Moreover, because holding positive self-regard constitutes a fundamental human motivation, such uncertainty and doubt about the self engender considerable negative affect that fuels a motivation to remove the uncertainty, hence elevating one's NFC. Acceptance of clearcut, radical world views restores the desired closure, and in the context of an intergroup conflict such world views tend to sharply demarcate between one's own in-group and its presumptive enemies, neglect the out-group's point of view, and justify aggression against it (through the mechanisms described above).

Study 1 examined these notions in an at-risk population of young Muslim immigrants (of Moroccan origin) in a disadvantaged neighborhood in southern Spain. Study 2 examined imprisoned Islamic militants in the Philippines: members of the Abu Sayyaf group (on the State Department's list of international terrorist organizations). Study 3 investigated hardcore members of the Liberation Tigers of Tamil Eelam (LTTE), another well-known terrorist organization, who were held in detention centers in Sri Lanka. Even though the contexts of these studies, the participants' culture, and the situations in which they found themselves were starkly different from each other, the findings of each study were highly similar. Specifically, Study 1 found that perceived maltreatment of one's own (Muslim) in-group by the Spanish population was positively related to NFC and to support for the Sharia law in Spain (an extreme attitude given that Spain is a devout Catholic country). Of particular interest, respondents' NFC mediated the relation between perceived maltreatment and support for the Sharia law. In other words, the higher respondents' perception of maltreatment suffered by the Muslims, the higher was their NFC, and in turn

---

[8] Analyses of the phenomenon of Chechnyan Black Widows or the case of Hnadi Taisir Jaradat who killed 21 and wounded 60, during her attack at the Maxim restaurant in Haifa, Israel in 2003, show that the loss of loved ones at the hands of the enemy preceded their radicalization. Having a close person wrested away from oneself in that manner is likely to induce a sense of powerlessness and aversive self-uncertainty that progress to the embracement and implementation of a closure providing extremist ideology that is easily accessible in their environment.

the stronger was their support for introducing Sharia law to govern Spain. Similarly, Study 2 found that sense of humiliation in detained members of the Abu Sayyaf group in the Philippines was positively related to their NFC and to Islamic extremism assessed via a reliable measure constructed in consultation with Islamic clerics. Moreover, the relation between participants' own sense of personal humiliation and endorsement of Islamic extremism was mediated by NFC: those participants who felt highly humiliated in their daily lives, thus experiencing a more pronounced loss of significance, tended also to have higher NFC scores than participants who felt less humiliated. In turn, detainees who had higher NFC scores tended to support Islamic extremism to a greater extent than detainees with lower NFC scores.

It is of interest to note here that whereas in the study with the Moroccan youth in southern Spain the loss of significance had to do with the perceived discrimination of their group (i.e., Muslims), in the second study, the loss of significance had to do with personally humiliating life experiences. Thus, it appears that the source of significance loss does not matter much; rather, it is the significance loss itself (of whatever origin) that may drive the radicalization process via NFC.

Study 3 in this series examined a sample of former members of one of the most violent terrorist organizations in history, known as the LTTE. Specifically, this research focused on a group of hardcore (highest risk category) members of the LTTE at a detention facility of Boosa in the city of Galle, Sri Lanka. Responses to the surveys administered to these detainees indicated that their sense of lost significance (indicated by their frequency of feeling ashamed and disgusted with oneself, resulting from experienced humiliation) was related to their NFC as well as to their support for an armed struggle against the Sinhalese majority. Moreover, NFC mediated the relation between significance loss and support for violence against the Sinhalese majority. These results again support the model whereby loss of significance increases one's need for certainty and closure, which in turn augments support for radical ways of dealing with the out-group.

3.3.4 Summary

The recent endeavors to apply NFC research to diverse real-world contexts characterized by pronounced intergroup conflicts have highlighted the pivotal role of NFC in the development of violent extremism, supporting the theory whereby NFC intensifies adherence to in-group narratives about the nature of the conflict, which in turn promotes extremist attitudes that justify aggression and violence against the adversarial out-group. Given that intergroup conflicts often involve considerable turmoil and aversive uncertainty that may heighten individuals' NFC, it appears that this psychological factor could be of particular importance in promoting extremism and violence against perceived detractors of the in-group. Additionally, in cases of intergroup conflict, humiliation (either personal or based on one's social identity) may intensify one's NFC, which in turn may augment extremism against the out-group.

4. CONCLUDING REMARKS
4.1 The recent progress

People's interaction with their physical and social environments is largely enabled through information they register and understand. Admitting or refusing such information, therefore, constitutes a fundamental juncture that feeds into our decisions and shapes the trajectories of our lives. The need for cognitive closure is the psychological mechanism fulfilling this gatekeeping function; it is not surprising, therefore, that it has been central to a wide array of research programs addressing the motivational bases of lay epistemics,[9] judgment and decision making, and individual cognition, as well as group and organizational dynamics. In recent years, a remarkable surge in both fundamental and applied NFC research has broadened the scope of this inquiry and highlighted the relevance of NFC to these diverse domains of human experience.

Specifically, new developments in basic psychological research have elucidated the motivational nature of NFC and its interplay with cognitive ability and capacity; these findings provide a useful conceptual framework for addressing issues of effort mobilization and cognitive performance, human knowledge formation, and judgment and decision making. Moreover, promising new directions integrating approaches from neuroscience and behavioral genetics are beginning to delineate the "hard-wired" sources and mechanisms that lie at the heart of fundamental NFC effects.

Beyond these advancements in fundamental research, recent inquiries in applied contexts have revealed NFC's relevance to major real-world issues of contemporary interest. Thus, research within the NFC framework has advanced our insights into how people function within a broad range of

---

[9] Recent studies on the role of NFC in lay versus expert epistemics in applied fields such as medical decision making (Roets, Raman, Heytens, & Avonds, 2014) corroborate that NFC primarily has an influence on judgments in less (vs. more) experienced decision makers.

organizational settings, including their coping with organizational change, their exertion and acceptance of leadership, and the effects of their motivational fit with their group on their satisfaction and performance.

At a broader level, the NFC concept has proven key to a better understanding of a number of universal social issues faced by societies around the world, such as intergroup prejudice and extremism. In particular, recent discoveries from NFC research have had substantial consequences for theorizing on prejudice and its underlying mechanisms, and especially for scientific perspectives on promising avenues of prejudice reduction. Finally, research on specific target groups engaged in intractable real-world conflicts has contributed to a better understanding of radicalization and violent extremism, expanding and complementing sociological and psychological theories concerning terrorism and political violence.

4.2 Challenges ahead

Notwithstanding the progress achieved thus far, research within the NFC framework is far from complete. Indeed, considerable challenges lie ahead. One problem that awaits further clarification is the *ability to achieve closure* and its precise workings. Though research suggests this particular ability has important consequences, its ingredients have not yet been fully identified. A promising avenue for research, therefore, would be to investigate further this particular ability and determine its components and modes of functioning.

Also, although recognition of the distinct role of AAC has resolved the psychometric problems with the original NFC scale (see Roets & Van Hiel, 2007), yielding a one-dimensional scale that exclusively taps into the *need* for closure as a broad construct, other aspects regarding the measurement of NFC are still unexplored. In particular, future research could take up the challenge of disentangling the tendencies to seize and freeze by developing specific scales that individually tap into these two fundamental processes in NFC theory.

Another issue awaiting further examination concerns the developmental origins of the NFC. Initial steps in this direction have been taken by Kossowska and colleagues (Kossowska, 2007a, 2007b; Kossowska et al., 2010), who demonstrated that individual differences in NFC are correlated with differences in working memory capacity, the latter presumably leading to the former. Also relevant here is research by Cheon et al. (2014; 2015) implicating genetic differences as a possible source of NFC differences, as well as Dhont et al.'s (2013) evidence for the intergenerational transmission of NFC. Nevertheless, the socialization and developmental antecedents of trait NFC remain largely unexplored. It seems plausible to speculate that aversive uncertainty experienced when growing up, for instance at times of war, dislocation, or economic downturn, may imbue certainty with particular value, thus inducing the NFC as a stable motivational predilection. It is also possible that family dynamics characterized by tense disagreements between one's parents or caretakers, creating a sense of confusion and uncertainty for the child, may contribute to NFC development. These issues deserve to be probed in future NFC research.

Continued brain research into the neural correlates of NFC, following the initial steps taken by Kossowska et al. (2014) and Viola et al. (2014), would also seem of particular importance. Given the centrality of the NFC to broad domains of human functioning, it is plausible that its arousal would reveal distinct patterns of brain activity. In a similar vein, Cheon et al. (2015) have recently started delving into the genetic underpinnings of NFC, providing some promising findings, but much work remains to be done to understand the role of genetics in the development and expression of NFC.

Finally, building on an advanced understanding of the NFC, its antecedents, and its consequences, a crucial goal of future NFC research should be to bring NFC to the "real world" and further translate these insights into interventions designed to improve human performance at individual, group, and societal levels.

ACKNOWLEDGMENTS

The preparation of this chapter was supported in part by a grant from the National Science Foundation—Flanders (Belgium) awarded to Arne Roets, and a grant from the National Science Center (Poland) DEC 2011/02/A/HS6/00155 awarded to Malgorzata Kossowska.

REFERENCES

Adorno, T. W., Frenkel-Brunswik, E., Levinson, D. J., & Sanford, R. N. (1950). *The authoritarian personality*. New York: Harper.

Allport, G. (1954). *The nature of prejudice*. Reading, MA: Addison-Wesley.

Altemeyer, B. (1981). *Right-wing authoritarianism*. Winnipeg, Canada: University of Manitoba Press.

Altemeyer, B. (1998). The other "authoritarian personality". *Advances in Experimental Social Psychology*, *30*, 47–92.

Anderson, M. C. (2003). Rethinking interference theory: Executive control and the mechanisms of forgetting. *Journal of Memory and Language*, *49*, 415–445. http://dx.doi.org/10.1016/j.jml.2003.08.006.

Anderson, M. C., Bjork, R. A., & Bjork, E. L. (1994). Remembering can cause forgetting: Retrieval dynamics in long-term memory. *Journal of Experimental Psychology: Learning, Memory and Cognition, 20,* 1063–1087.

Ariely, D., & Zakay, D. (2001). A timely account of the role of duration in decision making. *Acta Psychologica, 108,* 187–207.

Bar-Tal, Y. (1994). The effect on mundane decision-making of the need and ability to achieve cognitive structure. *European Journal of Personality, 8,* 45–58.

Bar-Tal, D. (2013). *Intractable conflicts: Socio-psychological foundations and dynamics.* Cambridge, NY: Cambridge University Press.

Bar-Tal, Y., Kishon-Rabin, L., & Tabak, N. (1997). The effect of need and ability to achieve cognitive structuring on cognitive structuring. *Journal of Personality and Social Psychology, 73,* 1158–1176.

Bar-Tal, Y., & Kossowska, M. (2010). The efficacy at fulfilling need for closure: The concept and its measurement. In J. P. Villanueva (Ed.), *Personality traits: Classification, effects and changes* (pp. 47–64). New York: Nova Publishers.

Belsky, J., & Pluess, M. (2009). Beyond diathesis stress: Differential susceptibility to environmental influences. *Psychological Bulletin, 135*(6), 885–908.

Botvinick, M., Braver, T., Barch, D., Carter, C., & Cohen, J. (2001). Evaluating the demand for control: Anterior cingulate cortex and crosstalk monitoring. *Psychological Review, 108,* 624–652.

Botvinick, M., Nystrom, L., Fissell, K., Carter, C., & Cohen, J. (1999). Conflict monitoring vs. selection-for-action in anterior cingulate cortex. *Nature, 402,* 179–181.

Brandt, M. J., & Reyna, C. (2010). The role of prejudice and need for closure in religious fundamentalism. *Personality and Social Psychology Bulletin, 36,* 715–725.

Brown, R., & Hewstone, M. (2005). An integrative theory of intergroup contact. *Advances in Experimental Social Psychology, 37,* 255–343.

Bruner, J. (1990). *Acts of meaning.* Cambridge, MA: Harvard University Press.

Bukowski, M., von Hecker, U., & Kossowska, M. (2013). Motivational determinants of reasoning about social relations: The role of need for cognitive closure. *Thinking and Reasoning, 19,* 150–177.

Cacioppo, J. T., & Petty, R. E. (1982). The need for cognition. *Journal of Personality and Social Psychology, 42,* 116–131.

Carter, C., Braver, T., Barch, D., Botvinick, M., Noll, D., & Cohen, J. (1998). Anterior cingulate cortex, error detection, and the online monitoring of performance. *Science, 280,* 747–749.

Chaiken, S., Duckworth, K. L., & Darke, P. (1999). When parsimony fails.... *Psychological Inquiry, 10,* 118–123.

Chao, M. M., Hong, Y., & Chiu, C. (2013). Essentializing race: Its implications on racial categorization. *Journal of Personality and Social Psychology, 104,* 619–634.

Cheon, B. K., Livingston, R. W., Hong, Y., & Chiao, J. Y. (2014). Gene x environment interaction in intergroup bias: The role of 5-HTTLPR and perceived outgroup threat. *Social Cognitive and Affective Neuroscience, 9,* 1268–1275.

Cheon, B. K., Livingston, R. W., Chiao, J. Y., & Hong, Y. (2015). *Genetic contributions to need for closure, implicit racial bias, and social ideologies: The roles of 5-HTTLPR and COMT Val158Met.* Nanyang Technological University, Submitted for publication.

Chirumbolo, A., Livi, S., Mannetti, L., Pierro, A., & Kruglanski, A. W. (2004). Effects of need for closure on creativity in small group interactions. *European Journal of Personality, 18,* 265–278.

Chiu, C., Morris, M. W., Hong, Y., & Melon, T. (2000). Motivated cultural cognition: The impact of implicit cultural theories on dispositional attribution varies as a function of need for closure. *Journal of Personality and Social Psychology, 78,* 247–259.

Cohen, A. R., Stotland, E., & Wolfe, D. M. (1955). An experimental investigation of need for cognition. *Journal of Abnormal and Social Psychology, 51,* 291–294.

Colzato, L. S., Waszak, F., Nieuwenhuis, S., Posthuma, D., & Hommel, B. (2010). The flexible mind is associated with the catechol-O-methyltransferase (COMT) Val[158]Met polymorphism: Evidence for a role of dopamine in the control of task-switching. *Neuropsychologia, 48*(9), 2764–2768.

Cornelis, I., & Van Hiel, A. (2006). The impact of cognitive styles on authoritarianism based conservatism and racism. *Basic and Applied Social Psychology, 28,* 37–50.

Cornelis, I., Van Hiel, A., Roets, A., & Kossowska, M. (2009). Age differences in conservatism: Evidence on the mediating effects of personality and cognitive style. *Journal of Personality, 77,* 51–88.

Cunningham, W. A., Nezlek, J. B., & Banaji, M. R. (2004). Implicit and explicit ethnocentrism. Revisiting the ideologies of prejudice. *Personality and Social Psychology Bulletin, 30,* 1338–1346.

Czernatowicz-Kukuczka, A., Jaśko, K., & Kossowska, M. (2014). Need for closure as a strategy of dealing with uncertainty in decision making context: The role of behavioral inhibition system and working memory capacity. *Personality & Individual Differences, 70,* 126–130.

DeDreu, C. K. W., Koole, S. L., & Oldersma, F. L. (1999). On the seizing and freezing of negotiator inferences: Need for cognitive closure moderates the use of heuristics in negotiation. *Personality and Social Psychology Bulletin, 25,* 348–362.

De Grada, E., Kruglanski, A. W., Mannetti, L., & Pierro, A. (1999). Motivated cognition and group interaction: Need for closure affects the contents and processes of collective negotiations. *Journal of Experimental Social Psychology, 35,* 346–365.

Dhont, K., Roets, A., & Van Hiel, A. (2011). Opening closed minds: The combined effects of intergroup contact and need for closure on prejudice. *Personality and Social Psychology Bulletin, 37,* 514–528.

Dhont, K., Roets, A., & Van Hiel, A. (2013). The intergenerational transmission of need for closure underlies the transmission of authoritarianism and anti-immigrant prejudice. *Personality and Individual Differences, 54,* 779–784.

Dhont, K., & Van Hiel, A. (2009). We must not be enemies: Interracial contact and the reduction of prejudice among authoritarians. *Personality and Individual Differences, 46,* 172–177.

Dijksterhuis, A., van Knippenberg, A., Kruglanski, A. W., & Schaper, C. (1996). Motivated social cognition: Need for closure effects on memory and judgement. *Journal of Experimental and Social Psychology, 32,* 254–270.

Drabant, E. M., Ramel, W., Edge, M. D., Hyde, L. W., Kuo, J. R., Goldin, P. R., et al. (2012). Neural mechanisms underlying 5-HTTLPR-related sensitivity to acute stress. *American Journal of Psychiatry, 169*(4), 397–405.

Dugas, M., Schori-Eyal, N., Kruglanski, A. W., Gelfand, M. J., Klar, Y., Roccas, S., et al. (2015). *The hurt justifies the means: Need for cognitive closure, group glorification, perceived victimhood and moral license.* University of Maryland, Submitted for publication.

Engle, R. W., Conway, A. R. A., Tuholski, S. W., & Shisler, R. J. (1995). A resource account of inhibition. *Psychological Science, 6,* 19–23.

Eriksen, B. A., & Eriksen, C. W. (1974). Effects of noise letters upon the identification of a target letter in a nonsearch task. *Perception & Psychophysics, 16,* 143–149.

Eysenck, H. J. (1954). *The psychology of politics.* New York: Praeger.

Falkenstein, M., Hohnsbein, J., Hoorman, J., & Blanke, L. (1990). Effects of errors in choice reaction tasks on the ERP under focused and divided attention. In C. Brunia, A. Gaillard, & A. Kok (Eds.), *Psychophysiological brain research: Vol. 1* (pp. 192–195). Tilburg, The Netherlands: Tilburg University Press.

Fallon, S., Williams-Gray, C., Barker, R., Owen, A., & Hampshire, A. (2013). Prefrontal dopamine levels determine the balance between cognitive stability and flexibility. *Cerebral Cortex*, *23*(2), 361–369.

Fiske, S. T., Cuddy, A. J. C., & Glick, P. (2006). Universal dimensions of social cognition: Warmth and competence. *Trends in Cognitive Science*, *11*, 77–83.

Ford, T. E., & Kruglanski, A. W. (1995). Effects of epistemic motivations on the use of accessible constructs in social judgment. *Personality and Social Psychology Bulletin*, *21*, 950–962.

Frenkel-Brunswik, E. (1949). Intolerance for ambiguity as emotional and perceptual personality variable. *Journal of Personality*, *18*, 108–143.

Freund, T., Kruglanski, A. W., & Shpitzajzen, A. (1985). The freezing and unfreezing of impressional primacy: Effects of the need for structure and the fear of invalidity. *Personality and Social Psychology Bulletin*, *11*, 479–487.

Gehring, W. J., Goss, B., Coles, M. G. H., Meyer, D. E., & Donchin, E. (1993). A neural system for error detection and compensation. *Psychological Science*, *4*, 385–390.

Gelman, S. A. (2003). *The essential child: Origins of essentialism in everyday thought*. Oxford, UK: Oxford University Press.

Giacomantonio, M., Pierro, A., & Kruglanski, A. W. (2011). Leaders' fairness and followers' conflict handling style. The moderating role of need for cognitive closure. *International Journal of Conflict Management*, *22*(4), 358–372.

Glick, P., & Fiske, S. T. (1996). The ambivalent sexism inventory: Differentiating hostile and benevolent sexism. *Journal of Personality and Social Psychology*, *70*, 491–512.

Glick, P., & Fiske, S. T. (1999). The ambivalence toward men inventory: Differentiating between hostile and benevolent beliefs about men. *Psychology of Women Quarterly*, *23*, 519–536.

Golec, A., & Federico, C. M. (2004). Understanding responses to political conflict: Interactive effects of need for closure and salient conflict schemas. *Journal of Personality and Social Psychology*, *87*, 750–762.

Golec de Zavala, A., Cislak, A., & Wesolowska, E. (2010). Political conservatism, need for cognitive closure, and intergroup hostility. *Political Psychology*, *31*, 521–541.

Golec de Zavala, A., & Van Bergh, A. (2007). Need for cognitive closure and conservative political beliefs: Differential mediation by personal worldviews. *Political Psychology*, *28*, 587–608.

Guan, Y., Deng, H., Bond, M. H., Chen, S. X., & Chan, C. C. (2010). Person-job fit and work-related attitudes among Chinese employees: Need for cognitive closure as moderator. *Basic and Applied Social Psychology*, *32*, 250–260.

Haidt, J., & Graham, J. (2007). When morality opposes justice: Conservatives have moral intuitions that liberals may not recognize. *Social Justice Research*, *20*, 98–116.

Hajcak, G. (2012). What we've learned from mistakes: Insights from error-related brain activity. *Current Directions in Psychological Science*, *21*, 101–106.

Hammack, P. L. (2011a). *Narrative and the politics of identity: The cultural psychology of Israeli and Palestinian youth*. New York: Oxford University Press.

Hammack, P. L. (2011b). Narrative and the politics of meaning. *Narrative Inquiry*, *21*, 311–318.

Haslam, N., & Levy, S. R. (2006). Essentialist beliefs about homosexuality: Structure and implications for prejudice. *Personality and Social Psychology Bulletin*, *32*, 471–485.

Heaton, A. W., & Kruglanski, A. W. (1991). Person perception by introverts and extroverts under time pressure: Effects of need for closure. *Personality and Social Psychology Bulletin*, *17*, 161–165.

Heinz, A., Smolka, M. N., Braus, D. F., Wrase, J., Beck, A., Flor, H., et al. (2007). Serotonin transporter genotype (5-HTTLPR): Effects of neutral and undefined conditions on amygdala activation. *Biological Psychiatry*, *61*(8), 1011–1014.

Herrmann, C. S., & Knight, R. T. (2001). Mechanisms of human attention: Event-related potentials and oscillations. *Neuroscience and Biobehavioral Reviews, 25*, 465–476.

Hess, T. M. (2001). Ageing-related influences on personal need for structure. *International Journal of Behavioral Development, 25*, 482–490.

Hockey, G. R. J. (1986). A state control theory of adaptation and individual differences in stress management. In G. R. J. Hockey, A. W. K. Gaillard, & M. G. H. Coles (Eds.), *Energetics and human information processing* (pp. 285–298). Dordrecht, The Netherlands: Kluwer Academic.

Hockey, G. R. J., & Hamilton, P. (1983). The cognitive patterning of stress states. In G. R. J. Hockey (Ed.), *Stress and fatigue in human performance* (pp. 331–362). Chichester: John Wiley.

Hogg, M. A. (2001). A social identity theory of leadership. *Personality and Social Psychology Review, 5*, 184–200.

Houghton, D., & Grewal, R. (2000). Let's get an answer—Any answer: Need for consumer cognitive closure. *Psychology and Marketing, 17*, 911–934.

Jamieson, D. W., & Zanna, M. P. (1989). Need for structure in attitude formation and expression. In A. Pratkanis, S. Breckler, & A. G. Greenwald (Eds.), *Attitude structure and function* (pp. 46–68). Hillsdale, NJ: Erlbaum.

Jaśko, K., Czernatowicz-Kukuczka, A., Kossowska, M., & Czarna, A. (2013). Uncertainty and motivation to reduce it in decision making: The role of behavioural inhibition system and need for closure. In *Paper presented at the EASP small group meeting: Motivational, affective, and cognitive sources of the knowledge formation process, 27–29 June, Krakow.*

Jost, J. T., Glaser, J., Kruglanski, A. W., & Sulloway, F. J. (2003). Political conservatism as motivated social cognition. *Psychological Bulletin, 129*, 339–375.

Juergensmeyer, M. (2000). *Terror in the mind of God.* Berkeley: University of California Press.

Kappenman, E., & Luck, S. (2011). The effects of electrode impedance on data quality and statistical significance in ERP recordings. *Psychophysiology, 47*, 888–904.

Keller, J. (2005). In genes we trust: The biological component of psychological essentialism and its relationship to mechanisms of motivated social cognition. *Journal of Personality and Social Psychology, 88*, 686–702.

Kerns, J. G., Cohen, J. D., MacDonald, A. W., Cho, R. Y., Stenger, V. A., et al. (2004). Anterior cingulate conflict monitoring and adjustments in control. *Science, 303*, 1023–1026.

Koessler, S., Engler, H., Riether, C., & Kissler, J. (2009). No retrieval induced forgetting under stress. *Psychological Science, 20*, 1356–1363.

Kosic, A., Kruglanski, A. W., Pierro, A., & Mannetti, L. (2004). The social cognition of immigrants' acculturation: Effects of the need for closure and the reference group at entry. *Journal of Personality and Social Psychology, 86*(6), 796–813.

Kossowska, M. (2007a). Motivation towards closure and cognitive processes: An individual differences approach. *Personality & Individual Differences, 43*, 2149–2158.

Kossowska, M. (2007b). The role of cognitive inhibition in motivation toward closure. *Personality & Individual Differences, 42*, 1117–1126.

Kossowska, M., & Bar-Tal, Y. (2013a). Need for closure and heuristic information processing: The moderating role of the ability to achieve the need for closure. *British Journal of Psychology, 104*, 457–480.

Kossowska, M., & Bar-Tal, Y. (2013b). Positive mood boosts the expression of a dispositional need for closure. *Cognition & Emotion, 27*, 1181–1201.

Kossowska, M., Bukowski, M., & Guinote, A. (2013). When people motivated to use stereotypes refrain from stereotypical thinking: The case of threat to morality. In *Paper presented at the Conference: Motivation in social context: Theory and practice, 29 June–3 July, Krakow.*

Kossowska, M., Czarnek, G., Wronka, E., Wyczesany, M., & Bukowski, M. (2014). Individual differences in epistemic motivation and brain conflict monitoring activity. *Neuroscience Letters*, *570*, 38–41.

Kossowska, M., Czarnek, G., Wyczesany, M., Wronka, E., Szwed, P., & Bukowski, M. (in press). Electrocortical indices of attention correlate with need for closure. *NeuroReport*.

Kossowska, M., Dragon, P., & Bukowski, M. (2015). When need for closure leads to positive attitudes towards a negatively stereotyped outgroup. *Motivation and Emotion*, *39*, 88–98.

Kossowska, M., Jaśko, K., & Bar-Tal, Y. (2012). Need for closure and cognitive structuring among younger and older adults. *Polish Psychological Bulletin*, *43*, 40–49.

Kossowska, M., Jaśko, M., Bar-Tal, Y., & Szastok, M. (2012). The relationship between need for closure and memory for schema-related information among younger and older adults. *Aging, Neuropsychology & Cognition*, *19*, 283–300.

Kossowska, M., Orehek, E., & Kruglanski, A. W. (2010). Motivation towards closure and cognitive resources: An individual differences approach. In A. Gruszka, G. Mathews, & B. Szymura (Eds.), *Handbook of individual differences in cognition: Attention, memory and executive control* (pp. 369–382). New York: Springer Science + Business Media.

Kossowska, M., & Van Hiel, A. (2003). The relationship between need for closure and conservative beliefs in Western and Eastern Europe. *Political Psychology*, *24*, 501–518.

Kruglanski, A. W. (1980). Lay epistemologic processes and contents. Another look at attribution theory. *Psychological Review*, *87*, 70–78.

Kruglanski, A. W. (1989). *Lay epistemic and human knowledge: Cognitive and motivational bases*. New York: Plenum.

Kruglanski, A. W. (1990). Motivations for judging and knowing: Implications for causal attribution. In E. T. Higgins, & R. M. Sorrentino (Eds.), *The handbook of motivation and cognition: Foundation of social behavior: Vol. 2* (pp. 333–368). New York: Guilford Press.

Kruglanski, A. W. (2004). *The psychology of closed mindedness*. New York: Psychology Press.

Kruglanski, A. W., Atash, M. N., De Grada, E., Mannetti, L., Pierro, A., & Webster, D. M. (1997). Psychological theory testing versus psychometric nay-saying: Comment on Neuberg et al.'s (1997) critique of the need for closure scale. *Journal of Personality and Social Psychology*, *73*, 1005–1016.

Kruglanski, A. W., Bélanger, J. J., Gelfand, M. J., Gunaratna, R., Hettiarachchi, M., Reinares, F., et al. (2013). Terrorism: A (self) love story: Redirecting the quest for significance can end violence. *American Psychologist*, *68*, 559–575.

Kruglanski, A. W., Dechesne, M., Orehek, E., & Pierro, A. (2009). Three decades of lay epistemics: The why, how and who of knowledge formation. *European Review of Social Psychology*, *20*, 146–191.

Kruglanski, A. W., & Freund, T. (1983). The freezing and unfreezing of lay-inferences: Effects of impressional primacy, ethnic stereotyping and numerical anchoring. *Journal of Experimental Social Psychology*, *19*, 448–468.

Kruglanski, A. W., Freund, T., & Bar-Tal, D. (1996). Motivational effects in the mere-exposure paradigm. *European Journal of Social Psychology*, *26*, 479–499.

Kruglanski, A. W., Gelfand, M. J., Belanger, J. J., Schori-Eyal, N., Moyano, E., Trujillo, X., et al. (2015). *On the psychology of extremism: Effects of humiliation and need for closure in three vulnerable populations*. University of Maryland, Submitted for publication.

Kruglanski, A. W., & Mayseless, O. (1988). Contextual effects in hypothesis testing: The role of competing alternatives and epistemic motivations. *Social Cognition*, *6*, 1–21.

Kruglanski, A. W., Orehek, E., Dechesne, M., & Pierro, A. (2010). Lay epistemic theory: Motivational, cognitive, and social aspects of knowledge formation. *Social and Personality Psychology Compass*, *4*, 939–950.

Kruglanski, A. W., Peri, N., & Zakai, D. (1991). Interactive effects of need for closure and initial confidence on social information seeking. *Social Cognition*, *9*, 127–148.

Kruglanski, A. W., Pierro, A., Higgins, E. T., & Capozza, D. (2007). "On the move" or "staying put": Locomotion, need for closure and reactions to organizational change. *Journal of Applied Social Psychology*, *37*, 1305–1340.

Kruglanski, A. W., Pierro, A., Mannetti, L., & De Grada, E. (2006). Groups as epistemic providers: Need for closure and the unfolding of group-centrism. *Psychological Review*, *113*, 84–100.

Kruglanski, A. W., Shah, J. Y., Fishbach, A., Friedman, R., Chun, W. Y., & Sleeth-Keppler, D. (2002). A theory of goal-systems. *Advances in Experimental Social Psychology*, *34*, 331–376.

Kruglanski, A. W., & Webster, D. M. (1991). Group members' reactions to opinion deviates and conformists at varying degrees of proximity to decision deadline and environmental noise. *Journal of Personality and Social Psychology*, *61*, 212–225.

Kruglanski, A. W., & Webster, D. M. (1996). Motivated closing of the mind: "Seizing" and "freezing". *Psychological Review*, *103*, 263–283.

Kruglanski, A. W., Webster, D. M., & Klem, A. (1993). Motivated resistance and openness to persuasion in the presence or absence of prior information. *Journal of Personality and Social Psychology*, *65*, 861–877.

Kuhn, T. S. (1962). *The structure of scientific revolutions*. Chicago: University of Chicago Press.

Lackner, C., Santesso, D., Dywan, J., Wade, T., & Segalowitz, S. (2013). Electrocortical indices of selective attention predict adolescent executive functioning. *Biological Psychology*, *93*, 325–333.

Leventhal, G. S. (1980). What should be done with equity theory? New approaches to the fairness in social relationships. In K. Gergen, M. Greenberg, & R. Willis (Eds.), *Social exchange theory* (pp. 27–55). New York: Plenum.

Levy, B. J., & Anderson, M. C. (2008). Individual differences in the suppression of unwanted memories: The executive deficit hypothesis. *Acta Psychologica*, *127*, 623–635.

Lewin, K. (1951). *Field theory in social sciences*. New York: Harper & Row.

Lind, E. A. (2001). Fairness heuristic theory: Justice judgments as pivotal cognitions in organizational relations. In J. Greenberg, & R. Cropanzano (Eds.), *Advances in organizational behavior* (pp. 56–88). Lexington, MA: New Lexington.

Lind, E. A., & Van den Bos, K. (2002). When fairness works: Towards a general theory of uncertainty management. *Research in Organizational Behavior*, *24*, 181–224.

Livi, S., Kruglanski, A. W., Pierro, A., Mannetti, L., & Kenny, D. A. (in press). Epistemic motivation and perpetuation of group culture: Effects of need for cognitive closure on trans-generational norm transmission. *Organizational Behavior and Human Decision Processes*. doi:10.1016/j.obhdp.2014.09.010.

Mangun, G. R., & Hillyard, S. A. (1988). Spatial gradients of visual attention: Behavioral and electrophysiological evidence. *Electroencephalography and Clinical Neurophysiology*, *70*, 417–428.

Mannetti, L., Pierro, A., Kruglanski, A., Taris, T., & Bezinovic, P. (2002). A cross-cultural study of the need for cognitive closure scale: Comparing its structure in Croatia, Italy, USA and the Netherlands. *British Journal of Social Psychology*, *41*, 139–156.

Mayseless, O., & Kruglanski, A. W. (1987). What makes you so sure? Effects of epistemic motivations on judgmental confidence. *Organizational Behavior and Human Decision Processes*, *39*, 162–183.

McCrae, R. R., & Costa, P. T., Jr. (1985). Openness to experience. In R. Hogan, & W. H. Jones (Eds.), *Perspectives in personality* (pp. 145–172). Greenwich, CT: JAI Press.

Medin, D. L. (1989). Concepts and conceptual structure. *American Psychologist*, *44*, 1469–1481.

Morris, M. W., Mok, A., & Mor, S. (2011). Cultural identity threat: The role of cultural identifications in moderating closure responses to a foreign cultural inflow. *Journal of Social Issues*, *67*, 760–773.

Neuberg, S. L., Judice, T. N., & West, S. G. (1997). What the need for closure scale measures and what it does not: Toward differentiating among related epistemic motives. *Journal of Personality and Social Psychology*, *72*, 1396–1412.

Neuberg, S. L., West, S. G., Judice, T. N., & Thompson, M. M. (1997). On dimensionality, discriminant validity, and the role of psychometric analyses in personality theory and measurement: Reply to Kruglanski et al.'s (1997) defense of the need for closure scale. *Journal of Personality and Social Psychology*, *73*, 1017–1029.

Nolan, K. A., Bilder, R. M., Lachman, H. M., & Volavka, J. (2004). Catechol O-methyltransferase Val158Met polymorphism in schizophrenia: Differential effects of Val and Met alleles on cognitive stability and flexibility. *American Journal of Psychiatry*, *161*(2), 359–361.

Onraet, E., Van Hiel, A., Roets, A., & Cornelis, I. (2011). The closed mind: 'Experience' and 'cognition' aspects of openness to experience and need for closure as psychological bases for right-wing attitudes. *European Journal of Personality*, *25*, 184–197.

Orehek, E., Fishman, S., Dechesne, M., Doosje, B., Kruglanski, A. W., Cole, A. P., et al. (2010). Need for closure and the social response to terrorism. *Basic and Applied Social Psychology*, *32*, 279–290.

Otten, S., & Bar-Tal, Y. (2002). Self-anchoring in the minimal group paradigm: The impact of need and ability to achieve cognitive structure. *Group Processes & Intergroup Relations*, *5*, 267–284.

Payne, J. W., Bettman, J. R., & Johnson, E. J. (1993). *The adaptive decision maker*. New York: Cambridge University Press.

Pettigrew, T. F., & Tropp, L. R. (2006). A meta-analytic test of intergroup contact theory. *Journal of Personality and Social Psychology*, *90*, 751–783.

Pettigrew, T. F., & Tropp, L. R. (2008). How does intergroup contact reduce prejudice? Meta-analytic tests of three mediators. *European Journal of Social Psychology*, *38*, 922–934.

Pica, G., Pierro, A., Bélanger, J. J., & Kruglanski, A. W. (2013). The motivational dynamics of retrieval-induced forgetting: A test of cognitive energetics theory. *Personality and Social Psychology Bulletin*, *39*, 1530–1541.

Pica, G., Pierro, A., Bélanger, J. J., & Kruglanski, A. W. (2014). The role of need for cognitive closure in retrieval-induced forgetting and misinformation effects in eyewitness memory. *Social Cognition*, *32*, 337–359.

Pierro, A., Cicero, L., Bonaiuto, M., van Knippenberg, D., & Kruglanski, A. W. (2005). Leader group prototypicality and leadership effectiveness: The moderating role of need for cognitive closure. *The Leadership Quarterly*, *16*, 503–516.

Pierro, A., Giacomantonio, M., Kruglanski, A. W., & van Knippenberg, D. (2014). Follower need for cognitive closure as moderator of the effectiveness of leader procedural fairness. *European Journal of Work and Organizational Psychology*, *23*, 582–595. http://dx.doi.org/10.1080/1359432X.2013.781269.

Pierro, A., Kruglanski, A. W., & Raven, B. H. (2012). Motivational underpinnings of social influence: Bases of social power and the need for cognitive closure. *European Journal of Social Psychology*, *42*, 41–52.

Pierro A., Sheveland A., Livi S., Kruglanski A.W. (in press). Person-group fit on the need for cognitive closure as a predictor of job performance, and the mediating role of group identification. *Group Dynamics: Theory, Research, and Practice*. http://dx.doi.org/10.1037/gdn0000022

Pierro, A., Mannetti, L., De Grada, E., Livi, S., & Kruglanski, A. W. (2003). Autocracy bias in informal groups under need for closure. *Personality and Social Psychology Bulletin*, *29*, 405–417.

Popper, K. R. (1934). *The logic of scientific discovery*. New York: Harper Torchbooks.

Pratto, F., Sidanius, J., Stallworth, L. M., & Malle, B. F. (1994). Social dominance orientation: A personality variable predicting social and political attitudes. *Journal of Personality and Social Psychology, 67,* 741–763.

Rangel, U., & Keller, J. (2011). Essentialism goes social: Belief in social determinism as a component of psychological essentialism. *Journal of Personality and Social Psychology, 100,* 1056–1078.

Raven, B. H., Schwarzwald, J., & Koslowsky, M. (1998). Conceptualizing and measuring a power/interaction model of interpersonal influence. *Journal of Applied Social Psychology, 28,* 307–332.

Richter, M., Baeriswyl, E., & Roets, A. (2012). Personality effects on cardiovascular reactivity: Need for closure moderates the impact of task difficulty on engagement-related myocardial beta-adrenergic activity. *Psychophysiology, 49,* 704–707.

Richter, L., & Kruglanski, A. W. (1998). Seizing on the latest. Motivationally driven recency effects in impression formation. *Journal of Experimental Social Psychology, 34,* 313–329.

Roets, A., Raman, E., Heytens, S., & Avonds, D. (2014). Effects of dispositional need for closure and training on medical decision making. *Medical Decision Making, 34,* 144–146.

Roets, A., & Soetens, B. (2010). Need and ability to achieve closure: Relationships with symptoms of psychopathology. *Personality and Individual Differences, 48,* 155–160.

Roets, A., & Van Hiel, A. (2006). Need for closure relations with authoritarianism, conservative beliefs and racism: The impact of urgency and permanence tendencies. *Psychologica Belgica, 46,* 235–252.

Roets, A., & Van Hiel, A. (2007). Separating ability from need: Clarifying the dimensional structure of the need for closure scale. *Personality and Social Psychology Bulletin, 33,* 266–280.

Roets, A., & Van Hiel, A. (2008). Why some hate to dillydally and others do not: The arousal-invoking capacity of decision-making for low and high-scoring need for closure individuals. *Social Cognition, 26,* 333–346.

Roets, A., & Van Hiel, A. (2011a). The role of need for closure in essentialist entitativity beliefs and prejudice: An epistemic needs approach to racial categorization. *British Journal of Social Psychology, 50,* 52–73.

Roets, A., & Van Hiel, A. (2011b). Item selection and validation of a brief, 15-item version of the need for closure scale. *Personality and Individual Differences, 50,* 90–94.

Roets, A., & Van Hiel, A. (2011c). Impaired performance as a source of reduced energy investment in judgment under stressors. *Journal of Cognitive Psychology, 23,* 625–632.

Roets, A., & Van Hiel, A. (2011d). Allport's prejudiced personality today: Need for closure as the motivated cognitive basis of prejudice. *Current Directions in Psychological Science, 26,* 349–354.

Roets, A., Van Hiel, A., & Cornelis, I. (2006). The dimensional structure of the need for cognitive closure scale: Relationships with "seizing" and "freezing" processes. *Social Cognition, 24,* 22–45.

Roets, A., Van Hiel, A., Cornelis, I., & Soetens, B. (2008). Determinants of task performance and invested effort: A need for closure by ability interaction analysis. *Personality and Social Psychology Bulletin, 34,* 779–792.

Roets, A., Van Hiel, A., & Dhont, K. (2012). Is sexism a gender issue? A motivated social cognition perspective on men's and women's sexist attitudes toward the own and other gender. *European Journal of Personality, 26,* 350–359.

Roman, P., Soriano, M. F., Gomez-Ariza, C. J., & Bayo, M. T. (2009). Retrieval induced forgetting and executive control. *Psychological Science, 20,* 1053–1058.

Rubin, M., Paolini, S., & Crisp, R. (2011). The relationship between the need for closure and deviant bias: An investigation of generality and process. *International Journal of Psychology, 46,* 206–213.

Salthouse, T. (1996). The processing-speed theory of adult age differences in cognition. *Psychological Review, 103*, 403–428.

Schori-Eyal, N., Halperin, E., Bar-Tal, D., Porat, R., & Kruglanski, A. W. (2015). *The place where we are right: Implications of need for cognitive closure for intergroup conflicts.* University of Maryland, Submitted for publication.

Schwarzwald, J., Koslowsky, M., & Ochana-Levin, T. (2004). Usage of and compliance with power tactics in routine versus nonroutine work settings. *Journal of Business and Psychology, 18*, 385–395.

Sedek, G., & Kofta, M. (1990). When cognitive exertion does not yield cognitive gain: Toward an informational explanation of learned helplessness. *Journal of Personality and Social Psychology, 58*, 729–743.

Sedek, G., Kossowska, M., & Rydzewska, K. (2014). The importance of adult life-span perspective in explaining variations in political ideology. *Behavioral & Brain Sciences, 37*, 329–330.

Shah, J. Y., Kruglanski, A. W., & Thompson, E. P. (1998). Membership has its (epistemic) rewards: Need for closure effects on ingroup bias. *Journal of Personality and Social Psychology, 75*, 383–393.

Singhal, A., Doerfling, P., & Fowler, B. (2002). Effects of a dual task on the N100–P200 complex and the early and late Nd attention waveforms. *Psychophysiology, 39*, 236–245.

Sorrentino, R. M., & Short, J. C. (1986). Uncertainty orientation, motivation and cognition. In R. M. Sorrentino, & E. T. Higgins (Eds.), *Handbook of motivation and cognition: Foundations of social behavior* (pp. 379–403). New York: Guilford Press.

Stroop, J. R. (1935). Studies on interference in serial verbal reactions. *Journal of Experimental Psychology, 18*, 643–662.

Tadmor, C. T., Hong, Y., Chao, M. M., Wiruchnipawan, F., & Wang, W. (2012). Multicultural experiences reduce intergroup bias through epistemic unfreezing. *Journal of Personality and Social Psychology, 103*, 750–772.

Tadmor, C. T., Chao, M. M., Hong, Y., & Polzer, J. T. (2013). Not just for stereotyping anymore: Racial essentialism reduces domain-general creativity. *Psychological Science, 24*, 99–105.

Tebbe, E. N., & Moradi, B. (2012). Anti-transgender prejudice: A structural equation model of associated constructs. *Journal of Counseling Psychology, 59*, 251–261.

Tyler, T. R. (1997). The psychology of legitimacy: A relational perspective on voluntary deference to authorities. *Personality and Social Psychology Review, 1*, 323–345.

Uher, R., Caspi, A., Houts, R., Sugden, K., Williams, B., Poulton, R., et al. (2011). Serotonin transporter gene moderates childhood maltreatment's effects on persistent but not single-episode depression: Replications and implications for resolving inconsistent results. *Journal of Affective Disorders, 135*, 56–65.

Van den Bos, K., & Lind, E. A. (2002). Uncertainty management by means of fairness judgments. *Advances in Experimental Social Psychology, 34*, 1–60.

Van Hiel, A., Pandelaere, M., & Duriez, B. (2004). The impact of need for closure on conservative beliefs and racism: Differential mediation by authoritarian submission and authoritarian dominance. *Personality and Social Psychology Bulletin, 30*, 824–837.

Vermeir, I., Van Kenhove, P., & Hendrickx, H. (2002). The influence of need for closure on consumer choice behaviour. *Journal of Economic Psychology, 23*, 703–727.

Viola, V., Tosoni, A., Kruglanski, A. W., Galati, G., & Mannetti, L. (2014). Routes of motivation: Stable psychological dispositions are associated with cortico-cortical functional connectivity. *PLoS One, 9*(6), E98010.

Wamberg, C. R., & Banas, J. T. (2000). Predictors and outcomes of openness to changes in a reorganizing workplace. *Journal of Applied Psychology, 85*, 132–142.

Webster, D. M. (1993a). Motivated augmentation and reduction of the overattribution bias. *Journal of Personality and Social Psychology, 65*, 261–271.

Webster, D. M. (1993b). Groups under the influence: Need for closure effects on information sharing in decision making groups. Unpublished doctoral dissertation. University of Maryland, College Park.

Webster, D. M., & Kruglanski, A. W. (1994). Individual differences in need for cognitive closure. *Journal of Personality and Social Psychology*, *67*, 1049–1062.

Webster, D. M., Richter, L., & Kruglanski, A. W. (1996). On leaping to conclusions when feeling tired: Mental fatigue effects on impressional primacy. *Journal of Experimental Social Psychology*, *32*, 181–195.

Weinberg, A., Riesel, A., & Hajcak, G. (2012). Integrating multiple perspectives on error-related brain activity: The ERN as a neural indicator of trait defensive reactivity. *Motivation & Emotion*, *36*, 84–100.

Wright, R. A., & Kirby, L. D. (2001). Effort determination of cardiovascular response: An integrative analysis with applications in social psychology. *Advances in Experimental Social Psychology*, *33*, 255–307.

Yeung, N., Botvinick, M., & Cohen, J. (2004). The neural basis of error detection: Conflict monitoring and the error-related negativity. *Psychological Review*, *111*, 931–959.

Yeung, N., & Cohen, J. (2006). The impact of cognitive deficits on conflict monitoring predictable dissociations between the error-related negativity and N2. *Psychological Science*, *17*, 164–171.

CHAPTER FIVE

The ABC of Ambivalence: Affective, Behavioral, and Cognitive Consequences of Attitudinal Conflict

Frenk van Harreveld[*,1], **Hannah U. Nohlen**[*], **Iris K. Schneider**[†,‡]

[*]Faculty of Social and Behavioral Sciences, Social Psychology Program, University of Amsterdam, Amsterdam, The Netherlands
[†]Department of Psychology, University of Southern California, Los Angeles, California, USA
[‡]Department of Psychology, VU University Amsterdam, Amsterdam, The Netherlands
[1]Corresponding author: e-mail address: f.vanharreveld@uva.nl

Contents

Abstract

In a world where individuals are continuously exposed to information, the experience of ambivalence has become an intricate part of human existence. Recently, the consequences of ambivalence have been the subject of considerable research attention. In this chapter, we provide an overview of this research and present the ABC (Affect, Behavior, Cognition) model of ambivalence that integrates recent insights into the affective, behavioral, and cognitive consequences of ambivalence. This research shows when and why ambivalence leads to negative affect and that this affective response is

Advances in Experimental Social Psychology, Volume 52
ISSN 0065-2601
http://dx.doi.org/10.1016/bs.aesp.2015.01.002

the fuel that drives subsequent effects of ambivalence on cognition and behavior. More-over, the reviewed findings reveal that the effects on cognition and behavior serve the purpose of either resolving ambivalence or mitigating the negative affective response. With the ABC model of ambivalence, we aim to identify the distinctive features of ambivalence in terms of what we feel, think, and do.

1. INTRODUCTION

Ambivalence is a wonderful tune to dance to. It has a rhythm all its own
Erica Jong

Evaluation is one of the most pervasive concepts in psychology. Not only is nearly all cognition and perception evaluative in nature (Markus & Zajonc, 1985), evaluations often take place quickly and without requiring much cognitive effort (Bargh, Chaiken, Govender, & Pratto, 1992). Evaluations serve important functions (e.g., Katz, 1960), such as preparing and guiding our behavior (Allport, 1935). They are based on a relatively stable set of associations that together form an attitude (Cunningham, Zelazo, Packer, & van Bavel, 2007). When associations are of the same valence, i.e., either positive or negative, evaluations form quickly and are seemingly effortless guides of human behavior (Armitage & Conner, 2000; Bargh et al., 1992). Often, however, attitudes are made up of positive and negative associations. Such coexistence of positive and negative associations within one attitude is what we call ambivalence. Ambivalence has recently seen a surge in research interest. This chapter will integrate this research and show that ambivalent attitudes can have important and distinctive consequences for what we feel, think, and do. This integration will culminate in a model that specifies when these consequences are most likely to occur.

Many scholars in the social sciences have argued that ambivalence is an intricate part of human existence. Freud (1930/1964) argued that all intimate relationships contain a certain degree of ambivalence, and, indeed, ambivalence has been shown in the context of parent–child relationships (Luescher & Pillemer, 1988; Maio, Fincham, & Lycett, 2000), marriage (Signorielli, 1991), and between lovers while sorting out their relationship (Wiseman, 1976). Ambivalence has also been shown in relation to a multitude of other topics, including abortion (Alvarez & Brehm, 1995), men (Feather, 2004; Glick & Fiske, 1999), women (Glick & Fiske, 1996), eating meat (Povey, Wellens, & Conner, 2001), presidential candidates (Lavine, 2001), pregnancy (Bruckner, Martin, & Bearman, 2004), dieting (Armitage & Arden, 2007), methadone treatment (Rosenblum, Magura, & Joseph, 1991), different ethnic groups (Katz & Hass, 1988), chocolate (Sparks, Conner, James, Shepherd, & Povey, 2001), drugs and condoms (Kane, 1990), smoking (Lipkus, Green, Feaganes, & Sedikides, 2001), physical exercise (Sparks, Harris, & Lockwood, 2004), among scientists (Mitroff, 1974), and toward the self (DeMarree, Rios Morrison, Wheeler, & Petty, 2011).

Research has extensively examined ambivalence as a structural property of attitudes (e.g., De Liver, van der Pligt, & Wigboldus, 2007; Katz & Hass, 1988; Lavine, Thomson, Zanna, & Borgida, 1998). Others have focused more on the consequences of ambivalence. This chapter will integrate insights into these consequences with more classic findings on the structural properties of ambivalence. This overview will culminate in the ABC (Affect, Behavior, Cognition) model, a comprehensive model of ambivalence that predicts what the affective, cognitive, and behavioral consequences of ambivalent attitudes are and how these consequences interact with each other.

2. WHAT IS AMBIVALENCE?

Research into ambivalence spawned from the observation that traditional bipolar measures of attitude (e.g., a semantic differential ranging from "good" to "bad") fail to distinguish between ambivalence and indifference. On such bipolar measures, both respondents who are torn between strong opposing evaluations and those who simply do not care will tick the midpoint of the bipolar scale (Klopfer & Madden, 1980), even though their evaluations are fundamentally different. Individuals who are indifferent have weak positive and negative associations, whereas those who are ambivalent have strong positive and negative associations (e.g., Cacioppo & Berntson, 1994; Cacioppo, Gardner, & Berntson, 1997; Kaplan, 1972; Priester & Petty, 1996). Empirical support for this notion is provided by research in which valenced primes (i.e., positive or negative) facilitated responses to ambivalent but not neutral (i.e., indifferent) attitude objects (De Liver et al., 2007).

Several definitions of ambivalence have been proposed. Gardner (1987, p. 241), for example, defined ambivalence as "a psychological state in which a person holds mixed feelings (positive and negative) towards some psychological object." Eagly and Chaiken (1993, p. 123) emphasized the cognitive inconsistency in ambivalence and defined it as "the extent of beliefs' evaluative dissimilarity (or inconsistency)." Wegener, Downing, Krosnick, and Petty (1995, p. 460) defined ambivalence as "the extent to which one's reactions to an attitude object are evaluatively mixed in that both positive (favorable) and negative (unfavorable) elements are included." Thompson, Zanna, and Griffin (1995, p. 367) referred to ambivalence as an inclination to "give it [an attitude object] equivalently strong positive and negative evaluations."

Although this list of definitions is by no means complete, two central elements of the psychological construct of ambivalence become clear. First, both positive and negative associations need to be present. Second, these associations can be (but not always are) relevant at the same time. Based on these two prerequisites, we make a distinction between the associative structure of ambivalence based on positive and negative association weights (objective ambivalence) and the experience of conflict due to this associative structure (subjective ambivalence). The latter is more closely related to defining ambivalence as simultaneously evaluating an object or behavior negatively and positively (cf. Kaplan, 1972; Thompson et al., 1995). We will return to this distinction between different kinds of ambivalence later.

The positive and negative evaluative components that together form ambivalence come in many flavors. As indicated by the aforementioned definition by Eagly and Chaiken (1993), both evaluative components can be cognitive in nature, but ambivalence has also been investigated in the context of inconsistencies between cognitive and affective elements (Lavine et al., 1998), between emotions (Fong, 2006; Larsen, McGraw, & Cacioppo, 2001; Vince & Broussine, 1996), between newly endorsed and older rejected attitudes (Petty, Tormala, Brinol, & Jarvis, 2006), and between inconsistent anticipations for the future (Priester, Petty, & Park, 2007). In our focus on the consequences of ambivalence, this chapter will not distinguish between these different kinds of ambivalence. Regardless of the kind of associations leading to ambivalence, the negative component tends to be more influential than the positive (e.g., Cacioppo & Berntson, 1994). This negativity bias is illustrated by the fact that highly ambivalent individuals are more persuaded by negatively framed messages (Broemer, 2002).

3. AMBIVALENCE AND ATTITUDE STRENGTH

This chapter focuses on the consequences of ambivalence, which came into the spotlight as a result of the extensive investigation of ambivalence as a dimension of attitude strength (Petty & Krosnick, 1995). In research on ambivalence as a dimension of strength, it is generally argued that ambivalent attitudes are one form of weak attitudes. This notion is supported by a large amount of research showing that ambivalence attenuates the relation between evaluations on the one hand and intentions and behaviors on the other (Armitage & Conner, 2000; Bruckner et al., 2004; Conner, Povey, Sparks, James, & Shepherd, 2003; Conner et al., 2002; Costarelli & Colloca, 2007; Shepherd, 1999; Sparks et al., 2001, 2004). Also, ambivalent attitudes have been found to be less accessible in memory (Bargh et al., 1992; Bassili, 1996) and more susceptible to persuasion attempts (Armitage & Conner, 2000).

Although this research seems to support the notion that ambivalence is reflective of a weak attitude, there are reasons to believe the matter is more complicated than that. First, studies found ambivalence to be related to stronger relations between attitudes and behavioral intentions, due to increased information processing (Jonas, Diehl, & Broemer, 1997). Specifically, ambivalence was associated with less confidence in one's evaluation, which led to a higher amount of cognitive elaboration. This elaboration (as reflected in the number of attitude-related thoughts), in turn, yielded a stronger relation between attitudes and behavioral intentions.

Second, a study on attitudes toward minorities (Maio, Bell, & Esses, 1996) found that ambivalence was associated with greater differentiation between strong and weak arguments. Such differential effects of strong and weak persuasive arguments have been related to systematic processing of information (Petty & Cacioppo, 1986), which requires the motivation to invest cognitive effort. This motivation is usually associated with strong rather than weak attitudes (e.g., Fabrigar, Priester, Petty, & Wegener, 1998; Petty & Krosnick, 1995).

Thus, although research on ambivalence aimed to show that ambivalence is a property of weak attitudes, it inadvertently revealed that ambivalence can have consequences (cognitive elaboration, strong relations between attitudes and intentions, differential effects of strong vs. weak persuasive messages) that are usually associated with strong attitudes. It has been argued (e.g., Maio et al., 1996) that the motivation to be evaluatively consistent underlies these findings. Research on, for example, cognitive dissonance (Festinger, 1964) and balance theory (Heider, 1946) has shown that people are motivated to reduce internal inconsistencies, and ambivalence has been assumed to have similar consequences (McGregor, Newby-Clark, & Zanna, 1999). And, indeed, it has been shown that ambivalent attitude holders are prone to engage in response amplification (exhibiting more extreme responses to a stigmatized individual, e.g., Monteith, 1993) and that this tendency is even more pronounced when there is a motive to reduce ambivalence (Bell & Esses, 2002).

Using similar reasoning, it has been argued that ambivalent attitude holders experience an internal evaluative inconsistency and, therefore, are motivated to extensively process information about the attitude object in an effort to reduce their ambivalence. This hypothesis has stimulated a considerable amount of research on the consequences of ambivalence. Ambivalence is no longer predominantly seen as a property of attitude strength; instead, ambivalent attitudes may ignite efforts to cope with their inherent inconsistency (Van Harreveld, Van der Pligt, & Liver, 2009).

4. CONSEQUENCES OF AMBIVALENCE

Despite the surge in research on the consequences of ambivalence, there have been few attempts to integrate this research. This chapter aims to do just that. Here, we discuss the consequences of ambivalence and integrate them along the lines of the traditional distinction in the literature on attitudes between affect, cognition, and behavior (e.g., Rosenberg & Hovland, 1960). In contrast to research on the tripartite structure of attitudes in which the causal relations between components are largely unresolved (e.g., Fiske & Pavelchak, 1986; Piderit, 2000; Zanna & Rempel, 1988), the proposed ABC model of ambivalence describes the affective, cognitive, and behavioral consequences of ambivalence and specifically predicts how the different components interact with each other.

4.1 A: Affect

The first category of consequences of ambivalence we discuss is affect. In the context of attitudes, affect has been defined as the "feelings, moods, emotions, and sympathetic nervous system activity that people have experienced in relation to an attitude object and subsequently associate with it" (Eagly & Chaiken, 1998, p. 272). In our consideration of the affective consequences of ambivalence, we take a similarly broad scope. Ambivalence can be related to affective responses in at least two ways. The first way is captured by one side of the aforementioned distinction between objective and subjective ambivalence. Whereas measures of objective ambivalence (i.e., Kaplan, 1972) assess the simultaneous existence of positive and negative evaluative responses in relation to an attitude object (e.g., "How positive (negative) are your thoughts and/or feelings with respect to X"), measures of subjective ambivalence (Jamieson, 1993; Priester & Petty, 2001) tap into the extent to which the attitude holder feels torn between both sides of the attitude object (e.g., "I feel torn between the two sides of X"). Objective ambivalence thus refers to the existence of conflicting associations, whereas subjective ambivalence refers to the (meta) experience of this conflict. The fact that measures of objective and subjective ambivalence do not always correlate highly (Armitage & Arden, 2007) reflects that ambivalence can either be salient (leading to an affective response) or remain in a dormant (and exclusively structural) state. Thus, subjective ambivalence is the form that elicits affect.

Subjective ambivalence is generally viewed as producing negative affect (e.g., Newby-Clark, McGregor, & Zanna, 2002; Van Harreveld, Van der Pligt, et al., 2009). This notion is of considerable importance to this chapter, and we discuss subjectively experienced ambivalence accordingly: as a reflection of ambivalence-induced negative affect. Also, most of the consequences of ambivalence discussed in this chapter have been obtained in the context of subjectively experienced ambivalence. Moreover, effects of objective ambivalence tend to be driven by subjective ambivalence (DeMarree, Wheeler, Brinol, & Petty, 2014). Although the existence of evaluatively incongruent associations (objective ambivalence) in our view is a prerequisite for experiencing subjective ambivalence, it is the more affective nature of the latter state that is the most consequential for what people think and do.

The second way in which ambivalence is theoretically linked to affective responses is via the aforementioned presumed human motivation to be consistent. Consistency violations can be experienced as unpleasant and lead to a negative affective response, as shown, for example, in the context of cognitive dissonance (e.g., Zanna & Cooper, 1974). Based on the similarities between ambivalence and dissonance (for an in-depth discussion of the similarities and differences between ambivalence and dissonance, see van Harreveld, Van der Pligt, et al., 2009), it has been suggested that ambivalence leads to negative affect as well (e.g., McGregor et al., 1999). Yet, although there are theoretical grounds to assume that ambivalence is unpleasant, the direct empirical evidence for the relation between ambivalence and negative affect is inconclusive.

On the one hand, several studies suggest that ambivalence is indeed unpleasant. For example, it has been found that when ambivalent attitude holders can attribute their discomfort to a placebo pill, they report less negative emotions than their counterparts who received a supposedly relaxing pill (Nordgren, van Harreveld, & van der Pligt, 2006), which suggests that ambivalence is experienced as negative. Also, racial ambivalence has been related to negative mood (Hass, Katz, Rizzo, Bailey, & Moore, 1992). Finally, in a recent EMG study (Nohlen, van Harreveld, Rotteveel,

Barendse, & Larsen, 2015), higher levels of subjective ambivalence were associated with less activation of the zygomaticus major, a facial muscle that pulls the corner of the mouth back and up (smiling).

On the other hand, however, it has been suggested that ambivalence may sometimes be evaluated positively. Maio and Haddock (2004) argued "Ambivalence may be desirable when an issue is controversial. In this situation, people who appear ambivalent may give the impression of being fair and knowledgeable" (p. 435). Consistent with this reasoning, ambivalence has been shown to be negatively related to physiological arousal (Maio, Greenland, Bernard, & Esses, 2001). Moreover, some studies indicate that ambivalence can be evaluated positively by others. Pillaud, Cavazza, and Butera (2013) showed that when participants had to present themselves positively (as opposed to negatively), they were more likely to express ambivalence on controversial issues, arguably because this may communicate a balanced view. In light of these conflicting findings, several researchers have focused not on whether but when ambivalence is associated with negative affect.

4.1.1 Causes of ambivalence-induced negative affect
Many people have ambivalent attitudes toward matters such as fast food, alcohol, exercise, the death penalty, or watching television, but most of these attitudes do not continuously make us feel conflicted. It has been argued that feelings of ambivalence only become unpleasant when the positive and negative components of the attitude are simultaneously accessible, because only then does one experience conflict (Newby-Clark et al., 2002).

4.1.2 Conflict
Whether both evaluations are indeed simultaneously accessible, and conflict occurs, depends on contextual factors. It has been argued, for example, that racial ambivalence is salient primarily in an intergroup context (Katz, Wackenhut, & Hass, 1986). In the aforementioned study on ambivalence and negative mood (Hass et al., 1992), the relation between the two was most pronounced when evaluative conflict was made salient by controversial (pro and con) racial statements. Other studies have shown that introspecting about one's attitude can also render ambivalence unpleasant (Schneider et al., 2013; Van Harreveld, Rutjens, Schneider, Nohlen, & Keskinis, 2014).

A likely cause of simultaneous accessibility of both evaluative components (and conflict) is highlighted by a comparison of ambivalence and dissonance (McGregor et al., 1999). An important difference between these concepts lies in the fact that dissonance is usually the result of a behavioral commitment that is in conflict with a preexisting attitude. Ambivalence is also defined by conflict, but within one's attitude and often not related to any behavioral commitment. For example, topics such as euthanasia and abortion may elicit ambivalent feelings, but it is likely that these mixed evaluations become irreconcilable mainly when people have to take an unequivocal stance, thus involving behavior. When the ambivalent attitude can no longer remain noncommittal, conflict between opposing associations arises, and ambivalence should become particularly unpleasant (Van Harreveld, Van der Pligt, et al., 2009).

Several lines of research support this line of reasoning. In the context of attitudes toward following a healthy diet, it was found that levels of ambivalence were higher when attitude holders were preparing for behavioral action than when they were in a precontemplative stage (Armitage, Povey, & Arden, 2003). Similarly, correlations between objective and subjective ambivalence are highest in stages of action and maintenance (Armitage & Arden, 2007). In other words, objective ambivalence becomes subjective ambivalence (with negative affect ensuing) when relevant behavior has to be executed and conflict between the opposing evaluative components has to be resolved.

4.1.3 Choice and conflict

The conflict that results from having to choose and resolve the cognitive competition between opposing evaluations has recently been investigated with a dynamic online measure of mental processing (Schneider et al., 2015). In three studies, participants' dichotomous evaluations with regard to a number of ambivalent and univalent attitude objects were assessed with a computerized task while measuring their movements of the mouse cursor over the screen. Tracking peoples' mouse trajectories can give insight into the mental processes accompanying the formation of an explicit evaluation (e.g., Freeman & Ambady, 2010; Freeman, Dale, & Farmer, 2011; Wojnowicz, Ferguson, Dale, & Spivey, 2009).

In a series of trials, participants were randomly and sequentially presented with ambivalent (e.g., abortion, organ donation, euthanasia, alcohol) and univalent (e.g., happy, holiday, depressed, disgust) attitude objects and in each trial were required to use their mouse to click on either the "positive" button or the "negative" button to indicate which of these best reflected their attitude. These buttons were presented in the top left and top right corner on the screen. During each trial, cognitive competition (conflict) between evaluations was operationalized as the degree to which the curvature of the trajectory deviated toward the unselected response (Maximum Deviation, MD, cf. Wojnowicz et al., 2009). The results revealed that, compared to univalent topics with only negative or only positive associations, ambivalent topics with both negative and positive associations showed a line that was attracted more to the nonchosen response options. In other words, mouse trajectories for ambivalent evaluations were drawn more to both responses compared to those for univalent evaluations. As a result, MD was greater for ambivalent compared to univalent attitude objects, reflecting more evaluative conflict. These studies directly show that, in a situation requiring a binary behavioral output, greater cognitive competition exists between opposing evaluative tendencies for ambivalent than for univalent attitude objects. These findings corroborate the earlier finding that ambivalent objects activate both positive and negative associations (De Liver et al., 2007) and extend this work by showing that these evaluations are continuously in conflict during response formation.

4.1.4 Choice and discomfort
It seems that the experience of conflict is paramount to the unpleasant nature of attitudinal ambivalence. Moreover, conflict is often the result being aware of the two conflicting sides of one's ambivalent attitude and having to choose between them. The notion that choice situations are therefore a likely cause of ambivalence-induced discomfort is the central tenet of the Model of Ambivalence-Induced Discomfort (MAID; Van Harreveld, Van der Pligt, et al., 2009). Direct empirical evidence was provided in studies in which ambivalent attitude holders wrote about the attitude topic at hand. In doing so, they were either forced to commit to one side of the attitude object by writing a one-sided essay or could stay uncommitted (Van Harreveld, Rutjens, Rotteveel, Nordgren, & van der Pligt, 2009). These groups, as well as a univalent control group, were compared in terms of their physiological arousal (Galvanic Skin Response). The results showed that ambivalent attitude holders only experienced more arousal than participants with univalent attitudes when they had to commit to one side of the attitude object. Moreover, the effect of ambivalence on arousal was fully mediated by feelings of uncertainty, further supporting the notion that it is the combination of ambivalence and choice that causes negative affect.

In a follow-up study, it was found that a number of self-reported negative emotions were increased by ambivalent choices. One of these was regret, which is an emotion likely to be associated with ambivalence for a number of reasons. Again, comparisons with cognitive dissonance can be drawn here. According to cognitive dissonance theory, subsequent to a decision, people immediately focus their attention on unfavorable aspects of the chosen alternatives and favorable aspects of the rejected alternatives, making regret likely (Festinger, 1964). Moreover, actions are associated with higher levels of regret than inactions (e.g., Gilovich & Medvec, 1994). For the ambivalent attitude holder, having to make a discrete choice is an action and thus is likely to lead to the anticipation of regret.

A recent neuroimaging study shed further light on the discomfort associated with ambivalent choices (Nohlen, van Harreveld, Rotteveel, Lelieveld, & Crone, 2014). In this study, participants were presented with several ambivalent (e.g., organ donation) and univalent (e.g., child labor, summer) concepts and were asked to judge each concept in terms of whether they were "for" or "against" it. Consistent with earlier research (Cunningham, Raye, & Johnson, 2004), greater activity was observed in the lateral PFC and ACC during ambivalent decision-making, reflecting the greater complexity of and conflict associated with the evaluation of ambivalent concepts. Interestingly, however, ambivalent decision-making was also associated with activity in areas that have been labeled a social-affective network, including the insula, temporoparietal junction, and precuneus/PCC. Activity in these areas was associated with lower levels of ambivalence on a subsequent measure. One way to interpret the observed activity in this social-affective network is that it was a reflection of efforts to reduce the unpleasant nature of ambivalence and cope with discomfort.

4.1.5 Relevance

Of course, decisions come in many shapes and sizes, and this applies to ambivalent decisions as well. In some cases, both evaluative components that together form ambivalence are relevant, such as when we are ambivalent about collaborating with a colleague who is both intelligent and dominant. In other cases, however, the two evaluative components may differ in terms of their relevance, such as when we have to decide whether or not this particular colleague is the right person to write a research paper. Although in this latter case, there are evaluatively opposing associations present, they are not likely to lead to the experience of ambivalence, because only one (intelligence) is directly relevant. In other words, different decisional contexts can put different weights on the associations and, as a consequence, determine whether objective ambivalence is translated into subjective ambivalence.

This line of reasoning was recently put to the test in an fMRI study in which objective ambivalence as well as the relevance of each of the components was manipulated (Nohlen, van Harreveld, Crone, & Cunningham, 2015). Participants first memorized profiles of four target persons that were either ambivalent (friendly, charming, lazy, dumb; or dominant, jealous, enthusiastic, intelligent) or univalent (friendly, charming, intelligent, enthusiastic; or dominant, jealous, lazy, dumb). In the scanner, participants then made dichotomous choices about each of the four target individuals, which elicited various degrees of subjective ambivalence dependent on the combination of question and target traits. It was shown that for someone who, for example, is friendly, charming, lazy, and dumb, a question such as "Do you think X can write a good newspaper article?" does not lead to subjective ambivalence, presumably because the positive traits are less relevant for writing a newspaper article. In those situations, ambivalence is temporarily resolved because more weight is given to the negative traits. However, if the question is "Would X be a good representative of your student union?" both the positive and negative traits are relevant and given equal weight, so resolution is difficult, and subjective ambivalence ensues.

Results revealed that regions in the posterior medial frontal cortex related to conflict detection and monitoring (anterior cingulate cortex) and higher executive control (superior frontal gyrus) were sensitive to questions that increased subjective ambivalence. Thus, objective and subjective ambivalence could be dissociated at a neural level. Additionally, ambivalent information for which conflict could be contextually resolved (low subjective ambivalence) engaged more anterior and posterior medial frontal cortex, as well as medial and left lateral frontal pole, than information that was only positive or negative. It seems, then, that the structural properties of ambivalent information require more effort to process even if they are not competing in the evaluation context.

In short, ambivalence leads to the experience of conflict and to negative affect when both evaluative components are of equal weight in a given situation. Although binary choice situations can put ambivalent decision-makers in a state of conflict because they have to trade off the evaluatively incongruent associations, to a large extent this depends on the relevance of the competing associations in the given situation.

4.1.6 Individual differences

Cultural and personality differences can also render the experience of ambivalence more or less unpleasant. For example, an inherent part of Buddhist and Confucian philosophies is dialectical thinking, defined as the tolerance for holding apparently contradictory beliefs (Peng & Nisbett, 1999). As a result, contradictions are perceived as natural and common in East Asia, while people from North American and European cultures, on the other hand, are known to have a lower propensity to accept duality (Peng & Nisbett, 1999). Interestingly, it has been found that people with an East-Asian cultural background show higher levels of potential ambivalence than those with a European background. Moreover, this effect of culture on ambivalence was mediated by dialectical thinking (Hamamura, Heine, & Paulhus, 2007). In other words, East Asians exhibit more ambivalence on questionnaires because they are more tolerant toward inconsistencies. Future research should examine whether this tolerance is also reflected in lower levels of subjective ambivalence. In accordance with this line of reasoning, it has also been shown that individuals with an Anglo-American background, who do not embrace duality, have less favorable attitudes toward a mixed emotional appeal than their Asian American counterparts (Williams & Aaker, 2002). This research indicates that the consistency motives that underlie ambivalence-induced discomfort are not universal and vary across cultures.

The tolerance for contradictions not only varies across cultures but also between individuals. In research that related ambivalence to individual differences, it has been found that individuals high in Personal Fear of Invalidity (PFI: the extent to which individuals are concerned with the cost of committing errors, cf. Thompson, Naccarato, Parker, & Moskowitz, 2001) are more ambivalent than those low in PFI, especially when the decision is high in personal involvement (Thompson & Zanna, 1995). This is a particularly interesting finding, as it further supports the notion discussed earlier that ambivalence is inherently tied to the anticipation of regret about potentially making the wrong decision (cf. Van Harreveld, Rutjens, et al., 2009). Need for Cognition (NFC: the extent to which individuals are inclined toward effortful cognitive activities, cf. Cacioppo & Petty, 1982) has also been related to ambivalence. Specifically, it was found that higher levels of NFC are related to lower levels of ambivalence, supposedly because high NFC individuals typically bring coherence to issues (Thompson & Zanna, 1995). On a related note, ambivalence has been associated with stronger feelings of discomfort for attitude holders who are high (vs. low) in preference for consistency (Newby-Clark et al., 2002), and ambivalence is associated with stronger response amplification for individuals low (vs. high) in tolerance for ambiguity (Nowlis, Kahn, & Dhar, 2002).

To summarize, as indicated by the distinction between objective and subjective ambivalence, the notion that ambivalence can be unpleasant (but not always is) is almost inherent to the construct. Although ambivalence sometimes is evaluated positively (e.g., Pillaud et al., 2013) and cultural and individual differences play a moderating role, many studies on the topic point toward ambivalence as a cause of negative affect when the positive and negative components of the attitude are experienced as in conflict with each other. Notwithstanding the multiple potential causes of such conflict, choice is a primary catalyst of both conflict (Schneider et al., 2015) and the ensuing discomfort (Van Harreveld, Van der Pligt, et al., 2009). The central tenet of this line of research is that ambivalence is associated with conflict when (a) attitude representations are given equal weight and (b) one has to commit to one side of the evaluative continuum. In such situations, one's conflicting thoughts and/or feelings become irreconcilable. The need to commit to one side leads ambivalent attitude holders to experience uncertainty-induced physiological arousal, potentially rooted in the anticipation of regret about the decision (Van Harreveld, Rutjens, et al., 2009).

4.2 B: Behavior

Although behavior is presumably predicted by attitudes (Ajzen, 1991), we have already discussed the moderating influence of ambivalence on the attitude–behavior relation (e.g., Conner et al., 2003, 2002). Interestingly, however, several studies have found a direct influence of ambivalence on behavior. For example, Lipkus et al. (2001) found that subjective (and not objective) ambivalence toward smoking was the best predictor of the desire to quit, even after adjusting for the attitude toward smoking. Similarly, subjective ambivalence has been directly related to reduced meat consumption, independent of the attitude (Berndsen & van der Pligt, 2004). Finally, in the context of environmental behavior, subjective ambivalence was associated with weaker intentions to adopt proenvironmental practices (Costarelli & Colloca, 2004). In this study, the relation between objective ambivalence and behavioral intentions was mediated by subjective ambivalence. The dominant role of subjective (rather than objective) ambivalence in these studies suggests that it is the affective nature of ambivalence that drives the effects. The question remains how the experience of ambivalence influences behavior. What kinds of behaviors are ignited by subjective ambivalence?

4.2.1 Body movement

Before we discuss the influence of ambivalence on intentional behavior, we first turn to the unintended behavior that can reveal ambivalence. In "The expression of emotion in man and animal" (1872), Charles Darwin defined attitude as a collection of motor behaviors—especially posture—that reflect an organism's evaluation of an object. Several lines of research have indeed shown that attitudes are reflected in body movement. For example, pride is reflected in a head tilted back and expansion of posture (Tracy & Robins, 2004), and liking of other people is reflected in a relaxed and open posture (Mehrabian, 1968). Positivity and negativity toward an affective image are, respectively, reflected in forward and backward leaning (Eerland, Guadalupe, Franken, & Zwaan, 2012; Hillman, Rosengren, & Smith, 2004).

Until very recently, research focused on one-sided evaluations, but neglected the question how our body responds to the experience of ambivalence. Nonetheless, there is reason to believe that ambivalence is physically expressed in a specific manner. When expressing ambivalence, people say that they are "torn" or "wavering" between two sides of an issue, and when reflecting on the opposing points of view regarding an ambivalent topic, they say: "on the one hand... but on the other hand" while gesturing with their hands alternatively (Calbris, 2008).

Whether these figures of speech indeed capture the physical embodiment of ambivalence was first examined in a study in which participants' movements were assessed by having them stand on a Wii™ Balance Board (Schneider et al., 2013, Study 1). Side-to-side movement was operationalized as the amount of x-flips (Dale & Duran, 2011), that is, the number of directional changes in mediolateral balance (i.e., shifting balance from left to right and vice versa). The experiment consisted of three phases. During the first phase, the participants read a fake newspaper article concerning a proposal to abolish minimum wages for young adults. For half of the participants, this message was unequivocally positive, but for the other half, the message was ambivalent in nature. During the second phase, subjective ambivalence was assessed (Priester & Petty, 1996). During the third phase, participants were asked to think about the topic of the article for 30 s, after which they evaluated the topic (either positive or negative) by leaning left or right on the board (evaluation phase). This last phase allowed for examining the effects of ambivalent choices on body movement. The results of this study clearly indicated that participants in the ambivalent condition moved more from side to side (i.e., had more x-flips) than those in the univalent condition, and this difference was obtained in each phase of the experiment.

In a follow-up study (Schneider et al., 2013, Study 2), the reverse relation was examined, i.e., whether body movement can influence ambivalence. Previous research has shown, for example, that people find cartoons funnier when their facial muscles are fixed in a smile (cf. Strack, Martin, & Stepper, 1988), but the influence of body movement on ambivalence had not yet been examined. In this study, participants were approached in an Amsterdam city park and asked whether they would like to participate in an experiment concerning Tai-Chi movements and information processing. If they complied, the experimenter handed them a clipboard holding a questionnaire assessing their ambivalence toward a self-chosen topic (cf. Van Harreveld et al., 2014). Subsequently, they were shown a film clip on a mobile video device. Participants were instructed to perform the shown movement while filling out the questionnaire. Dependent on experimental condition, participants saw and copied one of three movements: moving their body from side to side while keeping the feet to the ground (i.e., repeatedly swaying from left to right and vice versa), moving the body up and down while keeping the feet to the ground (i.e., repeatedly bending one's knees and then returning to the upright condition), or no movement. The results of this study indicated that participants moving from side to side reported more subjective ambivalence than those moving up and down and those not moving at all.

This line of research shows that our body movements are both cause and consequence of the experience of ambivalence. Strikingly, ambivalence can be influenced by behavior that is unrelated to the content of the attitude. An intriguing question concerns what causes this bidirectional relation. Research has shown that when people think of evaluative opposites, they mentally represent them at the opposite ends of a horizontal plane (Chatterjee, 2011). It could thus be that thinking about an ambivalent topic activates the opposing evaluations on this horizontal plane and thus also the accompanying motor patterns (cf. Miles, Nind, & Macrae, 2010). Conversely, the activation of motor patterns may activate the opposing evaluations on this horizontal plane, leading to more conflict experience and subjective ambivalence. An interesting potential implication of this logic is that physically curtailing movement over the horizontal plane could be a means to reduce subjective ambivalence and thus the negative affective nature of ambivalence.

4.2.2 Choice delay

Ambivalence also influences behaviors that are more deliberate in nature. Earlier, we discussed choice situations as a catalyst of ambivalence-induced negative affect. The type of behavior that is perhaps most directly aimed at (temporarily) resolving the unpleasantness of an ambivalent decision is delaying it (e.g., Van Harreveld, Van der Pligt, et al., 2009).

Research has shown that, in general, decisions and tasks are delayed when they are aversive, difficult, elicit negative affect, or when individuals are uncertain about the consequences of their decisions (e.g., Anderson, 2003; Hogarth, Michaud, & Mery, 1980; Milgram, Sroloff, & Rosenbaum, 1988; Solomon & Rothblum, 1984; Tversky & Shafir, 1992). These antecedents of delay also apply to ambivalent decision-making. In two field experiments, it was demonstrated that ambivalent choices are spontaneously delayed more often than univalent choices (Nohlen, van Harreveld, van der Pligt, & Rotteveel, 2015).

In the first study, people entering a supermarket were asked whether they wanted to participate in a small study. If they complied, they were presented with either ambivalent or univalent information about the possibility of free wireless Internet in the parks of Amsterdam. Subsequently, participants were asked whether they were for or against Wi-Fi in the parks and given the opportunity to either indicate their decision immediately or to delay it until after they finished shopping. The results indicated that, indeed, ambivalent participants were more likely to postpone the decision than their univalent counterparts, and that they did so particularly if they were frequent users of the parks, i.e., if the choice was consequential for them. This study is not only the first to show that ambivalent decision-making is associated with choice delay, but also that ambivalent decisions are especially associated with coping efforts if the decision is important. In a follow-up study, again people entering a supermarket were approached, now presenting them with ambivalent or univalent information about a fictitious food bank. Results revealed the same pattern, showing that ambivalent choices are delayed until after shopping, particularly if the decision at hand is personally relevant.

Indirect evidence suggests that these effects of ambivalence on choice delay are driven by ambivalence-induced negative affect, as it has been shown that difficult choices lead to negative feelings and avoidant behavior (Luce, Bettman, & Payne, 1997). In terms of how delay could mitigate negative affect, two opposing hypotheses can be formulated. On the one hand, individuals may simply mitigate negative affect through distraction, which would be in line with an emotion-focused coping style (Luce et al., 1997) and the traditional view of procrastination. On the other hand, it could be the case that ambivalent attitude holders delay to generate time to further ponder their decision. This would be a problem-focused coping approach and more in line with a strategic view of procrastination (Klingsieck, 2013). A study by Nohlen, van Harreveld, van der Pligt, and colleagues (2015) supports the first hypothesis. They manipulated subjective ambivalence with an introspective task (cf. Van Harreveld et al., 2014) and assessed how participants wanted to spend the time until they had to make a decision for or against the ambivalent topic. When participants could choose between (a) deliberating by writing down the pros and cons of the issue or (b) doing an unrelated, relatively boring distraction task in which they would describe the route from their house to the university, significantly more people chose the distraction task over the deliberation task. This pattern suggests that, in the context of ambivalence, delay may not serve the purpose of creating the opportunity to reduce ambivalence, but rather is a means to distract oneself and reduce the negative affective experience (cf. Luce et al., 1997).

Currently, the effectiveness of delay in mitigating negative affect is unclear. Some researchers have found that avoidant behavior is successful in reducing the negative affect that caused the procrastination to begin with (Luce, 1998), but others have found detrimental affective consequences of decision delay (Nohlen, van Harreveld, van der Pligt, et al., 2015). Future research should continue to investigate whether and how delay mitigates negative affect.

To summarize, different behaviors are both causes and consequences of the experience of ambivalence. With respect to body movement, an increase in body movement over the horizontal plane has been related to higher levels of subjective ambivalence, but it remains to be seen whether or not objective ambivalence is affected. Moreover, in order to elucidate the exact nature of the relation between body movement, affect, and ambivalence, future research should also determine whether curtailing movement has a mitigating effect on subjective ambivalence (and thus affect). Another issue for future research is to investigate the effectiveness of choice delay. Decision delay may under some circumstances mitigate negative affect, but is unlikely to change levels of objective ambivalence, because individuals who delay choose to distract themselves rather than contemplate their decision.

4.3 C: Cognition

Research into ambivalence-induced cognitions lies at the heart of research on the consequences of ambivalence. As noted previously, research interest in the affective consequences of ambivalence originated from the observation that ambivalent attitude holders engage in more elaborate processing of attitude-relevant information than participants with univalent attitudes (e.g., Jonas et al., 1997; Maio et al., 1996). It has been argued that the motivation to engage in this more effortful (or systematic) processing originates from the unpleasant nature of ambivalence. More specifically, it has been argued that people are motivated to reduce ambivalence, and new information relevant to the attitude may be functional in doing so and thus reducing discomfort (e.g., Van Harreveld, Van der Pligt, et al., 2009). Again, there are similarities with research on cognitive dissonance, where it has been shown that dissonance is reduced by bolstering consonant cognitions (Sherman & Gorkin, 1980) or trivializing dissonant cognitions (Simon, Greenberg, & Brehm, 1995).

4.3.1 Systematic processing

In terms of the effects of ambivalence on cognitive processes, several studies have shown that ambivalence is associated with increased systematic processing (Jonas et al., 1997), increased attention to discrepancy-related stimuli (Monteith, Devine, & Zuwerink, 1993), greater prefrontal cortex activity (Cunningham, Johnson, Gatenby, Gore, & Banaji, 2003; Nohlen, van Harreveld, Rotteveel, et al., 2014), and a larger difference in effectiveness between strong and weak persuasive messages (Maio et al., 1996). This latter study provided support for the notion that the relation between ambivalence and more systematic processing is driven by the motivation to reduce ambivalence, as it was found that the increased receptiveness of ambivalent attitude holders to a strong persuasive message helped to reduce subsequent feelings of ambivalence.

There is ample support for the idea that the motivation to reduce ambivalence underlies the relation between ambivalence and increased systematic processing. For example, ambivalence is known to lead to both elaboration and response amplification (i.e., the reduction of ambivalence; Hanze, 2001). Also, it has been shown that it is primarily subjective (and not objective) ambivalence, and the motivation to reduce it, that causes ambivalent attitude holders to have greater interest in attitude-relevant information (DeMarree et al., 2014). Along similar lines, egalitarian people who become aware of having prejudiced thoughts show increased attention to discrepancy-related information, supposedly with an aim to reduce this internal inconsistency (Devine, Monteith, Zuwerink, & Elliot, 1991; Monteith, 1993; Monteith et al., 1993).

The reduction of ambivalence through effortful processing can potentially be achieved by carefully weighing all alternatives and thus aiming to come to the best possible evaluation. This is known as unbiased systematic processing (van Harreveld, van der Pligt, et al., 2009). However, when issues are ambivalent, thinking about them extensively could increase ambivalence even further. Therefore, in such cases, biased systematic processing and the use of specific heuristics might be more effective. Biased systematic processing could involve selectively focusing on one side of the issue and thus tipping the evaluative balance within one's attitude to that side. This strategy may be especially fruitful because biased processing is cognitively less effortful than unbiased processing (van Harreveld, van der Pligt, et al., 2009).

Empirical evidence for the relation between ambivalence and biased systematic processing has been obtained in several studies. For example, ambivalent attitude holders have been shown to focus on proattitudinal information and avoid counter-attitudinal information (Clark, Wegener, & Fabrigar, 2008). In other words, ambivalent attitude holders use any slight evaluative inclination they may have and process information in accordance with it.

In a different study (Nordgren et al., 2006), information processing was directly related to ambivalence-induced discomfort. In this study, ambivalence was manipulated by means of a (fake) newspaper article discussing the pros and cons of genetically modified foods. Subsequent to reading this article and filling out a measure of their attitude, participants were given a placebo pill that (ostensibly and dependent on experimental condition) caused either relaxation or arousal. Finally, negative emotions were measured and participants were presented with a thought-listing task in which they wrote down their thoughts on the topic of genetically modified foods. The results not only indicated that participants reported fewer negative emotions in the condition in which they believed the pill was a cause of arousal, but also that participants who could not attribute their discomfort to an external source were more biased in their thoughts about the attitude object in the thought-listing task. As in the study by Clark et al. (2008) mentioned earlier, the direction of this bias was predicted by the attitude. In other words, ambivalent participants' (slight) inclinations toward the positive or negative end of the evaluative continuum predicted the evaluative nature of the thoughts reported on the thought-listing task. This pattern makes sense because it comprises the fastest route to a univalent attitude. Moreover, biased processing was effective in reducing ambivalence, indicating that it is indeed a way for ambivalent attitude holders to reduce their discomfort.

More recent studies have shed more light on this finding by showing that the effects of ambivalence on information seeking depend on knowledge about the ambivalent topic (Sawicki et al., 2013). Specifically, ambivalence was found to facilitate attitude-consistent exposure only when issue knowledge was low, arguably because less familiar information is perceived to be potentially effective in reducing ambivalence. However, when knowledge about the ambivalent topic was relatively high, more univalent attitudes were predictive of attitude-consistent information seeking.

4.3.2 Heuristic processing

Systematic processing can thus provide a way to reduce ambivalence, albeit a cognitively effortful one. A cognitively less demanding route toward univalence may be heuristic processing (Chaiken, 1980), such as conforming to a less ambivalent majority or taking the same unequivocal evaluative stance as someone viewed as an expert. Ambivalent attitude holders have indeed been known to process heuristically and reduce ambivalence accordingly. For example, the motivation to reduce conflict leads people to be less critical in examining the reliability of the source of information before being persuaded by it (Zemborain & Johar, 2007). Also, ambivalent attitude holders are more persuaded by consensus information than those who are not ambivalent (Hodson, Maio, & Esses, 2001).

4.3.3 Compensatory cognitions

Although reducing ambivalence is the most direct and permanent way of eliminating the problem of ambivalence-induced discomfort, coping with psychological threats such as inconsistency can also utilize strategies that are more distal to the threat itself, for example, through a process of affirmation. Affirmation is defined as:

> ...heightened commitment to alternative expected relationships following the violation of expected relationships. The affirmed expected relationships may share content with the violated relationships (e.g., affirming a controlling God after personal control has been violated) or share no content with the violated expected relationships (e.g., punishing a criminal more harshly following a visual anomaly)
> **Proulx, Inzlicht, and Harmon-Jones (2012, p. 285)**

As indicated in this definition, affirmation comes in many forms. For example, threats to personal control foster visual illusory pattern perception (e.g., Whitson & Galinsky, 2008) but also belief in human progress (Rutjens, van Harreveld, & van der Pligt, 2010). Because ambivalence is defined by the coexistence of evaluatively incongruent thoughts and/or feelings, which violates the consistency humans prefer in their world (e.g., Heider, 1946), the experience of ambivalence is inherently one of perceived internal (evaluative) disorders. Therefore, it has been argued that a potentially effective affirmation strategy could lie in (compensatory) perceptions of order.

In a series of studies, ambivalence was related to perceptions of order (Van Harreveld et al., 2014). In a first study, ambivalence (vs. univalence) was manipulated by an introspective task (cf. Schneider et al., 2013) in which we asked participants to think of a topic they felt ambivalent (univalent) about. Participants in the ambivalent condition were then presented with four numbered lines on which they could write their positive thoughts and/or feelings regarding their chosen topic and four numbered lines on which they could write their negative thoughts and/or feelings regarding their chosen topic. Participants in the univalent condition were presented with eight numbered lines on which they could write their thoughts regarding their chosen topic (without distinguishing them in terms of valence). Next, participants were presented with a snowy pictures task (Whitson & Galinksy, 2008) consisting of 24 grainy images. For each of the pictures, participants were asked to determine whether an image was hidden (and, if so, what it was). Of these 24 images, 12 actually contained an image, whereas the remaining 12 did not. Although ambivalent and univalent participants both were very adequate in detecting the actual images, there was an important difference in terms of false positives. Ambivalent participants were more likely to see an image where in fact there was none than were their univalent counterparts.

A subsequent study conceptually replicated this effect with a different measure of order perceptions: conspiracy beliefs. Conspiracy beliefs represent complex events in a simplified and often monocausal way. It has been argued that conspiracy theories assign causes and motives to events that are more rationally seen as accidents (Pipes, 1997). As such, conspiracy theories satisfy a need for order and predictability. In this study, we again manipulated ambivalence (vs. univalence) with an introspective task (cf. Schneider et al., 2013) and subsequently presented participants with a scale measuring several negative affective responses that can be elicited by ambivalence (uncertainty, anxiousness, irritation, doubt, nervousness; cf. van Harreveld, Rutjens, et al., 2009). Next, we presented participants with the same two scenarios that Whitson & Galinksy (2008) used to assess belief in conspiracy theories. In these scenarios, the protagonist was confronted with a positive or negative outcome. It was possible to interpret the outcome as the result of conspiratorial behavior of people around the protagonist, but the conspirational nature of the situation was ambiguous. The first scenario describes a negative outcome and the second a positive outcome. For both cases, participants were asked to what extent this outcome might be due to the actions of other people in the scenario. The results show that participants in the ambivalent condition are more inclined to interpret the outcome as the result of a conspiracy than their counterparts in the univalent condition. Importantly, the effect of ambivalence on conspiracy beliefs was mediated by the negative affective nature of ambivalence.

In the third and final study, we more directly examined the motivational nature of these perceptions of order by examining whether an affirmation of order subsequent to the ambivalence manipulation diminishes the need to perceive order (for ambivalent attitude holders). We replicated the finding that ambivalence fosters visual perceptions of order on the snowy pictures task, but additionally we also found that affirming participants' perceptions of order (by asking them to clean up their messy cubicle or not) makes ambivalent attitude holders less inclined to engage in compensatory perceptions of order. This finding is somewhat reminiscent of how self-affirmation can diminish the need to reduce cognitive dissonance through attitude change (e.g., Steele & Liu, 1983).

This final study supports the notion that ambivalence generates a need for compensatory order. The idea that order perceptions can help to reduce negative affect is supported by a study showing that, for men, belief in a just world is negatively related to emotional ambivalence about a female plaintiff in a gender discrimination case (Jost & Burgess, 2000). Arguably, a just world is more orderly than a world ruled by randomness and chance; therefore, these findings suggest that orderly perceptions of the world may help to mitigate ambivalence-induced negative affect.

Another compensatory coping strategy in the face of psychological threat is the assembly of unrelated meaning frameworks. Proulx and Inzlicht (2012) discuss assembly as a way of compensating for a threat to meaning through creating something (potentially unrelated) that does make sense to us. One specific form such assembly can take is the production of creative works. Although this is an area that has not yet been extensively examined, there are a few studies on other psychological threats that suggest that creativity may be enhanced by ambivalence (Markman, Lindberg, Kray, & Galinsky, 2007; Routledge & Juhl, 2012).

The relation between ambivalence and creativity is indirectly supported by research in which dialectical thinking (related to ambivalence; Hamamura et al., 2007) was associated with creativity (Benack, Basseches, & Swan, 1989). The most direct test of the relation between ambivalence and creativity was provided by two studies on emotional ambivalence (Fong, 2006). In a first study, participants who were asked to recall an event that elicited both happiness and sadness were better able to identify associations in a Remote Associates Task (Mednick, 1963) than participants who recalled an event eliciting only one of these emotions or neutrals. A second study replicated this effect, but also found lower creativity scores for the emotionally ambivalent participants who believed having mixed emotions was common than for those who thought it to be uncommon. This latter finding may suggest that rendering emotional ambivalence as something that is acceptable reduces the need to cope and thus creativity. Whether creativity is effective in mitigating the unpleasant nature of ambivalence is yet to be determined.

To summarize, ambivalence has various consequences for cognition that are driven by the negative affective nature of ambivalence. On the one hand, the motivation to reduce the unpleasant nature of ambivalence can lead to (biased or unbiased) systematic or heuristic processing. On the other hand, ambivalence has been found to lead to more distal forms of coping in the form of compensatory perceptions of order or creativity. Although the effectiveness of the former in terms of reducing ambivalence has been established, future research will have to determine whether the more distal compensatory coping efforts are effective as well.

Another matter that has to be investigated in the future is what determines whether ambivalence leads to systematic processing (and thus potentially to the reduction of ambivalence) or to more compensatory cognitions (aimed at reducing the unpleasant nature of ambivalence). We would predict that systematic processing is a more likely consequence when a decision has to be made, because this is when the opposing evaluations are irreconcilable and regret about making the wrong decision is anticipated. The ensuing motivation to reduce the likelihood of regret should make systematic processing a likely consequence (e.g., van Harreveld, van der Pligt, et al., 2009). However, when ambivalence is experienced for reasons other than having to make a decision, the motivation to resolve ambivalence should not be as strong, and compensatory coping processes may be more likely to ensue. Consistent with this reasoning, in the studies in which ambivalence was related to compensatory perceptions of order, ambivalence was manipulated through a process of introspection, and participants did not have to make a choice (Van Harreveld et al., 2014).

5. THE ABC OF AMBIVALENCE

It has become clear that ambivalence has a host of consequences for affect, behavior, and cognition. We now present the ABC model of the consequences of ambivalence, which summarizes how the affect, behavior, and cognition (1) relate to ambivalence and (2) relate to one another (Figure 1). The ABC model extends the aforementioned MAID (van Harreveld, van der Pligt, et al., 2009). Whereas the MAID model focuses on choice as a catalyst of affective consequences, the ABC model encompasses a wider range of affective, cognitive, and behavioral consequences. In the following section, we proceed with a description of each of the pathways in the ABC model.

5.1 Objective ambivalence causes negative affect when both evaluative components are accessible and conflict ensues

The first pathway in the ABC model is that from objective ambivalence to negative affect via simultaneous accessibility and conflict. The when and why of the relation between objective ambivalence and negative affect is a fundamental issue in the literature on attitudinal ambivalence. For example, the distinction between objective (Kaplan, 1972) and subjective measures of ambivalence (Jamieson, 1993) reflects the notion that

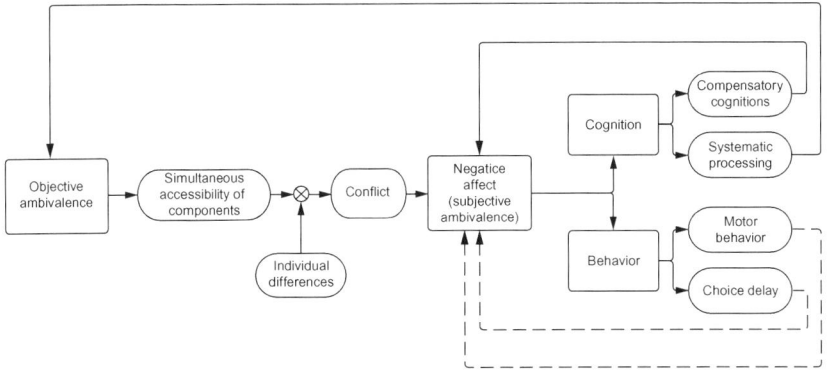

Figure 1 The ABC model of ambivalence.

ambivalence can either be experienced as unpleasant or remain in a dormant state without negative affect ensuing.

The relation between objective ambivalence and negative affect (or subjective ambivalence) hinges on whether the context renders both evaluative components salient and conflict arises. Specifically, ambivalence goes from the objective state to the more "hot" subjective state when individuals experience their positive and negative associations as conflicted. Such conflict can result from various sources, such as engaging in introspection (Newby-Clark et al., 2002; Van Harreveld et al., 2014) or having to trade off the positive and negative associations and come to one unequivocal evaluation (Schneider et al., 2015). Having to make a binary choice can render the two evaluations incompatible and lead ambivalence to be experienced as negative arousal, uncertainty, and feelings of regret (e.g., van Harreveld, Rutjens, et al., 2009). Recent research has indicated that not any binary . choice renders ambivalence unpleasant—both associations have to be relevant in the given choice situation (Nohlen, van Harreveld, Crone, et al., 2015).

Although individual differences can moderate the relation between ambivalence and negative affect (e.g., Thompson & Zanna, 1995) and ambivalence can sometimes be valued positively (e.g., Pillaud et al., 2013), the majority of studies on this issue point to ambivalence as a cause of negative affect. This negative affect is the result of the conflict ambivalent attitude holders experience when evaluatively opposing associations are equally relevant in a given situation. According to the ABC model, the negative affect that ensues from this conflict is the fuel that drives the subsequent effects of ambivalence on cognition and behavior.

5.2 Affect influences cognitions

The next pathway in the model is that from affect to cognition. We discussed various studies that relate ambivalence to different types of information processing and distinguished effects of ambivalence on systematic processing and compensatory perceptions of order. The effects of ambivalence on unbiased or biased processing of information seem to be driven by the desire to reduce ambivalence-induced negative affect (e.g., Nordgren et al., 2006; Sawicki et al., 2013). Likewise, the effects of ambivalence on compensatory order perceptions are also driven by ambivalence-induced negative affect (Van Harreveld et al., 2014). In short, although ambivalence has various effects on cognition, these effects are generally driven by the negative affective nature of ambivalence, which motivates its reduction. This is indicated by the fact that these effects are found only in the context of subjective ambivalence (e.g., Clark et al., 2008; Sawicki et al., 2013) or self-reported negative emotions (e.g., Nordgren et al., 2006; Van Harreveld et al., 2014).

5.3 Affect influences behavior

We also discussed various effects of ambivalence on behavior. Ambivalence was shown to influence physical behavior (Schneider et al., 2013), as well as delays in decision-making (Nohlen, van Harreveld, van der Pligt, et al., 2015). There is reason to believe that these effects are again driven by ambivalence-induced negative affect, as side-to-side movement on the Wii board was correlated with subjectively experienced ambivalence (Schneider et al., 2013). In the context of the relation between ambivalence and choice postponement, the evidence is more circumstantial. Manipulations of subjective ambivalence have affected decision delay (Nohlen, van Harreveld, van der Pligt, et al., 2015), and it has been found that difficult choices lead to negative feelings and avoidant behavior (Luce et al., 1997). These data suggest that the delay of ambivalent decisions may be driven by negative affect as well.

5.4 Cognition influences objective ambivalence and affect

In terms of the consequences ambivalence can have for cognition, we distinguish between effects on systematic processing of information on the one hand (e.g., Nordgren et al., 2006; Sawicki et al., 2013) and effects on compensatory cognitions on the other (Van Harreveld et al., 2014). As reflected in the model, we believe these paths have different subsequent effects. On the one hand, the effects of ambivalence on systematic processing seem to be guided by the motivation to reduce ambivalence altogether and obtain a more univalent attitude (e.g., DeMarree et al., 2014; Monteith, 1993). In other words, the ABC model predicts that systematic processing can directly influence objective ambivalence.

Compensatory cognitions, on the other hand, are not so much aimed at reducing objective ambivalence, but rather at making the experience less unpleasant. Empirical studies of the effects of ambivalence on compensatory cognitions are scarce, however, and thus there is little evidence for their effectiveness in terms of their ability to reduce the negative affective nature of ambivalence. It has been found that belief in a just world is negatively related to emotional ambivalence (Jost & Burgess, 2000). As a just world is more orderly than a world ruled by randomness and chance, it seems likely that compensatory order perceptions may indeed help to mitigate ambivalence-induced negative affect. Generally, in the literature on psychological threats, it is argued that compensatory cognitions do not mitigate the threat itself, but the affective nature of it (e.g., Proulx & Inzlicht, 2012). As a consequence, the ABC model predicts that compensatory cognitions influence affect (or subjective ambivalence) rather than objective ambivalence.

5.5 Behavior influences affect

We distinguished effects of ambivalence on two kinds of behavior: body movement and procrastination. The fact that subjective ambivalence increases as a result of physically moving from side to side indicates that behavior can influence subjective ambivalence. It remains to be determined whether curtailing such physical movement can also help to decrease the subjective experience of ambivalence (and thus negative affect). If this turns out to be the case, it would be compatible with the idea that the activation of motor patterns also activates the opposing evaluations on this horizontal plane (Schneider et al., 2013). At this point, however, this path remains a speculative rhombus in the model.

In terms of the subsequent effects of decision delay, there is some evidence suggesting that delay is successful in reducing the negative affect that caused delay to begin with (Luce, 1998), as well as some evidence to the contrary (Nohlen, van Harreveld, van der Pligt, et al., 2015). In the latter studies, however, when given the choice of how to spend the time generated by delaying the decision, ambivalent attitude holders preferred to distract themselves rather than to deliberate the decision. This finding suggests that choice delay may not be directed at resolving objective ambivalence directly. The ABC model therefore tentatively predicts that decision delay influences affect, although the effectiveness of decision delay requires further investigation.

5.6 Putting it all together

The ABC model of ambivalence not only describes the consequences of ambivalence for affect, cognition, and behavior, but also how these different categories relate to one another and to its source: the ambivalent attitude itself (i.e., objective ambivalence). The three different categories of consequences have different roles within the model. Of the three, affect (often operationalized with measures of subjective ambivalence) plays the most central role. In many ways, it is the engine that drives the subsequent effects of ambivalence on cognition and behavior. That is not to say that cognition and behavior play minor roles, as it is these factors that have been most directly related to subsequent levels of ambivalence and have influenced affect as well. In other words, although it is the unpleasant affective experience caused by ambivalence that drives the effects on cognition and behavior, the latter two mitigate the negative affective response and sometimes the underlying structure of the ambivalent attitude itself.

With regard to the ABC model, we discussed those pathways between the various factors that have actually been investigated. There are additional pathways that have not been included in the model because there is no empirical evidence to support them. In particular, one could argue that behavior and cognition may be related in the sense that people could deliberately perform the behavior in an attempt to reduce ambivalence. However, none of the participants in the study on ambivalence and physical movement (Schneider et al., 2013) expressed suspicion about the goal of the experiment, and there is no reason to believe people are aware of the effects of ambivalence on their physical behavior. Also, there is no evidence for ambivalent attitude holders to strategically procrastinate (e.g., Klingsieck, 2013) and delay the decision in an aim to generate the time needed to further ponder their decision. As such, there is no current evidence for the cognitive component influencing behavior or vice versa.

The ABC model reveals the experience of ambivalence to be a dynamic process, with ambivalent attitude holders showing various affective, behavioral, and cognitive responses, which can first render ambivalence unpleasant and eventually lead them to attain evaluative congruence or render the incongruence less unpleasant.

6. DISCUSSION

Holding evaluatively mixed associations is an intrinsic part of human existence. From daily temptations such as fast food, alcohol, and cigarettes to societal issues such as abortion, nuclear energy, and the death penalty; we are continuously confronted with things that elicit both positive and negative associations in ourselves. Such simultaneous existence of positive and negative associations is what we call attitudinal ambivalence, and, in this chapter, we have integrated research on the consequences of ambivalence for affect, behavior, and cognition. We discussed what these consequences are and presented the ABC model, which predicts (1) how they impact on ambivalence and (2) how they interact with each other. The model predicts that objective ambivalence can lead to negative affect, and that the effects of objective ambivalence on cognition and behavior tend to take place via this negative affective experience. Moreover, cognitive and behavioral processes can mitigate negative affect or the ambivalent attitude itself.

The added value of the ABC model is threefold. First, it is the only model that integrates the recent surge in research on the consequences of ambivalence. In doing so, it goes beyond the traditional conceptualization of ambivalence as a reflection of a weak attitude. Instead, the ABC model reveals that ambivalent attitudes have dynamic effects: They exert various influences on affect, cognition, and behavior that, in turn, can influence the weights of evaluative components, thereby (structurally or temporarily) changing the ambivalent nature of the attitude itself.

A second advancement of the ABC model is that it is a comprehensive model that makes specific predictions about each of the causal relations between the various components. There are broader theories in the realm of attitudes that predict relations between, for example, cognitions and behavior (Ajzen, 1991), behavior and cognition (Festinger, 1964), or affect and cognition (Zajonc, 1984), but very few that integrate all of these components and predict how they interact. There are exceptions, of course, such as Bagozzi (1982), whose volitional model not only predicts behavior from (among other things) cognition and affect but also predicts a number of interrelations between these variables. In the context of specific phenomena (such as ambivalence), comprehensive models are especially suitable, as their scope is limited enough to directly foster research into less established relations between the components and thereby increase understanding of the specific phenomena.

The third advancement of the ABC model is that it could feed future lines of research on ambivalence. We have shown that holding positive and negative associations especially becomes problematic once we become aware of both and they can no longer coexist because we have to make a binary behavioral choice. One matter that future research should further elucidate is how people aim to avoid such conflict. One way could be by compartmentalizing the opposing evaluative components that form their ambivalent attitudes. This could occur in different ways, for example, by strategically avoiding situations where both evaluations are likely to become salient (e.g., someone who is ambivalent about gun control may avoid discussions on this topic with advocates of both sides). Another example of such compartmentalizing is provided by the aforementioned study on contextual resolution of ambivalence (Nohlen, van Harreveld, Crone, et al., 2015), in which it was found that objective ambivalence (e.g., Bob is friendly, charming, lazy, and dumb) leads to subjective ambivalence only when both evaluative components are relevant in that particular context (e.g., Is Bob a good representative of your student union?). In situations where only one component is relevant (e.g., Is Bob the right person to write a newspaper article?), ambivalence is temporarily resolved, in this cause because more weight is given to the negative traits. It has to be investigated further whether ambivalent attitude holders strategically compartmentalize their opposing evaluations and thus avoid subjective ambivalence to ensue.

In terms of limitations, the current model's prediction about the causes and consequences of ambivalence-induced behavior is probably the most tentative and most in need of further investigation. The ABC model distinguishes two distinct types of behavior that may be the consequence of ambivalence-induced negative affect: motor behaviors and procrastination. There are various other kinds of behavior that may also be associated with ambivalence, but these have received limited research attention. For example, it has been found that when executives' evaluation of a strategic issue has both strong positive and strong negative evaluations, organizational action taking is more likely. Moreover, this predilection toward taking action facilitates more risky and novel behaviors (Plambeck & Weber, 2009). Whether risk-taking behavior is consistently facilitated by ambivalence and whether this effect is related to affect are issues that require future investigation.

We have discussed various ways in which behavior can potentially have an impact on ambivalence-induced affect. There is no direct evidence for an influence of motor behavior or decision delay on (objective) ambivalence itself. However, behavioral expressions of a more unequivocal attitude could reduce ambivalence as a consequence of biased processing driven by the motivation to justify one's behavior. In a line of studies on ambivalence and scapegoating, participants were put in the role of an "instructor" that required them to administer electric shocks to a black confederate. It was found that participants who were high on prejudice and high on sympathy (i.e., who were ambivalent) experienced guilt (i.e., negative affect) when administering the shocks and subsequently increased their prejudice, thus reducing ambivalence and justifying their behavior (Katz, Glass, & Cohen, 1973). Clearly, of the three types of responses associated with ambivalence reviewed in this chapter, the behavioral responses (and their consequences) are the most in need of future research attention.

The central role of affect within the model may seem in line with the notion that affect precedes cognition (Zajonc, 1984) and with the primary role of affect in the context of affective–cognitive ambivalence (Lavine et al., 1998). However, the ABC model focuses on affect as a primary consequence of ambivalence rather than on affect as one of the evaluative components of it. Moreover, although affect indeed has primacy over systematic and compensatory cognitions in the model, ambivalence-induced affect is dependent on the extent to which the opposing associations that determine objective ambivalence are both relevant in a given situation and thus lead to conflict. The role of cognition within the ABC model fits nicely within the Iterative Reprocessing model of Cunningham and Zelazo (2007). This model assumes stimuli to initiate an iterative sequence of evaluative processes, where the context determines the number of recursive feedback loops, and larger amounts of iterations lead evaluations to become increasingly reflective. In the context of ambivalence, we also propose that initial cognitions may objectively be in conflict, but may not always be experienced in that way. Contextual factors (such as having to make decision) can lead to additional processing, thereby leading individuals (1) to become aware of their ambivalence and (2) to generate subsequent cognitions aimed at coping with the ensuing negative affect.

A related matter is what defines ambivalence-induced affect. This negative affective response is reflected in measures of subjective ambivalence (e.g., "I feel torn between the two sides of this topic"; Jamieson, 1993), negative physiological arousal, and self-reported negative emotions (van Harreveld, Rutjens, et al., 2009). Regardless of whether these measures all tap into the same feeling, throughout this chapter it has been argued that objective ambivalence, the cognitive presence of evaluatively opposing associations, is a prerequisite for any subsequent effects of ambivalence. Crucially, however, situational factors determine whether these associations generate conflict. This conflict, in turn, arouses a negative affective response that requires some form of mitigation.

On the basis of the evidence reviewed in this chapter, it may appear at first glance that although attitudes generally may be functional (Katz, 1960), ambivalent attitudes do us more harm than good. First, they generate negative affect, and subsequently we have to go through effortful cognitive or behavioral processes to mitigate this affect. The question therefore presents itself: why do we have these ambivalent attitudes to begin with? The answer to this question is twofold. First, ambivalence may be of functional value, as it has recently been shown that emotional ambivalence increases receptivity to alternative perspectives, which, in turn, increases judgmental accuracy (Rees, Rothman, Lehavy, & Sanchez-Burks, 2013). This functional value of ambivalence is something that certainly deserves future research attention.

The second answer to the question why we hold ambivalent attitudes lies in the fact that they are almost inevitable. In modern society, we are exposed to an increasing amount of information, and the amount of evaluatively conflicted information increases as well. Research has indeed shown that, with an increasing number of attitude-related thoughts, the likelihood of evaluatively opposing thoughts increases as well (Van Harreveld et al., 2004). Further, as we have seen, ambivalence increases the motivation to take into account a large number of considerations (Jonas et al., 1997), which conceivably could produce a cyclical process through which ambivalence continuously reinforces itself.

As a consequence, ambivalence is more than ever an intrinsic part of human existence. In this chapter, we have shown that ambivalent attitudes are complex not only in their structure but also in their consequences. People have to come to terms with having ambivalent attitudes, and how they do this has a profound impact on what we feel, think, and do.

REFERENCES

Ajzen, I. (1991). The theory of planned behavior. *Organizational Behavior and Human Decision Processes, 50*, 179–211.

Allport, G. W. (1935). Attitudes. In C. Murchison (Ed.), *Handbook of social psychology* (pp. 798–844). Worcester, MA: Clark University Press.

Alvarez, R. M., & Brehm, J. (1995). American ambivalence towards abortion policy: Development of a heteroskedastic probit model of competing values. *American Journal of Political Science, 39*, 1055–1082.

Anderson, C. J. (2003). The psychology of doing nothing: Forms of decision avoidance result from reason and emotion. *Psychological Bulletin, 129*, 139–167.

Armitage, C. J., & Arden, M. A. (2007). Felt and potential ambivalence across the stages of change. *Journal of Health Psychology, 12*, 149–158.

Armitage, C. J., & Conner, M. (2000). Attitudinal ambivalence: A test of three key hypotheses. *Personality and Social Psychology Bulletin, 26*, 1421–1432.

Armitage, C. J., Povey, R., & Arden, M. A. (2003). Evidence for discontinuity patterns across the stages of change: A role for attitudinal ambivalence. *Psychology & Health, 18*, 373–386.

Bagozzi, R. P. (1982). A field investigation of causal relations among cognitions, affect, intentions, and behavior. *Journal of Marketing Research, 19*, 562–584.

Bargh, J. A., Chaiken, S., Govender, R., & Pratto, F. (1992). The generality of the automatic activation effect. *Journal of Personality and Social Psychology, 62*, 893–912.

Bassili, J. N. (1996). Meta-judgmental versus operative indexes of psychological attributes: The case of measures of attitude strength. *Journal of Personality and Social Psychology, 71*, 637–653.

Bell, D. W., & Esses, V. M. (2002). Ambivalence and response amplification: A motivational perspective. *Personality and Social Psychology Bulletin, 28*, 1143–1152.

Benack, S., Basseches, M., & Swan, T. (1989). Dialectical thinking and adult creativity. In J. A. Glover, R. R. Ronning, & C. R. Reynolds (Eds.), *Handbook of creativity: Perspectives on individual differences* (pp. 199–208). New York: Plenum Press.

Berndsen, M., & van der Pligt, J. (2004). Ambivalence towards meat. *Appetite, 42*, 71–78.

Broemer, P. (2002). Relative effectiveness of differentially framed health messages: The influence of ambivalence. *European Journal of Social Psychology, 32*, 685–703.

Bruckner, H., Martin, A., & Bearman, P. S. (2004). Ambivalence and pregnancy: Adolescents' attitudes, contraceptive use and pregnancy. *Perspectives on Sexual and Reproductive Health, 36*, 248–257.

Cacioppo, J. T., & Berntson, G. G. (1994). Relationship between attitudes and evaluative space: A critical review, with emphasis on the separability of positive and negative substrates. *Psychological Bulletin, 115*, 401–423.

Cacioppo, J. T., Gardner, W. L., & Berntson, G. G. (1997). Beyond bipolar conceptualizations and measures: The case of attitudes and evaluative space. *Personality and Social Psychology Review, 1*, 3–25.

Cacioppo, J. T., & Petty, R. E. (1982). The need for cognition. *Journal of Personality and Social Psychology, 42*, 116–131.

Calbris, G. (2008). From left to right: Coverbal gestures and their symbolic use of space. In A. Cienki & C. Müller (Eds.), *Metaphor and gesture* (pp. 27–53). Amsterdam, The Netherlands: John Benjamins.

Chaiken, S. (1980). Heuristic versus systematic information processing and the use of source versus message cues in persuasion. *Journal of Personality and Social Psychology, 39*, 752–766.

Chatterjee, A. (2011). Directional asymmetries in cognition: What's left to write about? In T. W. Schubert & A. Mass (Eds.), *Spatial dimensions of social thought* (pp. 189–210). Boston, USA/Berlin, Germany: Walter de Gruyter GmbH & Co.

Clark, J. K., Wegener, D. T., & Fabrigar, L. R. (2008). Attitudinal ambivalence and message-based persuasion: Motivated processing of proattitudinal information and avoidance of counterattitudinal information. *Personality and Social Psychology Bulletin, 34*, 565–577.

Conner, M., Povey, R., Sparks, P., James, R., & Shepherd, R. (2003). Moderating role of attitudinal ambivalence within the theory of planned behaviour. *British Journal of Social Psychology, 42*, 75–94.

Conner, M., Sparks, P., Povey, R., James, R., Shepherd, R., & Armitage, C. J. (2002). Moderator effects of attitudinal ambivalence on attitude–behaviour relationships. *European Journal of Social Psychology, 32*, 705–718.

Costarelli, S., & Colloca, P. (2004). The effects of attitudinal ambivalence on pro-environmental behavioural intentions. *Journal of Environmental Psychology, 24*, 279–288.

Costarelli, S., & Colloca, P. (2007). The moderation of ambivalence on attitude-intention relations as mediated by attitude importance. *European Journal of Social Psychology, 37*, 923–933.

Cunningham, W. A., Johnson, M. K., Gatenby, J. C. G., Gore, J. C., & Banaji, M. R. (2003). Neural components of social evaluation. *Journal of Personality and Social Psychology, 85*, 639–649.

Cunningham, W. A., Raye, C. L., & Johnson, M. K. (2004). Implicit and explicit evaluation: fMRI correlates of valence, emotional intensity, and control in the processing of attitudes. *Journal of Cognitive Neuroscience, 16*, 1717–1729.

Cunningham, W. A., & Zelazo, P. D. (2007). Attitudes and evaluations: A social cognitive neuroscience perspective. *Trends in Cognitive Sciences, 11*, 97–104.

Cunningham, W. A., Zelazo, P. D., Packer, D. J., & Van Bavel, J. J. (2007). The iterative reprocessing model: A multi-level framework for attitudes and evaluation. *Social Cognition, 25*, 736–760.

Dale, R., & Duran, N. D. (2011). The cognitive dynamics of negated sentence verification. *Cognitive Science, 35*, 983–996.

De Liver, Y., van der Pligt, J., & Wigboldus, D. (2007). Positive and negative associations underlying ambivalent attitudes. *Journal of Experimental Social Psychology*, *43*, 319–326.

DeMarree, K. G., Rios Morrison, K., Wheeler, S. C., & Petty, R. E. (2011). Self-ambivalence and resistance to subtle self-change attempts. *Personality and Social Psychology Bulletin*, *37*, 674–686.

DeMarree, K. G., Wheeler, S. C., Brinol, P., & Petty, R. E. (2014). Wanting other attitudes: Actual-desired attitude discrepancies predict feelings of ambivalence and ambivalence consequences. *Journal of Experimental Social Psychology*, *53*, 5–18.

Devine, P. G., Monteith, M. J., Zuwerink, J. R., & Elliot, A. J. (1991). Prejudice with and without compunction. *Journal of Personality and Social Psychology*, *60*, 817–830.

Eagly, H., & Chaiken, S. (1993). *The psychology of attitudes*. Orlando, FL: Harcourt Brace Jovanovich College Publishers.

Eagly, A. H., & Chaiken, S. (1998). Attitude structure and function. In D. T. Gilbert, S. T. Fiske, & G. Lindsey (Eds.), *Handbook of social psychology: Vol. 2*. (pp. 269–322). Boston: McGraw-Hill.

Eerland, A., Guadalupe, T. M., Franken, I. H. A., & Zwaan, R. A. (2012). Posture as index for approach-avoidance behavior. *PLoS One*, *7*, e31291.

Fabrigar, L. R., Priester, J. R., Petty, R. E., & Wegener, D. T. (1998). The impact of accessibility on elaboration of persuasive messages. *Personality and Social Psychology Bulletin*, *24*, 339–352.

Feather, N. T. (2004). Value correlates of ambivalent attitudes towards gender relations. *Personality and Social Psychology Bulletin*, *30*, 3–12.

Festinger, L. (1964). *Conflict, decision, and dissonance*. Stanford, CA: Stanford University Press.

Fiske, S. T., & Pavelchak, M. A. (1986). Category-based versus piecemeal-based affective responses: Developments in schema-triggered affect. In R. M. Sorrentino & E. T. Higgins (Eds.), *Handbook of motivation and cognition: Foundations of social behavior: Vol. 1*. (pp. 167–203). New York: Guilford.

Fong, C. T. (2006). The effects of emotional ambivalence on creativity. *Academy of Management Journal*, *5*, 1016–1030.

Freeman, J. B., & Ambady, N. (2010). Mousetracker: Software for studying real-time mental processing using a computer mouse-tracking method. *Behavior Research Methods*, *1*, 226–241.

Freeman, J. B., Dale, R., & Farmer, T. A. (2011). Hand in motion reveals mind in motion. *Frontiers in Psychology*, *2*, 1–6.

Freud, S. (1930). *Civilization and its discontents*. London: Hogarth (Original publication 1930).

Gardner, P. L. (1987). Measuring ambivalence to science. *Journal of Research in Science Teaching*, *24*, 241–247.

Gilovich, T., & Medvec, V. H. (1994). The temporal pattern to the experience of regret. *Journal of Personality and Social Psychology*, *67*, 357–365.

Glick, P., & Fiske, S. T. (1996). The ambivalent sexism inventory: Differentiation hostile and benevolent sexism. *Journal of Personality and Social Psychology*, *70*, 491–512.

Glick, P., & Fiske, S. T. (1999). The ambivalence toward men inventory: Differentiating hostile and benevolent beliefs about men. *Psychology of Women Quarterly*, *23*, 519–536.

Hamamura, T., Heine, S. J., & Paulhus, D. L. (2007). Cultural differences in response styles: The role of dialectical thinking. *Personality and Individual Differences*, *44*, 932–942.

Hanze, M. (2001). Ambivalence, conflict, and decision-making: Attitudes and feelings in Germany towards NATO's military intervention in the Kosovo war. *European Journal of Social Psychology*, *31*, 693–706.

Hass, R. G., Katz, I., Rizzo, N., Bailey, J., & Moore, L. (1992). When racial ambivalence evokes negative affect, using a disguised measure of mood. *Personality and Social Psychology Bulletin*, *18*, 786–797.

Heider, F. (1946). Attitudes and cognitive organization. *The Journal of Psychology*, *21*, 107–112.

Hillman, C. H., Rosengren, K. S., & Smith, D. P. (2004). Emotion and motivated behavior: Postural adjustments to affective picture viewing. *Biological Psychology*, *66*, 51–62.

Hodson, G., Maio, G. R., & Esses, V. M. (2001). The role of attitudinal ambivalence in susceptibility to consensus information. *Basic and Applied Social Psychology*, *23*, 197–205.

Hogarth, R. M., Michaud, C., & Mery, J. L. (1980). Decision behavior in urban development: A methodological approach and substantive considerations. *Acta Psychologica*, *45*, 95–117.

Jamieson, D. W. (1993, August). The attitude ambivalence construct: Validity, utility, and measurement. In *Paper presented at the annual meeting of the American Psychological Association, Toronto*.

Jonas, K., Diehl, M., & Broemer, P. (1997). Effects of attitudinal ambivalence on information processing and attitude-intention consistency. *Journal of Experimental Social Psychology*, *33*, 190–210.

Jost, J. T., & Burgess, D. (2000). Attitudinal ambivalence and the conflict between group and system justification motives in low status groups. *Personality and Social Psychology Bulletin*, *26*, 293–305.

Kane, S. (1990). AIDS, addiction and condom use: Sources of sexual risk for heterosexual women. *Journal of Sex Research*, *27*, 427–444.

Kaplan, K. J. (1972). On the ambivalence-indifference problem in attitude theory and measurement: A suggested modification of the semantic differential technique. *Psychological Bulletin*, *77*, 361–372.

Katz, D. (1960). The functional approach to the study of attitudes. *Public Opinion Quarterly*, *24*, 163–204.

Katz, I., Glass, D. C., & Cohen, S. (1973). Ambivalence, guilt, and the scapegoating of minority group victims. *Journal of Experimental Social Psychology*, *9*, 423–436.

Katz, I., & Hass, R. G. (1988). Racial ambivalence and American value conflict: Correlational and priming studies of dual cognitive structures. *Journal of Personality and Social Psychology*, *55*, 893–905.

Katz, I., Wackenhut, J., & Hass, R. G. (1986). Racial ambivalence, value duality, and behavior. In J. F. Dovidio & S. L. Gaertner (Eds.), *Prejudice, discrimination, and racism* (pp. 35–59). New York: Academic Press.

Klingsieck, K. B. (2013). Procrastination: When good things don't come to those who wait. *European Psychologist*, *18*, 24–34.

Klopfer, F. J., & Madden, T. M. (1980). The middlemost choice on attitude items: Ambivalence, neutrality, or uncertainty? *Personality and Social Psychology Bulletin*, *6*, 97–101.

Larsen, J. T., McGraw, A. P., & Cacioppo, J. T. (2001). Can people feel happy and sad at the same time? *Journal of Personality and Social Psychology*, *81*, 684–696.

Lavine, H. (2001). The electoral consequences of ambivalence toward presidential candidates. *American Journal of Political Science*, *45*, 915–929.

Lavine, H., Thomson, C. J., Zanna, M. P., & Borgida, E. (1998). On the primacy of affect in the determination of attitudes and behavior: The moderating role of affective-cognitive ambivalence. *Journal of Experimental Social Psychology*, *34*, 398–421.

Lipkus, I. M., Green, J. D., Feaganes, J. R., & Sedikides, C. (2001). The relationship between attitudinal ambivalence and desire to quit smoking among college smokers. *Journal of Applied Social Psychology*, *31*, 113–133.

Luce, M. F. (1998). Choosing to avoid: Coping with negatively emotion-laden consumer decisions. *Journal of Consumer Research*, *24*, 409–433.

Luce, M. F., Bettman, J. R., & Payne, J. W. (1997). Choice processing in emotionally difficult decisions. *Journal of Experimental Psychology. Learning, Memory, and Cognition*, *23*, 384–405.

Luescher, K., & Pillemer, K. (1988). Intergenerational ambivalence: A new approach to the study of parent-child relations later in life. *Journal of Marriage and Family*, *60*, 413–425.

Maio, G. R., Bell, D. W., & Esses, V. M. (1996). Ambivalence and persuasion: The processing of messages about immigrant groups. *Journal of Experimental Social Psychology*, *32*, 513–536.

Maio, G. R., Fincham, F. D., & Lycett, E. J. (2000). Attitudinal ambivalence toward parents and attachment style. *Personality and Social Psychology Bulletin*, *26*, 1451–1464.

Maio, G. R., Greenland, K., Bernard, M., & Esses, V. M. (2001). Effects of intergroup ambivalence on information processing: The role of physiological arousal. *Group Processes & Intergroup Relations*, *4*, 355–372.

Maio, G. R., & Haddock, G. (2004). Theories of attitude. Creating a witches' brew. In G. Haddock & G. R. Maio (Eds.), *Contemporary perspectives on the psychology of attitudes* (pp. 425–453). New York: Psychology Press.

Markman, K. D., Lindberg, M. J., Kray, L. J., & Galinsky, A. D. (2007). Implications of counterfactual structure for creative generation and analytical problem solving. *Personality and Social Psychology Bulletin*, *33*, 312–324.

Markus, H., & Zajonc, R. B. (1985). The cognitive perspective in social psychology. In G. Lindzey & E. Aronson (Eds.), *Handbook of social psychology: Vol. 1.* (pp. 137–230). Hillsdale, NJ: Erlbaum.

McGregor, I., Newby-Clark, I. R., & Zanna, M. P. (1999). "Remembering" dissonance: Simultaneous accessibility of inconsistent cognitive elements moderates epistemic discomfort. In E. Harmon-Jones & J. Mills (Eds.), *Cognitive dissonance: Progress on a pivotal theory in social psychology* (pp. 325–352). Washington, DC: American Psychological Association.

Mednick, M. T. (1963). Research creativity in psychology graduate students. *Journal of Consulting Psychology*, *27*, 265–266.

Mehrabian, A. (1968). Inference of attitudes from the posture, orientation, and distance of a communicator. *Journal of Consulting and Clinical Psychology*, *32*, 296–308.

Miles, L. K., Nind, L. K., & Macrae, C. N. (2010). Moving through time. *Psychological Science*, *21*, 222–223.

Milgram, N. A., Sroloff, B., & Rosenbaum, M. (1988). The procrastination of everyday life. *Journal of Research in Personality*, *22*, 197–212.

Mitroff, I. (1974). Norms and counternorms in a select group of the Apollo moon scientists: A case study of the ambivalence of scientists. *American Sociological Review*, *39*, 579–595.

Monteith, M. J. (1993). Self-regulation of prejudiced responses: Implications for progress in prejudice reduction effects. *Journal of Personality and Social Psychology*, *65*, 469–485.

Monteith, M. J., Devine, P. G., & Zuwerink, J. R. (1993). Self-directed versus other-directed affect as a consequence of prejudice-related discrepancies. *Journal of Personality and Social Psychology*, *64*, 198–210.

Newby-Clark, I. R., McGregor, I., & Zanna, M. P. (2002). Thinking and caring about cognitive inconsistency: When and for whom does attitudinal ambivalence feel uncomfortable? *Journal of Personality and Social Psychology*, *82*, 157–166.

Nohlen, H. U., van Harreveld, F., Crone, E. A., & Cunningham, W. A. (2015). Dissociation of resolved and unresolved ambivalence in fMRI. Under review.

Nohlen, H. U., van Harreveld, F., Rotteveel, M., Barends, A. J., & Larsen, J. T. (2015). Spontaneous affective responses toward ambivalent stimuli: Facial EMG responses to ambivalent stimuli in an evaluation and evaluation-free context. Under review.

Nohlen, H. U., van Harreveld, F., Rotteveel, M., Leliveld, G. J., & Crone, E. A. (2014). Evaluating ambivalence: Social-cognitive and affective brain regions associated with ambivalent decision-making. *Social Cognitive and Affective Neuroscience*, *9*, 924–931.

Nohlen, H. U., van Harreveld, F., van der Pligt, J., & Rotteveel, M. (2015). A waste of time? The prevalence and effectiveness of choice delay in ambivalent decision-making. Under review.

Nordgren, L., van Harreveld, F., & van der Pligt, J. (2006). Ambivalence, discomfort, and motivated information processing. *Journal of Experimental Social Psychology*, *42*, 252–258.

Nowlis, S. M., Kahn, B. E., & Dhar, R. (2002). Coping with ambivalence: The effect of removing a neutral option on consumer attitude and preference judgments. *Journal of Consumer Research*, *29*, 319–334.

Peng, K., & Nisbett, R. E. (1999). Culture, dialectics and reasoning about contradiction. *American Psychologist*, *54*, 741–754.

Petty, R. E., & Cacioppo, J. T. (1986). *From communication and persuasion: Central and peripheral routes to attitude change*. New York: Springer Verlag.

Petty, R. E., & Krosnick, J. A. (1995). *Attitude strength: Antecedents and consequences*. Hillsdale, NJ: Erlbaum.

Petty, R. E., Tormala, Z. L., Brinol, P., & Jarvis, W. B. G. (2006). Implicit ambivalence from attitude change: An exploration of the PAST model. *Journal of Personality and Social Psychology*, *90*, 21–41.

Piderit, S. K. (2000). Rethinking resistance and recognizing ambivalence: A multidimensional view of attitudes toward an organizational change. *Academy of Management Review*, *25*, 783–794.

Pillaud, V., Cavazza, N., & Butera, F. (2013). The social value of being ambivalent: Self-presentational concerns in the expression of attitudinal ambivalence. *Personality and Social Psychology Bulletin*, *39*, 1139–1151.

Pipes, D. (1997). *Conspiracy: How the paranoid style flourishes and where it comes from*. New York: Free Press.

Plambeck, N., & Weber, K. (2009). CEO ambivalence and responses to strategic issues. *Organization Science*, *20*, 993–1010.

Povey, R., Wellens, B., & Conner, M. (2001). Attitudes towards following meat, vegetarian and vegan diets: An examination of the role of ambivalence. *Appetite*, *37*, 15–26.

Priester, J. R., & Petty, R. E. (1996). The gradual threshold model of ambivalence: Relating the positive and negative bases of attitude to subjective ambivalence. *Journal of Personality and Social Psychology*, *71*, 431–449.

Priester, J. R., & Petty, R. E. (2001). Extending the bases of subjective attitudinal ambivalence: Interpersonal and intrapersonal antecedents of evaluative tension. *Journal of Personality and Social Psychology*, *80*, 19–34.

Priester, J. P., Petty, R. E., & Park, K. (2007). Whence univalent ambivalence? From the anticipation of conflicting reactions. *Journal of Consumer Research*, *34*, 11–21.

Proulx, T., & Inzlicht, M. (2012). Moderated disanxiousuncertlibrium: Specifying the moderating and neuroaffective determinants of violation-compensation effects. *Psychological Inquiry*, *23*, 386–396.

Proulx, T., Inzlicht, M., & Harmon-Jones, E. (2012). Understanding all inconsistency compensation as a palliative response to violated expectations. *Trends in Cognitive Sciences*, *16*, 285–291.

Rees, L., Rotham, N. B., Lehavy, R., & Sanchez-Burks, J. (2013). The ambivalent mind can be a wise mind: Emotional ambivalence increases judgment accuracy. *Journal of Experimental Social Psychology*, *49*, 360–367.

Rosenberg, M. J., & Hovland, C. I. (1960). Cognitive, affective, and behavioral components of attitude. In M. J. Rosenberg, C. I. Hovland, W. J. McGuire, R. P. Abelson, & J. W. Brehm (Eds.), *Attitude organization and change. An analysis of consistency among attitude components* (pp. 1–14). New Haven, CT: Yale University Press.

Rosenblum, A., Magura, S., & Joseph, H. (1991). Ambivalence toward methadone treatment among intravenous drug users. *Journal of Psychoactive Drugs*, *23*, 21–27.

Routledge, C., & Juhl, J. (2012). The creative spark of death: The effects of mortality salience and personal need for structure on creativity. *Motivation and Emotion, 36*, 478–482.

Rutjens, B. T., van Harreveld, F., & van der Pligt, J. (2010). Yes we can: Belief in progress as compensatory control. *Social Psychological and Personality Science, 1*, 246–252.

Sawicki, V., Wegener, D. T., Clark, J. K., Fabrigar, L. R., Smith, S. M., & Durso, G. R. O. (2013). Feeling conflicted and seeking information: When ambivalence enhances and diminishes selective exposure to attitude-consistent information. *Personality and Social Psychology Bulletin, 39*, 735–747.

Schneider, I. K., Eerland, A., van Harreveld, F., Rotteveel, M., van der Pligt, J., van der Stoep, N., et al. (2013). One way and the other: The bi-directional relationship between ambivalence and body movement. *Psychological Science, 24*, 319–325.

Schneider, I. K., van Harreveld, F., Rotteveel, M., Topolinski, S., van der Pligt, J., Schwarz, N., Koole, S. L. (2015). The path of ambivalence: Tracing the pull of opposing evaluations using mouse trajectories. Submitted for publication.

Shepherd, R. (1999). Social determinants of food choice. *Proceedings of the Nutrition Society, 58*, 807–812.

Sherman, S. J., & Gorkin, L. (1980). Attitude bolstering when behavior is inconsistent with central attitudes. *Journal of Experimental Social Psychology, 16*, 388–403.

Signorielli, N. (1991). Adolescents and ambivalence toward marriage: A cultivation analysis. *Youth & Society, 23*, 121–149.

Simon, L., Greenberg, J., & Brehm, J. (1995). Trivialization: The forgotten mode of dissonance reduction. *Journal of Personality and Social Psychology, 68*, 247–260.

Solomon, L. J., & Rothblum, E. (1984). Academic procrastination: Frequency and cognitive-behavioral correlates. *Journal of Consumer Research, 19*, 105–118.

Sparks, P., Conner, M., James, R., Shepherd, R., & Povey, R. (2001). Ambivalence about health behaviours: An exploration in the domain of food choice. *British Journal of Social Psychology, 6*, 53–68.

Sparks, P., Harris, P. H., & Lockwood, N. (2004). Predictors and predictive effects of ambivalence. *British Journal of Social Psychology, 43*, 371–383.

Steele, C. M., & Liu, T. J. (1983). Dissonance processes as self-affirmation. *Journal of Personality and Social Psychology, 45*, 5–19.

Strack, F., Martin, L. L., & Stepper, S. (1988). Inhibiting and facilitating conditions of the human smile: A non obtrusive test of the facial feedback hypothesis. *Journal of Personality and Social Psychology, 54*, 768–777.

Thompson, M. M., Naccarato, M. E., Parker, K. C. H., & Moskowitz, G. B. (2001). The personal need for structure and the personal need for invalidity: Historical perspectives, current applications, and future directions. In G. B. Moskowitz (Ed.), *Cognitive social psychology: The Princeton symposium on the legacy and future of social cognition* (pp. 19–39). Hillsdale, NJ: Erlbaum.

Thompson, M. M., & Zanna, M. P. (1995). The conflicted individual: Personality-based and domain-specific antecedents of ambivalent social attitudes. *Journal of Personality, 62*, 259–288.

Thompson, M. M., Zanna, M. P., & Griffin, D. W. (1995). Let's not be indifferent about (attitudinal) ambivalence. In R. E. Petty & J. A. Krosnick (Eds.), *Attitude strength: Antecedents and consequences* (pp. 361–386). Hillsdale, NJ: Erlbaum.

Tracy, J. L., & Robins, R. W. (2004). Show your pride: Evidence for a discrete emotion expression. *Psychological Science, 15*, 194–207.

Tversky, A., & Shafir, E. (1992). Choice under conflict: The dynamics of deferred decision. *Psychological Science, 3*, 358–361.

Van Harreveld, F., Rutjens, B. T., Rotteveel, M., Nordgren, L. F., & van der Pligt, J. (2009). Ambivalence and decisional conflict as a cause of psychological discomfort: Feeling tense when jumping off the fence. *Journal of Experimental Social Psychology, 45*, 167–173.

Van Harreveld, F., Rutjens, B. T., Schneider, I. K., Nohlen, H., & Keskinis, K. (2014). In doubt and disorderly: Ambivalence promotes compensatory perceptions of order. *Journal of Experimental Psychology. General, 143*, 1666–1676.

Van Harreveld, F., Van der Pligt, J., De Vries, N. K., Wenneker, C., & Verhue, D. (2004). Ambivalence and information integration in attitudinal judgment. *British Journal of Social Psychology, 43*, 431–447.

Van Harreveld, F., Van der Pligt, J., & Liver, De (2009). The agony of ambivalence and ways to resolve it: Introducing the MAID model. *Personality and Social Psychology Review, 13*, 45–61.

Vince, R., & Broussine, M. (1996). Paradox, defense, and attachment: Accessing and working with emotions and relations underlying organizational change. *Organization Studies, 17*, 1–21.

Wegener, D. T., Downing, J., Krosnick, J. A., & Petty, R. E. (1995). Measures and manipulations of strength-related properties of attitudes: Current practice and future directions. In R. E. Petty & J. A. Krosnick (Eds.), *Attitude strength: Antecedents and consequences* (pp. 456–487). Hillsdale, NJ: Erlbaum.

Whitson, J. A., & Galinksy, A. D. (2008). Lacking control increases illusory pattern perception. *Science, 322*, 115–117.

Williams, P., & Aaker, J. (2002). Can mixed emotions peacefully coexist? *Journal of Consumer Research, 28*, 636–645.

Wiseman, J. P. (1976). *The social psychology of sex*. New York: Harper & Row.

Wojnowicz, M. T., Ferguson, M. J., Dale, R., & Spivey, M. J. (2009). The self organization of explicit attitudes. *Psychological Science, 20*, 1428–1435.

Zajonc, R. B. (1984). On the primacy of affect. *The American Psychologist, 39*, 117–123.

Zanna, M. P., & Cooper, J. (1974). Dissonance and the pill: An attribution approach to studying the arousal properties of dissonance. *Journal of Personality and Social Psychology, 29*, 703–709.

Zanna, M. P., & Rempel, J. K. (1988). Attitudes: A new look at an old concept. In D. Bar-Tal & A. W. Kruglanski (Eds.), *The social psychology of knowledge* (pp. 315–334). New York: Cambridge University Press.

Zemborain, M. R., & Johar, G. V. (2007). Attitudinal ambivalence and openness to persuasion: A framework for interpersonal influence. *Journal of Consumer Research, 33*, 506–514.

INDEX

Note: Page numbers followed by "*f*" indicate figures and "*t*" indicate tables.

CONTENTS OF OTHER VOLUMES

Volume 51

Printed in the United States
By Bookmasters